**Malcolm Bradbury** is a novelist, television dramatist, literary critic and part-time Professor of American Studies at the University of East Anglia, where he also runs a programme in Creative Writing. His novels are *Eating People is Wrong* (1959), *Stepping Westward* (1965), *The History Man* (1975), *Rates of Exchange* (1983), *Cuts* (1987) and *Dr Criminale* (1992). His television drama includes *Porterhouse Blue* and two 'television novels', *The Gravy Train* and *The Gravy Train Goes East*. He has also written short stories, poems and parodies. Critical works include *Possibilities* (1973), *Saul Bellow* (1982), *The Modern American Novel* (1983), *No, Not Bloomsbury* (1987) and *From Puritanism to Postmodernism: A History of American Literature* (1991, with Richard Ruland). He has lectured internationally, was Chairman of the Judges for the Booker Prize for Fiction 1981 and was awarded the CBE in 1991.

**Andrew Motion** is a poet and biographer. From 1983 to 1989 he worked as Poetry Editor at Chatto and Windus. His poetry publications include *The Pleasure Steamers* (1977), *Independence* (1981), *Dangerous Play* (1984), *Natural Causes* (1987) and *Love in a Life* (1991). His biography, *The Lamberts George, Constant and Kit* appeared in 1986 and his authorised biography of Philip Larkin will be published by Faber in Spring 1993, as will his new long poem, *Lines of Desire*. He was co-editor with Blake Morrison of *The Penguin Book of Contemporary British Poetry* (1982).

*Also available in Minerva*

NEW WRITING edited by
Malcolm Bradbury
and Judy Cooke

# *New Writing 2*

edited by

## MALCOLM BRADBURY
and
## ANDREW MOTION

Minerva in association with the
British Council

**A Minerva Paperback**

NEW WRITING 2

First published in Great Britain 1993
by Minerva in association with the British Council
by Mandarin Paperbacks
an imprint of Reed Consumer Books Ltd
Michelin House, 81 Fulham Road, London SW3 6RB
and Auckland, Melbourne, Singapore and Toronto

A CIP catalogue record for this title is available from the British Library

ISBN 0 7493 9853 1

Printed and bound in Great Britain
by Cox & Wyman Ltd, Reading, Berks

# ▰ PREFACE ▰

*New Writing 2* is the second volume of an annual anthology founded to provide a much-needed outlet for new short stories, work in progress, poetry and essays by established and new authors working in Britain or in the English language. It was initiated by the British Council's Literature Department, who wished to respond to the strong interest in the newest British writing not only within Britain but overseas, where access to fresh developments is often difficult. Thus *New Writing* is not only a literary annual of important new work, but also an international shop window. Like all shop windows it can only display a proportion of the wealth of goods available within, a selective if significant sampling of the literature Britain is producing today. The aim is that over the years, and through changing editorships, it will provide a stimulating, variegated, useful and reasonably reliable guide to the work emerging from Britain and English-language writers during the 1990s.

The first volume, which appeared in 1992, was edited by Malcolm Bradbury and Judy Cooke. *New Writing 3*, to be edited by Andrew Motion and Candice Rodd, will appear in January 1994, and *New Writing 4*, edited by A. S. Byatt and Alan Hollinghurst, in January 1995. Though work is also commissioned, submissions (stories, verse, essays, literary interviews and sections of forthcoming works of fiction) for consideration are welcome. They should be sent (double-spaced, with a stamped addressed envelope) to *New Writing*, Literature Department, The British Council, 10 Spring Gardens, London SW1A 2BN. The annual deadline is 1 April.

IN MEMORIAM
ANGELA CARTER
1940–1992
and
GEORGE MACBETH
1932–1992

# CONTENTS

# *Introduction*

'New' writing, to deserve the name, must be more than recently-produced writing: several generations after Pound issued his celebrated edict ('Make it new'), writers worth their salt are still discovering ways of obeying it.

Conventional wisdom tells us that Pound's own efforts in this respect, like Eliot's, were repudiated by the dominant British writers of the middle of the century. Post-war, post-experimental, they clustered round the Union Jack raised by Larkin, snarling at the 'barbarity' of artists they felt helped them 'neither to enjoy nor endure' life as they knew it. In the last quarter of the century we can see that the long fuses lit by the Modernists are still alight. Bunting has been given the credit he deserves. Young writers have opened themselves up to Continental and international influences. There is a greater acceptance of the range of authentic voices at home.

These are the changes which help to shape what is 'new' in contemporary writing. They are also the developments Malcolm Bradbury and I have tried to reflect in this anthology – Malcolm Bradbury being, on the whole, responsible for the prose, me for the poems. Sometimes the newness revitalizes familiar-seeming forms – as when, for instance, the compression and contained wildness in the stories by John McGahern and Alison Habens make the familiar strange. Sometimes it is more overt – in the poems by Iain Sinclair, Peter Reading, Grace Nichol and Selima Hill. In every case, it is a sign not only of health but of growth – of a tradition strengthening as it diversifies.

# The Country Funeral

After Fonsie Ryan called his brother he sat in his wheelchair and waited with growing impatience for him to appear on the small stairs and then, as soon as Philly came down and sat at the table, Fonsie moved his wheelchair to the far wall to wait for him to finish. This silent pressure exasperated Philly as he ate.

'Did Mother get up yet?' he asked abruptly.

'She didn't feel like getting up. She went back to sleep after I brought her tea.'

Philly let his level stare rest on his brother but all Fonsie did was move his wheelchair a few inches out from the wall and then, in the same leaning rocking movement, let it the same few inches back, his huge hands all the time gripping the wheels. With his large head and trunk, he sometimes looked like a circus dwarf. The legless trousers were sewn up below the hips. Slowly and deliberately Philly buttered the toast, picked at the rashers and egg and sausages, took slow sips from his cup, but his nature was not hard. As quickly as he had grown angry he softened toward his brother.

'Would you be interested in pushing down to Mulligan's after a while for a pint?'

'I have the shopping to do.'

'Don't let me hold you up, then,' Philly responded sharply to the rebuff. 'I'll be well able to let myself out.'

'There's no hurry. I'll wait and wash up. It's nice to come back to a clean house.'

'I can wash these things up. I do it all the time in Saudi Arabia.'

'You're on your holidays now,' Fonsie said. 'I'm in no rush but it's too early in the day for me to drink.'

Three weeks before, Philly had come home in a fever of excitement from the oilfields. He always came home in that high state of fever and it lasted for a few days in the distribution of the presents he always brought home, especially to his mother; his delight looking at her sparse filigreed hair bent over the rug he had brought her, the bright tassels resting on her fingers; the meetings with old school friends, the meetings with neighbours, the buying of rounds and rounds of drinks; his own fever for company after the months at the oil wells and delight in the rounds of celebration blinding him to the poor fact that it is not generally light but shadow that we cast – and now all that fever had subsided to leave him alone and companionless in just another morning as he left the house without further word to Fonsie and with nothing better to do than walk to Mulligan's.

Because of the good weather, many of the terrace doors were open and people sat in the doorways, their feet out on the pavement. A young blonde woman was painting her toenails red in the shadow of a pram in a doorway at the end of the terrace, and she did not look up as he passed. Increasingly people had their own lives here and his homecoming broke the monotony for a few days, but then he did not belong.

As soon as the barman in Mulligan's had pulled his pint he offered Philly the newspaper spread out on the counter that he had been reading.

'Don't you want it yourself?' Philly asked out of a sense of politeness.

'I must have been through it at least twice. I've the complete arse read out of it since the morning.'

There were three other drinkers scattered about the bar nursing their pints at tables.

'There's never anything in those newspapers,' one of the drinkers said.

'Still, you always think you'll come on something,' the barman responded hopefully.

'That's how they get your money,' the drinker said.

Feet passed the open doorway. When it was empty the concrete gave back its own grey dull light. Philly turned the pages slowly and sipped at the pint. The waiting silence of the bar became too close an echo of the emptiness he felt all around his life. As he sipped and turned the pages he resolved to drink no more. The day would be too hard to get through if he had more. He'd go back to the house and tell his mother he was returning early to the oilfields. There were other places he could kill time in. London and Naples were on the way to Dahrain.

'He made a great splash when he came home first,' one of the drinkers said to the empty bar as soon as Philly left. 'He bought rings round him. Now the brother in the wheelchair isn't with him anymore.'

'Too much. Too much,' a second drinker added forcefully though it wasn't clear at all to what he referred.

'It must be bad when that brother throws in the towel, because he's a tank for drink. You'd think there was no bottom in that wheelchair.'

The barman stared in silent disapproval at his three customers. There were few things he disliked more than this 'behind-backs' criticism of a customer as soon as he left. He opened the newspaper loudly, staring pointedly out at the three drinkers until they were silent, and then bent his head to travel slowly through the pages again.

'I heard a good one the other day,' one of the drinkers cackled rebelliously. 'The only chance of travel that ever comes to the poor is when they get sick. They go from one state to the other state and back again to base if they're lucky.'

The other two drinkers thought this hilarious and one pounded the table with his glass in appreciation. Then they looked toward the barman for approval but he just raised his eyes to stare absently out on the grey strip of concrete until the little insurrection died and he was able to continue travelling through the newspaper again.

Philly came slowly back up the street. The blonde had finished painting her toenails – a loud vermilion – and she leaned the back of her head against a door jamb, her eyes closed as she gave her face and throat completely to the sun. The hooded pram above her outstretched legs was silent. Away, behind the area railings, old men wearing berets were playing bowls, a miniature French flag flying on the railings.

Philly expected to enter an empty room but as soon as he put his key in the door he heard the raised voices. He held the key still. His mother was downstairs. She and Fonsie were arguing. With a welcome little rush of expectancy, he turned the key. The two were so engaged with one another that they did not notice him enter. His mother was in her blue dressing-gown but she stood remarkably erect.

'What's going on?' They were so involved with one another that they looked toward him as if he were a burglar.

'Your Uncle Peter died last night, in Gloria. The Cullens just phoned,' his mother said, and it was Philly's turn to look at his mother and brother as if he couldn't quite grasp why they were in the room.

'You'll all have to go down,' his mother said.

'I don't see why we should have to go down. We haven't seen the man in twenty years. He never even liked us,' Fonsie said heatedly, turning the wheelchair to face Philly.

'Of course we'll go down. We are all he has now. It wouldn't look right if we didn't go down.' Philly would have grasped at any diversion, but the pictures of Gloria Bog that flooded his mind shut out the day and the room with its amazing brightness and calm.

'That doesn't mean I have to go,' Fonsie said.

'Of course you have to go. He was your uncle as well as mine,' Philly said.

'If nobody went to poor Peter's funeral, God rest him, we'd be the talk of the countryside for years,' their mother said. 'If I know nothing else in the world I know what they're like down there.'

'Anyhow, there's no way I can go in this,' Fonsie gestured contemptuously to his wheelchair.

'That's no problem. I'll hire a Mercedes. With a jalopy like that you wouldn't think of coming yourself, Mother?' Philly asked suddenly with the humour and malice of deep knowledge, and the silence that met the suggestion was as great as if some gross obscenity had been uttered.

'I'd look a nice speck in Gloria when I haven't been out of my own house in years. There wouldn't be much point in going to poor Peter's funeral, God rest him, and turning up at my own,' she said in a voice in which a sudden frailty only served to point up the different shades of its steel.

'He never even liked us. There were times I felt if he got a chance he'd throw me into a boghole the way he drowned the black whippet that started eating the eggs,' Fonsie said.

'He's gone now,' the mother said. 'He stood to us when he was needed. It made no difference whether he liked us or not.'

'How will you manage on your own?' Fonsie asked as if he had accepted he'd have to go.

'Won't Mrs O'Brien next door look in if you ask her and can't I call her myself on the phone? It'll be good for you to get out of the city for a change. None of the rest can be trusted to bring me back a word of anything that goes on,' she flattered.

'Was John told yet?' Philly interrupted, asking about their older brother.

'No. There'd be no use ringing him at home now. You'd have to ring him at the school,' their mother said.

The school's number was written in a notebook. Philly had to wait a long time on the phone after he'd explained the urgency of the call while the school secretary got John from the class-room.

'John won't take time off school to go to any funeral,' Fonsie said confidently as they waited.

To Fonsie's final disgust John agreed to go to the funeral at once. He'd be waiting for them at whatever time they thought they'd be ready to travel.

Philly hired the Mercedes. The wheelchair folded easily into its cavern-like boot. 'You'll all be careful,' their mother counsel-led as she kissed them goodbye. 'Everything you do down there will be watched and gone over. I'll be following poor Peter in my mind until you rest him with Father and Mother in Kil-leelan.'

John was waiting for them outside his front door, a brown hat in his hand, a gaberdine raincoat folded on his arm, when the Mercedes pulled up at the low double gate. Before Philly had time to touch the horn John raised the hat and hurried down the concrete path. On both sides of the path the postage stamp lawns showed the silver tracks of a mower, and roses were stacked and tied along the earthen borders.

'The wife doesn't seem to appear at all these days?' Philly asked, the vibrations of the engine shaking the car as they waited while John closed the gate.

'Herself and Mother never pulled,' Fonsie offered. There was dull peace between the two brothers now. Fonsie knew he was more or less in Philly's hands for the next two days. He did not like it but the stupid death had moved the next two days out of his control.

'What's she like now?'

'I suppose she's much like the rest of us. She was always nippy.'

'I'm sorry for keeping you,' John said as he got into the back of the car.

'You didn't keep us at all,' Philly answered.

'It's great to get a sudden break like this. You can imagine what it is to get out of the school and city for two or three whole days,' John said before he settled and was silent. The big Mercedes grew silent as it gathered speed through Fairview and the North Strand, crossing the Liffey at the Custom House and turned into the one-way flow of traffic out along the south bank of the river. Not until they'd got past Leixlip, and fields and trees and hedges started to be scattered between the new raw estates, did they begin to talk, and all their talk circled on the man they were going to bury, their mother's brother, their Uncle Peter McDermott.

He had been the only one in the family to stay behind with his parents on Gloria Bog where he'd been born. All the rest had scattered. Their Aunt Mary had died young in Walthamstow, London; Martin died in Milton, Massachusetts; Katie, the eldest, had died only the year before in Oneida, New York. With Peter's death they were all gone now except their mother. She had been the last to leave the house. She had first served her time in a shop in Carrick-on-Shannon and then moved to a greengrocer's cum confectioners on the North Circular Road where she met their unreliable father, a traveller for Lemons Sweets.

While the powerful car slowed through Enfield they began to recall how their mother had taken them back to Gloria at the beginning of every summer, leaving their father to his own devices in the city. They must have spent every summer there on the bog from the end of June until early September. Their mother had always believed that only for the clean air of the bog and the plain wholesome food they would never have made it through the makeshifts of the city winter. Without the air and the plain food they'd never, never have got through, she used to proclaim like a thanksgiving.

As long as her own mother lived it was like a holiday to go there every summer, the toothless grandmother who sat all day in her rocking chair, her shoulders shawled, the grey hair drawn severely back into a bun, only rising to gather crumbs and potato skins into her black apron, and holding it like a great cloth bowl, she would shuffle out on to the street. She'd wait until all her brown hens had started to beat and clamour around her and then with a quick laugh she'd scatter everything that the apron held. Often before she came in she'd look across the wide acres of the bog, the stunted birch trees, the faint blue of the heather, the white puffs of bog cotton trembling in every wind to the green slopes of Killeelan and walled evergreens high on the hill and say, 'I suppose it won't be long till I'm with the rest of them there.'

'You shouldn't talk like that, Mother,' they remembered their mother's ritual scold.

'There's not much else to think about at my age. The gaps between the bog holes are not getting wider.'

One summer the brown rocking chair was empty. Peter lived alone in the house. Though their mother worked from morning to night in the house, tidying, cleaning, sewing, cooking, he made it clear that he didn't want her anymore, but she ignored him. Her want was greater than his desire to be rid of them and his fear of going against the old pieties prevented him from turning them away.

The old ease of the grandmother's time had gone. He showed them no welcome when they came, spent as little time in the house as possible, the days working in the fields, visiting other houses at night where, as soon as he had eaten, he complained to everybody about the burden he had to put up with. He never troubled to hide his relief when the day finally came at the end of the summer for them to leave. In the quick way of children, the three boys picked up his resentment and suffered its constraint. He hardly ever looked at Fonsie in his wheelchair, and it was fear that never allowed Fonsie to take his eyes from the back of his uncle's head and broad shoulders. Whenever Philly or John took him sandwiches and the Power's bottle of tea kept warm in the sock to the bog or meadow, they always instinctively took a step or two back after handing him the oilcloth bag. Out of loneliness there were times when he tried to talk to them but the constraint had so solidified that all they were ever able to give back were childish echoes of his own awkward questions. He never once acknowledged the work their mother had done in the house which was the way she had – the only way she had – of paying for their stay in the house of her own childhood. The one time they saw him happy was whenever her exasperation broke and she scolded him: he would smile as if all the days he had spent alone with his mother had suddenly returned. Once she noticed that he enjoyed these scolds, and even set to actively provoke them at every small turn, she would go more doggedly still than was her usual wont.

'What really used to get her dander up was the way he used to lift up his trousers by the crotch before he sat down to the table,' Fonsie said as the car approached Longford, and the brothers all laughed in their different ways.

'He looked as if he was always afraid he'd sit on his balls,' Philly said. 'He'll not have to worry about that anymore.'

'His worries are over,' John said.

'Then, after our father died and she got that job in the laundry, that was the first summer we didn't go. She was very strange that summer. She'd take your head off if you talked. We never went again.'

'Strange, going down like this after all that,' John said vaguely.

'I was trying to say that in the house. It makes no sense to me but this man and Mother wouldn't listen,' Fonsie said. 'They were down my throat before I could open my mouth.'

'We're here now anyhow,' Philly said as the car crossed the narrow bridge at Carrick and they could look down at the Shannon. They were coming into country that they knew. They had suffered here.

'God, I don't know how she came here summer after summer when she wasn't wanted,' John said as the speeding car left behind the last curve of sluggish water.

'Well, she wasn't exactly leaving the Garden of Eden,' Philly said.

'It's terrible when you're young to come into a place where you know you're not wanted,' John said. 'I used to feel we were eating poor Peter out of house and home every summer. When you're a child you feel those sort of things badly even though nobody notices. I see it still in the faces of the children I teach.'

'After all that, we're coming down to bury the fucker. That's what gets me,' Fonsie said.

'He's dead now and belongs with all the dead,' Philly said. 'He wasn't all bad. Once I helped him drive cattle into the fair of Boyle. It was dark when set out. I had to run alongside them in the fields behind the hedges until they got too worn out to want to leave the road. After we sold the cattle up on the Green he took me to the Rockingham Arms. He bought me lemonade and ginger snaps and lifted me up on the counter and said I was a great gosson to the whole bar even if I had the misfortune to be from Dublin.'

'You make me sick,' Fonsie said angrily. 'The man wasn't civilized. I always felt if he got a chance he'd have put me in a bag with a stone and thrown me in a bog hole like that black whippet.'

'That's exaggerating now – he never did – and we're almost

there,' John said as the car went past the church and scattered houses of Cootehall, where they had come to Mass on Sundays and bought flour and tea and sugar.

'Now, fasten your seat belts,' Philly said humorously as he turned slowly into the bog road. To their surprise the deep potholes were gone. The road had been tarred, the unruly hedges of sally and hazel and briar cut back. Occasionally a straying briar clawed at the windscreen, the only hint of the old wildness. Philly slowed the car to a crawl, when the hedges gave way to the field of wild raspberry canes, and then stopped. Suddenly the bog looked like an ocean stretched in front of them, its miles of heather and pale sedge broken by the stunted birch trees, and high against the evening sun the dark evergreens stood out on the top of Killeelan Hill.

'He'll be buried there the day after tomorrow.'

The house hadn't changed, whitewashed, asbestos-roofed, the chestnut tree in front standing in the middle of the green fields on the edge of the bog; but the road was now tarred to the door, and all around the house new cattle sheds had sprung up. Four cars were parked on the street and the door of the small house was open. A man shading his eyes with his hand came to the doorway as soon as the Mercedes came to a stop. It was Jim Cullen, the man who had telephoned the news of the death, smaller now and white-haired. He welcomed the three brothers in turn as he shook their hands. 'I'm sorry for your trouble. You were great to come all the way. I wouldn't have known any of yous except for Fonsie. Your poor mother didn't manage to come?'

'She wasn't up to it,' Philly said. 'She hasn't left the house in years.'

As soon as they entered the room everybody stood up and came towards them and shook hands: 'I'm sorry for your trouble.' There were three old men besides Jim Cullen, neighbours of the dead man who had known them as children. Mrs Cullen was the older woman. A younger man about their own age was a son of the Cullens', Michael, whom they remembered as a child, but he had so grown and changed that his appearance was stranger to them than the old men.

'It's hard to think that Peter, God rest him, is gone. It's terrible,' Jim Cullen said as he led them into the bedroom.

The room was empty. A clock somewhere had not been stopped. He looked very old and still in the bed. They would not have known him had they not been told. His hands were enormous on the white sheet, the beads a thin dark trickle through the locked fingers. A white line crossed the weathered forehead where he had worn a hat or a cap. The three brothers blessed themselves, and after a pause John and Philly touched the huge rough hands clasped together on the sheet. They were very cold. Fonsie did not touch the hands, turning the chair round towards the kitchen before his brothers left the side of the bed.

In the kitchen Fonsie and Philly drank whiskey. Mrs Cullen said it was no trouble at all to make John a cup of tea and there were platefuls of cut sandwiches on the table. Jim Cullen started to take up the story of Peter's death. Already he had told it many times and would tell it many times again during the next days.

'Every evening before dark Peter would come out into that garden at the side. It can be seen plain from our front door. He was proud, proud of that garden though most of what it grew he gave away.'

'You couldn't have a better neighbour. If he saw you coming looking for help he'd drop whatever he was doing and swear black and blue that he was doing nothing at all,' an old man said.

'It was lucky,' Jim Cullen resumed. 'This woman here was thinking of closing up for the day and went out to the door before turning the key, and saw Peter in the garden. She saw him stoop a few times to pull up a weed or straighten something and then stand for a long time; suddenly he just seemed to keel over into the furrow. She didn't like to call and waited for him to get up and when he didn't she ran for me out the back. I called when I went into the garden. There was no sight or sound. He was hidden under the potato stalks. I had to pull them back before I was able to see anything. It was lucky she saw him fall.

We'd have had to look all over the bog for days before we'd have ever thought of searching in the stalks.'

'Poor Peter was all right,' Philly said emotionally. 'I'll never forget the day he put me up on the counter of the Rockingham Arms.' He was the only brother who seemed in any way moved by the death. John looked cautiously from face to face but whatever he found in the faces did not move him to speak. Fonsie had finished the whiskey he'd been given on coming from the room and appeared to sit in his wheelchair in furious resentment. Then, one by one, as if in obedience to some hidden signal or law, everybody in the room rose and shook hands with the three brothers in turn and left them alone with Jim and Maggie Cullen. As soon as the house had emptied Jim Cullen signalled that he wanted them to come down for a minute to the lower room, which had hardly been used or changed since they had slept there as children: the bed that sank in the centre, the plywood wardrobe, the blue paint of the windowsill half-flaked away and the small window that looked out on all of Gloria, straight across to the dark trees of Killeelan. First, Jim showed them a bill for whiskey, beer, stout, bread, ham, tomatoes, butter, cheese, sherry, tea, milk, sugar. He read out the words slowly and with difficulty.

'I got it all at Henry's. Indeed, you saw it all out on the table. It wasn't much but I wasn't certain if anybody was coming down and of course I'd be glad to pay it myself for poor Peter. You'll probably want to get more. When words gets out that you're here there could be a flood of visitors before the end of the night.' He took from a coat a large worn bulging wallet. 'Peter, God rest him, was carrying this when he fell. I didn't count it but there seems to be more than a lock of hundreds in the wallet.'

Philly took the handwritten bill and the wallet.

'Would Peter not have made a will?' John asked.

'No. He'd not have made a will,' Jim Cullen replied.

'How can we be sure?'

'That was the kind of him. He'd think it unlucky. It's not right but people like Peter think they're going to live forever.

Now that the rest of them has gone, except your mother, everything that Peter has goes to yous,' Jim Cullen continued as if he had already given it considerable thought. 'I ordered the coffin and hearse from Beirne's in Boyle. I did not order the cheapest – Peter never behaved like a small man when he went out – but he wouldn't like to see too much money going down into the ground either. Now that you're all here you can change all that if you think it's not right.'

'Not one thing will be changed, Jim,' Philly said emotionally.

'Then there's this key,' Jim Cullen held up a small key on a string. 'You'll find it opens the iron box in the press above in the bedroom. I didn't go near the box and I don't want to know what's in it. The key was around his poor neck when he fell. I'd do anything in the world for Peter.'

'You've done too much already. You've gone to far too much trouble,' Philly said.

'Far too much,' John echoed. 'We can't thank you enough.'

'I couldn't do less,' John Cullen replied. 'Poor Peter was one great neighbour. Anything you ever did for him he made sure you got back double.'

Fonsie alone did not say a word. He glowed in a private, silent resentment that shut out everything around him. His lips moved from time to time but they were speaking to some darkness seething within. It was a relief to move out of the small cramped room. Mrs Cullen rose from the table as soon as they came from the room as if making herself ready to help in any way she could.

'Would you like to come with us to the village?' Philly asked.

'No, thanks,' Jim Cullen answered. 'I have a few hours shuffling to do at home but then I'll be back.'

When it seemed as if the three brothers were going together to the village the Cullens looked from one to the other and Jim Cullen said, 'It'd be better if one of you stayed . . . in case of callers.'

John volunteered to stay. Philly had the car keys in his hand and Fonsie had already moved out to the car.

'I'll stay as well,' Mrs Cullen said. 'In case John might not know some of the callers.'

While Fonsie had been silent within the house, as soon as the car moved out of the open bog into that part of the lane enclosed by briars and small trees, an angry outpouring burst out like released water. Everything was gathered into the rushing complaint: the poor key with the string, keeling over in the potato stalks, the bloody wallet, the beads in the huge hands that he always felt had wanted to choke him, the bit of cotton sticking out of the corner of the dead man's mouth. The whole thing was barbaric, uncivilized, obscene: they should never have come.

'Isn't it as good anyhow as having the whole thing swept under the carpet as it is in the city?' Philly argued reasonably.

'You mean we should bark ourselves because we don't keep a dog?'

'You make no effort,' Philly said. 'You never once opened your mouth in the house . . . In Dublin even when you're going to shop it takes you a half-hour to get from one end of a street to the next.'

'I never opened my mouth in the house and I never will. Through all those summers I never talked to anybody in the house but Mother and only when the house was empty. We were all made to feel that way – even Mother admitted that – but I was made to feel worse than useless. Every time I caught Peter looking at me I knew he was thinking that there was nothing wrong with me that a big stone and a rope and a deep bog hole couldn't solve.'

'You only thought that,' Philly said gently.

'Then Peter thought it too.'

'Well then, if he did – which I doubt – he thinks it no more.'

'By the way, you were very quick to pocket his wallet,' Fonsie said quickly as if changing the attack.

'That's because nobody else seemed ready to take it. Take it if that's what you want.' Philly took the wallet from his pocket and offered it to Fonsie.

'I don't want it.' Fonsie refused the wallet roughly.

'We'd better look into it, then. We'll never get a quieter chance again in the next few days.'

They were on a long straight stretch of road just outside the village. Philly moved the car in on to the grass margin. He left the engine running. 'There are thousands in this wallet,' he said simply after opening the wallet and fingering the notes.

'You'd think the fool would have put it in a bank where it'd be safe and earning interest.'

'Peter wouldn't put it in a bank. It might earn a tax inspector and a few awkward questions as well as interest,' Philly said as if he already was in possession of some of his dead uncle's knowledge and presence.

With the exception of the huge evergreens that used to shelter the church, the village had not changed at all. They had all been cut down. Without the rich trees the church looked huge and plain and ugly in its nakedness.

'There's nothing more empty than a space you knew once when it was full,' Fonsie said.

'What do you mean?'

'Can you not see the trees?' Fonsie gestured irritably.

'The trees are gone.'

'That's what I mean. They were there and they're no longer there. Can you not see?'

Philly pressed Fonsie to come into the bar-grocery but he could not be persuaded. He said that he preferred to wait in the car. When Fonsie preferred something, with that kind of pointed politeness, Philly knew from old exasperations that it was useless to try to talk, and he left him there in silence.

'You must be one of the Ryans, then. You're welcome but I'm very sorry about poor Peter. You wouldn't be John, now? No? John stayed below in the house. You're Philly, then, and that's Fonsie out in the car. He won't come in? Your poor mother didn't come? I'm very sorry about Peter,' the old man with a limp behind the counter repeated each scrap of information after Philly as soon as it was given between his own hesitant questions and interjections.

'You must be Luke Henry, then?' Philly asked.

'The very man and still going strong. I remember you well coming in the summers. It must be at least ten years ago.'

'No. Twenty years now.'

'Twenty,' he shook his head. 'You'd never think. Terror how they go. It may be stiff pedalling for the first years but, I fear, after a bit, it is all freewheeling.' When Luke smiled his face became strangely boyish. 'What'll you have? On the house! A large brandy?'

'No, nothing at all. I just want to get a few things for the wake.'

'You'll have to have something, seeing what happened.'

'Just a pint, then. A pint of Guinness.'

'What will Fonsie have?'

'He's all right. He couldn't be got to come in out of the car. He's that bit upset,' Philly said.

'He'll have to have something,' Luke said doggedly.

'Well, a pint, then. I'll take it out to him myself. He's that bit upset.'

'What's this fucking thing for?' Fonsie said when Philly opened the door of the car and offered him Luke's pint.

'Nothing would do him but to send you out a drink when I said you wouldn't come in.'

'What am I supposed to do with it?'

'Put it in your pocket. Use it for hair oil. It's about time you came off your high horse and took things the way they are offered,' Fonsie's aggression was suddenly met with equal aggression, and before he had time to counter Philly closed the car door, leaving him alone with the pint in his hand.

Back inside the bar Philly raised his glass. 'Good luck. Thanks, Luke.'

'To the man that's gone,' Luke said. 'There was no sides to poor Peter. He was straight and thick. We could do with more like him.'

Philly drank quickly and then started his order: several bottles of whiskey, gin, vodka, sherry, brandy, stout, beer, lemonade, orange, and loaves, butter, tea, coffee, ham and breasts of turkey. Luke wrote down each item as it was called. Several times he tried to cut down the order – 'It's too much, too much' he kept muttering – then, slowly, one by one, all the time checking the list, he placed each item on the counter, checking it against the list once more before packing everything into several cardboard boxes.

Philly pulled out a wad of money.

'No,' Luke refused the money firmly. 'We'll settle it all out here later. You'll have lots to bring back. Not even the crowd down in the bog will be able to eat and drink that much.' He managed a smile in which malice almost equalled wistfulness.

After they'd filled the boot with boxes, they stacked more in the back seat and on one side of the folded wheelchair. Luke shook Fonsie's hand as he helped to carry out the boxes to the car. 'I'm sorry for your trouble'; but if Fonsie made any response it was inaudible. When they finished, Philly lifted the empty pint glass from the dashboard and handed it to Luke with a wink; Luke raised the pint glass in a sly gesture to indicate that he was more than well acquainted with the strange ways of the world.

'In all my life I never had to drink a pint sitting on my own in a car outside a public house. There's no manners round here. The people are savages,' Fonsie complained as soon as the car moved.

'You wouldn't come in and Luke meant only the best,' Philly said gruffly.

'Of course, as usual, you had to go and make a five or six-course meal out of the whole business.'

'What do you mean?'

'I thought you'd never stop coming out of the pub with the boxes. The boot is full. The backseat is jammed. You must have enough to start a bar-restaurant yourself.'

'They can be returned,' Philly said defensively. 'Luke wouldn't even take money. We wouldn't want to be disgraced by running out of drink in the middle of the wake. Luke said, everybody said, there was never anything small about Uncle Peter. He wouldn't want anything to run short at his wake. The McDermotts were always big people.'

'They were in their shite,' Fonsie said furiously. 'He made us feel we were stealing bread out of his mouth. But that's you all over. Big, big big,' he taunted. 'That's why people in Dublin are fed up with you. You always have to make the big splash. You live in a rathole in the desert for eighteen months, then you come out and do the big fellow. People don't want that. They want to go about their own normal lives. They don't want your drinks or big blow.'

There are no things more cruel than truths about ourselves spoken to us by another that are perceived to be at least half-true. Left unsaid and hidden we feel they can be changed or eradicated, in time. Philly gripped Fonsie's shoulder in a despairing warning that he'd heard enough. They turned into the bog road to the house.

'We live in no rathole in the desert,' Philly said quietly. 'There's no hotel in Dublin to match where we live, except there's no booze, and sometimes that's no bad thing either.'

'That still doesn't take anything away from what I said.' Fonsie would not relent.

Without any warning, suddenly, they were out of the screen of small trees into the open bog. A low red sun west of Killeelan was spilling over the sedge and dark heather. Long shadows stretched out from the small birches scattered all over the bog.

'What are you stopping for?' Fonsie demanded.

'Just looking at the bog. On evenings like this I used to think it was on fire. Other times the sedge looked like gold. I remember it well.'

'You're talking through your drainpipe,' Fonsie said as the car moved on. 'All I remember of these evenings is poor Mother hanging out the washing.'

'Wouldn't she hang it out in the morning?'

'She had too much to do in the morning. It shows how little you were about the house. She used to wash all of Peter's trousers. They never were washed from one year to the next. She used to say they were fit to walk around on their own. Often with a red sun there was the frost. She thought it freshened clothes.'

To their surprise there were already six cars on the street as they drew close to the house.

'News must have gone out already that you've bought the world of booze,' Fonsie said as they drew up in front of the door, and his humour was not improved by having to sit in the car while all the boxes in the boot were carried into the house before the wheelchair could be taken out.

John was getting on famously with the people in the house who had come while his two brothers had been away. In fact, he got on better with strangers than with either of his brothers. He was a good listener. At school he had been a brilliant student, winning scholarships with ease all the way to university; but as soon as he graduated he disappeared into teaching. He was still teaching the same subjects in the same school where he had started, and appeared to dislike his work intensely though he was considered one of the best teachers in the school. Like most of his students and fellow teachers he seemed to live and work for the moment when the buzzer would end the school day.

'I don't want to be bothered,' was a phrase he used whenever new theories or educational practices came up in the classroom. 'They can go and cause trouble with their new ideas elsewhere. I just want to be left in peace.'

Their mother complained that his wife ran his whole life – she had been a nurse before they married – but others were less certain. They felt he encouraged her innate bossiness so that he could the better shelter unbothered behind it like a deep hedge. When offered the headship of the school, he had turned it down without consulting his wife. She had been deeply hurt when she heard of the offer from the wife of another teacher. She would have loved to have gone to the supermarket and church as the headmaster's wife. Her dismay forced her to ask him if it was true. 'You should at least have told me.' His admission that he'd refused the promotion increased her hurt. 'I didn't want to bother you,' he said so finally that she was silenced.

When the two brothers came back to the house, he gradually moved back into a corner, listening with perfect attention to anybody who came to him, while before he had been energetically welcoming visitors, showing them to the corpse room, getting them drinks and putting them at ease. Once Philly and Fonsie came into the house he turned it all over to them. The new callers lined up in front of them to shake their hands in turn.

'I'm sorry about poor Peter. I'm sorry for your trouble. Very sorry.'

'Thank you for coming. I know that. I know that well,' Philly answered equally ceremoniously and his ready words covered Fonsie's stubborn silence.

Despite the aspersion Fonsie had cast on the early mourners, very little was drunk or eaten that night. Maggie Cullen made the sandwiches with the ham and turkey and tomatoes and sliced loaves. Her daughter-in-law cut the sandwiches into small squares and handed them around on a large oval plate with blue flowers around the rim. Tea was made in a big kettle. There were not many glasses in the house but few had to drink wine or whiskey from cups. Those that drank beer or stout refused all offers of cup or glass and drank from the bottles. Some who smoked had a curious, studious habit of dropping their cigarette butts carefully down the narrow necks of the bottles. Some held up the bottles like children to listen to the smouldering ash hiss in the beer dregs. By morning, butts could be seen floating in the bottoms of several of the bottles like trapped wasps.

All through the evening and night people kept coming to the house while others who had come earlier quietly left. First they shook hands with the three brothers, then went to the upper room, knelt by the bed; and when they rose they touched the dead hands or forehead in a gesture of leavetaking or communion, and then sat on one of the chairs by the bed. When new people came in to the room and knelt by the bed they left their chairs and returned to the front room where they were offered food and drink and joined in the free, unceasing talk and laughter. Almost all the talk was of the dead man. Much of it was in the form of stories. All of them showed the dead man winning out in life and the few times he had been forced to concede defeat it had been with stubbornness or wit. No surrender here, were his great words. The only thing he ever regretted was never having learned to drive a car. 'We always told him we'd drive him anywhere he wanted to go,' Jim Cullen said. 'But he'd never ask. He was too proud, and when we'd take him to town on Saturdays we'd have to make it appear that we needed him along for company; then he'd want to buy you the world of drink. When the children were young he'd load them down with money or oranges and chocolates. Then, out of the blue, he said to me once that he might be dead if he'd ever learned to drive: he'd noticed that many who drove cars had died, while a lot of those who had to walk or cycle like himself were still battering around.'

From the top of the dresser a horse made from matchsticks and mounted on a rough board was taken down. The thin lines of the matchsticks were cunningly spliced and glued together to suggest the shape of a straining horse in the motion of ploughing or mowing. A pig was found among the plates, several sheep that were subtly different from one another, as well as what looked like a tired old collie, all made from the same curved and spliced matchsticks.

'He was always looking for matches. Even in town on Saturdays you'd see him picking them up from the bar floor. He could do anything with them. The children loved the animals he'd give them. Seldom they broke them. Though our crowd are grown we still have several he made in the house. He never liked TV. That's what you'd find him at on any winter's night if you wandered in on your *ceilidhe*. He could nearly make those matchsticks talk.'

It was as if the house had been sundered into two distinct and separate elements, and yet each reflected and measured the other as much as the earth and the sky. In the upper room there was silence, the people there keeping vigil by the body where it lay in the stillness and awe of the last change; while in the lower room that life was being resurrected with more vividness than it could ever have had in the long days and years it had been given. Though all the clocks in the house had now been silenced everybody seemed to know at once when it was midnight and all the mourners knelt except Fonsie and two very old women. The two rooms were joined as the Rosary was recited but as soon as the prayers ended each room took on again its separate entity.

Fonsie signalled to Philly that he wanted to go outside. Philly knew immediately that his brother wanted to relieve himself. In the city he never allowed any help but here he was afraid of the emptiness and darkness of the night outside the house and the strange ground. It was a clear moonlit night without a murmur of wind, and the acres of pale sedge were all lit up, giving back much of the light it was receiving, so that the places that were covered with heather melted into a soft blackness and the scattered shadows of the small birches were soft and dark on the cold sedge. High up and far off they could hear an aeroplane and soon they picked it out by the pulsing of its white nightlight as it crossed their stretch of sky. The tall evergreens within the pale stone wall on the top of Killeelan were dark and gathered together against the moonlight. As if to give something back to his brother for accompanying him into the night, Fonsie said as he was relieving himself in the shadowed corner of the house, 'Mother remembers seeing the first car in this place. She says she was ten. All of them from the bog rushed out to the far road to see the car pass. It's strange to think of people living still who didn't grow up with cars.'

'Maybe they were as well off,' Philly said.

'How could they be as well off?'

'Would Peter in there now be better off?'

'I thought it was life we were talking about. If they were that well off why had they all to do their best to get the hell out of the place?'

'I was only thinking that a lot of life never changes. If the rich could get the poor to die for them the rich would never die,' Philly said belligerently.

It didn't take much or long for an edge to come between them, but before it could grow they went back into the house. Not until close to daylight did the crowd of mourners start to thin. During all this time John had been the most careful of the three brothers. He had drunk less than either of the other two, had stayed almost as silent as Fonsie, and now he noticed each person's departure and accompanied them out to their cars to thank them for coming to Peter's wake as if he had been doing it all his life. By the time the last car left, the moon was still in the sky but was well whitened by the rising sun. The sedge had lost its brightness and taken on the dull colour of wheat. All that was left in the house with the dead man and his three nephews were the Cullens and a local woman who had helped with tea and sandwiches through the night. By that time they had all acquired the heady, vaguely uplifting spiritual feeling that comes in the early stages of exhaustion and is often strikingly visible in the faces of the old or sick.

In the same vague, absent, dreamlike way, the day drifted towards evening. Whenever they came to the door they saw a light, freshening wind moving over the sedge as if it were passing over water. Odd callers continued coming to the house throughout the day, and after they spent time with the dead man in the room they were given food and drink and they sat and talked. Most of their talk was empty and tired by now and had none of the vigour of the night before. Mrs Cullen took great care to ensure that the upper room was never left empty, that someone was always there by Peter's side on this his last day in the house. Shortly after five the hearse arrived and the coffin was taken in. It was clear that Luke had been right and that most of the drink Philly had ordered would have to be returned. Immediately behind the hearse was a late, brief flurry of callers. Shortly before six the body was laid in the coffin and, with a perfunctory little swish of beads, the undertaker began the decade of the Rosary. The coffin was closed and taken out to the hearse. Many cars had taken up position on the narrow road to accompany the hearse to the church.

After they'd left the coffin before the high altar in the church, some of the mourners crossed the road to Luke's Bar. There, Philly bought everybody a round of drinks but when he attempted to buy a second round both Luke and Jim Cullen stopped him. Custom allowed one round but no more. Instead, he ordered a pint of stout for himself and Fonsie, but John shook his head to the offer of a second drink. Then when Philly went to pay for the two drinks Luke pushed the money back to him and said that Jim Cullen had just paid.

People had offered to put the brothers up for the night but Fonsie especially would not hear of staying in a strange house. He insisted on going to the hotel in town. As soon as they had drunk the second pint and said their goodbyes Philly drove John and Fonsie to the Royal Hotel. He waited until they were given rooms, and then prepared to leave.

'Aren't you staying here?' Fonsie asked sharply when he saw that Philly was about to leave him alone with John.

'No.'

'Where are you putting your carcass?'

'Let that be no worry of yours,' Philly said coolly.

'I don't think a more awkward man ever was born. Even Mother agrees on that count.'

'I'll see you around nine in the morning,' Philly said to John as they'd made an appointment to see Reynolds, the solicitor, before the funeral Mass at eleven.

Philly noticed that both the young Cullens and the older couple had returned from the removal by the two cars parked outside their house. Peter's house was unlocked and eerily empty, everything in it exactly as it was when the coffin was taken out. On impulse he took three bottles of whiskey from one of the boxes stacked beneath the table and walked with the bottles over to the Cullens' house. They'd seen him coming from the road and Jim Cullen went out to meet him before he reached the door.

'I'm afraid you caught us in the act,' Mrs Cullen laughed. The four of them had been sitting at the table, the two men drinking what looked like glasses of whiskey, the women cups of tea and biscuits.

'Another half-hour and you'd have found us in the nest,' Jim Cullen said. 'We didn't realize how tired we were until after we came in from looking at our own cattle and Peter's. We decided to have this last drink and then hit off. We'll miss Peter.'

Without asking him, Mrs Cullen poured him a glass of whiskey and a chair was pulled out for him at the table. Water was added to the whiskey from a glass jug. He placed the three bottles on the table. 'I just brought over these before everything goes back to the shop.'

'It's far too much,' they responded. 'We didn't want anything.'

'I know that but it's still too little.' He seemed to reach far back to his mother or uncle for the right thing to say. 'It's just a show of something for all that you've done.'

'Thanks but it's still far too much.' They all seemed to be pleased at once and took and put the three bottles away. They then offered him a bed but he said he'd manage well enough in their old room. 'I'm used to roughing it out there in the oilfields,' he lied; and not many minutes after that, seeing Mrs Cullen stifle a yawn, he drank down his whiskey and left. Jim Cullen accompanied him as far as the road and stood there until Philly had gone some distance towards his uncle's house before turning slowly back.

In the house Philly went from room to room to let in fresh air but found that all the windows were stuck. He left the doors to the rooms open and the front door open on the bog. In the lower room he placed an eiderdown on the old hollowed bed and in the upper room he drew the top sheet up over where the corpse had lain until it covered both the whole of the bed and pillow. He then took the iron box from the cupboard and unlocked it on the table in the front room. Before starting to go through the box he got a glass and half filled it with whiskey. He found very old deeds tied with legal ribbon as he drank, cattle cards, a large wad of notes in a rubber band, a number of scattered US dollar notes, a one-hundred-dollar bill, some shop receipts ready to fall apart, and a gold wedding ring. He put the parchment to one side to take to the solicitor the next morning. The notes he placed in a brown envelope he found and locked the box and placed it back in the cupboard. He poured another large whiskey. On a whim he went and took down some of the matchstick figures that they had looked at the night before, a few of the sheep, a little pig, the dray-horse and cart, a delicate greyhound on a board with its neck straining out from the bent knees like a snake's as if about to pick a turning rabbit or hare from the ground. He moved them here and there on the table with his finger as he drank when, putting his glass down, his arm leaned on the slender suggestion of a horse which crumpled and fell apart. Almost covertly he gathered the remains of the figure, the cart and scattered matches, and put them in his pocket to dispose of later in some anonymous place. Quickly and uneasily he restored the sheep and pig and hound to the safety of the shelf. Then he moved his chair out into the doorway and poured more whiskey.

He thought of Peter sitting alone here at night making the shapes of animals out of matchsticks; now those hands were in a coffin before the high altar of Cootehall Church. Tomorrow he'd lie in the earth on the top of Killeelan Hill. A man is born. He dies. Where he himself stood now on the path between those two points could not be known. He felt as much like the child that came each summer years ago to this bog from the city as the rough unfinished man he knew he must appear to be in the eyes of others: but feelings had nothing to do with it. He must be already well past halfway.

The moon of the night before lit the pale sedge. He could see the dark shapes of the heather, the light on the larger lakes of sedge, but he had no desire to walk out into the night. Blurred with tiredness and whiskey, all shapes and lives seemed to merge comfortably into one another as the pale, ghostly sedge and the dark heather merged under the moon. Except for the stirrings of animals about the house and a kitty-wake calling sharply high up over the bog and the barking of distant dogs the night was completely silent. There was not even a motor to be heard. But before he lay down like a dog under the eiderdown in the lower room he did not forget to set the alarm of his travelling clock to wake him at seven the next morning.

In spite of a throbbing forehead he was the first person in the dining room of the Royal Hotel for breakfast the next morning. After managing to get through most of a big fry – sausages, black pudding, bacon, scrambled eggs and three pots of black coffee – he was beginning to feel much better when Fonsie and John came in for their breakfast.

'I wouldn't advise the coffee though I'm awash with the stuff,' Philly said as the two brothers looked through the menu.

'We never have coffee in the house except when you're back,' Fonsie said.

'I got used to it out there. Their coffee is very good. The Americans drink nothing else throughout the day.'

'They're welcome to it,' Fonsie said.

John looked from one brother to the other but kept his silence. Both brothers ordered tea and scrambled eggs on toast.

'What did you two do last night?'

'I'm afraid we had pints, too many pints,' John answered.

'You had no pints, only glasses,' Fonsie said.

'It all totted up to pints and there were too many. This wild life doesn't suit me. How you are able to move around this morning I don't know.'

'That's nothing,' Fonsie said. 'And you should see yer man here when he gets going; then you'd have a chance to talk. It's all or nothing. There's never any turning back.'

As Philly was visibly discomforted, John asked, 'What did you do?'

'I thanked the Cullens.'

'More whiskey,' Fonsie crowed.

'Then I opened the iron box,' Philly ignored the jibe. 'I found the deeds. We'll need them for the lawyer in a few minutes. And there was another wad of money. There was sterling and dollars and a few Australian notes as well.'

'The sterling and dollars came from the brother and sister. They were probably sent to the mother and never cashed. God knows where the Australian came from,' John said.

'It all comes to thousands,' Philly said.

'When we used to go there you'd think we were starving him out of the place.'

'They probably didn't have it then.'

'Even if they did have it then it would still have been the same. It's a way of thinking.'

'The poor fucker, it'd make you laugh,' Fonsie said. 'Making pigs and horses out of matchsticks in the night, slaving on the bog or running after cattle in the day, when with that money he could have gone out and had himself a good time.'

'Maybe that was his way of having a good time,' John said carefully.

'It'll get some good scattering now,' Fonsie laughed at Philly.

'Are you sure?' Philly said sternly back. 'It all goes to Mother anyhow. She's the next of kin. Maybe you'll give it the scattering? I have lots for myself.'

'Mister Big again,' Fonsie jeered.

'It's time to go to see this lawyer. Do you want to come?'

'I have more sense,' Fonsie answered angrily.

The brown photos around the walls of the solicitor's waiting room as well as the heavy mahogany table and leather chairs told that the practice was old, that it had been passed from grandfather Reynolds to father to son. The son was about fifty, dressed in a beautifully-cut dark pinstripe suit, his grey hair parted in the centre. His manner was soft and urbane and very quietly watchful.

Philly had asked John to state their business, which he did with simple clarity. As he spoke Philly marvelled at his brother's clearness; even if it meant saving his own life he'd never have been able to put the business so clearly without sidetracking or leaving something out.

'My advice would be to lose that money,' the solicitor said when he had finished. 'Strictly, I shouldn't be giving that advice but as far as I'm concerned I never heard anything about it.'

Both brothers nodded their understanding and gratitude.

'Almost certainly there's no will. I'd have it if there was. I acted for Peter in a few matters. There was a case of trespass and harassment by a neighbouring family called Whelan a few years back. None of it was Peter's fault. They were a bad lot and solved our little problem by emigrating *en masse* to the States. Peter's friend, Jim Cullen, bought their land.'

Philly remembered a fierce black-haired Marie Whelan who

had challenged him to box on the bog road in one of those last summers, and John just nodded that he remembered the family.

'So everything should go to your mother as the only surviving next of kin. As she is a certain age it should be acted on quickly and I'll be glad to act as soon as I learn what it is your mother wants.' As he spoke he opened the deeds Philly gave John to hand over. 'Peter never even bothered to have the deeds changed into his name. The place is in your grandfather's name and this document was drawn up by my grandfather.'

'Would the place itself be worth much?' Philly's sudden blunt question surprised John. Mr Reynolds looked up at him sharply.

'I fear not a great deal. Ten or eleven thousand. A little more if there was local competition. I'd say fourteen at the very most.'

'You can't buy a room for that in the city and there's almost thirty acres with the small house.'

'Well, it's not the city and I do not think Gloria Bog is ever likely to become the Costa Brava.'

Philly noticed that both the solicitor and his brother were looking at him with withdrawn suspicion if not distaste. They were plainly thinking that greed had propelled him to stumble into the enquiry he had made when it was the last thing in the world he had in mind. Before anything further could be said, the solicitor was shaking both their hands at the door and nodding over their shoulders to the receptionist behind her desk across the hallway to take their particulars before showing them out.

In contrast to the removal of the previous evening, when the church had been full to overflowing, there were only a few dozen people at the funeral Mass. Eight cars followed the hearse to Killeelan, and only the Mercedes turned into the narrow laneway behind the hearse. The other mourners abandoned their cars at the road and entered the lane on foot. Blackthorn and briar scraped against the windscreen and sides of the Mercedes as they moved behind the hearse's slow pace. At the end of the lane there was a small clearing in front of the limestone wall that ringed the foot of Killeelan Hill. There was just enough space in the clearing for the hearse and the Mercedes to park on either side of the small iron gate in the wall. The coffin was taken from the hearse and placed on the shoulders of John and Philly and the two Cullens. The gate was just wide enough for them to go through. Fonsie alone stayed behind in the front seat of the Mercedes and watched the coffin as it slowly climbed the hill on the four shoulders. The coffin went up and up the steep hill, sometimes swaying dangerously, and then anxious hands of the immediate followers would go up against the back of the coffin. The shadows of the clouds swept continually over the green hill and brown varnish of the coffin. Away on the bog they were a darker, deeper shadow as the clouds travelled swiftly over the pale sedge. Three times the small snail-like cortège stopped completely for the bearers to be changed. As far as Fonsie could see – he would have needed binoculars to be certain – they were the original bearers, his brothers and the two Cullens, who took up the coffin the third and last time and carried it through the small gate in the wall around the graveyard on the hilltop. Then it was only the coffin itself and the heads of the mourners that could be seen until they were lost in the graveyard evergreens. In spite of his irritation at this useless ceremony that seemed only to show some deep love of hardship or enslavement – they'd be hard put to situate the graveyard in a more difficult or inaccessible place except on the very top of a mountain – he found the coffin and the small band of toiling mourners unbearably moving as it made its slow stumbling climb up the hill, and this deepened further his irritation and the sense of complete uselessness.

Suddenly he was startled by the noise of a car coming very fast in the narrow lane and braking to a stop behind the hearse. A priest in a long black soutane and white surplice with a purple stole over his shoulders got out of the car carrying a fat black breviary. Seeing Fonsie, he saluted briskly as he went through the open gate. Then, bent almost double, he started to climb quickly like an enormous black-and-white crab after the coffin. Watching him climb, Fonsie laughed harshly before starting to fiddle with the car radio.

After a long interval the priest was the first to come down the hill, accompanied by two middle-aged men, the most solid-looking and conventional of the mourners. The priest carried his surplice and stole on his arm. The long black soutane looked strangely menacing between the two attentive men in suits as they came down. Fonsie reached over to turn off the rock-and-roll playing on the radio as they drew close, but in a sudden reversal, he turned it up louder still. The three men looked toward the loud music as they came through the gate but did not salute or nod. They got into the priest's car, and, as there was no turning place between the hearse and the Mercedes, it proceeded to back out of the narrow lane. Then, in straggles of twos and threes, people started to come down the hill. The two brothers and Jim Cullen were the last to come down. As soon as Philly got into the Mercedes he turned off the radio.

'You'd think you'd show a bit more respect.'

'The radio station didn't know about the funeral.'

'I'm not talking about the radio station,' Philly said.

'That Jim Cullen is a nice man,' John said in order to steer the talk away from what he saw as an imminent clash. 'He's intelligent as well as decent. Peter was lucky in his neighbour.'

'The Cullens,' Philly said as if searching for a phrase. 'You couldn't, you couldn't if you tried get better people than the Cullens.'

They drove straight from Killeelan to the Royal for lunch. Not many people came, just the Cullens among the close neighbours and a few far-out cousins of the dead man. Philly bought a round for everyone and when he found no takers to his offer of a second round he did not press.

'Our friend seems to be restraining himself for once,' Fonsie remarked sarcastically to John as they moved from the bar to the restaurant.

'He's taking his cue from Jim Cullen. Philly is all right,' John said. 'It's those months and months out in the oilfields and then the excitement of coming home with all that money. It has to have an effect. Wouldn't it be worse if he got fond of the money?'

'It's still too much. It's not awanting,' Fonsie continued doggedly through a blurred recognition of all that Philly had given to their mother and to the small house over the years, and it caused him to stir uncomfortably.

The set meal was simple and good: hot vegetable soup, lamb chops with turnip and roast potatoes and peas, apple tart and cream, tea or coffee. While they were eating, the three grave-diggers came into the dining room and were given a separate table by one of the river windows. Philly got up as soon as they arrived to ensure that a drink was brought to their table.

When the meal ended, the three brothers drove back behind the Cullens' car to Gloria Bog. There they put all that was left of the booze back into the car. The Cullens accepted what food was left over but wouldn't hear of taking any more of the drink. 'We're not planning on holding another wake for a long time yet,' they said half humorously, half sadly. John helped with the boxes, Fonsie did not leave the car. As soon as Philly gave Jim Cullen the keys to the house John shook his hand and got back into the car with Fonsie and the boxes of booze, but still Philly continued talking to Jim Cullen outside the open house. In the rear mirror they saw Philly thrust a fistful of notes towards Jim Cullen. They noticed how large the old farmer's hands were as he gripped Philly by the wrist and pushed the hand and notes down into his jacket pocket, refusing stubbornly to accept any money. When John took his eyes from the mirror and the small sharp struggle between the two men, what met his eyes across the waste of pale sedge and heather was the rich dark waiting evergreens inside the back wall of Killeelan where they had buried Peter beside his father and mother only a few hours before. The colour of laughter is black. How dark is the end of all of life. Yet others carried the burden in the bright day on the hill. His shoulders shuddered slightly in revulsion and he wished himself back in the semi-detached suburbs with rosebeds in the gardens.

'I thought you'd never finish,' Fonsie accused Philly when the big car began to move slowly out the bog road.

'There was things to be tidied up,' Philly said absently. 'Jim is going to take care of the place till I get back,' and as Fonsie was about to answer he found John's hands pressing his shoulders from the backseat in a plea not to speak. When they parked beside the door of the bar there was just place enough for another car to pass inside the church wall.

'Not that a car is likely to pass,' Philly joked as he and John carried the boxes in. When they had placed all of them on the counter they saw Luke reach for a brandy bottle on the high shelf.

'No, Luke,' Philly said. 'I'll have a pint if that's what you have in mind.'

'John'll have a pint then, too.'

'I don't know,' John said in alarm. 'I haven't drunk as much in my life as the last few days. I feel poisoned.'

'Still, we're unlikely to have a day like this ever again,' Philly said as Luke pulled three pints.

'I don't think I'd survive many more such days,' John said.

'Wouldn't it be better to bring Fonsie in than to have him drinking out there in the car? It'll take me a while to make up all this. One thing I will say,' he said as he started to count the returned bottles: 'There was no danger of anybody running dry at Peter's wake.'

Fonsie protested when Philly went out to the car. It was too much trouble to get the wheelchair out of the boot. He didn't need drink. 'I'll take you in,' Philly offered his stooped neck and carried Fonsie into the bar like a child as he'd done many times when they were young and later when they were on certain sprees. He set him down in an armchair in front of the empty fireplace and brought his pint from the counter. It took Luke a long time to make up the bill, and when he eventually presented it to Philly, after many extra countings and checkings, he was full of apologies at what it had all come to.

'It'd be twice as much in the city,' Philly said energetically as he paid.

'I suppose it'd be as much anyhow,' Luke grumbled happily with relief and then at once started to draw another round of drinks which he insisted they take.

'It's on the house. It's not every day or year brings you down.'

Fonsie and Philly drank the second pint easily. John was already fuddled and unhappy and he drank reluctantly.

'I won't say goodbye,' Luke accompanied them out to the car when they left. 'You'll have to be down again before long.'

'It'll not be long till we're down,' Philly answered firmly for all of them.

On their way back to Dublin, in Longford and Mullingar and Enfield Philly stopped. John complained each time but it was Philly who had command of the car. Each time he carried Fonsie into the bars – and in all of them the two drank pints. John refused to have anything in Mullingar or Longford but took a reluctant glass in Enfield.

'What'll you do if you have an accident and get breathylized?'

'I'll not have an accident. And they can send the summons all the way out to the Saudis if I do.'

He drove fast but steadily into the city. He was silent as he drove. Increasingly, he seemed charged with an energy that was focused elsewhere and had been fuelled by every stop they had made. In the heart of the city, seeing a vacant place in front of Mulligan's where he had drunk on his own in the deep silence of the bar a few short mornings before, he pulled across the traffic and parked. Cars stopped to blow hard at him but he paid them no attention as he parked and got out.

'We'll have a last drink here in the name of God before we face back to the mother,' Philly said as he carried Fonsie into the bar. He set Fonsie on one of the low tables and went to get three pints from the bar. There were now a few dozen early evening drinkers in the bar; some of them seemed to know the brothers, but not well. John offered to move Fonsie from the table to an armchair but Fonsie said he preferred to remain where he was. John complained that he hadn't asked for the pint when the drinks were brought to the table.

'Is it a short you want, then?'

'No. I have had more drink today than I've had in years. I want nothing.'

'Don't drink it, then, if you don't want,' he was told roughly.

'Well, Peter, God rest him, was given a great send-off,' Philly

said with deep satisfaction as he drank. 'I thank God I was back.
I wouldn't have been away for the world. The church was
packed for the removal. Every neighbour around was at Killeelan.'

'What else have they to do down there? It's the one excuse
they have to get out of their houses,' Fonsie said.

'They honour the dead. That's what they do. People still
mean something down there. They showed the respect they had
for Peter.'

'Respect, my arse. Everybody is respected for a few days after
they conk it because they don't have to be lived with anymore.
Oh, it's easy to honour the dead. It doesn't cost anything and
gives them the chance to get out of their bloody houses before
they start to eat one another within.'

An old argument started up, an argument they had many
times before without resolving anything, the strength of their
difference betraying the hidden closeness.

Philly and Fonsie drained their glasses as John took the first sip
from his pint as he looked uneasily from one to the other.

'You have it all crooked,' Philly said as he rose to get more
drink from the counter. John covered his glass with his palm to
indicate that he wanted nothing more. When Philly came back
with the two pints he started to speak before he had even put the
glasses down on the table: he had all the blind dominating passion of someone in thrall to a single idea.

'I'll never forget it all the days of my life, the people coming to
the house all through the night. The rows and rows of people at
the removal passing by us in the front seat of the church grasp-
ing our hands. Coming in that small lane behind the hearse; and
then carrying Peter up that hill.'

Fonsie tried to speak but Philly raised his glass into his face
and refused to be silenced.

'I felt something I never felt when we left the coffin on the
edge of the grave. A rabbit hopped out of the briars a few yards
off. He sat there and looked at us as if he didn't know what was
going on before he bolted off somewhere again. You could see
the bog and all the shut houses to Peter's below us. There wasn't

even a wisp of smoke coming from any of the houses. Everybody gathered around, and the priest started to speak of the dead and the Mystery and the Resurrection.'

'He's paid to do that and he was nearly late. I saw it all from the car,' Fonsie asserted. 'It was no mystery from the car. Several times I thought you were going to drop the coffin. It was more like a crowd of apes staggering up a hill with something they had just looted. The whole lot of you could have come right out of the Dark Ages, without even a dab of make-up. I thought a standard of living had replaced the struggle for survival ages ago.'

'I have to say I found the whole ceremony moving, but once is more than enough to go through that experience,' John said very carefully. 'I think of Peter making those small animals out of matchsticks in the long nights on the bog. Some people pay money for that kind of work. They show figures like that in museums. Peter just did it out of some need.'

Philly either didn't hear or ignored what John said.

'It's a godsend they don't let you out often,' Fonsie said. 'People that exhibit in museums are artists. Peter was just killing the nights on the bloody bog.'

'I'll never forget the boredom of those summers, watching Peter foot turf, making grabs at the butterflies that tossed about over the sedge. Once you closed your hand they always escaped,' John said as if some waif-like quality long buried in him was drawn out. 'I think he was making things out of matchsticks even then, but we hardly noticed.'

'Peter never wanted us. Mother just forced us on him. He wasn't able to turn us away,' Fonsie said, the talk growing more and more rambling and at odds.

'He didn't turn us away, whether he wanted to or not,' Philly asserted truculently. 'I heard Mother say time and time again that we'd never have got through some of the winters but for those long summers on the bog.'

'She'd have to say that since she took us there.'

'It's over now. With Peter it's all finished. One of the things that made the last days bearable for me was that everything we were doing was being done for the last time,' John said with such uncharacteristic volubility that the two brothers just stared.

'I'll say amen to that,' Fonsie said.

'It's far from over but we better have a last round for the road first,' Philly drained his glass and rose, and again John covered his three-quarter-full glass with his palm. 'As far as I can make out nothing is ever over.'

'Those two are tanks for drink, but they don't seem to have been pulling lately,' a drinker at the counter remarked to his companion as Philly passed by shakily with the pair of pints. 'The pale one not drinking looks like a brother as well. There must have been a family do.'

'You'd wonder where that wheelchair brother puts all that drink,' the other changed.

'He puts it where we all put it. You don't need legs, for God's sake, to take drink. Drink only gets down as far as your flute.'

'Gloria is far from over,' Philly said as he put the two pints down on the table. 'Nothing is ever over. I'm going to take up in Peter's place.'

'You can't be that drunk,' Fonsie said dismissively.

'I'm not sober but I was never more certain of anything in my born life.'

'Didn't the lawyer say it'd go to Mother? What'll she do but sell?'

'I'm not sure she'll want to sell. She grew up there. It was in her family for generations.'

'I'm sure. I can tell you that now.'

'Well, it's even simpler, then. I'll buy the place off Mother,' Philly announced so decisively that Fonsie found himself looking at John.

'I'm out of this,' John said. 'What people do is their own business. All I ask is to be let go about my own life.'

'I've enough money to buy the place. You heard what the lawyer said it was worth. I'll give Mother its price and she can do with it what she likes.'

'We're sick these several years hearing about all you can buy,' Fonsie said angrily.

'Well, I'll go where people will not be sick, where there'll be no upcasting,' Philly said equally heatedly.

'What'll you do there?' John asked out of a desire to calm the heated talk.

'He'll grow onions,' Fonsie shook with laughter.

'I can't be going out to the oilfields forever. It'll be a place to come home to. You saw how the little iron cross in the circle over the grave was eaten with rust. I'm going to have marble put up. Jim Cullen is going to look after Peter's cattle till I get back in six months and everything will be settled then.'

'You might even get married there,' Fonsie said sarcastically.

'It's unlikely but stranger things have happened, and I'll definitely be buried there. Mother will want to be buried there as well some day.'

'She'll be buried with our father out in Glasnevin.'

'I doubt that. Even the fish go back to where they came from. I'd say she's had more than enough of our poor father in one life to be going on with. John here has a family, but it's about time you gave where you're going yourself some thought,' Philly spoke directly to Fonsie.

'If I were to go I'd want to go where there was people and a bit of life about, not on some godforsaken hill out in the bog with a crow or a sheep or a bloody rabbit.'

'There's no *if* in this business, it's just *when*. I'm sorry to have to say it, but it betrays a great lack of maturity on your part,' Philly said with drunken severity.

'You can plant maturity out there in the bog, for all I care, and may it grow into an ornament.'

'We better be going,' John said.

Philly rose and took Fonsie into his arms. In spite of his unsteadiness he carried him easily out to the car. Fonsie was close to tears. He had always thought he could never lose Philly. The burly block of exasperation would always come and go from the oilfields. Now he would go out to bloody Gloria Bog instead. As he was put in the car, his tears turned to rage.

'Yes, you'll be a big shot down there at last,' he said. 'They'll be made up. They'll be getting a Christmas present. They'll be getting one great big lump of a Christmas present.'

'Look,' John said soothingly. 'Mother will be waiting. She'll want to hear everything. And I have another home I have to go to yet.'

'I followed it all on the clock,' the mother said. 'I knew the Mass for Peter was starting at eleven and I put the big alarm clock on the table. At twenty-past-twelve I could see the coffin going through the cattle gate at the foot of Killeelan.'

'They were like a crowd of apes carrying the coffin up the hill. I could see it all from the car. Several times they had to put up hands as if the coffin was going to fall off the shoulders and roll back down the hill.'

'Once it did fall off. Old Johnny Whelan's coffin rolled half-way down the hill and broke open. They had to tie the boards together with the ropes they use for lowering into the grave. Some said the Whelans were drunk, others said they were too weak with hunger to carry the coffin. The Whelans were never liked. They are all in America now.'

'Anyhow, we buried poor Peter,' Philly said, as if it was at last a fact.

# Three Poems for J. R.

## Waif

You were a waif in our human mystery.
Your large eyes, so pleading and intense,
Looked from the Southern Cross
Like a dog's eyes
From its kennel— at home, and lost.

You moved with your muse
Inside what clothes you had put on
Like a howl inside a fugue.
Never enough Pacific Surf
Between the dry soles of your shoes.

Defending your family from your own wildness
As if Joan of Arc, in the flames,
Had begged God
To remember the innocent stake
And the poor sticks, no less.

You made even friendship seem like your first.
Your smile, like bomb-smoke, your Cheshire Cat grin,
Hovered afterwards. Or returned, pinned on the skull
Of a stone-age, Polynesian love-goddess— dug up
With a ten thousand year thirst.

## *Lovesick*

You barely touched the earth. You lived for love.
How many loves did you have?
Was there even one?

Or you just loved love.
Love, they say, meaning Dante's God,
Which has a sense in heaven— on earth, none.

Or Love, meaning biology: gene tactics
Of the reproductive system:
Faceless, mindless, almost the fire in the sun.

The Sun
Is its own Aztec victim, tearing for food
Its own heart out, eating only its own.

What was your love? Eyes, words, hands, rooms,
Children, marriages, tears, letters
Were merely the anaesthetics— the lulling flutes
As you fed your heart to its god.

No matter what happened or did not happen

You burned out. You reserved nothing.
You gave and you gave
And that included yourself and that
Was how you burned out
A lonely kind of death.

## Atavist

What you loved most
Apparently was the desert.
And the desert's brother— the sea.
The sea's eldest son— the stone.
And the Gulf— the old hoary father of all.

It was aboriginal incest
Of your firestick-naked, billabong spirit
That came bounding
Over the gibber flats
While your mother's dream lay moon open.

Or her immigrant pallor, in the downunder drought
 glare,
Drank the dark moisture and its shadow
From the black man's eye. Or her yawn
Had been violated, through the open window,
By snake-genes, blowing in the dust.

Maybe. You were feminist aggressive
With the best. But all the time
Your betrothed, the desert,
Was decorating you, night after night,
With his dead shells, and the inland sea

Slithered away off you
Every dawn, and the stone, shrinking again,
Left inside you the cold germ
Of the fossil fish.
Till the Gulf

Provoked by your reckless, hungry glances,
Your incantatory whisperings, your prayers to be
    carried off
By boundless Tao—
Came in the dream you just managed to tell,
Skull-eyed, big-winged, and took you.

## *Peerless Flats*

The first chapter of a novel to be published by Hamish Hamilton in Spring 1993.

Lisa, her mother, and her brother Max were dogsitting for a woman called Bunny who owned a house in the Archway. Bunny was away in America and was due back at any time.

Lisa's mother, Marguerite, went to the council when they first arrived in London. The council told her to come back when she was homeless. 'But we are homeless,' Marguerite had said. 'We're just not actually on the streets.' She explained about the dog who was an Alsatian and needed three meals a day. The council said to come back when she was absolutely homeless. When there was no roof of any kind over her head.

Lisa walked round to see her sister Ruby. Ruby was living two streets away with a boy called Jimmy Bright who dressed like a rockabilly in a white T-shirt and brothel creepers and wore his hair greased into a quiff. Ruby said that most people were terrified of Jimmy Bright. Jimmy despised the human race, with the exception of Ruby. 'He won't mind you eiver,' she reassured Lisa, 'cos you're me lil' sis.'

Ruby's accent had flourished in the two years since she left home and moved to London.

As Lisa walked up to Jimmy's flat she could see Ruby sitting on the floor in a sea of crumpled clothes. It was a ground floor flat that opened on to the street with a wall-sized sliding window. It was part of an entire row. Orange brick maisonettes with square, open gardens, and more were being built on the streets on either side. Jimmy didn't have curtains in his flat, and as Lisa approached through the derelict patch of garden, Ruby looked up and caught her eye. 'Hi babe.' She didn't stir as Lisa slid the door. 'Where's Jimmy?' She half expected him to rise up out of the debris and stop her in her tracks with his razor-sharp tongue. 'Dunno.'

Ruby was wearing a shirt with seven dwarfs all fucking each other on the front. Lisa sat and stared at it and wondered when it would get handed down to her. Everything Ruby had eventually got handed on to Lisa. Ruby was very generous with her things while Lisa was a hoarder by nature and found it hard to part with almost anything. She had once kept a box of plain chocolates she had won at a raffle and didn't like on the top shelf of her cupboard for two years. Eventually they had been discovered and distributed to the family as an after-dinner treat. Lisa pretended to be angry but really she had been relieved.

'How's Mum?' Ruby asked.

'All right.'

Marguerite and Ruby rarely saw each other and when they did, more often than not they argued. Lisa acted as their go-between. It was since Ruby left home, Lisa thought. Or before, since their mother's marriage to Swan Henderson, since Max was born . . . since . . . Lisa wasn't sure. She could remember Ruby and her mother getting on, somewhere in the distant past, but hard as she tried she couldn't place the memory.

Lisa had visited Ruby regularly in London while she waited for her sixteenth birthday. 'Don't tell Mum about this,' Ruby always ordered when they parted, and her mother's first question was inevitably, 'So how is Ruby getting along in London?'

Ruby was so unspecific as to what exactly she was to keep quiet about that Lisa never knew how to answer. 'Fine,' she said, and then at night she would lie awake worrying that if something terrible happened to her sister, it would be her fault for withholding vital information. Now that Lisa was in London herself she understood why Ruby had come back to school for the Christmas Fair, only six months after leaving, talking and swearing like a native East Ender and wearing a T-shirt for a dress and heels so high she couldn't walk down the hill to the pub. There had been no shortage of lifts on offer. Cars Lisa had never seen before swung open their doors.

Ruby was meant to be in London on a History of Art course. By the end of the first term she had already dropped out and was working in a shop that sold bondage trousers and plastic shorts and shirts with one sleeve longer than the other. People were whispering that Ruby was on drugs. That she was having an affair with a Sex Pistol. That it was a sacrilege to cut off that beautiful waist-length hair. Lisa felt immeasurably proud.

Ruby stood up and began searching the floor. 'Bastard,' she said, 'he's taken me fags.'

Lisa had a packet of ten John Player Special in her pocket. She smoked John Player because they had a scratch-and-reveal lottery in every packet to which she was addicted. She offered Ruby one. Ruby slouched through to the kitchen and smouldered it against the electric ring of the cooker until it caught. 'Mum wondered if you wanted to come round and have supper with us tonight,' Lisa said casually, passing on a message, investing nothing of herself in the request.

'Yeah I might.' Ruby pulled on her cigarette and changed the subject. 'Jim's old man gets out of the nick next week.'

'Oh.'

'This, you see, is his gaff.'

'Does that mean you'll have to move?'

Ruby sank back down to the floor, her thin white legs crossing.

'Jimmy says we can all live here, he says his Dad's all right. But I'm getting out.'

'You could come and stay at Bunny's,' Lisa said into the silence because she couldn't bear not to, and when Ruby didn't answer she added, 'but then again . . .'

'Yeah,' Ruby let her off the hook, 'anyway you'll be moving on yourselves soon, won't you?'

'That's true,' Lisa said and she stretched out a hand for a drag of Ruby's cigarette.

On the day Bunny returned from America, Lisa's mother went back to the council. Lisa took Max to the park. Max was five and was only really interested in foxes. Foxes were his main subject of conversation.

'Look, look there's a red fox in the pond with a fox tail and no ears and it's hungry and I'm going to eat you for my dinner. Are you a fox? I like foxes. I might be a fox when I grow up.'

Lisa tried to focus her mind on what he was saying and even attempted to answer his less obscure questions.

'How long is a fox tail?'

'Hmmm I don't know.'

'Is that fox very bad? Bad fox. Bad fox.'

'Quite bad.'

'Are you a fox?'

Lisa's patience never lasted long. 'No I'm not a fox. *Please* be quiet.'

'But if a bad fox came out of a hole in the ground in the middle of the night . . .' Max talked very fast with his words close together and his eyes staring straight ahead. It made Lisa feel crazy.

'Shut up.' She shook his narrow shoulders so that his teeth chattered. He continued anyway: 'There's a red fffox and a blllack fffox and two very big foxesss . . .'

Lisa gave him a final shove so that he fell back on to the grass with a thud. 'Shut uppp.'

'Shut uppp.' Max mimicked her exact tone and she knew that she was only winning because she was stronger than him. From the day Max learnt to talk he always won with the last word.

Lisa slumped back into the grass. 'I'm sorry.'

Max stared straight ahead with his flat black eyes.

'Would you like to know how to make a deluxe daisy chain?' she asked him.

He rolled over and waited while she reached around her, collecting the longest-stemmed daisies. He had a pale pointed face with two bright red patches on his cheeks like a child's drawing. His hair fell straight and black over his forehead in exactly the same way as his father's had. Lisa thought how strange it must be for her mother to be reminded daily of Max's father who at this moment was setting off on a round-the-world sailing trip with a Dutch nursery school teacher called Trudi.

When they arrived home Marguerite was waiting impatiently for them. 'They've given us a flat. They tried to put us into bed and breakfast, but then at the last minute they came up with a flat, a temporary flat, until they house us.'

'Bed and breakfast . . .' Lisa murmured mournfully, 'that could have been lovely.' Lisa had always longed to spend the night in a hotel, but to live in one, like a Parisian intellectual . . .

'You don't understand.' Marguerite said, 'it wouldn't be like that.'

Peerless Flats was in Peerless Street and was, as it turned out, just behind the Old Street roundabout. It was a faded 1930s block with stone staircases and bay windows and was hemmed in on every side by tower blocks. The man from the council was waiting. He glanced dubiously at the expectant faces of Marguerite and Lisa as they trailed after him with their plastic carrier bags of clothes.

There were two olive green doors on either side of each landing. Max ran from door to door head-butting the wood and shouting, 'I am the Foxman, I am the Foxman,' but no one appeared to complain.

The man stopped on the fourth floor and unlocked a door and for a moment they all stood crowded together in the tiny hall of the flat. The council man showed them wordlessly around. He pushed a door open into the sitting-room. It was oblong and empty with wooden floorboards and a window with small panes that cut the tower block opposite into squares. There was a bathroom and a narrow kitchen with flowers in orange, brown and yellow on the wallpaper all linked together with hairy green stalks. Max covered his eyes when he saw them. At the end of the kitchen was a toilet in a little room that hung out over the edge of the building.

The man from the council stood in the middle of the kitchen and clicked his tongue between his teeth.

'Where are the bedrooms?' Marguerite asked. The man widened his eyes questioningly as if he hadn't quite caught the gist of the conversation. 'There seem to be some rooms missing,' she said.

The man checked his form. 'You have been allocated a temporary homeless one-bedroom flat.'

'Well, where is it?' Marguerite demanded to know. 'This one bedroom, where is it?' And she kicked open the bathroom door to prove her point.

Lisa gulped. She hated a scene. 'Mum it's fine.' She felt her ears tensing up and her head filled with a high whine like a dying lightbulb.

The man walked briskly into the sitting-room. 'In council terms this is a one-bedroom flat,' he said, and then noticing Max, swinging viciously from the handle of the toilet door, he softened his tone, 'but I must ask you to remember, this is temporary accommodation and you will be re-housed in the shortest possible space of time.' He handed Marguerite the keys and left.

They returned the next night in the van loaded up with furniture. Marguerite had driven to the country to collect the things they had left stored in a garage until they had a place of their own. There was an iron bunkbed and the wooden base of a bed that had long since lost its legs. A fridge, a gas cooker and a tall wooden cupboard Marguerite had had for nearly twenty years. They had packed their books into boxes and the rest of the clothes from Bunny's into plastic bags.

As Lisa and Marguerite struggled up the staircase with the bed base between them, Lisa caught sight of something on the first landing, something oddly familiar. Marguerite stopped, jutting the frame into Lisa's side. 'Darling, aren't they yours?' she said, and in a horrible instant Lisa recognised a pair of her knickers. A green and white striped pair, the ones with the elastic gone in the waist. She nearly let the bed slide away from her down the stairs.

'I don't know.' She pushed to go on. 'Mum. Please.'

'But how did they get there?' Marguerite insisted.

At the same moment they both remembered the bags of clothes they had left propped against the wall of their new sitting-room. Marguerite stooped down and hoisted up a smudgy vest of Max's. 'Mum,' Lisa begged, and they began to heave on up.

In silence Lisa passed various grimy items that had once belonged to her. The sleeve of a jumper she had been knitting infrequently since she was twelve. It lay ragged in the crook of the stairs, collecting dust and cigarette ash, and still attached to its ball of wool by a long thread that wound its way down the staircase and out on to the street. Lisa disowned it. She cracked a little pot of blusher with her foot as she continued up.

The door of their flat was unexpectedly shut and locked. Lisa held Max back as they hovered in the doorway and listened. There was not a sound so they ventured in. Apart from the missing clothes, there was no other sign of a break-in.

'There's a fox swimming in the toilet,' Max shouted from the other end of the kitchen, and when Lisa went to investigate she found that the toilet door was locked. It was locked from the inside. If there is a fox in there, Lisa found herself thinking, he's gone and locked himself in. Lisa felt the skin on her face tighten as the door refused to give. She had a creeping feeling that there was someone holding on to the handle from the other side. Lisa's hand trembled as she unclasped it and backed away.

'Mum.' She wanted to stay calm for Max's sake. Max latched on to a person's fear and his eyes spun and his voice was louder than was bearable when he screamed.

'Mum . . .' Lisa called, 'I think there might be someone in the toilet.'

Marguerite strode over to prove her wrong. She took hold of the handle and pressed down and pushed up and banged on the door with her fists and called with her face close to the wood. 'Hello. Is someone in there? Hello.'

The more she shouted the braver her voice became. It even created a hollowness that echoed back at them through the wood. 'It must just be locked from the inside and someone very small must have climbed out of the window.'

'Someone tiny,' Lisa agreed, thinking of the window which she remembered as being one square pane of glass. The size of a rabbit hutch.

'Someone rabbit-sized,' Lisa suggested, and stopped herself as rabbits and thieving foxes, borrowed from Max's bubbling brain, began to chase across her mind.

They knocked, as a family, on the door of their neighbour. A young woman answered, pulling her matted wool dressing-gown across her chest as she inspected them through a slice of door.

'We've just moved in at number 52,' Marguerite told her through the crack.

The woman swung open her door. 'Well hello.' She had a high, Irish voice. 'I'm Frances.' She was as pale as milk with a turned up nose and skinny, skinny hair. 'Well, there's a hell of a crowd of you.'

Lisa nodded. 'But it won't be for long. They're going to re-house us as soon as they can.'

The woman smiled encouragingly. 'That's true all right. There's few that is here longer than three years.'

'Three years,' Lisa gasped. 'We were thinking more of three weeks. The man said . . .'

'Oh the man!' she interrupted, 'the man said I'd be out of here before the baby came and Brendan was to come over for the birth, but little Brendan is all of six weeks now and I've not heard a word.'

With that, little Brendan, as if hearing himself called, set up a thin wail from the other side of the wall and Frances hurried away to comfort him.

Frances's flat was identical to theirs with the same layout and overpowering wallpaper. The gas fire in the front room was blasting and the oven door was open, steaming up the hall and kitchen with a heat that made the empty flat feel full. Frances invited them to take a peep at little Brendan who lay staring at the ceiling with his blue rinsed eyes that were waiting patiently to change.

Lisa held Max at arm's length. Max hated babies and was liable to shout into their faces. Max only had respect for children older than himself. Unless they had turned into old ladies. Old ladies he took special pains to kick as he passed them in the street.

'Isn't he lovely,' Marguerite cooed, and Frances beamed with pride.

'It's just a great shame his father's not here to see him.' Frances flopped down onto the bed. 'But if he comes over before they offer me a flat we'll never get a place of our own. It's our only chance.'

'Couldn't he just come over for a visit?' Lisa asked, but Frances stared miserably into the fire and didn't answer. They sat for a moment in silence until the crash of a chair falling in the kitchen roused them. Max had been trying to get at a half-eaten Milky Way on the draining board.

Frances offered them the use of her toilet. 'Just knock three times,' and she laughed conspiratorially. She stood with Brendan in her arms and kept guard while Lisa and Marguerite unloaded the rest of the furniture. They squeezed one half of the bunkbeds into the bathroom as a bed for Max, in case he could be induced to go to bed before them, and set up the other half and the wooden base in the sitting-room.

Lisa spread the beds with blankets that were as familiar to her as anything she knew. They had made more homes than she could count feel like home with their unfolding. Frances brought them cups of pale tea and they stood around, chatting and smiling, and all the while straining for sounds of the burglar breaking out of the locked room.

Lisa and Marguerite lay against opposite walls pretending to be asleep and keeping their fear to themselves. The wooden window-frames creaked with every shock of wind and sent waves of possibilities through Lisa's chilled body. She listened so hard she thought her bones might crack. She twisted carefully in her sheets and heard her mother do the same. Lisa tried to remember when she and her mother had last slept in the same room. Not since she was a child and had slipped out of her own bed, wading through the silk of a black dream to climb in with her mother. Not since her mother had moved upstairs, first herself, then her few possessions, to Swan Henderson's shrine-like room with the king-sized mattress and the roll-top desk where, years later, Ruby had found the love letters addressed to 'Trudi my sweet.'

Lisa, Ruby and Marguerite had moved in with Swan Henderson as lodgers. They had moved in during the summer holiday when Lisa was nine. For almost a year they had been living in a large house on a bend in the road between one village and the next. It was a bend where cars frequently crashed. It was famous for it.

'We've been living here for ages,' Lisa had said to her mother as spring approached and she watched for the first time as her own daffodil bulbs, planted in the autumn, burst into flower. 'We've been living here for ages and ages. I'm bored,' Lisa tried again to prise a reaction from her mother. She put a moan into her voice although she wasn't sure how seriously she wanted it to be taken.

'I want to live in a house with my own garden so I can plant a blue rose bush and watch it grow up,' she had complained when they packed up from their last place and moved for the eleventh time in three years; but a part of her liked the excitement and the new people and a different bedroom and a different garden and a different lift to school almost every month.

'It looks like we will be moving,' Lisa's mother said, interrupting her thoughts, and taking her by surprise. 'At the end of the summer term.'

'Where to?'

Marguerite didn't know. 'But as always,' she said, 'something is bound to turn up.'

Lisa woke up with a start. The sun was streaming through the uncurtained window and her mother was still asleep with her face to the wall. Lisa's whole body ached and the moment she moved she was reminded of the locked room and the chair they had left jammed against the toilet door.

Max sat crosslegged on the kitchen floor absorbed in a game of Lego. Lisa tiptoed over him. She shifted the chair and tried the handle. Nothing had changed, but in the light of morning the locked door looked less sinister and she tapped at the wood happily with her fingers as she made her way to the bathroom to take a pee in the sink.

Lisa dressed Max and then herself and taking her brother with her for safety in numbers she walked out into Peerless Street to find a shop to buy some bread and milk for breakfast. It was Sunday and a strange, empty calm hung over the boarded cafés and the pillared basements of the tower blocks. Peerless Flats itself was still asleep. She kept a hand on Max's shoulder as they wound down the staircase avoiding the litter of her most personal belongings, and even kicking her green and white striped pants into a narrow corner as they passed.

They wandered hazily into Bath Street and through to Iron-monger Row where they discovered a Turkish Baths and a laundry but no shop. They walked slowly back across to City Road and turned in towards the Old Street roundabout. Max was unusually quiet, and stayed by Lisa's side, keeping up with quick padding steps of his plimsolled feet.

'I wonder if anyone except us lives round here,' Lisa said, and Max looked up at her with blank eyes.

There was a row of bus stops at the end of City Road with buses that went to the Angel and Highbury Corner. There was one bus, passing every twenty minutes, according to the time-table, that went up to the Archway and stopped at the end of Bunny's road. Lisa was tempted to wait for it and travel in its warm, red comfort to an area where people lived and shops opened, but she thought of her mother waking up in the empty flat, alone with the locked room, and she hurried on around the roundabout, scanning side streets for signs of life and peering into the deserted squares.

Marguerite stirred as she slammed the door. 'Did you get some milk?'

'No.'

'The foxes are dead,' Max explained, and for once Lisa was inclined to agree.

## Form

Trying to tell it all to you and cover everything
Is like awakening from its grassy form the hare:
In that makeshift shelter your hand, then my hand
Mislays the hare and the warmth it leaves behind.

## Icicle

Though the caddis fly does something similar with
                                                    hailstones
Knitting them into a waistcoat for her shivering larva,
The ants carry snowflakes inside their nest to make an
                                                    icicle
Which will satisfy the huge queen and her ignorant
                                                    grubs
And prove that the melting snowman was somebody's
                                                    child.

# Our Customs, Your Customs

'In the old days they sent the priest,' etc. We were allowed to talk amongst ourselves. And it was perhaps that more than anything else which caused my brother, Richard, to point out to my mother who had made the remark, that some of *those* had clearly been pretend priests; and my mother wrong-footed him again by saying that pretend priests had God as their ally whereas these others only had the State; though, she conceded, it was difficult to tell one source from the other. At the end of all this, a priest was shown in.

He wasn't someone we knew; a quick calculation: what did he know about us? Would we insist on knowing at least as much about him as he knew about us, to make the coming encounter more even? We would stress the aspect of the early priests far from home, the dress, the voice, the way they called on you at dinnertime and came back when the food was good – as it always was at my grandmother's, etc. At one time not only the Methodist but all the others had found their way to her door in Coderington. But now we were in another country, in their country, and the years, the decades had made a difference; my grandmother who never made the journey with us had been allowed to die, sort of, and the rest of us were kept waiting, far from Coderington, far from St Caesare.

There were four of us; mother, sister and two brothers: that could be said to be our family but, in another sense, there were fifteen hundred of us, which was the population of St Caesare, and we had to bring them with us, not just because they were family in some extended sense, but that each one depended on others to keep us all safe, to preserve or remember bits of family life that little units like ours, on our own, tended to forget. Let me give you an example, a simple one. When the house, my grandmother's old house in Coderington collapsed, the village came and took it away, plank by plank. And when I later visited the island I was taken to this house in the village, that house on the hill – house after house – that had incorporated a rafter from the old drawing-room, or the still new-looking boards that had been the partition between the spare room and the bathroom upstairs, behind my grandmother's bedroom. Fancy bits of the original verandah ringed this or that little house, perhaps making it look ridiculous, but all in all the place, though no longer visible on the skyline, was enjoying a new lease of life. That went also for the utensils, from breadroom to kitchen to the scales for weighing the cotton. Now, if you found a way of preserving things that were valuable to you, how could you do less for people?

So back to the family: either we were four or we were fifteen hundred, which was the environment in which the family made sense. This is what the problem was about, the great debate between their customs and our customs, and who was or was not allowed to be family. Earlier migrants had been caught out, had been tricked, had been encouraged to shed family, and now some were living to regret it. Like Flora Blessett. Remember Flora?

Miss Flora had struggled enough in her time so naturally when she had the opportunity to come over with her new husband she made a temporary arrangement for the child and took her chances. And when you're young you accept the usual sorts of assurances. But now look at Flora? Husband dead and here she is alone – child's family on the other side of the world – put in a home with people she didn't know, some of them put there even though they had family in this country, a state of affairs which made Flora feel she was being held there as punishment for something she had done early in her life. So she tried to recover her family; and they put a stop to that and said what was lost was better left forgotten; and they got strangers in to threaten her out of her rights of family, strangers who took her back to her point of entry in this country, the day, the hour, to what had accompanied her to this country – which was only the partner, the husband, now gone – and they convinced her that to

cling to anything that took place before that date was either
against the law or her interests or her sanity.

Now – we don't want to go on about it, but – Flora Blessett
was a woman in her thirties when she was transported; so what
does that do to her early life growing up in Coderington and
going to the Methodist School next to the graveyard, to the
Sunday School, the little wooden building behind Mr Lee's rum
shop, where the boys who were trying to be lay-preachers were
given the opportunity to preach on a Sunday night, to build up
their confidence? (Of course, most of them were doing it to pick
up women but that's another . . .) Flora was known to be sweet
on one of Professeur Croissant's boys – much younger than she;
it must have been the middle boy, not Cincinnatus who was
named after one of the Haitian Presidents who was assassinated:
Cincinnatus ended up in America, in Washington, and became
so American that he used to refer to his home as DC – just DC –
not even bothering with the Washington. It wasn't him, it was a
younger one that Flora had been sweet on. Anyway, that boy
eventually married someone else. Yet, they say he's good to his
family back home. So, where were we? Flora had been ordered
to forget all that. And other things: wasn't she in training at
some point to be a nurse or teacher or something, when the child
got in the way? Or was that someone else? We don't really know
the details; we weren't family. Anyway, she was in her thirties
when she married and made the trip abroad.

So here we were again, the family, in a room with a priest
who didn't look like a priest, the tell-tale sign being that he was
pretending to take an interest in the fortunes of Flora Blessett, as
recounted by us – the misfortunes, rather. You learn to be precise in this business, because what you say can be taken down
and used against you, and you never know who's laying down
traps to snare you. (Everyone remembers the case of that man
from Look Out who said Goodbye at the start of one of his
interviews. He said Goodbye instead of Good Morning, and you
know what happened to him! He had to spend the rest of his life
pretending that it was deliberate, and that when you met someone for the first time it was proper to say Goodbye. These were

the sorts of things which, over the years, made people a little suspicious of St Caesarians. But let's not get side-tracked, we're trying to be precise. I forget now the point we were making (I'm sure he's noting it all down) so let's stick with this thing of being precise: were there *four* or *fifteen hundred* in our little family? They will try again to trip us up over that; and of course, if you're unsympathetic, or just too busy to go into it, you could make a case for there being a serious discrepancy between being a family of four and a family of fifteen hundred. But that way of thinking, my sister Avril says (Avril is the juggler of the family, she's also something else) – that way of thinking is poor in spirit. Though it saddens us a little to hear Avril talk like this, because it sounds a little old for her, and it makes us conscious that time is passing. (In the words of my mother, 'Time waits for no man.')

And as you see, we've got caught again: who told us to be blabbing about Flora Blessett when we have our own problems to think about? Did we want to add her to our list? *No*. And yet it seems that one or two things we said about Flora weren't strictly accurate. Who was going to correct them? No, she didn't grow up in Coderington, after all, she grew up in Lower Barville where some of the poorer people in those days made their homes, in the forties and fifties, before the expatriates came and built their villas. But of course *we* were from Coderington, and when you were hazy about certain people you sometimes slipped into the habit of thinking that they were from Coderington, too, and that they had done this or that job of work for my grandmother. If we were wrong about Flora in this, maybe we were wrong about one or two other details as well. But then we never claimed to be right about everything on the island, and certainly not about people who had come on ahead of us, and that's why we tried to keep hold of the last fifteen hundred who were part of our story.

The priest who wasn't like a priest made us a proposal which was either subtle or insulting. We were a pretty sharp family by now with over three decades' experience of being interrogated. My sister was the sharpest but we were all pretty sharp. My mother, at the start, had had to deny that she was other people, everything from her own mother to the servant girl who used to bring her a glass of water in Coderington and not spit in it; and in the end she decided it was too boring to keep denying being this or that; that it was much more fun to become all these other people when the occasion arose; and now she was so good at it that when we met her we had to spend quite a bit of time guessing who she might be on that particular occasion. My sister, as I say, was both a juggler and something else, and we were so impressed by the something else that our nickname for her was Something Else. My brother won't let us talk about him from the point of view of security and I was the liar in the family. And it's a curious thing, that if you pronounce the word liar quickly or indistinctly, or put on an American accent, you could get away with people thinking you were a lawyer – but, of course, I don't overdo it. So, as I say, we were a pretty sharp family.

Of course, we were allowed to come and go on a temporary basis; we weren't confined to this little room, only we had to come back to be grilled, at regular intervals, and, hopefully, to acquit ourselves in such a way that in time we wouldn't have to come back to the room at all. And always the pressure was to repudiate members of the family – on the edge, so to speak – to save our own skin. There were many in this country – some from St Caesare itself – who blamed us for holding out, who revelled in the fact that they had, at the first sign of trouble, cut themselves loose; that they were now doing all right; that we had brought our own difficulties upon ourselves and that stories like Flora Blessett's were unrepresentative. All this was well known. It was also well known that our interrogators often tried to add to our list of family anyone – like Flora – whose bits of past we recognized floating about and tried to rescue, to pin down. We had to watch this because having had so much difficulty with our own fifteen hundred we couldn't afford to have that figure adjusted *upwards*. Which is what the new man (too boring to keep calling him a priest who didn't look like a priest) seemed to be encouraging us to do.

But no. He wasn't trying to make us add Flora Blessett to our list of essential family, making us in total fifteen hundred and one (or five); what he was suggesting was that we seemed close enough to Flora to substitute her for someone who had long been on our list, but had perhaps by now faded to a point whereby that person might no longer be perceived as family; for he recognised the need for us to rescue those bits of Flora that were being lost, those first thirty-odd years in Coderington or Lower Barville or wherever.

It was a trap. We could all think of people we could substitute for family. Friends; people in books. People on television. We could think of *objects* that, with good conscience, we could substitute for family! It was a trap, we knew, but we weren't fazed by this sort of thing. We weren't strange people; we weren't fanatical. We had long accepted that you couldn't just *add* to family *ad infinitum*, because in time – and they were giving us time – we should then embrace the whole world. So when the representative withdrew (that's better than priest . . . etc.) – when he withdrew, we prepared to discuss the matter seriously, to see who could be jettisoned from the old family to make room for Flora. (We started by affirming those who were sacrosanct: Grandmother. Uncles who had done this or that in various parts of the world, X, who used to do the washing and ironing in the big house, etc.)

I'm saving more time than you would think to say that we eventually came down in favour of Grandmother. *Grandmother!* Grandmother had always been the central member of the family, even though she had never travelled with us. She was so much part of us that, in a sense, we couldn't not bring her with us if we tried. So, really, there was no need to keep her name on our list. Mentally, it was forever engraved there, because when you came down to it, when you thought of Coderington – and we thought of Coderington often – we saw the house intact, and the five grafted mango trees at the edge of the front lawn, that she had planted for us, one each for my mother and for us children. You couldn't think of that without seeing her, sitting there at the top of the steps, the back steps, on the floor of her room, look-

ing down. Everything to do with the house, from the weighing
of the cotton, to auctions from the Animal Pound, to forbidding
the ironing of clothes on a Sunday – so the woman downstairs
had to be gentle with the flat-iron – recalled grandmother. As –
delicious memory – did the taste of brandy, which we, children,
were allowed to 'gargle with', diluted, when we had a tooth-
ache. Her memory clung to us, so we could pretend to let her go
– the authorities would like that – while we knew better. (In any
case, there were others, another branch of the family, trying
to get grandmother into another country; but we didn't trust
them.)

Following that sacrifice, we managed to save for the family
those who were at risk, those thought to be marginal: the girl
Madeleine, who used to bring my mother water and not spit in
the glass, for when you were in a strange country how could
you be sure that whoever brought you water wouldn't spit in
the glass? We managed to save the six or seven friendly people
on Rodney's beach, people who wouldn't look at you and say
you were too fat (considering your husband was away) or that
you had bad skin, or that you were a strange colour. (They
would say these things, but you would give as good as you got,
and not feel silenced.) We had our own individual treasures: I
saved mad Horace, who had the ability to dream my life, my
future life, peopling it with figures, unknown to me, who
repeatedly appeared in his dreams, but not in mine. So I had to
rely on him to describe my family to me, and hoped that he was
telling me the truth, and feared that he wasn't. I had to preserve
Horace, or lose that glimpse into the future. Collectively, we
saved characters like Great-uncle Neighton, who was the one
who didn't make it, of that generation. Some said he should
have gone to Panama or Haiti with the rest, instead of going
further north by way of Cuba. Or, like his brother, he may have
won the *borlette* in Haiti and had a few good years.

But, like others, Neighton, too, was a successful enough traveller, though he travelled mainly in his mind. He was testing the
strength of the family mind to travel vast distances – distances
beyond being a doctor or a preacher – and he had got bogged

down, years ago, in Egypt. Egypt, he used to say, was as good a place as any to live in. So, in memory of Great-uncle Neighton who never made it, we children used to memorise bits of the experience that from time to time fell out of his mind. And even now, in middle age, with other distractions, we were prepared to fight our corner over the relative merits of Amen-hetep III (1402–64) and his prosperous and tranquil empire stretching from the Euphrates in the north to Napata in the Sudan. Some-one of us would defend him against a brother, a sister who would insist that he had inherited it all and that the real figures of interest were Amen-hetep II and Tuthmosis IV. This way we could preserve the mental toughness that Great-uncle Neighton promised and lost. (After a recent discussion, in our exiled room, we decided to go on the offensive: when our interrogator arrived we would open with a discussion on the influence of Amen-hetep II's sun disc image on sun-worship and creation of a new god under Amen-hetep III. But my sister, sharp in her juggling, said we'd be playing into his hands, we'd be accused of triumphalism. My sister was Something Else.)

And then certain things happened in the world that you might not want to hear about. The result was that the family reinstated *Grandmother*, because really, we didn't want to be seen to be chipping away at our base, at our dates, and making ourselves too provincial in time, for Great-uncle Neighton had seemed a little exposed without Grandmother. And also, how could we trust the other branch of the family, trying to get her into another country, to succeed? (And really, we couldn't have pre-vented the moving of Flora Blessett from the home she didn't like, into something worse.)

So, when the man returned to confront us in the room, we reinstated *Grandmother*, and we retained responsibility for Flora Blessett whose growing-up in Coderington had been in doubt. Now, we were reconciled to being a family of *five* or, if you like, *fifteen hundred and one*, and growing.

## *Four and a Half Dancing Men*

She knows how to fold
and turn the paper,
guiding the scissors with care
to create for her son
five little dancing dolls.
Toe by toe, hand in hand,
*ring a ring a rosy*,
watch them caper

across the plain and up,
up over the mountain –
five happy men
to amuse a small boy in bed –
so cross, so bored, for
all that, a little blond god,
with the shifting realm
of his risen knees to govern.

The fauna buried in his
landslides, the cities
swallowed by his earthquakes
no longer divert him.
He monitors the marching
of five chained men
with silent intensity,
grave as his liquid eyes.

Up and down, up and down,
his to command,
one, two, three, four
manikins spring by.

He tears from the fifth
an arm, and then a thigh.
The troupe trips on,
though sagging at one end.

Four and a half dancing men,
and the half he made
with an act of his hand
seems to please him best.
He smiles. The same
can be done with the rest.
Four blind men, and a half,
unafraid, unafraid.

# A Silver Christening Mug

Of all his dreadful colleagues, whom Lubowicz considered a bunch of emotionally retarded, dangerously repressed and un-relentingly snobbish middle-class Oxford academics, he found Porbright the most difficult to deal with. Porbright seemed to be the epitome of the breed; or rather, the exaggeration or carica-ture which occurs when the outsider of a club devotes his whole life to becoming an insider.

Porbright had arrived in Oxford on a Rhodes scholarship shortly after the Second World War, a first from Canberra in his pocket, a proven track record in rugby, and an insatiable desire in his loins to conquer that world that had been too much for his bankrupt and emigré father. With a giddy swiftness, he set about losing his nasty Australian twang, the cheap and unpleasant cig-arettes, the oversharp blazers and ties. He acquired a reputation for the finest plus-fours in Oxford, became a master of etiquette, and cultivated membership of a multitude of dining societies and flatulent clubs.

In time, he became more of an 'Oxford chap' than the Oxford chaps themselves. He became the institution's conscience, the sort of spiritual *primum mobile* of his college. It was to Porbright that people went when they wanted to check up on the exact wording of the Latin grace for the feast of St Swithin; to Por-bright that they went when they wanted to know the correct form of address for a lesser cousin of the royal family, or the Baroness of Sutherland. And it was to Porbright they went when they wanted to discuss any little matter of college busi-ness, such as the allocation of rooms, or the deployment of a legacy from the city. So profound was his transformation that he ingested the language of his chosen home, and spoke it more fluently than its authors. It was Porbright who composed the Christmas address, and scribed the college bulletins, such masterpieces of erudite and infantile wit as could only be penetrated by one who had spent at least twenty years absorbing the Biggles slang and classical references of Eton after-the-match teas and Master's sherry parties on summer evenings on the long college lawns.

And Porbright's life, occupied in this fashion, was a happy one. He was fulfilled, successful, satisfied. In time, he acquired, as a finishing touch to his portrait of himself, a deep plummy bass which succeeded in intimidating undergraduates from the North or young academics who had come up through the state schools. He married the daughter of a former Conservative Cabinet minister. And he acquired a long wonderfully polished rosewood pipe, from which this bass, replete with billowings of smoke, would boom out to the terror of young students of Tacitus and Pliny; for Porbright taught, of course, the gentleman's subjects: Classics and Ancient History.

Lubowicz, a Polish Jew by origin, who had come from Israel to work in Oxford, could not say when his loathing of Porbright had first begun. It had been going on for several years now, and had become one of those institutionalised obsessions, those incursions of madness into the flat landscape of the everyday, which you no longer examine.

If pushed, Lubowicz would have said he hated the man's pomposity, his pretentiousness, his vaunting, vacuous and obscene pride. The gnawing snobbery which was at the very vitals and heart of the man, driving him ever on to further peaks of folly. And then, if questioned further, he would have added more quietly, that Porbright might be a fool but he was also dangerous. That he might be a caricature of something, an antediluvian obsolescence, but that it was not so very long since the good old heady thirties – apparently the romantic core of his value system – when he would have been a member of clubs where no Jews nor blacks nor women were allowed. That he was a believer in Empire, and that it was a great disappointment to him that he had to relinquish the system of race distinction for that of class distinction in making his day to day judgements about people. And that of course he was one of those historians who consider it in very bad taste to try to prosecute old Nazis living peacefully in Britain fifty years after the events they are accused of are over and all decent gentlemen have come to a polite agreement to drop the subject.

Generally, Lubowicz's hatred took the form of avoidance. Porbright was too powerful a member of college to have as an open enemy; so he engaged in the only thing possible under the circumstances – flight. He avoided high table dinners where he might be forced to listen to Porbright's booming drone, or contemplate his magnificent profile slowly turned for every-one's inspection, where the similarity between its chiselled splendour and that of his great hero, Alexander the Great, could not possibly be missed by anyone except those ciphers of the classically illiterate, who unfortunately seemed to have been worming their way through the college portals over the last few years. He avoided the college quad as much as was possible, and especially on those days when Porbright would do ostentatious perambulations there with visiting dignitaries. He cut his attend-ance at college meetings to a bare minimum, and avoided those most dull of Oxford parties, where Porbrightianism – complete with small armies of aspirant new members booming and guf-fawing, flexing twenty-year-old calf muscles clad in the thickest of tweeds, dropping Latin phrases as regularly as a hen drops turds – might be uncontrolledly rife.

The policy worked in the main, and his irritation level was kept to a minimum. But then one day – it was a clear bright autumn day, with golden trees and fresh white clouds scudding high across a blue sky, a day in which you forgot about college and college matters – Lubowicz's policy of containment was over-turned with one fell blow; a blow which struck him down into an abject position of dependence and overturned that delicate emotional homeostasis of hatred and superior detachment which had taken him so long to achieve. The long and the short of it was that Lubowicz fell off a ladder, cricked his back, and Porbright rescued him; thus placing him in a position of indebtedness which he found completely intolerable.

Lubowicz fell while trying to hang up a painting in his college room. He was at the top of the stepladder when it slid away from him and he was left without so much as a picture rail to hang on to. Porbright, going past at the time to visit his friend the bursar to discuss the financing of a new Keasby bursary to keep 'young gentlemen at Oxford University in the style of living to which they are accustomed', heard the bang – 'prodigious' as he said afterwards – and came bustling immediately to the site of the accident. With great alacrity and energy, he took charge of the situation. 'Dear fellow! Dear fellow! Allow me!' Picking Lubowicz off the floor, where he was grounded in agony, he helped him drag himself to the sofa and covered him in some moth-eaten old college blankets. He ordered up his own doctor, a back specialist, and presided over the diagnosis and the prurient visits of half his colleagues, who loved, as Lubowicz well knew, nothing more than a sick bed (failing a death bed), as a relief to academic tedium, and the only thing left in life that still gave them a sensation of their own vitality. Then Porbright drove him home, despite protestations, and when Lubowicz tried to thank him, insisted on the whole thing being 'Gratis, my dear fellow, gratis. *Egregium sanctumque virum qui donet amico* and so on . . .' the meaning of which phrase Lubowicz did not know.

After he had recovered sufficiently to move around, Lubowicz determined to buy Porbright a large present to get rid of the unpleasant sensation of indebtedness he felt, and also the resentment at having been seen flat on his back on the floor, like a bug that can't turn over, and at having been buried by him, with whatever excuse, under a pile of stinking old blankets.

And he spent some time thinking what this present should be. At first he considered an artistic gift – a gift which would show his good taste and sober 'chappiness'; some fine old hunting print in a gilt frame, a picture of the college, or one of those old maps which were then the fashion, of Saxon or medieval

Oxford. But the more he considered these, the more he found them too dull. God knows how many such things Porbright already possessed – they were probably something he had aspired to in some former life and rejected now as a sign of the tawdry culture of the nouveau riche. And Lubowicz wanted to give something a little striking, a little startling, as befitted his own more bold and striking personality, not something expensive and wholly unlovely, to be slid away into some dusty corner of bland English bric-a-brac.

He next thought of chocolates. He considered the fabulous hand-made chocolates of Gerard Ronay – he could go up to London and buy some – the exquisite sweetmeats with subtle striated colourings, and shaped in the form of shells and flowers and corals. He could buy a whole box of them, a complete set, monogrammed possibly in copperplate. A gastronome would find them a delight of course, an ultimate aesthetic experience, and would recognise the tastefulness and delicacy of the gift. But would Porbright?

When Lubowicz got to considering this, he became uneasy. He recollected those interminable meals after Latin grace, innumerable courses of crucified meats, deconstructed vegetables, and tapiocacised puddings, consumed beneath the arrogant gaze of former Masters, who stared down from their gilt frames with craggy features twisted in 'Socratic' contempt for things of the flesh. (Despite the spattering of port-shattered veins across their withered cheekbones.) No, Porbright would eat the most disgusting food with great relish, gustily praising the college kitchen. On second thoughts, the chocolates seemed a bad idea. He probably wouldn't realise what he was getting, and he might even think – here Lubowicz shuddered – that after all his help it was a bit of a shabby present.

After much heartache and anxious scrutiny, Lubowicz decided on a crate of champagne. The gift was a good one on several counts: it had an air of doing things in style, in a rather grand style, a style which Porbright would not hitherto have associated with Lubowicz; the champagne was fine if not ostentatious; and, unlike the chocolates, it carried its price tag with it.

So Lubowicz bought the champagne, and with a decided feeling of relief after all this time, and almost of exuberance, took it round to Porbright's room.

'My dear fellow! How charming of you!' Porbright greeted him. 'But I just don't *drink* the stuff. Haven't been able to stand it for years – too fizzy you know. Affects the digestion. But a very kind thought, very kind. Really, you must take it away and drink it yourself, with some of your young undergraduate friends.'

He held his line, and couldn't be prevailed on to accept the champagne. He assured Lubowicz that getting the doctor was nothing, that he was paid princely sums to attend to his own, Porbright's, back, and so it made little difference to do a quick 'jiggery pokery' on the far more youthful back of Lubowicz. That Lubowicz must just accept the favour with his compliments, for what were one's colleagues for if they could not help one out of a jam, and that in short, if Lubowicz wished to express his thanks for so small a service, the best thing he could do would be to honour him with his presence at a small sherry party that he and his dear wife were holding for a few friends on the following Sunday evening.

Lubowicz could think of no excuses. He was in a fluster, deflated and bothered. He struggled back to his own room with the crate of champagne, which he promptly gave to his cleaner with an air of lordly unconcern; and then regretted it all afternoon, because the man probably wouldn't be able to tell a reasonable champagne from white Lambrusco, and the whole thing had, after all, cost more than a hundred pounds.

On Sunday, still in the same state of anxiety and dull resentment, he turned up for Porbright's party. It was just the sort of party he liked to avoid. A gathering of mini-porcs, as he called them in his mind. Twenty-one-year-old octogenarian buffers, the down still soft on their cheeks, and the ideology already as hard-wired in their heads as the feeding habits of a plankton. They were Porbright's acolytes; milky youths fresh from the playing fields of Eton, who, having served their apprenticeship of years of bullying, beating, buggering and browbeating, were determined now to enter into their manly inheritance.

Lubowicz found himself a corner over by the window and set in for some heavy drinking.

But he was disturbed in this occupation by Porbright himself, who came up in a resplendent new pair of tweed bloomers, and an air of magisterial patronage.

'Lubowicz, my dear fellow! How nice of you to come! And how's the back? A little better I hope. No twinges and creaks. No? Wonderful, absolutely wonderful . . . Now, you must come and meet Anthony Pantie, a very interesting young man, son of Pantie the minister for trade and industry. Studying classics, of course, like his father before him . . . up in '57, did you know?'

Lubowicz was directed over to the centre of the room where a short boy, with round glasses and an inveterately baby face, was delivering pronouncements on world politics to his fellows in a thin arrogant drawl, with an air of papal infallibility.

'Oh no!' thought Lubowicz, with a sinking feeling. 'This is going to be bad.'

But at this point he was saved by a sudden high-pitched scream in the garden outside the drawing-room, and the sight of two children running very fast across a flower bed. One was a girl, with long brown hair which flew out behind her, skinny legs, and a red dress; the other was a stout little boy, who was puffing obsessively as he ran and was pursuing her with something which he held tightly grasped in his right fist.

They disappeared from sight. There was a pounding of footsteps in the corridor, and they appeared, panting, in the doorway.

At the sight of the room full of guests, the girl, who was about seven and several inches taller than the boy, stopped abruptly in the doorway, turned and hit her brother behind her to stop him doing whatever he was doing. Then she began to compose herself into the picture of a demure young lady in a red dress with black patent shoes and a black velvet bow in her hair. She was only foiled in this effort by an air of irrepressible wickedness which flashed out from her large downcast eyes; and her ill-hidden sadism towards her brother.

'Ah Sophie – and Charles! You little savages, what are you getting up to?' said Porbright. 'This is a sherry party you know. There is a . . . ha . . . decorum . . . a certain decorum . . . ha ha.' He turned to Lubowicz.

'Lubowicz, meet my grandchildren – Sophie – and Charles.' He introduced them separately and ceremoniously, with great pride.

Lubowicz found himself looking into a pair of very large amber-flecked eyes, fringed by thick sooty lashes. The eyes looked up at him with sly curiosity, rested on him for a moment with the blinding attention of children, and then looked down again; there followed a small giggle as he shook her hand, a twisting of long pale fingers, and a shifting of the black patent shoes.

'And this is Charles,' Porbright boomed, bringing up little Charles, who had been standing watching his elders with wide eyes and an open mouth, and the seat of his trousers hanging somewhere down round his knees.

'But Charles!' he said as Charles came up, the round eyes still fixed on Lubowicz and a long tube of grey snot hanging down from a very tiny cold-reddened nostril.

'What on earth is *that*?'

Charles broke his gaze for the first time, and looked down now to where his grandfather was staring. Laconically, as if trying to study what it was that should produce the effect, he surveyed his own round dimpled fist, which held in its fat grasp a long pink wriggling worm.

Sophie gave a sniff and turned her head away on a long and perilously slim white neck. She asserted in a tone of chilly precision:

'He was trying to chase me with a worm. He's dis*gust*ing.'

Charles shifted his gaze to his sister and blinked vacantly several times.

'Charles!' boomed Porbright. '*Were* you trying to chase your sister with a worm?'

Charles blinked again, and looked around him. He had a baffled air, as if events were going out of his control, and he could not find a handle.

'*Were* you Charles?' repeated Porbright.

Charles took a big sniff. The tube of snot shot up into his nose for a fraction of a second, and then reappeared again, in exactly the same position.

'She p-p-put a . . .' He sniffed again. 'She p-p-put a p-p-plastic b-b-bag– ' Another big sniff. 'She said: "L-lets go down the g-g-garden and see wh-what h-happens if we put a p-p-p-lastic b-b-bag on your head." '

There was a small silence when Charles finished his deposition. Porbright stared at him for a moment, and then turned to Sophie, who had flashed her brother a look of pure hatred and menace, and then turned her head away at a severe angle, adopting an expression of icy and transcendent contempt.

'Is this true Sophie?' said Porbright more gently, for Sophie was evidently a favourite with him. 'Is this true?'

She did not answer straight away, but remained standing, with her fine brow puckering in suppressed frustration, and her small chin, which was faintly receding, tilted in defiance.

'Is this true Sophie my dear? Did you try to put a plastic bag on your brother's head?' Porbright continued portentously.

At this point something broke in Sophie. She gave a toss of her head, which made her long hair in its bow leap and fall, crossed her arms defiantly, and glowered down at Charles.

'He tried to hurt Nobody!' she asserted with great and self-righteous force. 'He deserved it. He tried to hurt Nobody!'

Everyone absorbed this piece of information. Then she continued in the same tone of righteousness. 'He pulled his wings to try and make him fly, and poked him with a stick and made him run until he fell over! It was *horrible*. And then he poked him in the eye with a blade of grass. He had no right to do that to Nobody! No *right*!'

The ferocity of the girl's opinion held everyone's attention for a while. Porbright, struggling now to keep his magisterial control, turned lumberingly round to Charles again.

'*Did* you do that to Nobody, Charles? *Did* you do that to Nobody?'

But by this stage Charles had had enough. He took one look at his grandfather's craggy and grandiose face bent down towards him, a sort of swimming look at the group of adults around him – all these mythical great giants arranging and disposing of the world in volcanic voices many feet above his head – and burst into tears. The snot jetted out of both his nostrils, and the worm fell out of his fist and on to the floor. Momentarily, the cocktail chatter stopped and people turned to stare.

'O my God Humphrey, look! There's a worm crawling across the floor!' said someone.

'I do believe there is,' said someone else in a tone of mild wonder and pleasure. 'My golly, I do believe there is.'

'Oh . . . em . . . er,' said Porbright. 'Now Charles, now Charles, don't cry, dear boy. There's a good chap. Don't cry, eh, good little fellow. Stiff upper lip eh . . . Mary! Mary!' he bawled for the child's mother, who came rushing from the kitchen.

Lubowicz meantime picked up the worm and threw it out of the window into the garden. He turned to Sophie, who was standing unaffected by her brother's tears, her expression of transcendent contempt, if anything, deepened.

'So who's Nobody?' he inquired conversationally, finding her rigour on the subject of tears rather intriguing.

Nobody was a small duckling, one of a litter of nine which had been born a week ago to Sophie's duck Jemima. Nobody had been born blind, with one leg shorter than the other and clipped stunted wings. He could not keep up with the others when they waddled after their mother, could not compete with them for food, and could not see his way to the water trough. So he had been christened Nobody by Sophie, and had been taken into her special care and attention.

'Oh yes!' asseverated Porbright, relaxing now that Charles had been whisked away by his mother. 'Nobody is a very special duckling. He is spoilt, I can assure you, quite spoilt. He has to have the best straw, and the best milk, the best grass and bowls of warm water to swim in. No one is allowed to harm him, and when he falls behind the others, Sophie picks him up and runs along and puts him first in the queue, just behind the mother.'

'Oh yes,' he continued, lighting his pipe and looking as mellow as Lubowicz had ever seen him, and almost human in his forgetfulness of self. 'Nobody has a fine life. Sophie makes sure of that. A fine life.'

Sophie, who had lost her chilly disdain during the course of the exchange and accomplished one of her instantaneous transitions from demure young lady to seven-year-old girl, now looked up eagerly into Lubowicz's face. 'Do you want to see him?' she asked with shy excitement.

'Oh yes, I would be honoured.' She gave a big smile, twisted her hands again, shifted her black patent shoes, blushed.

'Yes, you *are* honoured,' came Porbright. 'Not everyone is allowed to see Nobody. Not everybody by any means. Only Sophie's particular favourites.'

At this point Charles, who was having a horrible time – his buttons buttoned up so tightly his chin was pinched, his laces knotted, his trousers yanked up round his waist till they bit into his crotch, his face rubbed down with a flannel so vigorously his little nose was inflamed, broke free and interrupted. 'I want to come! I want to come! Can I come? Sophie? Can I come?'

Sophie considered this gravely. A frown appeared on her face. 'Only if you're not stupid,' she said eventually. 'Otherwise I'll never let you again.'

It was a fine frosty late afternoon. The sun was still shining in the beeches, in the hazel copses, on the fallow rose-beds. It polished the bright berries of hawthorn and holly and made them flash blood in their tawny thickets. The air was piercing, crystalline, and small skeins of starlings were unwinding across the sky, and then folding shut again into the topmost branches. Snitches of woodsmoke drifted across from neighbouring bonfires; and leaves were scattered, flame and organdy, not yet rotted. The world was in transition, on the brink of something. It held itself still and startling as a vision.

Sophie led the way directly to the copse of hazels at the bottom of the garden where a small hen hutch stood tilted against a tree trunk.

'In there,' she whispered, dropping onto her knees a few feet from the hutch. 'In there. They're all in there now. You can hear them.'

Lubowicz lowered himself on to his knees in the thick wet grass, and Charles, who had adopted him the minute they left the house, stuffing his hot little hand in his own, plumped himself down beside him. In his buttoned-up anorak and muffler, he seemed to throw off an amazing amount of heat. Lubowicz felt he was snuggled up against a hot little potato.

They all leaned forward carefully, and peered through the door inside the hutch.

Lubowicz could not see or hear anything to begin with. The milky grey shadows of the interior were opaque. There was a strong smell of fowl-droppings, rather sweet and warm.

'Look!' whispered Sophie. 'Look! There they are! If you look like this, you'll see them.' Tactfully, she tugged Lubowicz by the sleeve, until he had adjusted his position to gaze at an oblique angle through the door.

Inside, he made out a darker density in the shadows, which he took to be a creature, surrounded by a thin bluish line, sinuous and soft. The line gradually took on the form of a duck, wing-tip to tail and neck, very fine, like a piece of calligraphy from a Chinese painting. It seemed huge, ruffled out and swollen. And he made out a jewelled eye, gleaming at him mistrustfully from the darkness.

'Now watch!' whispered his companion.

'Quack, quack!' she went sharply. 'Quack! Quack! Quack!' And scattered some crumbs of dried bread at the doorstep of the hutch.

Now Lubowicz's sense of hearing came alive. He was aware of a tiny series of sounds at extremely high frequency, almost too high for audibility; and in the same moment, was aware that these sounds had been going on for some time. Now they intensified, until they formed a swarm of noise, a multitude of tiny high-pitched cheeps, desperate, raw, almost terrifying in their insistence. There was a deeper answering quack from the mother. And then the line of Chinese calligraphy decomposed itself. A large ruffled shadow loomed up against the door. And suddenly, streaming out from all directions, flapping tiny unformed wings, with little beaks held fantastically ajar, came a multitude of clamouring cheeping tiny, soft creatures, thronging the door and stumbling into the light.

'You see!' said Sophie triumphantly. 'You see!'

Followed sedately by the mother, they swarmed on to the grass and began to peck up the bread. They followed the line of bread that Sophie had scattered, and stumbled over each other to get at it. Lubowicz was so absorbed in the ferocity of their greed, and its clamour, that he did not immediately notice the irregularity: a duckling that had been left behind, was still struggling to stand up, and was not getting any of the bread.

'That's Nobody!' said Sophie, ran towards him and gathered him into her palm. 'Nobody.'

'Nobody,' repeated Charles happily in the same reverent tone. 'Nobody. Nobody.'

'And they're so mean. Always shoving you out of the way, and trampling on you. I hate them.'

And she began to feed Nobody choice morsels of bread from the palm of her hand. He was so weak he could scarcely take them. His beak, with its tiny punctured breath-holes, waggled about aimlessly. His eyes were scarfed up with a film of bluish skin. And he flapped his wings continuously in an effort to give strength to his legs which could scarcely support him.

Sophie held him towards Lubowicz, and the latter stroked his head to please her.

'They always leave him behind,' she said, her voice full of confusion, as she addressed Lubowicz, and communicating to him the child's private universe of trauma. 'Always. They peck at him, to keep him away from the food. Even when there's lots

of it. Even when there's lots. They drive him away from it, peck
at him.'

She nuzzled herself to Nobody, and gave him another kiss.

Then she caught sight of the other ducklings, all falling into
single file behind the mother, who was waddling off to the
water trough.

'And there they go again,' she broke out. 'Leaving you last
again.'

She ran behind the ducks and dropped Nobody into line
directly after the mother, where he wobbled unsteadily on his
feet, flapped his wings, stumbled, and began to be trampled on
by the fast-succeeding others.

'But I'll make you first,' she said, bending to help him along.
'I'll make you first. Always.'

Lubowicz gave the duckling a week, at the most.

When he went back to the house, Lubowicz found himself much
mollified by the whole escapade with the children. Sophie had
invited him to her birthday party the following Sunday, when
she would be eight, and he had accepted. Charles had trudged
along with his hot hand in his, and offered him one of his most
treasured possessions, a torn and sticky postcard of Diplodicus
diplodicus, the dinosaur. And although they were now taken off
by their mother for supper and baths, the glow they had created
stayed with him. He felt much altered towards the whole party
and Porbright in particular, who had unaccountably progeni-
tured such charming children. What a stupid fuss about the present, he thought to himself. What a neurotic fool I have been.

And when he entered the drawing-room he gave Porbright a
broad smile, as if to signify his approval.

'Ah Lubowicz, you're back! Well, my dear fellow, now
Sophie has let you out of her clutches, I must get you into mine.
I know you're a man of refined taste, a man with a love of the
arts, so you must come and tell me what you think of my . . .
ah . . . little collection.'

Porbright led the way rumblingly through the drawing-
room, now thick with smoke and the voice of Anthony Pantie

discoursing very loudly about how Israel must 'buck up its act' towards the Palestinians, to a small room which adjoined it. The room was cold and narrow and rather sombrely decorated in a thick hessian of olive green and brown. All over the walls, in elaborate gilt and mahogany frames, were paintings and drawings. They stretched from the floor to the ceiling, all shapes and sizes, colours and mediums.

Porbright now indicated them with a debonair flourish. 'My . . . ah . . . collection,' he said. 'Now, I don't want you to hurry, dear chap. Take as long as you like. I want you to examine them for me, so to speak.' He smiled coyly. 'And then give me your opinion – your true opinion as a man of the arts, mind you, one must never lie about these things – as to likeness, composition, chiaroscuro and so on.'

He rubbed his hands gleefully, and boomed as he moved towards the door. 'Now take your time, dear chap. Take your time.'

It took Lubowicz a little while to realise exactly what he was looking at, because he couldn't immediately believe his first intuition. But after surveying the whole gallery from top to toe, from the biggest oil painting placed above the fireplace, to the last little pastel sketch tucked in a corner, he could see that there was no doubt about it, no doubt at all. Every last one of them. Not a sketch, or a line, a dash of oil, or a smudge of charcoal, that was not devoted to the stupendous profundity, the classically noble Alexandrine profile, that king of craniums, Porbright himself.

It would have been hard for Lubowicz to say why what happened next in the room really happened. If he had had to track down the chain of causation, he would have muttered uneasily about the smoke and noise from the other room, how the fresh air perhaps had gone to his head, how he was drunk and his head was spinning. He would have mentioned a sudden memory of Porbright burying him beneath the blankets in his own room and booming 'Don't drink the stuff.' And then the arrogant drawl of young Anthony Pantie which penetrated easily to the cool room – 'Israel . . . the Jews . . . really must understand . . . don't play cricket . . . all that Moses and the mountain stuff . . . a superiority complex . . . whining self-pity. . . .'

All of which Lubowicz might have been capable of remarking on himself at another time and in another language. But somehow it was the effect of it, the imperial arrogance of the voice with its drawling iterations, that same voice that had resounded in fly-blown offices in Cairo, Damascus, Jerusalem and carved up empires, that had boomed along the quays of Akko and Haifa with bureaucratic instructions that turned back ships from Germany. The portraits began to spin in front of him. The vacant and overweening features began to dislimb and disliver themselves. They split and curved and grew and writhed. The bloodshot eyes came running down towards him from the walls, coming to get him, to pulverise, to consume.

And caused Lubowicz, standing dizzy in the cool and shadowy room, to reach out his hand towards a softly gleaming silver mug standing beneath the portrait above him, and slip it unaccountably, without rhyme or reason, into his breastcoat jacket pocket.

And that was when Porbright came back into the room, unable to wait any longer for Lubowicz's opinion; whisked him back into the main room, pumped him full of more sherry and insisted he give his views on his 'humble gallery', and also the Israel question being discussed so ably by young Anthony Pantie. Lubowicz, conscious of the mug in his pocket as if it were a tumour growing externally on his body in full view for everyone to see, suffered agonies of self-reproach and terror. He capitulated on the question of the gallery, and admired every piece. 'Yes, fine likenesses,' he heard himself say. 'Good compositions, yes, a powerful grasp of form . . .' And he allowed himself to be browbeaten by young Pantie, who was determined to be stern and stiff and not run away from this live Israeli in front of him – never mind that this Israeli had left his country some time ago and seldom went back – and bludgeoned into his head every last one of the world's scruples on Israel's treatment of the Palestinians. Lubowicz's head was dinning; the room was swimming; and his hands sweating.

Finally, he broke free, saying he must hurry home now for another appointment. He knew he should go back to the gallery, and deposit the mug, but when he got to the doorway, he heard voices inside. He thought briefly of just leaving the mug in the kitchen, the toilet, on a window sill, in the dining-room. But everywhere he looked people were milling around, and it seemed to him that they looked at him strangely, as if they could see right through him to his horrible tumour. Porbright came over and hovered boomingly by his side; his heart was pounding; he really must get out.

'Kind of you to come old chap . . . Don't mention it. Delighted to be of service. And if it plays you up again, don't hesitate to call.'

Then, just as he was leaving, from behind him in the hall, came a high clear voice. 'You will remember my party, won't you? I'm going to be eight. You won't forget?'

And looking up he saw Sophie, in a pair of striped pyjamas, swinging over the banisters, and smiling down at him shyly. Beside her was Charles, also dressed for bed and squatted down with his head stuck through the banisters. He was pointing repeatedly down at the crowd of adults, whom he seldom saw from such a height, and found highly entertaining. 'There's one! There's one! There's one!' he was saying, pointing at one bright pink bald patch after another, and rocking with giggles.

'I wouldn't miss it for anything,' Lubowicz called up.

And then he was out again, the door closed, the fresh night air stinging his lungs, with only the reek of Porbright's tobacco and the bulge in his jacket, to show he had ever been there.

It was not until he got back to the safety of his own flat that Lubowicz examined his plunder. Sitting down, for his heart was still pounding and his legs weak from the prolonged stress, he took out the mug and stared at it on the kitchen table.

It was a very fine Georgian silver christening mug; a tankard set on a faintly bell-shaped base like the cushion of a Doric pillar.

It was decorated at base and rim with garlands of vine-leaves, entwined with nuts and fruits, and in the centre it contained the image of a bird of paradise, a lovely creature with a long plumed arabesque tail and its beak wide open in song. Lubowicz found it a beautiful object altogether, extremely handsome – with its chased silver, and the fine workmanship of its classical motifs. He turned it in his hand, enjoying its cool mass, and let it catch the light.

And as he did so he caught the thin hieroglyphs of an inscription. He bent closer. It was an elaborate flowing copperplate, with scrolls and loops like tiny dancing zephyrs, and letters that ran forward like a ship in full sail.

'To our darling Sophie,' it said. 'On her christening. May 14th 1975.'

It was clear to him that he should take this beautiful mug straight back to her. It was precious and lovely, and would quickly be missed. But how? Should he wrap it up and present it to her at her birthday party on Sunday. Saying . . . Saying . . . well, that it had got mislaid, that it had jumped into his pocket by purest accident, that it was an impudent cup, and didn't know its place. She would find that very funny. She would think it was a good joke. And she would understand it perfectly well, with the fine penetrating intelligence of children, which understands everything, while understanding nothing. And she would smile at him shyly, giggling, then take him by the hand, and invite him to play a game.

But then how was he to . . . ? The thought stung him so badly he jumped out of his seat and began to pace around the room. Oh no . . . Oh no . . . that was just not possible! Just not possible! Not at all. My goodness, the talk of high table for the next five years! Oh yes, how many nasty little unspoken suspicions would it corroborate, those little suspicions that hang around like coiled snakes in the water tank of the supposedly liberal imagination. Oh no . . . oh no indeed. . . . And he imagined their voices. 'Did you hear the one about? . . . invited him to a party and popped a bit of silver in his pocket . . .

helped him out with a crick in his back . . . walked off with the kitchen spoons. . . .'

It was out of the question! And he was so disturbed by the sequence of images that he walked very fast up to the kitchen table, and brought his hand down sharply on its edge. Lubowicz now felt feverish. All the excitement had given him the shivers and he felt both dizzy and hectic, weak and energetic all at the same time. His forehead was throbbing. To keep himself warm, he lit a fire, and considered what he should do. Already the thought of discovery was sending cold trickles of horror up and down his spine. Porbright would know immediately that the mug had gone, he was deeply possession-conscious. And if he didn't, his wife would surely. From there it would be a small step to enumerating the few people who had been in that room, and from there it would take only an intuitive leap to arrive at him, Lubowicz. And then what? Lubowicz shuddered, and jumped up again out of his chair.

He couldn't take the property back. He couldn't send it through the post. That would compound the embarrassment. He couldn't leave it somewhere in the street for the girl to find, because, although she would be perfectly happy to find it in this manner – indeed delighted, to come upon it sitting up by a lamp-post in some obvious position, or on a little wall or a dustbin where someone must have put it just ready for her to be walking by – they would ask her where she had found it. And then they would know immediately that it was him. People guess that sort of thing. They make stunning dare-devil leaps across chasms of ignorance; he had often remarked it.

There seemed no possible avenue of escape. His thoughts, keeping erratic time with the leaping flames, whirled and tumbled and doubled back on themselves like fugitives in a dark alley.

Finally, he made a decision. Or at least, he did not make a decision. The decision arrived in him, and communicated itself through his whole body before any other restraining force had time to act. He went over to the table, picked up the mug, and stoking the fire up to its maximum heat and making a kind of furnace with shovelfuls of fresh coals, he placed the mug in the very heart of the heat, and allowed it to burn.

It was a long time burning, an agony to watch. The flames licked about it, smoked and blackened it without altering the structure. Swearing, he bent forward, and taking up the ornamental bellows from the wall, began to pump oxygen madly into the centre of the flames. The heat intensified. The coals glowed redder. And finally, the flames took. The silver of the mug began to sizzle and snap. He saw large cracks appearing, and dark metal beneath. He saw the fine chased overlay peel away in ugly green slicks; and finally, he saw the thin fine lines of the inscription, 'To our darling Sophie . . . May 14th . . .' curl up, shrivel and disappear in smoke.

It was enough. Enough. The cup was completely unrecognisable. Turning it gingerly in the grate with the poker, he then picked it up, ran through to the kitchen and fetched out some newspaper. Very quickly, almost hysterically, he wrapped it up in wad upon wad of the sheets. He wrapped and wrapped until he had a large amorphous shape, a bale of paper. Then he went out onto the fire escape which led down the side of the house to the dustbins, and ran down the stairs. Lifting the lid of the first bin, he threw in his parcel.

It was pitch-dark now and very cold in the streets of North Oxford. Here and there soft yellow lights shone out of the dark, as if at each other, and up above them the colder fiercer light of the stars was scattered fantastically across the black heavens. Putting back the lid of the dustbin, Lubowicz stopped suddenly and was seized by a thought. 'Are you mad!' he almost hissed to himself. 'Are you completely off your head?' And everything he had just done whirled in front of his vision like a flow of hideously grinning carnival masks: alien and grotesque. He tamped the lid back tightly on the bin. 'You are mad!' he hissed at himself. 'Disgusting character! Insane!' And it seemed to him that all the yellow lights shining from the solid brick houses had turned into eyes; and that all those eyes were training on him, focussing on him, and that they would search him out, and see into the innermost core of his being.

Suddenly a cat leapt from a wall on to the dustbins. With a frozen ring, a lid slithered to the ground; the cat let out a yelp of outrage. With a start, and a burst of adrenalin, Lubowicz ran quickly back up the fire escape stairs, and slammed the door.

## For Graham Cable's Funeral

Death is this Dickensian flunkey pacing along
               in his polished top hat,
The four pallbearers bowing to each other
               like mannequins at a minuet,
The music box starts and it's bed time and night time.

And the puzzle's little pieces are floating in free fall
               riding the extent
Air of the body whose guy-ropes have snapped
               collapsing the tent
Of inner air, and it's bed time, it's night time.

To think how many pieces the human spore comprises,
               vague scents and sharp clauses
That never will join to assemble the semblance. The actor is
               one with his ill-timed pauses,
His script half forgotten. Here is the night time

Where only the small hard seed of being can weigh down
               the body no longer
A body, but memory of memory, the unshrinkable good
               that's the only thing stronger
Than bed time or night time.

## Accordionist

The accordionist is a blind intellectual
carrying an enormous typewriter whose keys
grow wings as the instrument expands into a tall
horizontal hat that collapses with a tubercular wheeze.

My century is a sad one of collapses.
The concertina of the chest; the tubular bells
of the high houses; the flattened ellipses
of our skulls that open like petals.

We are the poppies sprinkled along the field.
We are simple crosses dotted with blood.
Beware the sentiments concealed
in this short rhyme. Be wise. Be good.

# A Question of Crime

P.D. James, Britain's leading detective story writer, discusses crime and detective fiction with fellow crime novelist Joan Smith.

**PDJ**: Joan, you've written three detective novels, *A Masculine Ending* (1987), *Why Aren't They Screaming* (1988), and *Don't Leave Me This Way* (1990), featuring the woman academic Loretta Lawson, and you're now working on your fourth. You've chosen to write more or less within the conventions of the traditional British detective novel – which I'd define as involving the central mysterious death, a closed circle of suspects, a detective, sometimes professional, but in your books an amateur, and by the end of the story a credible solution, which the reader can himself arrive at by logical deduction from the clues. You are a younger novelist, and regarded as one of the most interesting of the newer British women writers in the genre. May I ask you what it is that attracts you, a younger writer, to this rather well-worn form?

**JS**: I think what attracted me first was the strong narrative drive that exists in the detective novel. I love stories. As a child I loved hearing stories from my mother, I loved reading them, listening to them on the radio. I read masses of Greek mythology, all kinds of fairy stories. I liked that sense of wanting to know what happened next. That's one of the things that attracted me to journalism, where my career started. It was an opportunity to interview people, a licence to ask them intimate questions, to find out what had happened to them, why they'd done what they had, and then write it down. Then there comes a point where you don't want to write other people's stories any more. You want to write your own, make them up, and they start coming into your head. Then I've always been interested in crime – the way crime rends the fabric, the way murder, this extraordinary event, strips everyone of their polite surface, the kind of face we show the world. That's what has always interested me: the chance to write about people in a raw emotional state.

**PDJ**: Yes, I quite agree. I also share that interest in the stripping away of the individual's protective carapace. Murder is a unique crime, and it carries this huge weight of atavistic horror; and there are no privacies respected in a murder investigation. But what I think some critics still find extraordinary is the continued hold the detective genre has on the modern reader's imagination, as it obviously does. We both enjoy writing detective stories. But why do so many people so love reading them? And here I mean not the crime novel, but the detective story, the story of an investigation, itself.

**JS**: I think first there's the attraction of the plot, the basic mystery. We like mysteries, and also like to think we can take chaotic events and make sense of them. There's a very strong human drive – you could say it's the position of humanism – which wants to believe we can really understand the world in which we live. The detective novel starts out by setting a puzzle. It allows you to identify, follow in the footsteps of, the detective as he or she grapples with the mystery and finds some sense. But it's more than that. Detective fiction raises serious issues, even though it is genre fiction. This is pre-eminently a genre that does confront the fact of death, and it's a subject we're not very good at facing in a society that has lost much of its religious faith. Today death is something we prefer to forget or trivialize. And there has been a huge change in the detective novel, and the crime novel generally, over the last twenty years. In the so-called Golden Age of detective novels – the Agatha Christie novels, the work of Ngaio Marsh, Dorothy L. Sayers, Margery Allingham and so on – death was almost another life event.

There was really no sense that murder was real or tragic, it was just the source of the puzzle. Now, in your novels, and Ruth Rendell's, and those of Margaret Millar, for instance, there is a real sense of death as this tragic, shattering event which makes you as a reader think about your own mortality. So, although the critics generally treat the detective story as a kind of minor genre, it is important, because it brings you face to face with issues which are often dodged in straight fiction.

**PDJ**: I agree absolutely about the so-called Golden Age of detective fiction, those cosy novels in which you don't for one moment imagine that the blood or the pain are real; the fictional village, Mayhem Parva, never really loses its essential peace or innocence. But isn't it surprising that even with the modern detective story, which treats death more realistically, the detective novel is still basically thought of as entertainment, as a relief from reality, the literature of escape not the literature of involvement?

**JS**:  I think some readers certainly have that expectation. I was very amused by a letter I got from an American reader about my second novel. The complaint was that essentially it was too close to reality. This reader said: 'It's bad enough that murderers get away with it in real life without it happening in fiction as well', and more or less demanded his money back. What was interesting was that he clearly expected the detective novel to be an entertainment, and was shocked by my attempt to reflect the real world, a world in which an awful lot of murderers do get away with it. The resolution that Agatha Christie was aiming for, the sense of comfort at the end of the book, the reassurance that these terrible events can be absorbed – I don't have that sense at all. We live in a very violent society, a society which is divided, where there is an underclass, where there is violence, where there is unfairness. Terrible things do happen, and not all murderers get caught, and I want to reflect that uncomfortable reality. Some readers are very disturbed by it; they probably put down my books and go back to reading Agatha Christie or

Dorothy L. Sayers with a great sense of relief. But I think there are readers who appreciate what I'm doing, and see that the crime novel, the detective novel, can be used to reflect the contemporary dilemmas we live with.

**PDJ:** There are some reviewers, including some notable ones, who judge the detective story solely as a puzzle and who would go so far as to say that it has no right to concern itself with psychological subtlety and atmosphere, or with the horror of real-life murder, that it has a limited potential, and should fulfil that potential and attempt nothing more. But even the most realistic detective story surely offers one comfort. It affirms our belief that we live in a rational universe, that problems can be solved, not by luck or by supernatural intervention, but by human intelligence, human courage, human perseverance. As a journalist you covered the particularly horrible Ripper murders in the North of England and came close, thankfully not too close, to real-life murder. Do you feel you could deal in fiction with a psychopathic murderer?

**JS:** I have wondered about that because I think one of the effects of covering the Yorkshire Ripper murders was that I'm not able to regard death in a trivial kind of way, and I want to reflect its impact in my novels. I am interested in the serial killer, I suppose primarily because the serial killer is a man who kills women, and that fact says interesting things to me as a feminist about the kind of culture we live in. I worry about writing a book about a serial killer because so many of these books are titillating, a rather cheap and lurid way of writing about sex and sex murder. But I have in the back of my mind the notion that I would perhaps like to write about a serial killer from the point of view of the women who might be his victims. I was very conscious, when I was working in Manchester as a journalist and covering these murders, that I was in a curious double position, unlike the male journalists working on the case with me. I saw myself as a potential victim as well as a commentator on the horror, and that was a very peculiar dual role. I felt at the time that the murders weren't being reported properly, the police were making a mess of the case, which subsequently was shown to be what happened. I wrote about it in non-fiction, and that was very painful, but I'm glad that I did it. It is in the back of my mind that I may some day come back to the serial murder as a subject, but I think that it has to be approached very, very delicately indeed.

**PDJ:** Some people would argue that the psychopathic killer has no central place in the detective story because, without a rational murderer, there's no moral choice. It is the conflict between good and evil, the moral choice, which fascinates me; people faced with appalling problems and the reason why they choose one way out, including murder, rather than another. I was interested in what you said in your book *Misogynies* about these murders – the way in which the police made a distinction between innocent victims and prostitutes. I'm not for one moment suggesting that the police felt that the prostitutes deserved to be murdered, but there was an underlying suggestion that some victims were more deserving of sympathy than others. You describe yourself as a feminist, and of course Loretta Lawson, your heroine, is a feminist. When you created her – and that begs the question of what I mean when I use the word 'created' – when you decided to write about her, did you make a conscious decision that she should be a feminist?

**JS:** The way Loretta came into being was that I visited a flat in Paris which belonged to a friend and arrived there late at night, as Loretta does in the first novel *A Masculine Ending*. I woke up next morning thinking it was an immensely spooky place and something terrible could easily have happened there. I'd arrived with a friend, but I thought about what it would be like to arrive there as a woman alone late at night. Then I began to wonder, if she had arrived here alone, what kind of woman would she be? And quite quickly it came into my head that she would be an academic. That was because I didn't want her to be a journalist, which was what I then was; I didn't want her to be me, though there are elements of me in her. I think the strongest element of me that's in her is her feminism, and I would have found it very difficult to create a character I was going to live with for some years who didn't reflect my values, which are feminist values. But I didn't want to preach about it. What I wanted to do, I think, was to use this woman character to show what it's like to be a woman in a world still largely dominated by men, the kind of trivial everyday annoyances one encounters, and the assumptions that are made about a woman. It's so integral to Loretta's character that I'm not sure it ever was a conscious decision. She came into my head, and I saw her as a vehicle for showing people what it's like to be a woman in the world in the 1980s and 1990s. So the feminism is important but it wasn't really a conscious decision. She sort of appeared, and there she was, this independent-minded, slightly sheltered academic who was a feminist and was rather uncomfortable with the world. And, as her life has continued, she remains uncomfortable with the world.

**PDJ:** She would be categorised as an amateur detective as opposed to detectives, like my own Adam Dalgliesh, who are professionals. Is that how you think of her?

**JS:** That's a very interesting question because I don't think of her as an amateur detective at all. I think of her almost like a friend whom I knew maybe ten or twelve years ago, who lived near me and who would pop round late at night and tell me about her life. Then we drifted apart but every so often I think about her, and I want to know what she's been doing, and I find out what's been going on in her life. Each time that happens she has a story to tell. One of the criticisms that is made of my books is that Loretta doesn't investigate things properly, she doesn't know what to do. That puzzles me, because I don't see her as a detective at all. I think of her as what she is, an academic who is getting on with her life, and these things happen, and of course she doesn't know the rules of an inquest, of course she doesn't know about police procedures because that's not what she does.

It's not exactly even a series of episodes in her life, it's a series of stories about this one person, and I almost forget when I write about her again the details of the previous crime she was involved with.

**PDJ:** I very much like the fact that Loretta isn't knowledgeable about police procedures and coroner's laws and all the details of criminology, and I think that adds very much both to her attraction and credibility. Like many crime writers, particularly women, you keep the same detective in all your novels. There are, of course, advantages in keeping one character going through a series of books. Would you like to talk about that?

**JS:** The advantage of having a character who appears in several books, and keeping him or her going, is that you develop a quite detailed and intimate knowledge of the character. It is a process of discovery, of revelation. You know initially who they are, where they live, the kind of things they like. But as you live with them year in and year out – and you're living with them when you're not writing a book – it's almost like that sentence at the end of a comic saying 'the story continues'. It does, and you don't necessarily write all of it down. I know things now about Loretta's life, about her past, that I didn't know when I began writing the books. I probably won't put some of the things I know about her into the books, but this intimate knowledge does let me write about her as a fairly rounded and realistic character. And certainly the readers write to me as though she's a real person. Sometimes that's very flattering; sometimes it's rather disconcerting because they ask questions about her to which I don't know the answer. But I think that is the advantage. She becomes very real to me, and I think you can only write about characters in a realistic way if they become real to you.

**PDJ:** If you have a character who does go through a series of books, there's either a great deal of you in that character or at least you like that person. If the writer doesn't like a continuing character, gets bored with him or her, then certainly the readers will. It's interesting that Agatha Christie got very bored with Poirot, and I think with good reason.

**JS:** I do agree about Poirot. He is a very two-dimensional, cardboard character with all his little traits; there's no development. He goes on talking about his little grey cells for about forty years. There is no sense of Christie discovering more about her character. I have a sense of her thinking 'Oh goodness me, I'd better get him out of the box again.'

**PDJ:** You've said your heroine is a feminist and her feminist viewpoint is important to her. Do you think there is such a thing as a feminist detective novel? Is it reasonable to talk about feminist writing if we're thinking of novels and not polemical books about feminine issues?

**JS:** My impression is that feminist ideas have permeated so far and widely that it's very hard to make a distinction. There are crime novels and detective novels by women who are self-identified as feminists, and writers like Sara Paretsky, Gillian Slovo, Val McDermid, would probably identify themselves, like me, as feminists, and are writing books in which there are feminist ideas. But it seems to me that the spread of those ideas, which in some ways are quite radical and in others are simply common sense, is now so wide that it's very difficult to draw a distinction. If a woman is writing a novel which happens to have strong independent characters and reflects the changes in women's lives – that there are now more women MPs though not enough, the way women are moving to the top in industry – if the book reflects all these changes, is it fair to call it feminist? Would the author call it feminist? Or does it simply reflect the fact that women's position has changed quite radically and drastically in the last twenty or thirty years? I find it very hard to know, and in a way it's slightly disappointing to be pigeon-holed not just as a detective-story writer, but as a feminist detective-story writer. One feels that one is being put into a category, and I think – well I hope – that the books do have a much wider appeal than that. But one can't deny that these feminist values are very important to the fiction.

**PDJ:** It's irritating enough to have this critical dichotomy between detective and crime novels and the so-called straight novel without introducing a new category of feminist detective story. Some of the women you mention, Sara Paretsky in particular, and Sue Grafton, in the States, have detectives who are very different from the stereotype of the British female detective. They're very feisty, they carry guns, they can fight effectively, they operate in a violent society. Do you think this just reflects the difference in our two societies, or the difference in the attitudes of the women who write detective fiction?

**JS:** When I first read Sara Paretsky and Sue Grafton, I did like their books a great deal and I've gone on liking them. But I do have reservations about them, particularly the character in Sara Paretsky's books. These private eyes are much more like men and I suspect there is a kind of anxiety on the part of the author about whether her character really is a man. One of the things I've noticed about the Paretsky V.I. Warshawski novels is that they're completely obsessed with details of dress. We're constantly told that V.I. is putting on her high-heeled pumps and her Chanel suit and so on; I almost think it's a nervous signal to the reader that this is a woman, not a man. I do believe that the private eye novel has severe limitations to it. There are one or two in England now – in fact I suspect there are probably more female private eyes in fiction than there are in real life. The one that I actually like rather a lot is Liza Cody's heroine, Anna Lee, because she's a private detective who works in the seediest, most dingy office, and instead of being asked to investigate sensational murders or vast insurance frauds, she's sent off to investigate people passing-off retread tyres and jobs like that. I quite enjoy the way that Cody plays with that set of clichés. I agree that the books are very violent and I think that the genre doesn't translate all that happily to having a female protagonist. In one of Sara Paretsky's books there is a scene where her heroine goes to see a gangster and he slashes her face, and it's a very nasty scene. But I think that at that point in real life she would have been raped, and that is a problem for women writers. One doesn't want to write titillating scenes of sexual violence, and that imposes a limitation on what one can write. If you put women detectives into these very violent situations you're going to get into that area of sexual violence and it's a very uncomfortable one. So I think that there are very severe limitations to what you can do with a private eye character.

**PDJ:** One of the things I find fascinating about detective fiction is the need to construct. I love construction in novels, this need to do a great deal within ninety thousand words, to have a beginning, a middle and an end, to present and solve a puzzle. The detective story presents interesting technical problems. For that reason some writers have seen detective fiction as a kind of apprenticeship before moving to, presumably, higher and better things. I don't personally take this view, but there have been writers who do. Are you ever tempted to feel like that? Do you aspire to leave detective fiction behind at some stage and to write the so-called straight novel?

**JS:** I'm not very happy with the idea that writing detective fiction is a sort of apprenticeship, then you make the leap and write the straight novel. I think any kind of novel-writing is a way of learning, a way of discovering what you can do. I'm not sure that writing can be taught. If people have stories they want to write it is possible to give them tips and show them short-cuts. But the wonderful thing about any kind of creative writing is that, as you gain more confidence, you are able to do more things, you are able to turn away from the single imperative, from 'Can I write a novel at all?' to 'What kind of novel can I write?' What I have noticed is that when I began writing I wasn't aware of the joy of getting the emotional rhythm of a book going. That for me is the great moment where suddenly, without even planning it, the book actually works in a series of scenes, and when you look back at what you've written, you can see that there is a kind of emotional pattern of ups and downs and things happening without even having planned it out very much. That's when the writing is going really well and when you enjoy it most. I think the question of whether or not one wants to write another kind of novel betrays a misapprehension about the way in which novels come to you. You write the story that comes to you, the story that seems most powerful to you, and whether that happens to have a crime in it or be some other kind of novel doesn't really matter. For me it's having a scene in my head, having a few characters in my head, and knowing vaguely what's going to happen to them and wanting to get it down, it's almost a challenge to myself. The story's there, can I get it out in a way that's convincing to other people? The question of genre and what I'm writing doesn't really arise for me. Sometimes a book comes into my head and it isn't a novel, it isn't fiction at all, but a set of ideas I have to write about. I suppose I always have three or four ideas for fiction in my head at any one time, and probably one or two ideas for non-fiction, and it's when one of them becomes incredibly powerful and gripping that I sit down and write. Maybe one day that story won't be about a murder, it won't be a crime novel, but I really don't know.

**PDJ:** When you're writing your detective stories, are you aware of the conventions? And how far do you think you are influenced by the past? Those of us who are writing detective fiction today are certainly writing a very different kind of detective fiction; but we carry with us a great weight of tradition and much of it, in a sense, feminine tradition. Do you feel you are aware of that tradition or influenced by it in any way?

**JS:** If I am influenced by tradition I think it's in a negative way. If you look at the novels of the so-called Golden Age you can see the expectations they're working with and the limitations they accept. And I think that what's happened in the last twenty or thirty years is that writers have been challenging those traditions and those confines and saying, why is it the case that you have to do this in a detective novel? Where I am conscious of tradition I feel it as a constraint, something I bump up against. Quite often when I'm writing a novel I suddenly realise that what I'm about to do is different from what would have been done in the Golden Age, and that quite pleases me. With the novel I'm writing at the moment, the fourth one, I was wondering about the detectives, the professional police detectives, who would be involved in the case. It suddenly occurred to me that on a big murder enquiry there would be forty or fifty detectives, and instead of the same person always coming round and having a friendly – or maybe an adversarial – relationship, it might be interesting to have a different detective calling every time, and that's what I've been doing so far. And that's really quite disconcerting, because there is an expectation that your character will form a relationship with the police investigating the case, whether it's a happy relationship or not. What I'm trying to do with this book is to avoid that. It has quite a strange and rather alienating effect on my characters, and makes them feel disconcerted. So I think that if I am aware of traditions, it is to question them. This can, of course, sometimes be unsettling for the reader, but then I think there are other readers who have seen the limitations of the Golden Age detective novel, and like the sense that the author is challenging and playing with them.

PDJ: I think there are peculiar difficulties in writing detective novels which have an amateur, because the police are necessarily going to be involved with the murder and you have the problem of making sure that the interest stays with your amateur detective who, after all, isn't going to be told very much by the police or taken into their confidence, as, for example, Peter Wimsey was in the so-called Golden Age. Do you find that? Do you see that as one of the technical difficulties?

JS: Yes, very much so. What makes it easier for those of us who are writing now is that our characters are much more engrossing in themselves. If in a Christie story you didn't have the kind of detective who was liaising with the police and being constantly given titbits of information, you'd lose interest in the book altogether because there isn't really very much there apart from plot. But one of the advantages we have is that crime novels these days contain memorable characters. If you have that sense of interesting people, real people going about their lives and reacting to what they find out, you probably can get away with it. I also think you can create menace and fear by the very fact that your character doesn't know what is going on. It means that the reader is in a relationship both with the amateur detective and with the police, and doesn't know who to trust. It can create a kind of ambivalence and tension which adds something to the novel.

**PDJ:** Each decade or so critics prophesy the demise of the classical detective story. I think it was at the end of the nineteenth century when, reviewing the latest Conan Doyle, a reviewer wrote: 'Considering the difficulties of hitting on any fancies which are decently fresh, surely this sensational business must shortly come to a close.' Well, the sensational business continues. What do you see as the future of the detective story? Shall we continue to get closer to the straight novel while remaining within the conventions? Or do you think in the end the conventions themselves will change and go?

**JS:** There will probably always be an appetite on the part of readers for detective novels and I think the changing nature of society means that every generation has a new type of crime to write about. It's very noticeable, if you look at real-life crime in the nineteenth century, that a high proportion of the notorious murders were committed by spouses who couldn't get rid of their husbands or wives. The classic nineteenth-century murderer is a woman who puts arsenic in her husband's kedgeree because she simply can't stand him and can't see any other way out. But in our own century we've seen vast changes, particularly this horrible thing we were talking about before, the rise of the serial killer who really is a mid- and late-twentieth century phenomenon. The fact that crime changes, that motives for crime change, means that the crime novel is a very contemporary form; it reflects the society that the author is writing about. There has been in recent years a number of interesting and very nasty planned murders. I'm thinking particularly of the Jeremy Bamber case where a man killed his adoptive parents and his sister, and did it very carefully and set it up so that his sister would be blamed, and initially she was – that kind of crime is particularly fascinating to write about. As long as there is crime there will be interesting material for detective novelists. What is happening is that the boundary between crime novels and what is regarded as the straight novel is blurring. Agatha Christie trapped the crime novel in a sort of cosy sub-literary genre and it has taken years for it to escape. There will always be people who write what are virtually Golden Age novels, who just want to provide a puzzle and who don't aspire to write anything more. But the blurring will continue, and I think anyone who writes off the detective novel is ignoring the fact that there is a huge appetite for them among the reading public.

**PDJ**: An inevitable question which we are always asked, and I rather hate being asked: Why are women so good at detective novels and, in particular, British women?

**JS**: Yes, I think this is the question that crime novelists dread more than any other. I sometimes think we should all agree on an answer and type it on a postcard and hand it out. The first thing to say is that women have always been very good at novel writing. Women took to fiction very early. If you look at the eighteenth century, people like Fanny Burney, and the early nineteenth century, Jane Austen, this is a form that women were able to do because it didn't require any training, it didn't require any equipment, it's not like being a sculptor or being a violinist where you have to have training, you have to have materials. It was something women could do, as Jane Austen did, scribbling on tiny pieces of paper in between the other parts of their life. I think the rest of it is probably a matter of what interests women and what interests men. The thing that strikes me about good crime novels by women is that they deal very much with emotion, that they analyse people's feelings, that they're not afraid, they're not just about the surface. Someone whom I admire tremendously, John Le Carré, does go deeper in his spy novels, but an awful lot of thrillers are simply about rather mechanical characters rushing around the world hiding things and seducing each other and avoiding real feelings. What you get in very good crime novels by women is the sense that the emotions are explored, that they're not ducked, that people are sometimes horrible to each other, that even nice characters can behave in bad ways. You were talking earlier about moral dilemmas and I think the crime novel does face people with a moral dilemma and it asks – okay, people create a public face, they create a persona which is what they choose, and that is what they show to the world. When the crime erupts, that's when they're tested, that's when you see what they're really like; sometimes they'll disappoint you, and sometimes they'll rise to it. That's the really interesting thing, and women have never been afraid of emotion. This is probably cultural, and I've noticed that men are getting better at it too – for example, in Michael Dibdin's novels, I think he's very good at writing about emotion. But the male crime novel still tends to be a Dick Francis-type adventure where there's lots of violence and lots of glamour, not so much introspection and the things that women are good at.

**PDJ:**   Orwell said: 'Murder, the unique crime, should arise only from strong emotions', and I agree with you that women are good at the strong emotions and that it is the strong emotions which make the novel. I also feel, Joan, that there's something about the structure which women find emotionally supportive. I sometimes wonder whether I would feel as ready to deal with violent and, sometimes in my books, terrible deaths if I were writing outside the detective novel.

**JS:**   I'm not sure about that. I think I would find it possible to write about death outside the genre because I'm not quite so aware of that framework as perhaps you are. Perhaps the sense in which you are right is that it is often asked, why do women write crime novels given that men commit the vast majority of crimes? The point that question misses is that women are often the victims, women actually do live in fear of crime, yet traditionally women are almost completely excluded from the investigation. I was very conscious of this during the Yorkshire Ripper investigation – the people who were investigating the murders were men, the people who were writing about the murders were in the vast majority men, and women didn't seem to have a voice. The actual victims were necessarily silent, and other women didn't have any part in the investigation or reporting of the crimes. Yet I felt that if women's voices were listened to, they'd have quite interesting things to say that might actually have helped the investigation. Maybe the crime novel gives us this voice. It allows women to have their own input, to explain their feelings about crime, to say: this is why we think people commit crimes, these are the pressures under which people buckle and commit this terrible act. Perhaps it gives us the chance to meditate and contemplate something which is a very real fear for us, and, in a sense, take control of it.

## CAROL RUMENS

# Threnody for an Action Doll

The mother we were free to hate is dead.
The last we saw of her, her face was breaking:
Only the palace of her hair still stood.
Her sons threw off their sullenness and cheered.
Her daughters, too, denied their hearts were aching.
We knew she'd leave us nothing. She loved men
Next to herself, and we were none of hers.
But yes, we'd thought her of some consequence:
Stronger than us, because she'd had to be,
Stronger than men. This proves the fallacy:
Her triumph, like her wealth, was all men's making,
And now she's in their funny cupboard world,
Upside down, her voice a box of holes,
Blue sparklers jammed in the hollow of her head,
While they charge round the room with guns and
                                        shrieking,
Swearing they'd sooner die than play with dolls.

# Reinventing the British Disease

Britain in the Eighties was a country in the grip of a fever. Infused with Thatcherism, the body politic experienced little peace. It was a decade of much disordered writhing at the hands of a single politician. And the effects linger on after the fever has receded. The patient cannot avoid still being a little touched. But that is not the most noticeable condition of Britain. The difference in the Nineties is that the country is returning gratefully to sleep.

Mrs Thatcher seldom permitted sleep. The voice hacksawed its way relentlessly into the public mind, and lost none of its searing power as the eleven years unfolded. This was a leader, primarily, of turmoil. She broke many rules of British governance but none so completely as the rule that the people must at all times be reassured. If she offered comfort, it would be available only several years later, after the proper suffering had been endured. Her preferred style was combat, her rarest faculty the power of unreason. She was the most unreasonable, though not unreasoning, leader the country ever had. Although socially punctilious, in politics she rejected orthodoxy and exalted lunatic as well as potent ideas, and the orthodoxy she rejected with most determination was the belief that the leader's duty was to be liked. She disdained liking, and the attitude was returned by a country she declined to try and charm. As a result, the pulse-rate of the nation remained high. She made sure Britain stayed awake.

After years of this kind of treatment, any country would tend to favour a period for reflection. The rhythms of life are as natural to peoples as to people. This is the call not just of psychology but of political effect. Years of social upheaval seem to demand at some stage a few years of relative inertia during which the new order is allowed to settle down. And the Thatcher upheaval lasted longer, displaying more persistent kinetic energy, than any in post-war Europe, with the single, and quite differently circumstanced, exception of Adenauer's Germany. What was remarkable about the huge Conservative election victories in 1983 and 1987 was not so much the familiar fact that they produced the longest-lasting British prime minister in the twentieth century, but the endorsement they gave to a radical programme. This was eleven years not merely of unbroken government, but of the kind of government that exhausted rather than mollified the people.

So the people needed a break. Yet all the same, the conservatism that has engulfed them returned with surprising speed. What are the sources of this descent into narcolepsy? First of all, there is plenty to be conservative about. The years of upheaval left many voters with a vested interest in entrenching what those years had done for them. Between 1979 and 1992, according to surveys conducted by Mori, the physical and economic condition of the British underwent some pretty striking improvements. The number of voters classifiable in the upper market-research categories known as A, B or C1 grew from 33 per cent to 42 per cent over the period. Owner-occupiers rose from 51 per cent to 68 per cent of the population, and shareholders from 7 per cent to 23 per cent. These people have a lot to lose. They are happy with the new status quo in their own lives. Yet another cycle of radical politics, whether administered by triumphalist Conservatism or – perish the thought – by a Labour government bent on a counter-revolution, was a far more disturbing prospect at the end of the Thatcher years than it had been at the beginning. Many specifics of the revolution, moreover, were a long way from complete. There was a widespread sense that across the field of social policy, deep changes had been set in train whose effects could not yet be judged. Violations of sacred orthodoxy, such as Mrs Thatcher's interference with the National Health Service, came to enjoy the blessing of passive approval. Much debated in the election, they disappeared entirely from the agenda once the mandate had been decided. Let's see how the thing works, the people said. This is telling evidence of a country already dosed up on the post-revolution-ary soporific.

The rhythm of politics reinforced a deep strain in the national character, which tends, in any case, to be socially and politically pacifist. Mrs Thatcher's hostilities were conducted against a people who are by nature docile. That was why someone, per-ceptively early in her time, said that she was prime minister of the wrong country. Without this natural docility, indeed, the British would never have put up with her assaults upon them. In few other countries would the Thatcherite programme have been tolerated when positive support for it barely exceeded 40 per cent at the ballot box or 30 per cent among the population as a whole. Three times running, the leader received the most qualified of national mandates. But this in no respect deterred her; and more to the point, it did not provoke much indignation among the people, save at the most isolated times and places. By suffering the revolution in silence, they showed their true temper: masochistic, stoical, inertly bloody-minded.

The ultimate proof of this was found in Scotland. In Scotland, Mrs Thatcher had a positive anti-mandate. The vast majority actively rejected her, year after year. They elected Thatcherite politicians only in fragmentary numbers, who nevertheless pro-ceeded to govern with a suave disregard for Scotland's verdict. Yet there was no important price to pay. Even the fiery Scots could manage no more by way of rebellion than the mild com-plaints that could be made at by-elections. They stood meekly by as the rage was visited upon them. They were awake all right. Nobody could avoid that. But they continued to sound and behave like the congenitally sluggish people whom Mrs Thatcher saw it as her destiny to shake up.

Such were the tendencies towards conservatism – the opposite, in the Eighties, of Conservatism – among which the new leadership of the nation began to find itself in 1990. Britain was readier for a rest than it had ever recently been. Previous transitions had not been marked by the same passionate desire to relapse into a sort of quietism. When the Labour Government petered to a halt in 1979, it was seen as the end of a failed regime, and the general sense that something needed to be done was enough to bring an alarming lady to power. When the Heath Government declared war on the unions in 1974 and was itself ousted, the country could be said to have voted for peace and a quiet life, but few people contended that a revolution had run its course. Labour's defeat before that, in 1970, was accompanied by a sense of impatience, if not outrage, at the empty presumptions of Harold Wilson. The result was a vote for modest galvanising.

In 1992 it was quite different. John Major, unlike Mrs Thatcher, is prime minister of the right country. After the warrior leader, the man of peace; after the stern grimacer, the quick smiler; after the conviction woman, the consensus man; after she who would be hated, he who must be liked. Once he won the 1992 general election, and was no longer the appointed creature of a handful of Conservative MPs, Mr Major had a proper claim to speak for the nation. Leaders do sometimes personify nations and, to an eery extent, for the Nineties Mr Major does personify what this one is most comfortable at being.

The passion for brutal modernity, to begin with, is in retreat. For a better future, Mr Major looks significantly to the past. Nineties Britain harks back to Sixties Britain and earlier, in some of the symbols people care most about. The old county names are returning, after twenty years' supplanting by alien constructs such as Avon and Humberside. Old regiments are saved from the museum, especially if they're Scottish. The railways will soon be running in the different liveries of regional branches long since dead and which even the oldest inhabitants have forgotten, but which the political leadership sees more than sentimental merit in resurrecting. It is almost as if the dream of some Trollopian idyll is to come vestigially to life. Not many people read Trollope these days. But he is the prime minister's favourite author. Days at the cricket and, he would have us believe, evenings at Barchester Towers are the leader's own most public proofs that he, although a child of the Thatcherite fever, yearns for a haven of rest.

The products of the fever have not disappeared, and cricket is an instance of it. The sport is now dominated by the business imperative. Commerce and television have drained every big sport of its romantic associations. The emblematic cultural battle of the Nineties is being fought not over the level of subsidy to the arts, still less over the proper direction which après–post-modernism should take in the empty galleries along Cork Street, but about who should have the right to televise and who to watch big-time football. Should it be shown by national broadcasters and continue to be universally available as part of the television service everyone was used to, or should it be sold to the highest bidder for showing only to those willing to buy it by the hour? The greatest mass medium, near-free to the millions, faces destruction at the hands of financiers egged on by politicians. In this, the emollient Nineties do little to divert the inexorable logic of the Eighties. The primacy of the accountant's bottom line in every transaction, which was the lesson Thatcherism sought to apply across the complete range of human conduct, has hardly been overturned in Major's Britain. He was, after all, an integral part of it as both pupil and master. But the face of the bank manager in Downing Street disarms all ruderies. He is the epitome of sweet reason. He reassures us that nothing truly alarming need ever happen. Whether smiling from the pavilion balcony, or uttering platitudes from the soap-box outside his front door, he speaks for a people only too pleased to feel torpidly at ease with itself once again, the economy notwithstanding.

An equivalent recession has taken place on the other side of the argument. Because the challenge has softened, so has the response. Of all European countries, Britain has always tended to register the most trivial level of engagement between intellectuals and politics. The ascendancy of the parties has excluded the contribution that could be made to politics from a world not professionally involved in the trade, and the British distaste for political ideas has erected an almost invulnerable barrier between the thinkers and the men of action. One of the attractions of the Eighties was that this form of cultural apartheid was broken. Mrs Thatcher stood for a politics of ideas, and these ideas were often extravagantly offensive to the assembled cohorts of the academy. At one level, therefore, the Thatcher years produced some genuine intellectual combat, in which affronted professors fought for old orthodoxies against a generation of parvenus who had the supreme advantage of access to the prime minister's ear. At another level, there was sheer jealous outrage, which was not especially edifying but did contribute to a real disturbance of the nervous system. Bitter blood was spilt. But the wounds have been staunched with remarkable speed. The intellectuals who abused Mrs Thatcher heap gratitude on her successor, and seem less serious as a result. Only now does the *ad feminam* quality of their onslaughts become fully clear. One hears little anger directed from any quarter against Mr Major and his government even though the impact of the Eighties, not least in the universities, has not changed and shows no sign of improvement in the future. After their brief excursion into the forum, British intellectuals have returned to where they are more at home, cultivating their garden. Whether this is through pessimism or habit is hard to say. But the effect is the same. They ensure that controversy has no sharp edge, while the blander, gentling orthodoxies of Mr Major are bedded in.

These are planted round two governing ideas. They are the only ones that distinguish him from what went before, but they have a pervasive effect on the public life of Britain.

The first is an idea about Europe. Mr Major, like most voters of his age and below, has no difficulty in regarding Britain as a European country. To him the Channel is not an unbridgeable chasm between the continental land mass and its north-west offshore island extension. He is the first prime minister for eighty years without the inextinguishable deposit of European war in his personal memory. His predecessor had that memory but, far from impressing her with the necessity of closer union between the states, it persuaded her of the opposite: that the nation-state, especially the British nation-state ranged against its war-time enemy in an expanded German nation-state, must at all costs preserve itself. She became fanatically committed to this, and it contributed to her downfall. Mr Major has not forgotten that event. He does not trifle with the atavistic feelings about nationhood that the majority of his party continues to take very seriously. In the fluid waters of European union, which have receded from the high tidemark established in the putative Treaty of Maastricht, he has been a subtle navigator. But he experiences no fury at what some Europeans want. His style is to manoeuvre around it. He says hardly a word to excite his own people against the European future he believes to be theirs beyond argument. The project will have its ups and downs: may, indeed, have descended to a plateau from which any new climb will be long delayed. But Mr Major has removed much of the heat from the issue. He articulates a consensus it is hard, in any but the short term, to oppose. The familiar British combination of scepticism and indifference meets a leader whose habits make a natural match with it: pragmatism, caution and endless reassurance.

His second big idea, on the home front, is almost equally anaesthetic. Again it seems on the face of it like quite an abrupt departure from what went before. For Mr Major is a believer in the old-fashioned concept of the public good. This is a phrase that never sullied the thinking of Mrs Thatcher. If she was prepared to contemplate it, it was only in the sense of an aggregation of individual goods that might make for a better economic environment. There is no such thing as society, she unapologetically asserted. This is a sentiment which Mr Major, the son of a circus conjurer without trace of aldermanic pedigree, would not begin to understand and would not allow anyone to write for him. He believes, instead, not merely in the necessity but the desirable excellence of public services. To securing this end he sets his government. He invents the Citizen's Charter not just out of opportunism, although he is the most political of men, but through what passes for conviction. It is the idea he regards as the leitmotif of his administration: making the citizen see himself as a customer whom the civil servant, the hospital administrator, the train driver has a duty to satisfy. Yet this does not alter very much. It promises no shift in the mortal struggle to contain public spending. It is accompanied by no great revision of the old impulses which say that state intervention should if possible be avoided, and prefer privatised to public bodies. It is also, in its own terms, hard to disagree with. Like motherhood, making the trains run on time, even if there are fewer of them, is an incontestable social good. Hearing that that's the plan, the country offers a tolerant wave and returns, with a sigh of relief, to its unabrasive business.

There is a final player in this drama of the essentially undramatic, this conspiracy of cool. Britain, although an amenable society, is highly political. Politicians, their words transmitted through their allies in the media, are the people who determine what important arguments take place. If politicians don't disagree, the routes are few by which anyone else can influence the public discourse. If the status quo is to be rescued from slumbering acquiescence, the opposition parties are supposed to be the ones to make it happen.

The banner under which the Labour Party fought the 1992 election said 'Time for a Change'. At first sight this seemed a neat truism. It had the quality good political slogans need: it plausibly expressed what people perhaps ought to have been feeling, after thirteen years of Tory rule. It also united the party, no small feat, and offered the least alarming proposition to the nation. It was, in other words, very like the politics of Major himself. And yet that, on reflection, proved to be its downfall. For what does the slogan actually mean? That the Labour Party can think up no positive challenge which it dares to stand behind. The slogan was intensely negative. If this was the crystallised essence of anti-Majorism, it supplied pathetically little for serious opponents of the reigning orthodoxy to get their teeth into. It said that Labour was quite uncertain of the alternative it offered. And a great deal of what Labour did offer turned out to be an echo not a choice. Its most earnest efforts went into saying how little it would dismantle of Majorism, not how much. The public, Labour decided, above all wanted reassurance, something which it was in the end unable to supply. It did make an attempt to portray itself as an egalitarian party, with a plan for raising taxes, but its failure to catch the public mood only reinforced the broader point. In the Major era, neither Labour nor anyone else has found the ideas or the language to wrest the nation out of the unalarmed tranquillity it habitually prefers.

The reasons for alarm are on the face of it quite great. The British economy languishes well behind most of its biggest competitors. Consistent growth still eludes it, and it came worse than many out of the world recession that started the Nineties. The manufacturing base remains cripplingly reduced. Education, from schools through to universities, is in a crisis that won't soon be resolved, part of which is a crisis of resources. The British workforce is still the worst-trained in the western world, an appalling harbinger for economic performance in the twenty-first century. Homelessness and poverty are far worse in the mid-Nineties than they were in the late Seventies, islands of shameful deprivation in the rising plenty that swirls around them. The urban squalor in which many people live disgraces a civilised society. The failure of this society to come to grips with other challenges – from destruction of the healthy environment, from the demand for better-funded culture, from the degeneration of law and order – might be enough in other times and places to provoke outrage. But the Nineties are not a time for outrage. The Eighties had many faults, but at least they were a time when outrage was in fashion. There was some equivalence between the scale of the problems and the emotional energy that confronted them on every side. It wasn't comfortable and it wasn't British. It didn't always produce the results. But it broke through the protective skein of illusion and defined a state of crisis. That state we no longer want to recognise. It is no accident that we have a leader with the same benign preference, agreeable at all costs, as we quietly watch the sun go down.

## *Shoe*

I saw Posterity the other night
looking along the length of my left leg
to where my beautifully polished shoe
asserted its eternal shoeness
from the casual station of my foot.

I saw it as it might be
in some future museum,
absolute clarity, lonely, labelled

> c.1990, leather, brogue-type,
> prob. British (right missing)

recalling all its ancestors I'd seen
under dusty glass in county towns,
those black things with silver buckles,
and how my own life
might be only leather at the last . . .

Slick bloody stand-in,
in tomorrow's showcase performances
you tell your schoolparties this:
boys, this is no shoe you see,
but the forsaken site of a past foot
once as quick and as corny as your own.

# Timothy Bagshott – a tale for TV

Picture the scene. Frame it in your mind's eye. We are looking at a great new development to the East of the City, with the eye of a TV cameraman (we will call him Les) who loves the very idea of it, who sees beauty in a tower block slanting cool and clean into a windy sky, and in the blossom drifting from the instant trees of the Garden Centres, and in the majesty of a great steel and glass structure so vast he can hardly lose it from his frame, even if he wanted to, even if he was paid to, which you may be sure he isn't; symbol of the city's wealth and busy-ness. Les sees no point in dwelling on the 'To Let' or 'For Sale' signs, or the homeless who drift like the blossom up against the concrete walls, already stained by soot, weather and urine, or on the rats which nose up out of the flooding sewers; Les prefers to focus his lens on the beautiful faces of the PR women and the gently crumpled Armani suits of their employers, and who wouldn't? His shots are disciplined, beautifully framed. He's one of the best around.

But what's this? We're into fiction now? Thank God for that. We need no longer take anything seriously. We know all that other bad news, don't we; indeed, we're pleased, to know it so well. How are the mighty fallen, we rejoice! Serve them right, we cry – the bastards, the property developers, sticky fingers in the pension fund: serve them right for being richer than us, for sending their useless unecological spires into the godless sky. Forget all that. We have a story to tell. Let's turn our cameras West a little: while we consider our children, all our victims. Let's turn our minds to the tale of young Timothy Bagshott, son of Jim Bagshott, property developer, swindler, charmer. Les, are you on line? Sound man; are you there? Paul, are you happy? (Most sound men are called Paul, and Directors always say

'Paul, are you happy?' and Paul always replies 'yes'. So I have a vision of all Pauls as happy men or liars, take your pick.)

Paul is giving us the sound of schoolchildren singing, a little further to the west of the great city development to which we have been referring. Paul has located a school of the new regime: they're singing a Christian song as required under the 1990 Education Act at morning assembly. Their innocent voices carol: this is what they sing:

> 'So here hath been dawning
> Another blue day,
> Think, wilt thou let it
> Fly useless away?'

So far so good; the Protestant work ethic still about its perfectly decent business. But what is this? What are they singing now?

> 'Or wilt thou use it
> For profit, and say
> Hasten the dawn
> Of another blue day?'

What has got into their voices, their hearts, their souls? What view is this of their own existences? Do they no longer want to go to heaven? Do they want heaven on earth, these kids? Do they want their oats now, not later? Good God, how will we keep our youth in order, if they have adopted the hopes and aspirations of their elders and betters, Mr Maxwell, Mrs Thatcher and her fine son Mark, all those city folk whose names we have already forgotten, stabbed in the back by their colleagues, the insider dealers, the fraudsters, the goers to sea in sleazy yachts? The new robber barons. Weep, children, weep for your lost souls. Trust Les to be hot on Paul's heels, getting them into shot. What's happened is that Paul and Les have a new master now: the stern director Angus, and a commission from the BBC, though it scrapes its barrel for funds. Oh yes, we're into fiction now. We're allowed a glimpse of the terrors of reality.

Here, little sister to Canary Wharf, we see Bagshott Towers, an unfinished development complex striving to survive recession. Once it was the little river port of Parrot Pier: a pretty place; a miniature Greenwich, albeit on the wrong side of the river. Parrot Port boasted a Georgian house or so, and an old playhouse, some bonded warehouses, a host of railway cottages and navy dwellings. Gone, all gone: in their place a cluster of concrete structures rise out of a river of mud. If Les will only point his camera where Angus requires, we can see what can only be a group of anxious structural engineers teetering on the still unfinished thirteenth floor of a residential block, wondering whether or not it's entirely safe. Too late, in any case – from the ground floor up to the twelfth the habitation units are already occupied; here now dwell the desperate human overflow from the Inner City (the local council hires in homeless from other city boroughs for a substantial fee, hires out its own homeless to others for a lesser one, and so mysteriously makes a profit: it has something to do with the river view and Poll Tax levels).

Listen hard, and hear the hurrying feet of Rupert Oates, the social worker, driven by pressure of overwork to speak his thoughts aloud, at our expense. Les, where are you? Paul, Paul, pick up Mr Oates' thought patterns, if you please. Paul, are you happy?

'More than happy, Mr Angus, sir. I call you "sir" because you as my director are equipped to take an overview, earn more than I do, are not staff but work freelance, and can engage the bosses in conversation. I, who do not have the benefits of your education, your background, your capacity for chutzpah, am only fit to lick your boots, be told what to do and develop biceps, which my girlfriend hates, by swinging the sound boom overhead. She does not like me to be muscley, macho. More than happy, sir! What option do I have? The thoughts in Mr Rupert Oates' head run thus: "Listen, folks, I have a tale to tell of Bagshott Towers, I know it well. Being the welfare man round here: kept sadly busy too, I fear. Here, where once stood Parrot Pier and village pond and willows dear, now soars the height of Bagshott Towers, stressed concrete takes the place of bowers – " You live in a flowery house called The Bowers, I believe, Mr Director Angus, over on Hampstead Hill, next door to "The Cot" where Mr Bagshott used to live, before he was carted away for corruption. Bagshott tore down his dovecote, according to the gutter press, and put in a swimming pool and re-named The Cot "Amanda" after his girlfriend – and why not, Mr Director? Mr Bagshott was a vulgarian, as am I: happy Paul the soundman. Mr Oates has a word or two to say on that. They go like this: "The grass of course is greener on the other side, where the gentry of the world reside. But listen, folks, we have a tale to tell, of how the rich and mighty fell. The property speculators' bubble produced this land of mud and rubble. And Timothy Bagshott's dad, I fear, is much to blame for all that's here, and now he languishes in jail, so let Jim himself take up the tale." '

'Les,' says Angus, 'that's more than enough of Paul. Can we reconstruct Amanda three months ago, when the fraud squad swooped at five that summer morning, and eased Jim Bagshott out of bed, and put him in a police car and sped him off to meet his just deserts? And can we do it within budget?'

You, the viewer, will have seen similar scenes on TV many times. The camera, following the vanishing car, seldom turns back to the house to see the forlorn figures of those left behind, waving goodbye on the step: in this case it's young Timothy Bagshott and his dismal Aunt Annie. Or, as Rupert Oates observes, 'My tale's of Timothy Bagshott, son of Jim, and how misfortune came to him, and how the lad faced up to perils great, and how at least he conquered cruel fate.' Paul the soundman swears this is what goes on in Rupert Oates' head, and Paul has the acuity of the really happy. 'Paul, are you happy?' 'Happy as Larry, Angus.' There is hope, you see: there is always some underlying happy refrain, if only we can hear it. Let's for God's sake get on before the light goes.

'I'll have something to say to my solicitor,' says Jim, and who should he find sharing his open prison cell, of course, but Clive his solicitor, so this is how the word or two went:

'What are you doing here?' asked Jim.

'Six years,' said Clive. 'For fraud. And you?'

'Twenty years,' said Jim, 'for bribery and corruption.'

'Last time we met,' said Clive, 'we had champagne and chips for breakfast. Remember that.'

'And now,' said Jim, 'we are reduced to porridge. But, knowing us, we'll soon have cream on it. My only worry is the boy. Poor Timothy, poor motherless boy. The house sold over his head: his school fees left unpaid. Nothing between him and destitution but my sister, his Aunt Annie, and all she cares about is herself, but then who doesn't?'

'But he's got the Welfare, Jim,' said Clive. 'Let us not forget the Welfare. It's what we paid our poll tax for, or failed to, as the case may be.'

'What's to become of the boy?' asked Jim again. A tear or two fell from his eyes.

'The criminal classes often weep for the sorrows of children,' Angus the director says in a note to the actor playing Jim, 'although they have caused the sorrows themselves.' The actor yawns.

Ripple dissolve to a month ago – Angus favours ripple dissolves: they remind him of his childhood and save re-writes – when on the step of the shuttered 'Amanda' Timothy Bagshott stood alone, his smart pigskin suitcase by his side, the very model of a smart city gent in uniform, only slightly miniatured by virtue of his lack of years. And zooming up in a battered mini-van, with *Department of Youth* writ large upon its rusty side – nothing rustier than the Welfare, these days, in any city in the world – and in the van our good friend Rupert Oates himself. Paul, happy Paul, pick up his thoughts!

'See, here I come, the Welfare Man, in the County Council van, though Bagshott is a cursed name round here, still Timothy does deserve my care.'

And Timothy and his poor Aunt Annie, a nervous, plain, unmarried lady in her middle years, much burdened by black plastic sacks into which are crammed all her worldly belongings and such of Timothy's as she could be bothered to bring, step into the van. The lad would not be seen in public, even on the steps of a disgraced and shuttered house, with a black plastic sack. He would rather die than lose his dignity. This is what private education does to a lad.

And off the van goes, through the dilapidation of poor Parrot Pier, to the slightly less broken structures of the new estate. Here removal vans abound: the hopeful and the hopeless, the repossessed and unpossessed: have you got them in shot, Les? You're not doing a promotional video now: this is real life. 'Till Timothy's fortunes we decide,' thinks Rupert Oates, 'it's been judged best that he reside, for such are fate's ironic powers, with his Aunt in Bagshott Towers. A council rent book! Oh what a shame, to those with Bagshott as a name.'

Les captures the faces of Timothy and his Auntie Annie, as they stare up the soaring, if truncated, face of Audrey Tower, their future home. Twelve floors finished and twenty-five hoped for.

'Most of us,' observes Rupert, 'of course are glad to take what there is to be had, but Audrey Tower I have to tell is where the problem families dwell, and as a pleasant place to live is quite the worst the Council has to give.'

The arrival of the Bagshott aunt and nephew and Mr Oates in Council towers is observed by one Jon-Jon Ooster, a 16-year-old punk of some charm and intelligence, albeit white-faced, grimy and hung with leather, chains and nose rings. Jon-Jon, a vegetarian, smokes a cigar in the corridor he is to share with the Bagshotts (and a dozen others, of course, but they're too in terror of Jon-Jon to leave their apartments to put in an appearance). Paul, a snatch of conversation, please. Are you dreaming? We have to hear as well as look.

'I'm certain there'll be a shortage of oxygen this high up,' said Aunt Annie. 'If Timothy's asthma returns I shall hold you responsible, Mr Oates.'

'I didn't know you had asthma, Timothy,' says Mr Oates.

'I haven't,' says Timothy.

'Yes, he has,' declares Aunt Annie. 'It started the day his mother left home. He was only seven. Do you remember that day, Timothy?'

'Not if I can help it,' observes Timothy.

'See? How he suffers!' says Aunt Annie. 'Poor little Timothy! Poor wee boy!'

Aunt Annie has decided that the mercy directed at Timothy, by virtue of his childish state, shall include her too, by reason of the sympathy and concern she clearly shows for her nephew. Aunt Annie is not without a soupçon of her brother Jim's self-interested genes.

Into the flat they go, gene sharers both, sister and child of brother Jim, and find it bleak, and sparse and grim. The view's terrific, even so.

'Is this really how the workers live?' asks Annie. 'Come away from the window, Timothy, it isn't safe. Timothy suffers from vertigo. Don't you, Timothy?'

'No,' says Timothy.

'You must understand, Mr Oates,' says Aunt Annie, 'that it's impossible for us to live here.'

'All flats on the Bagshott Estate are of standard size and shape, Miss Bagshott,' observes Mr Oates. 'You are very lucky indeed to have anywhere at all to live. Bed and breakfast is the best that you could have reasonably hoped for. I had to plead your case most strongly at the last Council meeting to get you even this.'

'But my brother built the place,' says Aunt Annie.

'Exactly,' says Rupert Oates.

'Ingratitude!' exclaims Aunt Annie. 'And how are we expected to live? I am penniless, you understand. All my money was in my brother's companies.'

'So was the Council's,' says Mr Oates. 'The Social Security office is not far. Try to attend early, otherwise a queue builds up.'

'I must live on charity?' asks Annie.

'It's that or work,' says Rupert Oates. 'The same for you as it is for everyone. Nor can the Council continue Timothy at his private school: last term's incidentals, we notice, came to £1,500. Timothy must say goodbye to riding lessons, stables for his mounts, music and fencing tuition, and a log fire in his study. Timothy must go to the local comprehensive, like anybody else. To Bagshott School.'

Les, turn your camera to the comprehensive school; a structure twenty-five years old, once pride of Parrot Pier, now in excessive disrepair, except a recent council grant of £150,000 paid through Jim Bagshott's companies has recently effected some meagre improvement. Graffiti sours the walls, the scuttle of cockroaches unnerves the listening ear.

'A boy with Bagshott as a name at Bagshott School? It seems unkind but that's the rule,' muses our friend and Timothy's, Rupert Oates, who now uses his mobile phone to get in touch with Mr Korn, headmaster of Bagshott School. Picture Mr Korn, frame him in shot: a good man, the hope of the nation, of middle class origin and working class aspirations: he has children's art upon his walls: night and day he fights for the rights of his pupils and the survival of civilisation, in the face of finance cuts, the irrationality of the parent classes and the original sin of his pupils. He's tired but he won't give up. What's he saying, Paul?

'I'd like to oblige but I can't. The second year's full and I'm understaffed as it is. I know, Mr Oates, that it's my happy duty to educate all the kids in this area regardless of race, colour, creed and handicap. If there were only something special about him. There is? What is it? His Dad's in prison? So are all the Dads in prison. What's that you say? Jim Bagshott's boy? Impossible! I won't be responsible. He'll be lynched, and I'll be blamed.'

But Mr Oates puts the pressure on and so the second years squeeze over to make room for Timothy Bagshott. On his way down twelve flights of stairs – the lift is broken – Mr Oates has a word or two with Jon-Jon Ooster, who keeps him company.

'I had a letter from your headmaster, Jon-Jon.'

'Two thousand pupils and Mr Korn writes about little me! *Quel honneur!*'

'You can hardly count as a pupil, Jon-Jon, since it seems you seldom attend.'

'They go on at you if you're there,' says Jon-Jon, 'and they go on at you if you aren't. So what does it matter one way or another?'

'Tell you what, Jon-Jon,' says Mr Oates, 'since we're all in this together, how about you keep a helpful eye on young Timothy Bagshott, your new neighbour. You're a good boy at heart. Help him settle in.'

And Jon-Jon laughs and says, 'Yes, me and my mates, we'll help settle any Bagshott in.'

'Ingratitude, complaints,' thinks Rupert Oates, 'what else can be expected. We have so far from nature's way defected, the Bagshott lift in Bagshott Towers is often stuck for hours and hours; they piss into the shaft and rust soon turns all moving parts to dust.'

'I say,' said Timothy Bagshott to his Aunt Annie as dirty water from the loo bubbled up into the sink, 'I'm sure the Pater never imagined his own family would end up here or he'd have seen to everything very differently. Tell you what, try running the bath: sometimes it's a simple matter of an airlock,' but both are distracted by cries of help from the Ooster household and a sudden blow is directed upon the thin front door, which splinters, and there stands Jon-Jon.

'My mum,' says Jon-Jon, 'cannot abide it no more. Every time you empty your bath her loo fills up.'

'Too bad, old chap,' says Timothy, and shuts the door in Jon-Jon's face.

'People like that having the nerve to complain!' remarks Annie. 'Why, they're nothing but a Problem Family!'

Another blow upon the door: a burst of splinters in the room: Jon-Jon enters in unasked, and with him brothers both older and younger.

'Ooster's the name,' says Jon-Jon, 'and this is Joe-Joe and this is little Ripper, and as for me, I'm Jon-Jon.'

'What quaint names you have round here,' says Timothy.

'None so quaint as Bagshott,' observes the middle Ooster lad. 'Ripper's called Ripper for a reason, and Joe-Joe's back from Borstal where they taught him love of animals and how to have a cold shower every day. We Oosters get about, enjoy life: they suspend our sentences more often than not, to save the prison service aggro.'

'How fascinating,' observes Timothy.

'I am reliably informed,' says Jon-Jon, 'that you are about to attend Bagshott Comprehensive. I am a pupil there myself. If I were you, I'd get your Auntie Annie not to take a bath from now on, because my Mum don't like it when she does.'

'I'll think about it,' says Timothy, and closes what's left of the door and tries not to tremble.

News of his family's predicament flies fast to big bad Jim, but how can he help his little son?

'Lovely piece of renovation we did on that school,' observes Jim. 'He shouldn't have too hard a time. Renamed in my honour. A deal of asbestos in the assembly hall walls and high aluminium joists as well; not too good at stress-bearing but economical. Perhaps I should mention it? What do you think, Clive? Imprisonment makes me indecisive. I blame the Courts!'

'*Quietus non movere*,' replies Clive, which, being translated, is 'let sleeping dogs lie.'

'A lot of glass in that assembly hall,' muses Jim. 'What with the roof. They may have had the impression it was anti-ultra-violet glass, but the contractors let me down. What could I do?'

'*Quietus non movere*,' says Clive.

'A fuss about nothing, a scare, this ozone layer,' says Jim. 'If a boy gets skin cancer it's easily cured. I blame his mother; she had no business walking out on me. Everything a woman could want – a fur, a chauffeur, nannies, holidays. Ingratitude! The boy takes after his mother, Clive, and that's the truth of it. All that money spent on his education, and not a flicker of gratitude: has he been to visit me? No! He thinks himself a cut above me: always did. Sneered at me from behind the bars of his cot. I hope his Aunt Annie's coping. Perhaps I should get in touch with his mother?'

'*Quietus non movere*,' is all Clive says, and Jim fears his friend means to sleep the years of his sentence away . . .

An evening or two later (Angus deals with the passage of time on screen by flicking over the days in a calendar; that simple nostalgic device) and there's Auntie Annie removing soup stains and ironing a secondhand school uniform for Timothy to put on in the morning for his first day.

'Black, grey and navy blue,' observes Timothy. 'How dreary; necessary, I daresay, amongst the great unwashed or why would those in charge choose it? And supposing I get head lice, or impetigo? What then? Perhaps I should aim for a quick medical discharge?'

'Timothy dear,' says Auntie Annie. 'Try to be sensible. Co-operate. Don't put on airs. Be like the others. If you ever want to escape from Bagshott Estate you must work hard and pass exams, and I must be here to help you. There is some talk of a cut in our subsistence allowance, of my going out to work; but my work is here with you, helping you get an education. You look on me as a mother, don't you, Timothy dear?'

'Of course I do, dear Aunt,' says Timothy. 'Never let it be said that a Bagshott worked from nine to five.'

'Or seven to midnight,' said Auntie Annie, 'now the Shop Act is cancelled and a crust is so very hard to earn.'

'I will do what I can for you, Aunt,' says Timothy. 'I will aim for suspension rather than expulsion. Needs must and all that. But I will not willingly keep the company of the Oosters of this world.'

Even as he spoke, a great convulsion shook the corridor, indeed the very structure of the dwelling block, the elevator quivered between its rusty girders and fell an inch or so: Maisie Ooster was rounding up her boys. Maisie Ooster was twenty-four stone and perfect with it, if loud. Annie stuck her head out of her splintered front door.

'Take no notice of me,' cried Maisie Ooster. 'I washed these lads last night and I can't do a thing with them today', and she laughed so loud and heartily that Annie joined in, but not Timothy, and so night fell, and the full moon arose over Bagsh-ott Towers, and made all things so boldly brilliant and beautiful even the rats and the cockroaches paused in their rustling, and the human scavengers lifted up their hearts, and even the mug-gers paused to consider the nature of creation, and the wild creatures of the night slept, thinking it was day: and those who normally slept by night awoke, including Rupert Oates; in the morning Paul had his thoughts on tape ready for playback to Angus. Paul's tapes are like some film, really sensitive, and just as film will pick up scenes that never were, so Paul's tapes pick up sound. He is always in employment. Perhaps that's why he's so happy. 'Night falls on Bagshott Towers,' mused Rupert Oates that moonlit night, 'on good and bad and in between, as most of us are seen to be. And who's to blame? Your poor old mum? No. She had a mum herself, you know, and is what she was made, as are we all. Moon on Bagshott Towers! And there's a fox, and there the night owl flies. Listen; the wild life of the city cries – and morning breaks, and unreality breaks in, on this strange world we're living in.'

The moon set. The sun arose. Cameraman Les, up bright and early, uninstructed by Angus, who has a hangover, is filming the kids of Bagshott Comp. arrive – some on crack and some still clutching teddy bears: some pregnant and some virtuous still, and all shockable one way or another, either at the innocence of some, or the knowingness of others.

'Children of Bagshott Towers,' says Rupert in his heart, 'school's not so bad. It's warm and there is dinner to be had. Your teachers want to help you, honestly they do. I've asked them and they say it's true.'

Angus arrives, apologetic, and the film crew sets up in the corridor outside Mr Korn's office, where Timothy stands disdainful and alone. The headmaster appears – 'Please, sir – ' says Timothy, but Mr Korn is already inside and the door is shut. Even the best of teachers develop deafness to the pleas of pupils: it is not the teachers' fault. Children are no different from adults, other than in scale and lack of experience; their clamour, their tugging at the conscience and coatstrings of those they see as powerful, render dazed, punch drunk and rude those who are paid to suffer it.

And coming down the corridor, framed by Les, observed by Timothy, a smallish, pimply, owlish child called Twitcher, son of an optician.

'I've had enough,' says Twitcher, 'of this day.'

'Already?' enquired Timothy, quite alarmed.

'Ten minutes in this place is always enough. Already my eye is twitching. My mother said if it happened I was to go home.'

'Well!' says Jon-Jon, Joe-Joe and Ripper, fast approaching, 'Well, well, well. If it isn't little Twitcher: off home are we, darling, nice back home with Mummy. Twitcher wears a vest,' they say, and so on, and then, 'Tell you what, Twitcher, give us a dance and show us how happy you are!'

'I don't know how to dance,' says Twitcher.

'Then we'll jump on your toes,' says Jon-Jon, 'and teach you, unless by any chance you have dinner money to spare. Just a borrow, of course, until tomorrow.'

'I don't take school dinners,' says Twitcher, 'because someone always takes the money. I bring packed lunch instead, with egg and curry filling that nobody likes, not even me. But at least I don't starve.'

'Better than what our mum gives us,' says Ripper.

'A biff on the communal lughole. If you got no money, you gotta dance. If you can't dance, then we gotta stamp.'

'Now look here, you fellows,' says Timothy Bagshott, 'bullying a little fellow like this. It simply isn't on.'

Six cold eyes focus in upon Timothy Bagshott; Twitcher dodges away and who can blame him.

'If it isn't my neighbour Timothy Bagshott,' says Jon-Jon. 'Fairdo's. You let Twitcher go so it's up to you to see us right.'

'You'll get nothing from me,' says Timothy Bagshott.

'We will,' says Jon-Jon, ''cos we'll smash your face in else. All you've got and more; your Dad dines on champagne and chips, you've got a lot to spare.'

'But he's in clink,' says Timothy boldly.

'We know his sort,' said the Ooster boys. 'Some men are born to champagne and chips as the sparks fly upwards,' says Jon-Jon, who'd been in Mr Korn's high-flyers' special English class until his fifteenth birthday, the day he went on mental and moral strike and they let him into the cinema to see '15' films. The porn he takes home for the video and the subtleties of 'Pause'.

'Hand over what you've got and we'll have your trainers too, unless you want to dance.'

'I wish you boys wouldn't dance in the corridor,' says Mr Korn, emerging from his room. 'Just stand quiet, boy, until I've time for you.'

In post-production, we are allowed merciful release from scenes of teenage torture; Angus tactfully intercuts a scene between Maisie and Annie which, according to Paul's sound tape, carried above even the sound of Bagshott plumbing. The two women had got together with a book of *Plumbing Made Easy* to solve the bath/loo problem.

'A wire like this, Miss Bagshott,' Maisie said, 'must have a dozen uses. Say you had a dress shop with a fair size letterbox, you could pull it through and hook your winter outfit out in no time at all.'

'You have a lively mind, Mrs Ooster,' said Miss Bagshott.

'If you were married to my Barley,' said Mrs Ooster kindly, 'no doubt you'd have the same. A wife contrives as best she must.' And with a gurgle and a splodge the blockage was cleared; that the water supply and the sewage now intermingled on the floor below was no concern of theirs. Annie thanked Maisie and Maisie remarked, 'My Gawd, you could do with a thing or two in here. Telly, video, three-piece, cocktail cabinet. My Barley can get things cheap.'

'Thank you,' said Annie primly, 'but we Bagshotts don't like to be indebted. We're cosy as we are.'

'Don't put on airs,' said Maisie. 'Your brother's doing time, like anyone else.'

'That's rather different,' said Annie. 'My brother is no criminal.'

'I call it criminal,' said Maisie Ooster outright, 'when other people's drains come up my sink, and who's doing that but your brother?'

'I accept your censure, Mrs Ooster,' said Annie, 'or may I call you Maisie? The fact of the matter is, I used to live a lonely life up at "Amanda"; my brother always away on business, and Timothy learning to be a little gent at boarding school. But here!

Why, even the dole queue is quite jolly. And I packed little Timothy his favourite lunch: egg and curry sandwiches.

'My boys never bother with lunch,' said Maisie. 'They pick something up on the way, they say. They're such good boys. We believe in discipline, Barley and me. Take the stick to them often and hard, they grow up good as gold.'

'Sir,' says Timothy the while, entering Mr Korn's office unasked and unabashed. 'I will not continue to wait outside; it was you who wished to see me, not I you. In the circumstances, I'd be glad if you said what you had to, and let me begin the education the State so kindly provides, and not waste the tax-payers' money, nor my valuable time, keeping me waiting.'

'You'll be Timothy Bagshott,' murmured Mr Korn.

'And you'll be Mr Korn,' replied Timothy.

'I was only going to welcome you to the school, Timothy,' said Mr Korn.

'I'd rather you called me Bagshott,' said Timothy. 'We are not friends.'

'Boy,' said Mr Korn, 'is it your intention that I suspend you?'

'It is, sir.'

'Then you will have to do better than that, Timothy. My threshold of natural indignation is high. Are you perhaps having trouble with the Ooster boys? Joe-Joe, Jon-Jon and Ripper? The family is not easy, but they are all our responsibility, and yours perhaps more than anyone, your name being Bagshott.'

'Guilt by association, sir?'

'A matter of cultural, family and communal guilt. Your father and his like are responsible for many social ills round here: bad housing for a start; the breakdown of family life in general; the squalor of our streets and schools.'

'So the sins of the father are to be visited on the children?'

'I think you'll find they are, my boy, whenever you enter the toilet block. The sewers leak: the plastic pipes are all too permeable. There you are, Mr Hobbs!'

Enter Mr Hobbs, the PE teacher: a karate expert, shaven-headed with an evil mien, as are too many of his ilk.

'Mr Hobbs,' said Mr Korn, 'we have a problem or two to

deal with today. When the indoor swimming pool overflowed because of the stuck ballcock, electrical damage was clearly done. The fire alarms have rung six times already today – '

'I thought that was your little joke, sir,' said Mr Hobbs, 'to keep us on our toes.'

'My sense of humour is quite, quite gone,' said Mr Korn. 'And the automatic doors to the assembly hall are working in reverse. They close when anyone approaches.'

Timothy laughed.

'I'm glad you find that funny, Timothy,' said Mr Korn. 'Trust a Bagshott! Let me introduce you to your head of year, our Mr Hobbs. Mr Hobbs doubles as caretaker at this, your father's school, in order to pay his mortgage. Timothy, if I might give you a word of advice: a slight note of diffidence, even of apology, might help you get along with pupils and with staff.'

'I have nothing of which I need be ashamed,' said Timothy. 'I am proud of my father, as any son might be.'

'He's a lucky lad,' said Mr Hobbs. 'I'll let him be first on the wall-bars since he's new. They carry quite an electric charge; the wiring in the gym being what it is, after the flooding, and even before.'

'Perhaps I am just a little ashamed,' said Timothy. 'Sir.'

Now what of Timothy's mother? Doesn't she care? Surely she's read of Jim Bagshott's disgrace, arrest and imprisonment in the press: surely she'll care, do something to rescue the flesh of her flesh, love of her love?

'Meanwhile the Welfare, ever tender-hearted,' observes Rupert Oates, 'seeks to trace our Timothy's mum, long departed, and find her – what surprise! – not so far away though feeling unmaternal, sad to say.'

Audrey, for such is her name, works as the barmaid at the local pub, the Bagshott Arms – the landlord is in trouble with Equal Opportunities for describing her as barmaid, when it should be barperson. No one has yet got round to insisting that he be called the landnoble which presumably is the non-gender specific of landlord. But who cares about that? On with the story. Are you happy, Les? Paul? Angus? Happy, happy, happy, in the execution of our craft. What other happiness can there be?

'Rhubarb, rhubarb, rhubarb,' says Rupert now, for although Paul swore he was happy, his boom proved faulty. Let it just be said Rupert Oates put the child's plight to the mother and the mother denied all knowledge of the child. Some mothers are like that, and a lot of fathers too. Children are plentiful, since parents must opt out of parenthood, not opt in: the former is a boring, expensive, time-consuming thing to do. But Rupert Oates persevered, and finally Audrey grudgingly acknowleged she had borne a child to a property developer of note and criminality, Jim Bagshott of Bagshott Towers and Bagshott School.

Where Mr Hobbs now addressed his class in language vile, insulting and persuasive, as was his custom.

'First one to talk gets a detention,' said Mr Hobbs, 'and the one sitting next to him. Both sides. Anyone who thinks my bark is worse than my bite is mistaken. My little darlings, my sensitive children, welcome back. How many walls did you deface in the holidays? How many old ladies did you mug, cars did you joyride, reefers did you inhale and raves attend? I've brought an extra little playmate for you today; young Timothy Bagshott. He's son of Jim, perpetrator of your fate. Once you lived in squalor in slums upon the ground, now you live up on high, in half-completed tower blocks. The rest of Europe gave up the habit years ago, of housing its riff-raff in the sky, but Jim Bagshott told your elected representatives the old ways were the best, that is to say the cheapest, and your elected representatives, mesmerised like the snakes they are – '

'Sir,' said Timothy, 'isn't it the snakes who do the mesmerising, and the rabbits who get mesmerised?'

'Take a detention, lad,' said Mr Hobbs. 'Have it your own way. Your father is a snake and the Council are rabbits. And it is thanks to your snake of a father that the PE wing is flooded and I am teaching History to form Thirteen, a class well known throughout the school to be composed of spastics and pygmies.'

'Sir,' said Timothy, 'I really must protest. You shouldn't call people pygmies. Say rather people of restricted growth, or the vertically challenged. '

'Another detention, boy,' said Mr Hobbs. 'I call you lot what I like and so long as it's not racist and I don't lay a finger on you, no one can say me nay. Spastics and pygmies, the lot of you!'

Mr Hobbs left the class to check the basement's pumps in case the central heating blew.

'If you tear Timothy Bagshott limb from limb, class,' said Mr Hobbs, 'you'll only get probation. Why don't you have a go?'

Form Thirteen, so familiarly called because it was understood to be unlucky in that its members had Mr Hobbs as year tutor, personal counsellor and careers' officer, turned to stare at Timothy, undecided as to its group response. The toilets in both school and home were so often out of order that even the young ones had noticed – it is one thing to defecate in lifts and corridors out of choice, in a spirit of defiance, quite another to have nowhere else to go. And there always has to be someone to blame, and how seldom is that person not just in the room with you, but on the same scale? Mr Hobbs had given permission to hate, and to not a few in the class Mr Hobbs was a hero. The oppressed soon learn to lick the oppressor's boot. It was, in other words, a tense moment.

'I expect,' said Timothy, 'you get quite a few days off because of the structural difficulties inherent in the rehabilitation of any educational institution.'

Jaws dropped.

'That is to say,' said Timothy, 'if you ask me, my Dad cocked up this sodding school on purpose. My Dad hates schools.'

The moment passed. Ordinary mayhem broke out, and Twitcher was its target, not our Timothy. Twitcher got his glasses broken but that was nothing unusual. All knew Twitcher's father was an optician, and could easily acquire more. Class Thirteen, the other side of their culture and conditioning, were quite reasonable and thoughtful lads, whose habit it was to take justice into their own hands, since society afforded so little evidence of it. And pleasure likewise, since so much of what they did was frowned upon.

Up at the Bagshott Arms the while, Rupert Oates wrestled with the soul of Audrey Bagshott.

'So what if I ran off with the chauffeur,' cried Audrey. 'I chose love, not money, didn't I? Isn't that what a girl is supposed to do? And don't tell me Jim turned criminal when I left; he was born like that: devious, greedy and grungy. And he always did the plumbing himself, liked to turn his hand to a real man's job, so "Amanda" was always awash with water. My built-in cupboards filled up with water. My shoes and my furs were always awash. And I couldn't take Timothy with me: the chauffeur didn't like kids. You know what kids are like in cars, never at their best.'

'He's thirteen now,' said Mr Oates. 'I had him in my own car. He made no trouble.'

'But I'm with the landlord now,' said Audrey, 'and you have to be eighteen to get in for a drink. And I know those boys from Bagshott Comp. Nasty, thieving little hooligans, lacing their cokes with rum if you so much as look the other way.'

It is always hard to reason with the not altogether reasonable, but on the other hand the least reasonable make the warmest mothers, so Mr Oates persisted, and on hearing that the lad lived in a block of flats named in her memory, and perceiving that Jim Bagshott's heart was still tender towards her, she consented to visit both her child and her husband.

And Mr Oates was relieved, because he knew only too well for any child to be in Mr Hobbs' class was a strain upon that child's source of cheerfulness, and cheerfulness in Bagshott Towers was the rarest and most precious of all commodities.

'Sticks and stones,' said Rupert Oates in his heart, 'may break my bones, and words can always hurt me. And who it is who says they don't can only mean to bruise me. Flesh and bones will heal at last, but insults past stay with me.'

Mr Oates did not like Mr Hobbs. Neither did Mr Korn, but Mr Hobbs was on a fixed contract, and could not be fired other than for gross professional negligence, which he took care not to show. And, besides, Mr Hobbs was a dab hand at keeping the boilers going. Disgraceful people often develop very rare and precise skills, so that others will be obliged to put up with them.

Mrs Ooster, in spite of the wild and aggressive mien of her very large sons, was an agreeable person indeed. Angus cuts gratefully away from Rupert Oates' light verse musings – which Angus feels are somehow happy Paul's fault, and totally out of order, considering the overall style of the piece – to Aunt Annie's new home and the arrival of Mrs Ooster with a daintily pale pink TV set with a built-in aerial like a leaping dolphin. 'So kind of you, Maisie,' Aunt Annie is saying. 'The only people who ever came up to "Amanda" were those bearing writs and solicitors' letters. No one ever seemed to like us, for all Jim was forever throwing parties. Why did you say the TV didn't have a back, Maisie? It seems to me to have a back. I imagine one could get quite a shock if it didn't. All those nasty wires.' 'Things which fall off lorries,' said Mrs Ooster enigmatically, 'don't have backs. Never mind. You'll learn, now you live in Audrey Tower. Would you care to come to Bingo with me tonight?'

'I've never gambled in my life,' said Auntie Annie.

'It's not a gamble,' said Mrs Ooster. 'The Caller is a very good friend of mine.'

And Aunt Annie was glad that Mrs Ooster had a very good friend, because she'd had a glimpse of Mr Ooster and thought him a surly and miserable fellow indeed.

Angus prefers to look through his viewfinder at Audrey who, although into her forties, is blonde, well-bosomed and high-heeled, rather than at staid (so far) Auntie Annie and vast Mrs Ooster – agreeableness is a quality that can get you lost on the cutting-room floor, but sexiness keeps anyone in shot. So visiting hours at the open prison are here and Audrey's sitting opposite Jim, who doesn't seem one bit pleased to see her. The Rupert Oates of this world, in spite of the harmonies inside their heads, can be naive, believing that others are as they are: that is to say, really nice if a trifle power-hungry.

'I've come all this way,' says Audrey, 'and you aren't one bit pleased to see me.'

'Because I know what you want,' says Jim. 'And it's the same as everyone else wants.'

'What's that?' asks Audrey.

'Money,' says Jim. 'The only thing I've ever had to offer. So now you come running to me for the fees, so your boy can go to boarding school and be a little gent.'

'Such a thing never crossed my heart, Jim,' says Audrey.

'Then it should have,' says Jim. 'What sort of mother are you? Running out on your own child. That boy's going to spend the rest of his life searching for an absent mother figure.'

'What's got into you, Jim?' asks Audrey.

'Psychology classes,' says Jim. 'There's nothing else to do round here. I wasn't much of a father myself. He'll be searching for an absent father figure too. Not much of a husband either. A workaholic like me leaves a trail of personal disasters behind.'

'You go on saying things like that, Jim,' says Audrey, 'and I'll be on the step waiting when you come out.'

'As to the fees,' says Jim, 'I'll see what I can do. I haven't been fair to him. Bringing him up posh then pushing him in the deep end.'

Audrey expresses admiration that a man in prison could still get his hands on money; Jim expresses his anxiety about the swimming pool at Bagshott School – chlorine might eat away at the new style insulation of the underwater electrics – and suggests Timothy be warned not to take a dip. And so love, affection and trust is re-established between the two. Angus makes a note to establish a heart-shaped frame around the pair in post-production.

Aunt Annie has packed a very special lunch for Timothy today. He eats it in the safety of the Art Room. Twitcher is there, together with a small group of boys in need of quiet and protection. The Art Room door affords some protection against the clanging and banging, the shouting and screaming, the pushing and shoving in the corridors outside.

'Anyone care for a chicken leg?' enquires Timothy. 'Seasoned with salt and lemon, roasted in butter and basil. Only 40p the piece, and a bargain at the price.'

'Sounds foreign to me,' says Twitcher.

'Then how about a cigarette?' asks Timothy, '25p each or three for the pound.'

'Why are three more expensive than one?' asks Twitcher.

'Because I have my father's blood in me,' says Timothy.

'He's inside, isn't he?' says Boy 1.

'He is indeed,' says Timothy,. 'Left to rot by a corrupt authority, a society indifferent to the rightness of his case.'

'Open prison?' asks Boy 2.

'Of course,' says Timothy.

'Then it doesn't count,' says Boy 3. 'My dad's doing thirty years in high security, and not even a political.'

Boys 1, 2 and 3 will have to double as prison attendants (trainees, of course; they will have to age down for the one, age up for the other). This is not a lavish production, and extras are expensive. The producer can see no merit in having Boys 1, 2 and 3: the dialogue could have been accomplished with just the one bit-part player. But Angus says the way to look lavish is to be lavish.

'Besides,' says Boy 2, 'it's not fathers that count in here, it's mothers. How's yours?'

'Run off,' says Timothy.

'That's nothing,' says Boy 2.

'It was to me,' says Timothy sadly.

All contemplate the truth of this. Angus studies each face at some length to get the value of their hiring and keep the producers in their place. The Ooster boys at this point lean on the Art Room door so it collapses inward, being made none too solidly, and deprive the already dismal group of their dinner: chicken legs, ham rolls, crisps, Ryvita and cheese slices, and a bottle of Montrachet Cadet which Timothy has been keeping to himself. Well, the Ooster boys have to live too, and Mrs Ooster is too busy keeping Mr Ooster happy in the mornings to do much in the way of providing lunch, nor does their father see why he should provide men younger, bigger and more energetic than he with funds simply because they are his sons. Rupert Oates' voice shivers over the scene: 'Children remember this, that childhood ends. When you grow up, at least you'll choose your friends.'

Mr Oates then appears in conversation with Aunt Annie, offering her a change of residence: he has organised it so that she and Timothy can exchange dwellings with a family living on the outskirts of town, almost in the country; Timothy can be taken out of Bagshott School and go to Parrot High: a smaller and altogether milder institution in a better area, so much so that it is soon to become a Direct Grant School. But Aunt Annie, to Rupert Oates' surprise, will have none of it. She is happy, she says, as Mrs Ooster's neighbour: she's on her way to Bingo and, besides, she's come to fancy the view from the twelfth floor and Timothy no longer suffers from vertigo.

'But I'm offering you a thatched cottage,' says Rupert Oates, and all Aunt Annie says, pushing past, is 'nasty, germy things, thatches'. Mr Oates inhales the fetid air of the Ooster level, as it's known at the Council offices, and marvels. The Ooster boys are active and healthy eaters and drinkers and seldom make it inside their home before being overtaken by the call of nature. The lift is so often out of order, their own door so seldom opened promptly to them (Mr Ooster has the lock changed frequently) they can hardly be blamed for this lack of control. So far one can get, no farther. Requests to the Council by Mr Oates that common lavatory provision should be made at the entrance to Audrey Tower convulsed the Supplies and Facilities Dept. with mirth. How many hours would such constructs survive the vandals? Let the corridors stink: there was nothing to be done about it.

Angus decided against attempting to dramatise this sorry state of affairs. Producers, viewers and indeed Les would resist anything too graphic, so Mr Oates was merely left sniffing the air and wincing; Angus then cut away to a scene at Bagshott School, where the French class was in process, cheerful enough, if punctuated by cheers, jeers, Kung Fu kicks and the sound of breaking windows. A student teacher, pretty and eighteen, and in her first year at college, stood weeping in front of the class, who thought it best to tactfully ignore her distress. The lads were not unkind but no doubt thought the sooner she toughened up the happier everyone would be. That, or get out of teaching. Timothy sat at the back of the class, reading.

'Tim,' muttered the boy next to him, 'what are you reading?'

'A book called *Teach Yourself French*,' said Timothy. At which point Mr Hobbs erupted into the room, shouting, swearing, thwacking everyone in sight. 'Dregs and rabble!' he shouted. 'Class Thirteen, the dross of the streets: what's the point of teaching them French, they can't even speak their native tongue. The sooner they're out on the streets and on crack the better. Their mothers are, *et tes grandmères*.' The class fell silent, shocked and stunned, and the student teacher ran from the room and out of the profession altogether. Had it not been for Mr Hobbs, she would have toughened up perfectly well in her own good time.

It was this particular scene which causes the TV critic of *The Times*, who later became editor of *Punch* – a humorous magazine, now deceased – to become almost incoherent in his outrage: the film, he complained, was a vicious attack against the educational system of the nation. Schools such as Bagshott Comprehensive did not exist. A foul fabrication! Everyone knew schools were places where calm and kindly teachers, in an organised fashion, set about the business of teaching and socialising the docile and grateful young. Else what were the taxpayers paying their taxes for? But that is by the by. Just why *The Tale of Timothy Bagshott*, a play for TV, was never repeated and wiped from the BBC archives. Just as Les could not bring himself to turn his camera on what we had better call defecatory matter, nor could the critic of *The Times* face truth. Why should he be expected to do better than Les?

The cookery class at the Open Prison was doing rather better: Clive and Jim were baking £50 notes into a cake tin. Clive extracted them from between the pages of a cookery book called *Easy Steps to Home Baking* and handed them to Jim, who dipped them one by one into a rather over-vanillaed mix before laying them in the tin. He sang as he dipped. He was in love, and for a man to fall in love with his own wife is a happy experience. Can electrified fences a prison make, or cookery classes a cage?

And because new love flies through the universe, turning all things rosy, tipping the spires of the Bagshott Development, and even the poor, unfinished, stunted growth of Audrey Tower itself, with gold, Aunt Annie looking out over what to many was the debris of a ruined city and a languid slime of murky river and seeing only charm, progress and infinite possibility, said to Timothy, 'Oh, by the way, a postcard came for you. It's from your mother.' She'd meant just to forget its arrival. She'd never liked Audrey, even before she ran off with the chauffeur and so upset Jim.

The postcard was what's known as a sixteenth-century Dutch interior, a woman sweeping clean a yard, forget the yard's outside not inside. See ya soon, kid, the message on the back said in its enchantingly quivery red-biroed writing. The hand of his mother. Timothy rejoiced in his heart, felt his father's blood surge more strongly in his veins, and his mother's too, and the very next day took Mr Hobbs aside and offered him and his wife a free holiday for two in the Bahamas, through certain travel agencies known personally to the Bagshott family, in return for Mr Hobbs desisting from libelling Class Thirteen.

'Schedule flight or charter?' asked Mr Hobbs.

'Schedule,' replied Timothy.

'Club Class or Economy?' asked Mr Hobbs.

'Club,' said Timothy, and so the deal was done. That Mr Hobbs knew his time was up in teaching, that Mr Korn – following a doctor's report relating to the traumas suffered by the pretty student teacher (I'm not saying her prettiness had anything to do with the advent of natural justice: merely that it helps), which she had the courage to attribute to Mr Hobbs and not the pupils – finally had sufficient evidence to apply to the Council for Mr Hobbs' dismissal, was neither here nor there. One thing to be said for Mr Hobbs was that he was not proud, and another was that he knew which side his bread was buttered. It is important to keep looking for good in people, otherwise one might succumb to despair.

We next see Rupert Oates visiting Audrey Tower with a cake, a gift for Annie, baked by her brother Jim in prison. A nice scene this: Annie's surprise and gratification at her brother's thoughtfulness: her mixed pleasure (once Mr Oates was gone – no Bagshott was born yesterday) and disappointment at finding her mouth more full of money than cake: the internal struggle as to whether or not just to swallow the note that said the money was to take Timothy out of Bagshott School and pay for his private education, or just keep the money herself, and the eventual triumph of good. Aunt Annie decided to act unselfishly, and do as her brother wished. People make this kind of decision all the time, though cynics think they don't. The assumption that the great men of the people act only in their own interest is a plague of our time.

Meanwhile, it's packed lunch time in the Art Room, and Timothy stands on a chair and exhorts fans and doubters both to direct action. The power of the union, the will of the workers, so fast fading in the adult world, will find its revival in our schools: it is a prophecy; not a difficult one, if you consider the state of our schools. Rather like a Western scientist impressing a native tribe by predicting an eclipse.

'Fellow pupils,' cries Timothy. 'Comrades! Have you no courage, no common sense? Are you sheep or are you men? Packed lunchers all, have you no pride? Daily we are subjected to these Ooster raids: it is too much. We must unite against these bullies: singly we are powerless, united and organised, who can stand against us? The formation of the Bagshott Protection Agency is underway – membership 50p, payable to me. Twitcher here will make a note of it. An offence against one is from now on an offence against all. The Teamsters' Union was better than none. Ask any US baggage handler.'

'We'll get found out,' said Boy 1.

'We'll get into trouble,' said Boy 2.

'We'll get sent to Mr Korn,' said Boy 3.

'But you'll get to eat your dinner,' said Timothy Bagshott, and as the faces of Boys 1, 2 and 3 broke into smiles, Les lingered long upon them, at Angus's request.

Happy Paul took care to record the conversation of the Ooster boys as they approached the Art Room, the dinner of others on their minds. It went like this:

Ripper: 'Jon-Jon, big brother, there's something I want to know.'

'What's that?' asked Jon-Jon.

Ripper: 'If our mum ever won at bingo, instead of always losing, would we get chicken legs for dinner, like Timothy Bagshott?'

'Spastic,' said Jon-Jon, 'you are a spastic. Our mum always wins at bingo. She just tells us she doesn't.'

Tears came into Ripper's eyes. Boys depend dreadfully upon their mother's love, no matter how much taller than their mothers they become. Joe-Joe said nothing. He was a silent lad, and had spoken very little since the day his pet rabbit produced a litter of twelve and Barley Ooster flushed the lot down the toilet. It had been a miracle birth: how can a single pet rabbit produce a litter without divine intervention? And indeed, the problems with Audrey Tower plumbing dated from that traumatic day, though the tenants preferred to blame Jim Bagshott.

As the Ooster boys leant heavily through the Art Room door and splintered it for the third time that term, they were set upon by the Bagshott Protection Society, in united and organised protest, and forcibly thrown out again into the corridor, bruised, surprised, and without their trainers.

'It's a madhouse, this school,' said Jon-Jon.

'You can't even get dinner when you're hungry,' said Ripper. But Joe-Joe said, he who had been silent for so long, 'If we asked Mr Oates, he'd get us free cooked dinners every day.'

Money, time and patience ran out for Angus at this stage. There was trouble with the crew. Paul had another job to go to: Les lost interest once he had perceived there was nowhere for the story to go but to a happy ending, and began to frame his shots sloppily and forgot to renew the batteries before they ran out, thus holding everybody up intolerably, and to the detriment of the shooting schedule. Angus was obliged to forgo the dramatic (fairly) scenes in which Timothy Bagshott gave the cake money back to his Aunt Annie, and told Mr Korn he wanted to stay on at Bagshott School, which now he had organised a little he had come to love. He was certainly finding it profitable. Viewers never got to see how Jim confessed to the Parent Governors that the school swimming pool was potentially dangerous and how in return, and for health reasons, he was let out on parole. How Audrey and Jim (reformed by love) and Timothy returned to 'Amanda', to run a centre for the homeless. How Aunt Annie ran off with Barley Ooster – why do you think she wouldn't move to a thatched cottage? – to Mrs Ooster's great relief. Mrs Ooster had come to dislike sex and Annie had all her years of celibacy to make up for, which suited everyone. Mrs Ooster was now able to give all her love and affection to her boys, who became model members of society. How Twitcher's father paid for him to have his short-sightedness cured by the new Soviet method of paring away the cornea, so the lad was no longer obliged to wear glasses. How Joe-Joe's rabbit gave birth to another set of miraculous young, which Joe-Joe, now his father was happy with Aunt Annie, was allowed to raise: how a vandal-proof toilet was installed at the entrance to Audrey Tower and its remaining seven floors constructed without undue torment to those already living there, and so forth. All these happy occurrences were left drifting in the hopeful air – too expensive to be nailed on film and, besides, as everyone knows, good news is no news. So forget it. Who cares about dramatic form?

'Paul, are you happy?' enquired Angus for the last time, and Paul replied yes with some sincerity, for with the end of filming he was at last free to return to the arms of his girlfriend, and as his parting shot gave Angus a few more lines from Rupert Oates' head.

> Though socialism's dead and gone, they say
> Yet still shall justice and compassion win the day.
> How else can man (and woman too) live with him (her) self?
> Only by understanding, empathy, good management, these
> three,
> Shall come the proper sharing out of wealth:

The best will, not the worst will, of the people be set
free.
No one's a villain, but the world has made him so.
No one's a villain, but if you ask him won't say no,
Who, me?

Thank you, Rupert Oates, you'll be late for your meeting.

# A Conversation for the Nineties

*HUSBAND:*

If I were a warrior
And not weak, as I am.
I would slaughter an adventurer
Who came for your child, or your life.
I would roast his bones
For your dinner.

Why, therefore,
When I am consumed
By a discriminating appetite,
Will you not freely
Open the hairy gates of your belly
To my probing?

*WIFE:*

Because I, too, am weak,
An exchange of services
Is only possible between the hungry.
If I desired
Your steaming thickness
Up to its root in my body
I would hire a machine-pistol
And slaughter an adventurer
Who came for your child, or your life.
I would poach his testicles
For your breakfast.
So there.

## ADVENTURER:

I am an adventurer
With a red hot poker
Up my bottom,
Intercourse can be nasty, too.
I recommend that you both
Become vegetarians, and celibate.

This is not a time
To make a powerful enemy.
The devil is out, looking
For astray sexual organs
To make a stew for his dog.

So beware.


# The Sick

The sick are like the old. When muscles waste
They end as famished shadows of themselves.
Their skin goes cold, the colour of the paste
That seventies put on to look like twelves.

A second childhood comes. And then a third.
Steel wheelchairs carry babies to their meals
Where eating means extrusion of a turd.
The costive athlete squirms on useless heels.

Imagine, then, the evening traffic jams
These dream of, where they idle, browse and talk,
The stirrup-cups they manage, the young lambs
They seem like when their mounted bodies walk.

Yes, walk. Some dream they walk again through a door,
Even dance a fox-trot on a slippery floor.

## Last Orders

She was a bulbous bottle, unreliably stoppered, and any move-ment away from the strictest upright provoked the geni into shooting acrid slop up to her epiglottis. So she stayed vertical, and when night came propped herself against a bank of bolsters like an Anglo-Saxon afraid of death's approach during sleep.

These night hours unrolled reams of poor but heavy slumber, thick and threadbare like hessian, coarse curtains which fanned open occasionally on to thresholds of glimmering incomprehen-sion. The dreams were of release, violent and half-baked, there was one where she was flat as a flounder with eyes on the same side of her nose, shifting along an inch above the seabed, and then she would wake into the half-light with a strong aversion to duality and everything to do with bifurcation.

This had been a bad night, spiralling down through threats of knives and stomach-globes. The easy tears streaked her cheeks, cheap as dew. She lay and languished, watching the forked radish which was Patrick pulling on his trousers in the gloom.

'Twelve days late now,' she said. 'My body doesn't work.'

'Yes it does,' said Patrick, scrabbling through a dish of loose change. 'Babies come when they're ready.'

'How would *you* know,' she said, turning her big white clumsy face into the pillow.

'The doctors say so,' he said, as usual, strapping on his watch. 'Sorry, got to rush, I'm late.'

'Good luck with the Brisbane blockbuster,' she said. 'Where's lunch?'

'Let The Good Times Roll.'

'You lucky devil.'

'Don't forget we're off to the Bengal Tiger tonight.'

She groaned.

'Worth a try,' he said. 'Whenever anybody hears you're late, they mention hot curry. If it works we'll call him Vindaloo.'

She lay in bed for an hour after he had gone, dipping back into drifts of half-sleep, trawling her memory again for more specific details of the wish-gone-sour tale which surfaced every morning now. There was a withered old man imploring some ringleted goddess to release him. He had been granted his wish for eternal life, but had forgotten to ask for eternal youth at the same time, and now, as he hobbled across her gleaming marble halls on wrinkled feet, tears trickling down his walnut face and silvery waist-length beard, he pleaded for the ordinary power to die.

Watching the summer light strengthen at the margins of the bedroom curtains, she wondered why this story kept returning to her, since it did not concern birth, but death. When she started to worry again that her body would never work, that she would simply grow bigger and bigger, then she commenced the laborious business of getting dressed.

The telephone rang.

'*Still* nothing?' came the incredulous voice of her aunt. 'It'll have a beard and long toe-nails by now.'

'Any day,' she said, automatically, as she had been saying every day for the last month.

Now that the official hospital date, the baby's Estimated Time of Arrival, had come and gone, it was like life after death. Only she had not yet laid down her life. This was limbo. She was not currently living inside real hours and minutes. Perhaps this was what was meant by living on borrowed time. She had run out of credit with her waiting relatives, anyway; they almost jeered at her when they telephoned now. Invalid in both senses of the word, she lumbered out into the little back garden. These days, walking was like wading through sea water up to the thighs.

Bees boomed inside the freckle-throated foxgloves. From the lime trees came a rustle like stiff silk tussore, and a sweet soap-and-talcum-powder smell. Already the garden was a pocket of heat. This was the hottest June for twelve years, as everybody kept saying. There was a menacing innocence, a pre-war stasis about it.

'*Still* not had it?' The old lady who lived next door appeared at the fence, her leech-black eyes peering through the trellis of honeysuckle. 'You must be very worried by now.'

'I'm all right,' she said, taking a step back towards the kitchen door. 'How are you?'

'As you know. Lonely as hell since Reg died,' said Mrs Pightle. 'Sometimes I get so bored I wish even something nasty would happen.'

Wanting to avoid infection by contact with Mrs Pightle's misery, she took another step back.

'Mustn't grumble though,' said Mrs Pightle, eyeing her bulk sharply as though suspecting her of fraudulent practices, a cushion up her teeshirt. Then, unnervingly, she snapped, 'I kill each day as it comes.'

'There's the telephone,' she said, and scuttled back inside.

'*Well*?' came her mother's voice. 'Are you going to tell me you've had it?' She held the receiver at arm's length for a moment, as gingerly as if it had been a scorpion.

Twelve days ago had been the promised day. The flat was perfectly clean for the first time in its life, she had even polished the windows and mirrors; she had piled two pounds of glossy cherries into the green glass dish and had put a vase of straight-backed tulips in each of the rooms. It had felt like her birthday. Patrick had brought home a slice of Brie, almost ripe – 'I thought you might like it for your first meal after the baby,' he had said, 'Since you've been complaining for nine months about how you wish you could have a little bit of soft cheese.' He had made her feel like Ben Gunn, whose first request after years of being marooned on a desert island was for some crumbs of toasted cheese. Ben Gunn, too, had had a long beard and toe-nails, she thought confusedly. Later that morning they had gone to the hospital for her forty week appointment. The baby's head had not engaged, said the registrar; the absence of Braxton Hicks contractions was absolutely no cause for concern. It'll be a few days yet, he had advised, we'll have to wait for the cervix to ripen; don't look so disappointed, you've got a marvellous hae-moglobin count.

A week later the tulips were swooping drunkenly, stems curving in art nouveau arabesques so that their splayed flowerheads touched the dust-gathering surfaces at last, almost inaudibly, and fell to pieces, each petal a glamorous painted coracle. The cherries grew bruised, then rotten. She threw them away. After nine days, when it had lost in form what it had gained in odour, Patrick ate the Brie. She had to dust again, and kicked the bag she had packed for hospital six weeks ago, now standing sad and ridiculous in the corner of the bedroom like a cancelled holiday. At her forty-first week appointment, they gave her a graph-paper kick-chart to fill in; she ticked a square for each movement the baby made until the tenth square was attained, which was always before midday; and then she had nothing to do except field the phone calls. They told her to be patient, and she gave a wan sneer. She was clearly nothing but a bad joke on two legs, a joke without a punchline.

It was galling now to see the sunny patch of garden through the doorway and know that Mrs Pightle would get her if she put her nose outside. She hadn't been more than five hundred yards from the house for more than a fortnight now, so convinced had she been that the baby would appear at its appointed time to the sound of empyreal trumpets, trailing clouds of glory. She had refused plans to meet anyone because they might have to be cancelled, and her only contact with the outside world for the last fortnight had been via the telephone wire and Patrick, or from sending out letters like messages in bottles. Prevented by Mrs Pightle from watching the grass grow, she had instead monitored the progress of her nail and hair lengths, like Rapunzel waiting for rescue from the witch's tower.

She sat down with her book on *How to Have a Baby*, and the baby inside her woke up and started its bulging movements. It, too, was a prisoner in a tower, of course. They were in a double bind. Strange, to be lounging around in this summer torpor, lazy as an aquarium, while just round the corner waited bloody scenes of violence and danger and life at its most portentous.

The telephone rang.

'Are you still in one piece? Never mind, they're bound to

induce now. Make the most of your last days – this is the last time alone you'll ever have. I haven't had a minute to myself since Maisie was born. And remember, the first six weeks are *awful*. Impossible to describe, but *you'll* see. It's *chaos*. It gets better gradually. After about a year. Have you tried sitting on a washing machine during the spin cycle?'

She went back to her book and looked up induction in the index. 'The doctor will snag a hole in the membranes which surround your baby with an instrument like a long crochet hook, and the waters will then gush out,' she read.

She went to the bookcase and pulled out an old exercise book. A long time ago she had copied out a poem written in the Tower of London by a man who knew he was going to be executed the next morning. Here it was, and it was by twenty-eight-year-old Chidiock Tichborne hanged in 1586 before he had had time to write much at all.

> My prime of youth is but a frost of cares,
> My feast of joy is but a dish of pain,
> My crop of corn is but a field of tares,
> And all my good is but vain hope of gain;
> The day is past, and yet I saw no sun,
> And now I live, and now my life is done.

I'll never see Mexico, she thought, the jointed armadillo running across the sand. I won't be able to try hang-gliding in case I leave an orphan. I haven't *done* anything yet.

> My tale was heard and yet it was not told,
> My fruit is fallen and yet my leaves are green,
> My youth is spent and yet I am not old
> I saw the world and yet I was not seen;
> My thread is cut and yet it is not spun,
> And now I live, and now my life is done.

The telephone rang. It was Patrick, calling from a phone box on his way to lunch.

'Do we *want* a baby?' she asked.

'Of course we do! More than anything else in the world! I'm so happy I'm almost scared.'

'I never seem to feel the right thing at the right time. I'm unnatural.'

'No you're not. But it'll be all right, you'll see. Have you any *idea* how much I love you? You're mine now.'

The pips went and she used this as an excuse to put the phone down. She heard herself swearing and cursing.

'Hormones,' she said flatly.

> I sought my death and found it in my womb,
> I looked for life and saw it was a shade,
> I trod the earth and knew it was my tomb,
> And now I die, and now I was but made;
> My glass is full, and now my glass is run,
> And now I live, and now my life is done.

The telephone rang again.

'It's Wendy here, *you* know, from the antenatal class. Just ringing to let you know I've had it. It's a boy, eight pounds six ounces. I know, he wasn't due for another two weeks, but he couldn't wait, could he. Funny really, even though he'll be older than yours now, when you think about it yours has actually been *alive* a whole month longer. . . . What was it like? Do you *really* want to know? I don't think I should tell you. Oh, all right. It was horrible, not a bit like the classes said. At least it was quick, well, eight hours. I started getting pains about two forty-five on Saturday. Geoff wanted to go off to the gym for his circuit training, and by the time he got back I said, this is it, we've got to go to hospital. Anyway I don't think I'll go into details with you in your condition – I'm so glad *I* wasn't late, I couldn't bear it – but don't believe them when they say it doesn't hurt. I was screaming my head off at the end. Then it shot out at 10.50 p.m. I remember Geoff said, just in time for last orders.'

Come pain, welcome pain, she thought as she put the phone down. I want to be cool and free again, lean and Atlantic-salted.

I want to lose this fish-like, full-throated extra under the chin. I wish I could run like the wind across frost-crusted grass, or lunge and bump at will in the night. I want to say goodbye to this batwing mask of pregnancy across my nose and cheeks.

The telephone rang. It was Wendy again, suggesting that she drive at thirty miles an hour over sleeping policemen since this had worked for the woman in the bed next to hers at St Mary's, and she had been two weeks overdue.

Taking up another baby book, emotional rather than technical this time, along with a handful of raisins for lunch, she read, 'When you refuse to leave your breast-fed baby with a bottle and a sitter in order to go out and enjoy yourself, it isn't self-sacrifice but self-protection. While you and your baby are interlocked in this way, you can only be happy if she is happy.' She let the book rest in her lap and stared hungrily at the open door. This was what people had said before when she had voiced doubts about missing pubs, parties, dancing, travel; they always smiled as though she were odd or innocent, and said, 'You'll see; you won't *want* to.'

You will not be you any more, her ego told her id. Not only will you have produced somebody else from inside you, someone quite different and separate, but you yourself will change into somebody quite different and other, overnight – a Mother.

Her id held its sides and screeched with laughter. Pull the other one! it pleaded, weak with mirth.

What if she failed to feel misery at the thought of a bottle and a sitter? What if they seemed fair exchange for a bottle and a party? *Would* she feel the necessary 'interlock' that would turn her into a stay-at-home?

Thinking back to that last outing a month ago, she realised it had been, among other things, a wake for her old self without her realising it. She had taken a valedictory taxi back to the flat, sitting upright on the high-backed seat in the purring darkness, exhausted by the baby beating away in protest since early evening, but humming and happy too.

'Enjoy yourself while you can,' said the taxi driver over his shoulder. He was the cold, light-eyed virile sort with steely grey hair and an air of grim fitness.

'Oh, that was the last party for a while,' she had said airily. 'I'm about to have a baby. Have *you* got any children?'

'I wish I'd drowned them at birth,' he had said. 'Look at it like this. Two people get together, they get on well. Out to the cinema, out to the pub, go to bed together; out to the pub. Then the little bleeder arrives. It's meant to bring you closer together, but does it? Does it ****. *You* say, let's go down the pub. *She* says, ooh no, the baby's feeding pattern, or something like that. She says, *you* go down the pub. Nah, you say. You sit around a bit. Then you think, okay, just for half an hour. So you're down there, you think, well, this is fun, it's a bit lively. Next thing you're talking to someone who's *not* the old lady. And you hear people say they bring you closer together! Still, not a lot you can do about it at this stage in the game by the look of you. Tell you what, I'll give you a tip. Give it a few spoons of Benelux – not too often – just when you really need a couple of hours' peace. Night Nurse is too strong.'

Well, she was going out tonight, wasn't she. 'Positively my last appearance,' she muttered. 'Like some old music hall star who doesn't know when to call it a day.'

Patrick brought home the Australian author whom he had taken out to lunch. They both had the withered eyelids and kamikaze air of people who have been drinking during daylight and who intend to go on against their better judgment.

'Hope you don't mind,' whispered Patrick. 'I meant to ring and warn you, but he's been like a limpet and he keeps on telling me how he doesn't know anybody in London.'

'The more the merrier,' she yawned. They shuffled off down the road to the Bengal Tiger, the men creeping along to keep her company, one on either side, like the royal escort of an ancient monarch.

Once on the threshold of the restaurant she looked around ravenously at this fresh landscape, noticing that all eyes skidded off her bulk and that she had become a visual embarrassment now she was out in public after so long. She did not care. It was somewhere different. She admired the filigree metal of the basket holding poppadoms, and watched Patrick and his author devouring stuffed paratha. They were discussing differences in national humour, comparing Australian with English.

'Ours is a bit cruder, a bit brasher,' said the Australian earnestly, popping an onion bhaji whole into his mouth. 'Our jokes are not exactly subtle. For example, would you find this funny? I do, but my humour is very Antipodean.'

Patrick cocked his ear in the attitude of one about to enjoy a treat.

'Well, here's Sheila and she's standing on the edge of Sydney Suspension bridge and she's about to jump off. Bruce comes running up, all concern, shouts, "Why Sheila, *why*?" "Because I'm pregnant," says Sheila. "Jeez, Sheila," says Bruce, "Not only are you a bloody good lay but you're a bloody good sport too, Sheila." Now you either find that funny or you don't.'

Patrick was looking at her uneasily, but she liked a joke, even an ideologically unsound joke, and she was sniggering into her chicken dhansak. Relieved, Patrick laughed and crowed and said, 'Well, have *you* heard the one about the man who's drinking alone in a pub and he wants to go off and have a pee, but he's scared someone'll steal his pint, so he props a little note against it saying, "I have spat in this beer." '

'No,' said the Australian, grinning attentively and gulping lager.

'When he gets back from the Gents his beer's still there but somebody's scribbled "So have I" on the note. Ha, ha, ha!'

The two men rocked with laughter. To her surprise, she was prickling with alarm. She heard his voice again down the telephone: 'You're *mine* now.' The baby heaved up against her ribs like a barge. She restrained herself from lifting Patrick's pint and pouring it over his head.

'Excuse me,' she said, the syllables glacial in her burning mouth, and waddled off down a spiral staircase to the Ladies.

There, she locked herself into a cubicle and leant her forehead against the gleaming marble-tiled walls, and wept, and swore, and maundered for release.

## The Café-Bookshop

It's taught in schools: how the equestrian statues
Were lethal, the riders were all wanted men,
And one opened a slot in the belly of his horse
And hibernated there, waking to the river distantly
Cracking and fussing like the preparations
Grandparents make. He welcomed himself
As a hero, limping into the spring sunshine.
Under the new dispensation statues were pedestrian.
In the brass of the night he stood like a drunk
Signposting emptily under the map of stars.

Pedestrian statues lie broken, remembered,
The most public ridden by the children of children.
This one who is pasting snot into bronze nostrils,
He is hungry and cold, like a skater who has left
His lunch behind; yet his eyes are bright
With the infamous glissades of revolution.
Our city looks new-made, as under a fall of snow.
Teachers are chatting to parents in the streets:
Note the frisson of joint enterprise when the sons'
Names are pronounced. Daughters are also mentioned,

Their days off work, their love letters uncrumpling
On the fire. We all mutter the hurtful song,
The *samizdat* hymn in the blood. We have lived long.
'Hey, face-ache!' Rough words laden with love,

Spoken by a father who has roused himself
From a daydream, a great tumbledown thaw of books,
Fielding, Trollope, Galsworthy and the rest
Of those who knew the burden of masculinity,
All the solitary souls patient in a café-bookshop,
Which breaks into a smile when the rain starts.

## *Else the Isle with Calibans*

This island's mine, by Sycorax my mother, and all the fruit trees
on it. Teazels too that clamp the hair, and mangusteen, and
tamarisks that smother near the shore, all these I own. Thrift,
and crimson grannie's bonnet, oranges like golden lamps alight.
Shells, feather, shards of bone. Fowl, the things that scuttle
under stone or others in the trees, go screaming from me branch
by branch as if their arms were legs. All, all's my own, now that
I'm free again.

When my love and I walk this domain of ours, we hear the
apes cry each to each. Me thinks they do resemble me in part,
except in this – they have no speech and cannot answer us.

My kith and I oft watch these leafy-brains coupling like dogs,
all snarling though in pleasure's weal, as if their genitals were
pained to yield their joy away.

This very day, I'm idling on a headland, having swum, a hairy
fish beneath the bay. Though I'd not wish to change an acre of
this ground of mine for endless furlongs of brine wane, I love its
mystery.

Yet Fano, eldest son for whom shellfish are finest venison,
propounds this jest: 'The sea or sky, pa – which is best?'
Answers he relenting at my bafflement: 'The sea's the king – you
cannot find a welk in all the welkin.'

So roll we, chins under fundaments, with mirth and wonderment elate, until a direful spectacle sobers straight our glee.

I know not why the sea's so warm and calm. But as my love
saith, with its charm the wave wins our forgiveness after storm,
like to that poet, nails begrimed by ink, who with internal
rhyme and melody captures our reveries and earns his grace
when we have traced the rapture of his song.

And in that calm, a clatter carrying across the bay speaks of an
anchor plunging through the spray to wound our softling sand.

Then from our eyrie high bestowed in ocean's bosom, we espied a longboat rowed by sailors from a galleon. The flag of Naples fluttered at its bow. Already but a reach away, the oars were sure to gain our beach!

O woe! I jumped as if bereft of sense awhile! Who were these mariners? 'Tis well-known happiness has no past tense and, in my careless sovereignty of isle and wife Miranda, Present is the time I wear . . . Lo, many ancient fears leapt from their charnel place. Upon their winding sheets emblazoned was – the name of Prospero!

Yes, he! Vile exiled duke, who from Milan came to the still unvexed Bermoothes to plague me. Ere his arrival, Sycorax unseen, my blue-eyed mother, Sycorax, source of sweet spells which made the island tame, was queen of all . . . And I, her little prince – although malformed, a happy brat – essayed to ape her tricks to summon wood nymphs mild and suchlike sprites to play. But Prospero – blind to our rustic magic – must too soon supplant my dam, while he himself with all technology equipped.

Thus I became his slave Neanderthal, to follow him about, doglike, early or late: apt to fetch timber, chop his wood, or from an amber pool tickle a wily trout to fill his plate . . . Many a morning cool, I dreamed that I were out of pain and free. Then woke, and wept that I might dream again.

'Tis half a score of years since Prospero called up a storm and quit the isle, his tortures at an end. He drowned his magic books full fathom five. My pulses warm and live, I took dominion then, of everything. My bruises mend. And on his fair Miranda, ho, I peopled then the isle with Calibans! Am I not King? Comes he now back, that magusman? I run to hide, to snare in thickest brake my trembling self, lest he decide my soul to take again.

My childish tribe, with whimpers each, dive into the pleached bowers where honeysuckle and the wild cherry flower.

Ensconced in that dim uncertain shade, I watch the armèd men. More do parade than I have fingers. Martial are they with swords display'd, and led – yes, there's that noble head, that rote-learnt face – these pallid flat Italian chops are like as herrings. Yet, peer I through my hedges at misfortune's brother, Ferdinand . . . Rich Ferdinand, I say, none other, he, all privilege . . . His merest look doth call back yesterday, bids grief return.

Grey in his beard – he tastes the salt of time. Wrath in his eye – he tastes the puke of jealousy. On his curled lip, the call to crime. All haste! I must to my Miranda . . . Warning her that Mars arrives upon no mercy spree. His armour, dullened like his face, squeaks against bracken as they pass. I run and never slacken in my pace.

Hurdling fast as hounds o'er broken ground, I beat my head to summon up all past unhappy things. When Ferdy – so she called him – came before, he lusted for her, put on courtly airs to charm. All, Prospero commanded. With Ferdy, if I don't mistake – the past's all fog, a foreign tongue, to me – came those who were my friends. Stout Stephano, descendant from the Moon, and with him Trinculo, whose lip was gallant with a bottle. Why, his sip could dredge from neck to dregs. Where are they now? Of that old courtly band, whose fulsome clothes with gold did smoulder, ashore is only Ferdinand, with vengeance on his shoulder.

So panting like a cur come I, into our palace. There, with creepers decked, embowered in rose, and beds that share a shelf whereon the wild thyme blows, our habitation is an oak – that self-same tree wherein old Prosper penned myself. But now made kind in country style. And there my honey-quimmed Miranda lies meanwhile, the fringed curtains of her eyes pulled close in sleep. The idea of her life so sweetly creeps, I leap upon her in my lust and she, like one who dreams to wake and wakes to dream, receives me heartily.

Ah, this is ample golden age, that love showers from my golden wench, increase of appetite doth grow by what it feeds on. She and I do clench as hand in glove or blind mole in its tunnel. The sword of joy is such we prick ourselves alive at every touch and in our sweat baste life itself.

As sings she then for cheer, I clutch Miranda, all undressed:

> The nightingales are singing in
>    The orchards of our mothers
> And wounds that festered long ago
>    Mayhap fester on others.
> Summer cozens our repose –
> How we live here no one knows.
> Sea nymphs hourly plight our troth
> Where the gladsome waves do froth.
>    Ding-dong bell!

Alas, that face, that voice, they conquer me as always. Lie I deep within her arms and do rejoice, forgetting. So, by small ways and devious do Ferdinand and crew creep to the tree and with their grievous metal points surround us.

How we tumble, she and I! But she's allowed to rise.

Then does this royal son use me as footstool. 'Ape,' cries he, 'with forehead villainous low, lie still. Your hours are all sucked dry.'

It's with more venom yet he turns his eye and speech to her he courted once. Says he, 'Wretched Miranda, poor seed of your line, in outcast, downcast state, do you remember me?'

That lower lip I oftimes clipped with mine shakes like a tiny leaf whose stalk the spiralled snail attacks. She says, 'Despite that arrogance of talk, I cede that you are Ferdinand who, in my former life enclosed – that life of solitude and learning by my pa imposed – were son of Naples' king.'

'And now am King, my father being finally disposed to quit this mortal scene.'

Cowering I watch, to see her terror leave her, while her gaze blazes at his.

'You came in former time with meeker brow, all syrup tongued, yet gentle to me. Why, now that you've the crown, you force a sterner mode, and must with armoured men entreat discourse.'

At that he laughs as if a load bore down his humour. This new-made king declares, 'No more entreaties in this later day. Miranda – how your very name still rises up before me, mist-like – think you that your brow is still unwrinkled, pillowed limbs still virginal and slim, or eye still clear with innocence, as when we first did meet through Prospero's enchantments? Like his, your own enchantments now are ended, much as the baseless fabric of a dream is torn by waking. Think you to sleep with apes improves your style? All that was fine in you, I see, as meat is thrown to wolves, you tossed to this Neanderthal, this witch's welp. And he, with his vile instrument, has fatted you how many times . . . Till all that's left is flesh, beyond time's help.'

'And soul.' She smiles, more haughty now than he. 'Rest your regard, so sourly stern, upon this jade whose whole experience rides roughshod o'er that thing men prize – virginity. Sir, Eros hath a gentler touch than Time – the hours are lost where Cupid is not cossetted! You boast a deficit in flesh. What eats you, royal Naples slave, so profligate and thin? Desire, ambition, hate that dances round some grave of sin, perpetually to dig it up again, as jackals do their carrion? I see the blow-fly in your glance.'

With covered eye, the soldiery seek one another's gaze, not daring openly to welcome such a thrust. Despairing, Ferdinand, 'I expeditioned to this unmapped strand solely to meet again – I sought to meet – one who in mem'ry sweet did fill – ' Dead falls his thought.

His look is ill as, dried of words, he turns away his head.

He curses, kicks, and spits, and yet I see that Ferdy knows full well what all men understand; there is no bush of circumstance so valued as a bird in hand. Compared with love and wholesome mate, the Naples throne is but a counterfeit.

Then we are bound. Her arm and mine, my left, her right, are touching 'gainst the round oak's bark. This is the ship, when launched in flame, will carry us beyond our mortal shore, our life submerging into night. Our children roar, and as the torches flare, from undergrowth emerging, caper on the leaze for mercy.

Here's Fano, Trink, and little Iris, dear doe daughter, as bright water nimble. All now trip and tumble, pleading that our bonds be cut. In agitation, in their humble way they clown, death to deny, for the greater glory of the day. Their rich moist eyes rain supplication.

Whereupon, the savage Neapolitan plunges his blade into my Fano's breast. The others flee, to crouch with partridge and the speckled snake in nested lair, while Fano in his blood chokes out his soul.

My groans resound through all the oaken grove. Now do the twigs, well heaped with gorses too, about our toes catch fire, to hiss the villainy of what they do.

All eager with desire does Ferdinand lean his crazed face into the growing blaze and shout, 'Miranda, tell me while your life delays, you took me in – why didst thou throw me out?

'For at that moment all were reconciled and Prospero had drowned his books – indeed, as boatswain was prepared to bend his rowers' backs and bear us safely from the wild and then to Naples. At that living moment, oh, your hand slipped out of mine . . . You turned and ran from off the strand. I called. My cries awoke the beach. I searched, but with you out of reach we had to leave. Ten years have dragged their hapless pomp along, and still that wrong afflicts me. Speak, why didst thou make me grieve?'

Mild was her answer then.

'I am not ceremony's bride who was informal nature's child.'

The smoke that hides her lovely face lifts like a veil. All modesty, Miranda sighs, 'I thought you first a thing divine. Your noble clothes, your seemly tongue, enchanted when we met. How much you promised then. Oh, I should be the Queen of Naples and I'd wear . . . this gem and that, I quite forget. But when I grew to know you more I realised your robes and rings and thrones were pageants, mere material things. In that moment on the shore, about to leave this little land, *I thought of Caliban.*'

'That brute!'

'Oh yes. "That brute" – whom all despised, eternally my father's slave, beaten and maltreated, like me bereft of mother – yet my friend, well-prized above all others. Who was it taught me laughter, played a flute, was antic when it suited, tamed a hare! Who named me all the pleasures of the isle, the fresh springs, marl-pits, mushrooms that enchant? My Ban alone! What's more, when pa had turned his alchemistic back, my Banny teased me with much sport in naughty ways, and in my crack his finger tickled qualms I knew not that I sought.'

'So in that moment by your boat – the mariners with oars all poised – I found I did not want your promises. What do I care for ceremonial? Rather, here I'd live and die. I dote upon this isle's remoteness. That's why I ran – praise fate – to find with Caliban within our little plot pleasures of nature that would please you not.'

Burning within as we without, he sighs. 'Not all the harlots that comprise my court and nation's pride can wash you from my contemplation.'

And as he speaks, I free one hand. The flames fly up. But at a stroke, I summon forth from crackling tree my brother Ariel. In his divinity he does descend, swift as an owl by night upon its prey, piercing the air, to douse the flames and scare the men away with awful shrieks and spears of light. Vesuvius sparked less fiercely than my Ariel.

Only the King of Naples stands his ground, till spirits in the shape of dog and hound pursue him from the scene. As all do bark, cries Ariel, 'Silver, Fury, there. Go fetch! Hark, Tyrant, hark!' And in uproar, all chase him till he gains the shore, his cloak and sword forgotten.

With Ariel and sweet Miranda, I do follow where the tide, now slack, casts on the yellow sands a necklace of seawrack. We there take hands and watch the sad invader row with undue haste away.

He stands all reckless in the craft to call in accents choked and gruff, 'I loved you once, Miranda . . .'

From our beach I shout back, rough with pride, 'Then that must serve enough.'

His cry returns, now faint below the screech of gulls, to haunt us to our dying day, 'Nothing in life is ever enough . . .'

The gleaming distance bore his boat away.

## *Prospero Caliban Cricket*
(for CLR James)

Prospero batting
Caliban bowling
and is cricket is cricket in yuh ricketics
but from far it look like politics

Caliban running up
from beyond de boundary
because he come
from beyond de boundary
if you know yuh history

Prospero standing
bat and pad
thinking Caliban is a mere lad
from a new-world archipelago
and new to the game

But not taking chances
Prospero invoking de name
of W. G. Grace
to preserve him
from a bouncer to the face

Caliban if he want
could invoke duppy jumbie
zemi baccoo douen all kinda ting,
but instead he relying
just pon pace and swing

Caliban arcing de ball
like an unpredictable whip.
Prospero foot like it chain to de ground.
Before he could mek a move
de ball gone thru to de slip,
and de way de crowd rocking
you would think dey crossing de atlantic

Is cricket is cricket in yuh ricketics
but from far it look like politics.

Prospero remembering
how Caliban used to call him master.
Now Caliban agitating de ball faster
and de crowd shouting POWER

Caliban remembering
how Prospero used to call him knave and serf.
Now Caliban striding de cricket turf
like he breathing a nation,
and de ball swinging it own way
like it hear bout self-determination

Is cricket is cricket in yuh ricketics
but from far it look like politics.

Prospero wishing
Shakespeare was the umpire,
Caliban see a red ball
and he see fire
rising with glorious uncertainty.
Prospero front pad forward with diplomacy.

Is cricket is cricket in yuh ricketics
but from far it look like politics.

Prospero invoking
de god of snow,
wishing a shower of flakes
would stop all play,
but de sky so bright with carib glow
you can't even appeal for light
much less ask for snow.

Is cricket is cricket in yuh ricketics
but from far it look like politics.

# Different

Grey. High, grey walls rising sheer from the railway lines. Inaccessible cliffs in which there were, nevertheless, a few lighted slots, nooks in which people – could it be? – lived out their unknowable lives. Stirred by the idea of these alien existences, the girl peered upwards through the rain-spotted glass of the train. Grey walls, weak lights in the wet morning, grey sky in which night had been only half-heartedly replaced by day. Now the train was slowing; giant letters crawled by on the wall: *Gare St Lazare*.

Lazarus. Lazar houses. Leprosy. Sickness, Poverty. The Dead. She felt sickish herself from the hours in the heaving Channel, from lack of sleep, from the excitement of arrival, the dread of the new people she must meet and the undesired life that awaited her here. But, most of all, from the nebulous fear that had accompanied her for the last six months – no, not quite six – ever since Mummy, since my mother . . . '*You see, my mother . . .*' How, ever, to explain? Even in English, let alone in French.

'*Paris. What a lucky girl!*' That had been aunt Dorothy. And other people too. If only, she thought, they wouldn't all go on as if it was wonderful for me to be sent away now to a foreign country, I might not mind it so much. '*Such a lovely city . . . So gay, such fun . . . You'll come back with such a dress sense . . . Such fun to be there with other girls, I wish I'd had the chance when I was your age, but of course the War . . . You'll have a wonderful time . . .*'

Are they all quite stupid? Or do they think I am? Do they think I don't know why Daddy wants me out of the way now? Or are they too silly to realise it for themselves?

The station. The luggage. Crowds. Her new high-heeled shoes made her self-conscious, teetering like a grown-up in her best coat at Daddy's side while he carried the cases and peered about, for once seeming a little lost himself.

'I told Henri and Madeleine not to meet us as the train gets in so damned early,' he said, sounding disappointed all the same that they were not there. 'We'll get a taxi.'

In the taxi he said, as he had said several times already: 'You'll like Henri and Madeleine. They're very old friends. They were awfully good to us in Paris in the old days. We had terrific fun together.'

*The old days.* That meant, at the end of the War. Daddy had been with the British Army and Mummy with the Red Cross. They had met in Paris and it had all been very romantic. Mummy, at any rate, had given the impression that nothing afterwards had ever quite matched up to that period. But then Mummy had always – well, for years and years anyway – talked as if time, the sheer accumulation of days, formed some great barrier cutting one off from happiness and friends and fun and 'the things one used to do.' Daddy, on the other hand, tended to behave as if everything went on being there for ever and what was true at one time was just as true at another, whatever else had happened in between. She suddenly found herself worrying that, when they got to the address, Henri and Madeleine would long ago have moved away.

It seemed to be taking ages to get there. The taxi turned to the right, bore to the left, circulated another roundabout, yet they seemed to be always in the same street, wide but choked with traffic, between tall, heavy buildings with portcullises, and iron-work on the tiers of windows. Daddy kept looking at the meter, and remarked several times on the huge price that was clocking up. She said patiently:

'You know, Daddy, the franc probably isn't worth the same as when you were last here.'

'Too right it isn't. Nor is the pound. You know, don't you Pussycat, how much all this is going to cost?'

'You told me, Daddy.'

'Madame Thing – Duvernet – where you're going to board certainly isn't cheap, but Madeleine did write and say she's the

best butter. So mind you make the most of it, Pussycat. It isn't
every girl who's lucky enough to be finished in Paris, but it's
what – ah – Mummy and I always wanted for you.'

'I know, Daddy.'

*Finished in Paris.* It's a ridiculous phrase. A ridiculous idea,
too. It belongs with being presented and catching a husband and
having-a-little-job-just-till-you-settle-down. Life isn't like that,
these days. It's 1963, for goodness' sake. . . . And why does he
go on about how much it's going to cost him? That's not a bit
like him, he's usually easy about money, likes to be generous.
Oh, I suppose it's because he wants me to think it's all so marvellous. Stupid, because if I wasn't being packed off here then I'd
still be costing him money at boarding school. That is, I'd probably still be there now, in the Sixth, doing A-levels, if I hadn't
had to leave at the beginning of last year. If Mummy hadn't . . .
If. If.

When she had stopped going to school because Mummy
couldn't be left on her own, he wasn't like he was now. 'Darling, I'm afraid you'll just have to stay at home for a bit,' he had
said, looking drawn and puckered and older than he used to, and
yet at the same time like a small boy who, if she were too
sympathetic, might suddenly cry. 'I'm afraid Mummy does
need you about the place . . . And so of course do I. I mean, she
can't cope with the cooking and so on at the moment, poor
dear . . . I'm so sorry, darling, but there it is. Perhaps we can
find you a tutorial class, for the time being. And then later,
when Mummy gets better . . .'

Of course she hadn't really minded leaving school and staying
at home and cooking his supper for him each evening. It was
different, it was being grown-up. Didn't he notice she enjoyed
it? Or did he just think she was being good. They both had to
be very good to Mummy, that was his line. Because Mummy
couldn't help it.

She thought now, in a moment of bleak revelation, I've no
idea if she could help it or not. But she didn't get better in the
end, after all, and now it doesn't seem to make any difference.
Because, except for the odd time he mentions her in connection

with the past, when they were young, Daddy seems to have forgotten all about her.

Oh, that's ridiculous. Of course he can't have. But he certainly seems to have forgotten about other things – about even grown-ups not being able to help the way they are and about being grateful to me for being such a big girl and a comfort to him and understanding. Instead, he says things like 'Don't look so down in the mouth, Pussycat, no one likes a girl who's dreary!' He's calling me 'Pussycat' again, like he did when I was six. And he even said once, in front of Elaine, it was, otherwise I don't think he'd have had the nerve to: 'The trouble with you is, you're self-centred and self-pitying. Why can't you be like other dollies your age?'

Elaine. Oh, I won't think of Elaine. Indeed, I can't, because when I try to a terrible weight settles on my chest, as if I'd swallowed something impossible to digest, a lump of under-cooked potato or a hard-boiled egg. Actually, Elaine *is* rather like both those things. Her skin is white and floury and sort of pulpy, like a fruit that's been sitting in the bowl too long and ought to be thrown away. I'm sure that inside she must be going soft and nasty . . . But on the surface there's lots of red lipstick and nail-polish and blue eye shadow. She thinks these things make her look young: I've heard her say so – '*Of course always having looked young for my age . . .*' I don't know why she thinks she needs to look young. She isn't, and she's probably going to marry Daddy (yes, yes I do know that, though I'm not supposed to) and he's not young either. So why should she need to pretend?

I don't wear lipstick or nail-polish – I mean, who does, these days? – and Elaine seems to resent that. She's always going on about my clothes and my hair and what a sight I look, as if I were about ten, as if she had the right to. I wish someone would tell her that it's rude to go on like that, at anybody. I wish *I* could . . . I can't. I can't. . . . . I do hope Madeleine doesn't turn out to be like Elaine. If she does, I don't think I can bear it.

The street – not wide, now, but narrow with rods of rain, wet laurels soughing behind high, dark railings. The building: one of those like the way into a castle. The lift – a cramped cage, shuddering with the weight of luggage. The wrong floor. Then the right one and, at last, Madeleine. Not like anyone, thank God. More like a cheerful, wrinkled monkey, smelling of Chanel Number Five when she kisses me on both cheeks. And Henri like a great soft animal of a different sort, a sloth perhaps, watching everyone.

The girl sensed at the start, before getting to know them confused her view, that they had had no children and that this had made Madeleine a little sad. But, being a quite different sort of person from Mummy, she covered this up so that no one would ever know. And the girl sensed that Henri too, though he seemed friendly and easy, had sometimes made Madeleine unhappy. Not that he would care, but it was so.

I don't know exactly how people make other people unhappy. I just know they do. Did Daddy make Mummy unhappy? When she died in that terrible way, he kept saying to me for the first day or two 'You don't think it was my fault, do you darling? I hope to God you don't think that.' And I kept saying 'Of course I don't, Daddy,' for how could it have been his fault? He was at work at the time. And anyway Mummy never said it was anyone's fault – no one else's and not hers, certainly not her own. Instead she would talk about 'my illness', 'my problem', 'this depression' as if it were some tiresome creature that had been wished on her and was really nothing to do with her at all. Nothing she could do anything about. That's why we had to be so sorry for her.

I tried. I did try. But I had a lot else to do. There was the house, the shopping, the cooking. The French classes I had to get to. Mummy didn't like being left alone for hours and made it difficult. She used to say she didn't know where I was and tried to find out if I'd been meeting A Man. Pretending to be still in charge. She used to go on about 'life' and look at me sideways as if I might know something she didn't. As if she was afraid I had somehow deserted her and joined the others and she was trying to make me feel bad about it . . . Oh, perhaps I wasn't sorry enough for her, after all.

Standing in the bathroom, which seemed antiquated and
exotic, with odd-shaped taps, the girl thought: I mustn't think
about Mummy. Not any more. And not here, especially,
because here no one is supposed to Know. They know she's
dead of course. But not how. It's supposed to have been an
accident.

She stood running cool water over her wrists for so long that
Daddy came to look for her. He stood in the doorway and said,
in that gruff voice he used when he didn't want to talk about
something:

'Come on, for goodness' sake. Everyone's waiting. We're
going out to pick up some other people and then to lunch in a
restaurant.'

'Daddy – I'm tired. Must I come? Can't I just stay here?'

'Of course you must come. Good for your French.'

'But I'm going to be here – oh, for months.' She swallowed
hard. 'Must I have good done to my French *today*?'

She saw his face in the mirror, watching her's. He looked
anxious and a little mad, smiling and frowning at the same time,
head jerked back, like he used to when Mummy went on at him,
when she had had too much to drink or taken too many
pills . . . *Now* she thought, *now*: if I shout and make a scene he'll
have to listen to me. He'll have to stop pretending everything's
ordinary, an ordinary father taking his ordinary daughter to stay
in Paris and learn French in an ordinary way – *what a lucky girl*.

She said nothing. I can't. I can't.

In his stern-Daddy voice he said:

'Now come on, miss, we can't have any nonsense here. Madeleine and Henri are both being extremely kind to us, do you
want them to think you're an ungrateful little so-and-so? Pull
yourself together.'

*Pull yourself together*. That was the phrase above all which one
had not been allowed to say to Mummy. If anyone did say it, she
knocked things over and started to scream. The doctor had said
it once – so Daddy had told the girl at the time when he was still
explaining things to her, confiding in her – and so of course they
had had to find another doctor. Of course.

Daddy had been very upset when Mummy was dead. Of course. His tears had been genuine: the girl knew that. But now that that was all over, months and months ago, Daddy had to have someone new to fuss over. Of course. So he had Elaine. That was, it seemed, the way things were.

At lunch in a restaurant in what she was told was the Bois de Boulogne, though it didn't seem like a wood, French and French-English punctuated with gusts of laughter rolled around her. The food was consoling; she ate greedily. Occasionally she stuck out her head like a tortoise and concentrated on a snatch of conversation, before she got lost and had to retreat again. Further up the table, she could see that Daddy was having something of the same difficulty. Several times he looked across at her and winked, and once he made a thumbs-up sign. Either he was sorry for how he had spoken in the bathroom, or else he was simply pleased to see her looking more cheerful. He found it very hard to cope with people who weren't being cheerful, always had.

A woman sitting next to her, a woman with dark purplish hair and a lighter purple dress, said:

'Of course, dah-leeng, I knew your Mummee long before you wuz born.'

'Oh did you?' She tried to inject a little enthusiasm into her voice. She had noticed already in England that people seemed to think she might want to talk about her mother. She didn't. Why should she? They meant well of course.

'Oh my goodness, ye-es. So clever and amusing, your Mummee. So spiritual. What a lucky girl to have had such a mother.' She dropped her voice to the register the girl had come, in the last six months, to recognise as the inquisitiveness-disguised-as-sympathy one, and went on:

'You must miss her?'

Perhaps it was the delicious mussels she had eaten for hors-d'oeuvre or the steak she had had next, or the wine she had drunk (her neighbour on the other side had kept politely refilling her glass), or perhaps it was the sleepless night of travel or simply the noise of French going on over her head, insulating her from everyone else. Whatever it was, the girl suddenly heard herself say:

'Would *you* miss someone who tried to drown herself in the bath while you were downstairs cooking supper?'

'To drown . . . ?' The purple woman gaped at her, and drank some water. Presently she said, eyeing the girl carefully as if afraid she were not quite sane:

'One cannot drown oneself in a bath. Not on purpose.'

'Well of course you can't, that's what I mean. It was perfectly stupid of her to think she could.' Drunk with the power of what she had just uttered, she added after a moment:

'In the end, she jumped under a train. That was much more sensible of course. But not a very nice thing to do. I mean – the poor driver.'

The woman turned quickly to talk to the man on the other side of her.

Two days later, when she had been deposited in Madame Duvernet's mirror-haunted apartment and Daddy was due to go back to London and to his own new life there, they had dinner in Henri and Madeleine's flat. Madeleine made some excuse to take her into the bedroom and then said with warmth:

'Try to be a brave girl when you say goodbye to your father tonight. I know it is rather hard for you to be left on your own here, so soon after your mother's death. But he means well and he too will miss you, you know, when he gets home. You have been a great help to him.'

She's a nice woman, thought the girl, and she may even know now what Mummy did. She's trying to tell me: *I know he's rather childish. You did your best.* If she knew about Elaine . . . But I'm sure she doesn't know, because, two nights before we left London, Daddy made a big thing to me about how 'his relationship' with Elaine was still a personal, private thing and I wasn't to mention it to anyone.

It's supposed to be absolutely all right, that Elaine's there, and I'm to be polite to her and not let on that I know he must have known her for ages, since long before Mummy . . . Mummy . . . But at the same time she's not really supposed to be there at all. So is it all right for people to behave like Daddy and Elaine or isn't it? How on earth is one meant to know. It's like Mummy's illness. You had to be really nice about it, and yet at the same time pretend to everyone else that it didn't exist.

Oh how sick I am of it all. I want to be somewhere else altogether. Another sort of life. Different. Is Paris going to be different? I don't know yet. I don't know.

I'm tired. That's the trouble with me, I think. Really tired. It's the wine, and all these streets in Paris all looking alike, and having to meet so many people. That's why I keep feeling I want to burst into tears.

Madame Duvernet wore black, and had other boarders who had the advantage of being Roman Catholic – a dull Canadian, and two Belgian girls who talked to each other in Flemish between their teeth. Madame Duvernet had made the girl a little speech of welcome when she arrived and signed her up for lessons in Culture with an elderly gentleman who came three mornings a week, but after that seemed to forget about her. The girl quickly realised, rather to her relief, that it made no difference to anyone if she were there or not. The pretence here seemed to be that they were all impeccably well-brought-up girls of a background situated in provincial France somewhere between the wars. It was assumed that none of them would dream of going out after dusk unaccompanied by one of the others, or indeed should have any preoccupation or interest of her own beyond a little tepid interest in suitable young men – not actually provided by Madame Duvernet, but archly referred to by her as *des flirts*.

The girl told the Canadian, with whom she shared a room, that her mother had died of Asian 'flu. She invented a brother who was a medical student and another who played the guitar in a group. She said that her father had been too attached to her mother ever to marry again. The Canadian said that she thought that was such a lovely way to feel, and coyly mentioned 'a boy I know back in Toronto.'

Really alone for the first time in her life, the girl drifted about Paris by day, learning its relentlessly urban patterns that were like some petrified geological structure. She soon began to avoid the boulevards, the big shops and the café terraces, drawn instead to the web of older streets where the irregular houses reared up like natural rock formations. Bubbling streams ran in the gutters in the early mornings. Damp sweated through old stone; the occasional wrought-iron *pissoir*, survivor of a vanishing time, added its own pungent natural scent. Semi-decipherable letters proclaimed wood, wine and coals for sale from darkened establishments over which the shutters had been closed for the last time, but adjoining premises were loud with juke-box music and new plastic chairs. Hungrily she sniffed bitter coffee and the fresh grease of cheap food. From alleys in some parts of the town came eddies of Arab music and the backwash of spice. She noticed particularly beggars, and those who slept oblivious and ignored on the gratings from which came the warm, tainted air and the roar of the Metro beneath.

*Such a lovely city . . . so gay, such fun . . . You'll come back with such a dress sense . . .*

She took to wearing flat shoes and her old duffle coat, as if to make herself as invisible to passers-by as those bodies on the Metro gratings. But men looked at her in the streets because she was pretty, and because she seemed dreamy and unoccupied. A few of them stared boldly at her, or tried to speak to her. She was not certain what to do about this. One was not supposed to 'speak to strange men', but this dictum might just be more grown-up lies and rubbish, and their presence stirred her. It was as if they were trying to tell her something she needed to know. To introduce her, even, to some different way of living.

Presently it occurred to her that for the first time in many months she was no longer afraid, which was very nice. She could do anything, now.

One late afternoon she found herself back by the Gare St Lazare and remembered those inaccessible high windows hanging over the lines. Under a bloody sunset she wandered round to the back of the station to see if she could find the blackened blocks where people led such other lives from any she had so far found. In the street, a thin, dark young man with large eyes and bad teeth fell into step beside her, exchanging small talk almost as if he knew her. She followed him docilely into another street, and when he said hesitantly but insistently '*Tu viens chez moi?*' she nodded her head.

The stairs were dark and became darker as they went up, turning in iron circles past stained walls and small landings with barred doors, repetitive as in a dream. She felt glad she had abandoned her high-heeled shoes and her best coat at the back of one of Madame Duvernet's mirrored cupboards, far, far away. Perhaps, now, she would never need to go back for them.

When they reached the right landing at last there was a tap at the end that dribbled over a green-encrusted drain as if the building were some sort of mountain and this a spring. He seized her hand in the pitch-dark corridor, drew her onwards a few blind paces and then opened a door on to the abrupt light of the declining day. An unmade bed, clothes hanging from nails, a window open on to the last red streaks of the sky. She went eagerly over and looked down – on to the railway lines and the trains.

When he came up behind her and gripped her with uncertain fervour, she was not even quite sure, for a disorientated instant, whether he was going to project her forwards into that luminous void beyond the window, down, down under the sunset and into the path of a train. When, instead, he pulled her towards the tumbled bed, she collapsed backwards among the grubby quilts in weak relief, gratitude and a willing abandonment. Another sort of life might really be quite easy, after all.

## Blackout

Blackout is endemic to the land.
People have grown sixth sense
and sonic ways, like bats,
emerging out of the shadows
into the light of their own flesh.

But the car headlamps coming towards us
make it seem we're in some third world movie,
throwing up potholes and houses exaggeratedly,
the fresh white painted and grey ramshackle
blending into snug relief.

And inside, the children are still hovering,
hopeful moths around – The flickerless Box,
immune to the cloying stench of toilets
that can't be flushed. The children,
all waiting on electric-spell to come
and trigger a movie, the one featuring America,
played out endlessly in their heads.

While back outside, coconut vendors decapitate
the night, husky heads cutlassed off
in the medieval glow of bottle lamps.

And everywhere there are flittings
and things coming into being,
in a night where footfall is an act of faith –
A group of young girls huddled
in a questionable doorway;
The sudden dim horizontal of an alleyway;
And the occasional generator-lit big house,

obscenely bright –
hurting the soft iris of darkness
in this worn-out movie, slow reeling

Under the endless cinema of the skies.

# Nuptials

As he walked along the street, little bits of grit blew into his face. Through watering eyes he saw the roof tiles of the houses shining in the sun. For a moment they reminded him of the tortoise he and his sister had kept as a child. They called him Cuchulain, and for fun they would put him on top of the oil tank, and watch as he crept across to the edge where he invariably came to a dead stop. They would wave carrots and lettuce leaves in front of his still, reptilian head, but not an inch further would he go.

He had to stop and blink. Around him he was aware of other pedestrians – a woman holding down her skirt, a man chasing after his tam-o'-shanter that was bowling along the street, a young girl wrestling with an umbrella which had turned inside out. Somewhere he heard a tile shattering on the pavement.

On the telephone to him in Dublin, the secretary from the university had warned of summer storms.

'Awful weather we're having in the north these days,' she had said and added, in an appalling mock-cockney accent, 'raining cats and dogs.'

Walking on with eyes narrowed against the wind, he suddenly remembered the lines of Jonathan Swift;

'Drown'd Puppies, stinking Sprats, all drench'd in Mud,
Dead Cats and Turnip-Tops, came tumbling down the
    Flood.'

The theme of his lecture was to be how the differing traditions of Ireland – English and Irish, Scots-Ulster and Gaelic – nourished one another. Could he start with cats and dogs, Swift and rhyming slang? But however he began, his point was that the people of the island now had more in common, uniting them, than they had separating them.

Having agreed to speak, he had come to Belfast now to meet the organisers. But first he was going to call at the second-hand bookshops which he always visited when he was in the city. There were several of them and they were all near the university, in a street which had been totally redeveloped. 'The sanitisation by British architecture of the problem of violent dichotomy,' was how he had referred to the area in one article.

He bent down and pulled up one of his socks. It was cotton, with a black and red pattern, like a Malevich painting. He liked to dress well, and buying clothes was his only frivolous pleasure. He had bought the socks in Stockholm when attending a conference on 'Regional Variation and the Nation State'.

Just then, he heard the girl's cries. Turning, he saw that on the other side of the street, thirty yards or so away, she was being dragged out of a photocopying shop towards a lamppost. She was shouting and laughing, and the group who were pulling her were also shouting. A Rag Week stunt he thought. He stood up, and putting the briefcase under his arm, walked into the first bookshop. As the door clanged shut behind him, he carefully wiped his shoes on the brown mat and sniffed the air. He was immediately assailed, first by the unmistakable odour that clings to every secondhand bookshop – a mixture of dust, old paper and cloth – and then by the sight of the books themselves on the shelves; rows of old orange and green Penguins and American hardback novels with gold writing on their spines, nineteenth-century calf-bound editions of the classics and first editions from the Left Wing Book Club with their bright yellow covers. This was a good moment, and one he could always conjure up when sitting alone at his desk at home.

He turned to the section nearest him: 'Literature – Unsorted – Various.' After gazing along several rows, he lifted down an early edition of Aldous Huxley's *Eyeless in Gaza*. He opened the contents page, now off-white, and covered with brown spots. He had never read it. He relied on his intuition when he bought fiction. Outside, he could still hear shouting.

He stared at the title below him, turned to the first page and read the beginning: 'The snapshots had become almost as dim as memories.' He turned to the last page: 'He put a couple of eggs on to boil, and sat down meanwhile to bread and cheese. Dispassionately, and with a serene lucidity, he thought of what was in store for him. Whatever it might be, he knew now that all would be well.' It interested him but he also needed a price. The cost was not marked. He looked around for the owners and saw that they were at the window. He walked over to the pair. The woman was in her fifties and wore orange lipstick and thick mascara. Her hair was heavily hennaed, but at the roots traces of grey and brown showed through. Her husband was a thick-set man, with a bald egg-shaped head balanced on an egg-shaped body. He was wearing a blue jersey bearing the insignia of a well known Belfast rugby club and, as he stood looking into the street, he revolved the heavy gold signet ring on his thick little finger.

'Cutting up rough over there, aren't they!' the man said.

The woman made a face of disgust and made room for Michael at the window.

He looked across the road; the girl had now been strapped to the lamppost with brown tape. The crowd had started around her shoulders, and in one continuous spiralling motion, had wound their way down her body, trapping her hands by the side of her hips. Her feet were bare and her skirt was caught up in the tape, exposing her white knickers. Another girl was applying make-up aggressively to her face, whilst a third was simultaneously emptying out the contents of a silver carry-out tray onto her head. Then a bag of flour was flung over the girl. The crowd around the lamppost laughed and cheered. It was like a horrible perversion of the Maypole dancing he had once seen at Windsor. He felt sick.

'So what do you think of Belfast?' growled the man.

Michael sighed and shook his head ambiguously. The fact was, although he would never have admitted it, either privately or in his lectures and articles, he did not care for the people of the north, their province, or their largest city. With the exception of some university colleagues, he thought them a vile, nasty, violent pack of sects, who had besmirched his country. It was also loathsome how they hogged any attention that was directed to Ireland, not for any positive reasons – not for what they had done to help mankind – but because they reached for the gun when they wanted to settle a dispute, rather than heading for the conference table. Their crimes were unspeakable; they were not to be trusted; and their charm, if one could call it that, was at best dour and at worst stoney. And now this.

'Nice people, aren't we,' continued the man in the jersey.

'I don't know,' said Michael, and the man laughed sardonically.

The owners moved away from the window and he continued to watch the grotesque spectacle.

On the far side of the road, the girl with the make-up box stepped back, as if to consider her handiwork, and someone produced a plastic red nose and forced it on to the girl's face. She shook her head violently. This only improved the entertainment for those around her. The girl herself had long since stopped laughing.

The crowd of about eight or so now formed a circle around the girl, and two of them suddenly lifted a bucket up and tipped it out over her. As the water drenched the miserable figure tied to the lamppost, he knew immediately how cold it was: he could tell from the way her body went rigid, and the way she screamed. Her wet teeshirt was moulded against her body by the wind. A cheer went up.

Without thinking he returned the Huxley to its shelf, and then clasping his briefcase under his arm, marched out through the door.

Outside he noticed two policemen standing under the eaves of a bank, clutching their rifles, their backs to the wind. One of them was directing a tourist, while the other was gazing down the street. They appeared resolutely disinterested in what was happening. He looked back up the road and saw the girl was alone, still strapped to the lamppost, and the crowd were gone.

There was a gap in the traffic and he began to cross carefully. There were big puddles on the tarmac, and he worried momentarily about wetting his new leather button boots, recently purchased in Milan.

On the other side of the road an old woman with a shopping trolley was staring at the girl, shaking her head in disbelief. She walked away muttering to herself. He stepped forward. The girl's feet were bare and, with unexpected consideration, her tormenters had slipped a piece of cardboard under them. Her toe-nails were red. There was flour on the pavement and a strong smell of curry. Her legs were bare and white, with a bruise the colour of a plum showing on one thigh between two brown bands of tape. Her bare arms were goose-pimpled. From the other side of the road he hadn't taken in how small she was. Her hair was smeared with flour and curry and hung down in rat's tails. Her face was small and angular and probably quite pretty, he thought, but now with her lips crudely daubed with red lipstick, her eyelids coated with green mascara, and the false red nose, she looked both pathetic and surreal. She couldn't have been much older than eighteen.

'My God, it's cold,' she said, quite normally.

'What's going on?' he asked, coming closer.

He saw that she realised he was appalled. 'I'm getting married on Tuesday, and this is what some ones like to do here,' she said, trying to make light of her situation. But she was also embarrassed and looked away.

'Does this always happen?' Michael asked.

'No.'

'Will this happen to your fiancé?'

'I expect so. Probably worse'll happen to him.'

He felt confused and uncomfortable.

'What time is it?'

'I'm sorry, my watch is broken,' he apologised.

'Are you up from Dublin?' the girl asked, noting his accent. But then not waiting for a reply she sighed, 'My God! How much longer?'

He shifted uneasily from one foot to the other and swopped his briefcase to the other arm. This was absurd.

The door of the photocopying shop opened and out came the

girl who had applied the make-up. There was a gold cross hanging from her neck, and from her thin wrist dangled a black camera.

'Come on Aoife, give us a smile?' said the girl, lifting the camera. 'One for Seamus.'

'Fuck off,' Aoife shouted back, turning her head away.

'Oh, come on now,' he heard the girl calling, playfully, teasingly.

'Let me go. I'm cold. Come on Colette, you've had your fun.' She was getting angry now.

'Ah no, didn't we say four-thirty?' Colette was enjoying her power. He looked again at her gold cross. He presumed both girls were Catholic, like himself.

'Would you like this done to you?' he asked Colette as she folded away her camera.

'Next time round I'll not let anyone know I'm getting married,' she laughed, 'but I had this – worse actually – last year.' Then she added, 'Anyway, it's only a bit of fun.'

'Colette, I'm fucking cold,' said Aoife.

'Let her go,' he said, 'Go on, let her go.'

He aimed to sound persuasive but he sounded like a schoolmaster.

'No,' said Colette curtly. She turned on her high heels and clipped back into the shop.

'Cut me loose, will you, mister?' said Aoife. Her teeth were chattering.

He had a small penknife which he used for cleaning out the bowl of his pipe. He unbuttoned his green felt hunting coat, undid his tweed jacket, reached a finger into the top left pocket of his waistcoat and pulled out the knife. It was like a silver fish.

He opened out the short blade and went behind the lamppost. He started to saw the tape which held her shoulders. Nothing happened. The tape had too many layers, and his blade was blunt. Why hadn't he got a Swiss Army knife? he wondered, cursing.

He jabbed the knife at the middle of the taut tape, and to his delight it went through with a pop. He made another stab, then a third and a fourth. Hurrah. Someone came out of the door of the shop, and Michael suddenly felt he had been caught doing something wrong.

'What are you doing?' said a voice sharply – a male voice which unnerved him.

He stabbed violently with the blade, not looking up. The knife travelled faster than before, struck the lamppost and snapped in two. The blade fell down to Aoife's feet.

'I said, what do you think you're doing?'

Michael started to bite at the tape. He felt frustrated. He was also fearful and on the verge of panic. He was aware that more people had emerged from the shop.

'You'd better stop,' Aoife said to him.

He straightened up and saw that they had all come out of the shop. They seemed a large crowd. One was a middle-aged woman in her fifties and that surprised him. He hadn't noticed her before.

'She's a bit cold,' he said quietly and, he hoped, unthreateningly.

The faces stared at him. He could not tell if they agreed.

With the toe of one of his boots he moved the broken blade towards himself, and then, looking sideways, caught a glimpse of himself in the shop window. He looked ridiculous in his elegant clothes, with his briefcase between his feet.

From the group three youths stepped out, all with short, aggressive haircuts and pimply faces. Michael noticed their huge trainers.

'Why don't you just piss off, mister,' one of them said.

'Leave him alone, William,' called the middle-aged woman, 'he's a stranger, and he doesn't know what he's about.'

'I'm not here to argue with you,' said Michael, defensively.

'Well then, fuck off,' shouted another, and smirking he added, 'Mick.'

Beside him Michael heard Aoife whisper, 'Go, mister, get away.' She looked apprehensive and fearful. 'Go on,' she said again, 'it's only a bit of fun.'

He slowly started to walk away. He would not show his fear.

He slipped his hand into his jacket pocket and found his fountain pen. He took off the top and then held the pen by its stem, nib upwards. If anyone came up behind him, he would plunge it backwards, striking the forehead and, if he was lucky, even the eye of the assailant. But no one ran up and he walked on, all the way to the safety of the University, his pen pointing skywards, the nib gleaming like a dagger.

## *After*

After the horse that stands with its back to the rain,
after the rain that smells of lilies and urine,
after the urine-blood has a trooper draw rein,
after the rein has snapped and one stirrup-iron

hangs over the saddle-post (or, the saddle-*horn*)
after the horn has sounded the rout at Bull Run,
after the run of bass run through by a heron,
after the great blue heron itself ends its reign –

after all that I wait in line for a bagel
with lox and a schmear. Lox and a schmear. No pickle.

## St Patrick's Daughter

The first chapter of a novel to be published by Hodder
& Stoughton in March 1993

For traitors, my mother was full of sympathy and understanding. We often talked about Delilah, how nervous she was that
night as she lay there with her eyes closed, waiting for Samson
to drop off. Even though the Philistines were set to pay her,
more than Judas Iscariot, Delilah must have felt that shopping
Samson was all in the public interest. My mother identified
with her anyway. There was nothing mighty or hairy about my
father, but still she thought she should have done something
similar when she'd had the chance, got out of bed in the middle
of the night to brand his chest with a warning for other women:
'This man will be a bitter disappointment to you.' Not that they,
the other women, or she, the wife, should have needed such a
warning. It was obvious, from the day she met him, that Eugene
Murphy wasn't up to much.

He stole books from the shop in Dublin city where she
worked as an assistant. One morning her boss, a Mr Foley, put
his mug of coffee down on the till and said:

'Maria, you and I know there's a special corner in hell for
bookstealers, but do you know something else?'

'No,' said Maria, and she was only being a little bit
untruthful.

'Our lanky friend's going to get his reward on Earth.'

Her boss had been making plans. Next time the thief called
Mr Foley was going to challenge him, and at that challenge an
already primed policeman was going to step out into the shop
from his hiding place in the stock room.

Mr Foley was dying to see the look on the apprehended culprit's face, but Maria couldn't share in his excitement. She was inhibited by a strange sympathy for the bookstealer, strange because his thieving was her loss, directly relevant to the weight of her own wretched pay packet. Strange also because she had no sympathy for the thief as a poor lover of learning. Although she liked the smell of new books, Maria herself was generally indifferent to their contents. Surrounded by the latest offerings from every solvent publisher in the English language, she just grazed among the diet paperbacks, counting up the calories of all the foods she was ever likely to eat. In fact it was her lack of intellectuality that had impressed Mr Foley at the interview. She didn't look right for the job: people always said she could have been an air hostess. But Mr Foley reckoned that such an incongruously wholesome-looking assistant would be good for business. Glancing over at her, a Natalie Wood with a Dublin accent, his customers could reassure themselves that books did you no harm.

Having climbed out of love, it was hard for Maria to remember exactly what it was that had made her fall in. There may have been an oedipal dimension to it: Mr Foley took such a fatherly interest in her welfare that she was almost bound to take a lover he didn't approve of. But that was only a small factor. In the final analysis she had to admit that the main impulse had been physical. Eugene Murphy was certifiably tall, dark and handsome. More crucially, there was something touchingly qualified about his maleness. He was as thinly and finely built as an antelope, and he was very pale. It was his gaunt stalk of a neck that often came into focus when Maria summoned up her first impression. This pathetic quality was reinforced by the dark, oversized clothes that he wore then, good for the thieving of course, but also adding to the hunted, cold look. She had this urge to warm him up.

Maria knew that he retired to St Stephen's Green to read the stolen books because during her lunch breaks she regularly saw him there, sitting on a bench by the pond. His long legs reached out almost to the far side of the path alongside the bench, so that he often had to shift his focus in order to wind them up for other strollers. On the day of Mr Foley's confidence she went there on spec. If he was lolling in the usual place, she would warn him; if not, fate had it in for him.

Eugene was watching the coots when Maria went to seek him out, and when she sat down beside him he lifted his coat up to make more room for her. She just sat there for a time because she was suddenly gripped by the humiliating realization that whereas he was already a preoccupation of hers, she was completely unfamiliar to him.

'Excuse me,' she said, and he turned to her with a look of cool but polite attention, 'but I work at the Pedagogues' Corner . . .'

He nodded and said that must be nice for her.

'Well I just thought I'd let you know that Mr Foley, the owner, is on to you and he's going to have a Guard at the back of the shop on Thursday.'

'Is he now?' That was Eugene's response. There was no anxiety or repentance, yet alone gratitude. She had to remark upon the weather several times before he invited her for a coffee.

The table they sat at had just been vacated by an elderly priest who had left fifty pence behind him as a tip for the waitress. Eugene pocketed it and put a ten penny piece down in its place. That was a slithery moment, in terms of Maria's slide into love. It was the waitress, in all probability another poor woman like herself, who had been robbed of the priest's generous tip by Eugene Murphy, but Maria persuaded herself that it was really the Church which had been expropriated.

What she remembered of their conversation was not very scintillating. Apparently he noticed her studying the cakes on the tiered stand in the centre of their table, so she explained that she was working out the calories in each one and told him how a buttered sticky bun is just as fattening as a cream cake. She was impressed when, in spite of the metabolic consequences, he ate two éclairs, so impressed that it was years before she decided to resent the fact that she'd ended up paying the bill. At the time she thought it was great the way he seemed to take everything she said so seriously. Another significant thing about this meeting was his way with his hands. Eugene had hard white hands, with long fingers and chiselled knuckles, the sort of hands you expected artistic, sensitive things of. When he saw that Maria was aroused by these hands, he made it easier for her to admire them by holding them out over the tablecloth, as if it were a keyboard.

On the day of the showdown Eugene Murphy slipped into the bookshop in a suspiciously roomy duffle coat to spend the usual amount of time rubbing himself up against the paperbacks in the European drama section. He looked convincingly startled and nervous when Mr Foley pounced upon him, the Garda prematurely at his back, and asked if he could examine the contents of his coat. Eugene calmly removed the duffle coat. Then they all watched Mr Foley feeling through it, as if he half-hoped for a delightful surprise for himself.

Mr Foley squealed as he brought forth a copy of Lorca's *The House of Bernarda Alba*, but Eugene Murphy didn't look at all worried. He reached into the inner lining of the sports jacket he was wearing under the duffle coat, and pulled out the wallet containing a receipt for his purchase of this same book from another shop that morning.

After this defeat Mr Foley went through a personal crisis. The whole business had been a terrible blow to his confidence. But he started to believe in stories about police corruption and he took some consolation from the fact that Eugene Murphy had never insisted on an apology, which, if he were truly innocent, he would have been entitled to. In the meantime, Maria's fear of being spied by Mr Foley when she was arm-in-arm with the bookstealer added piquancy to the romance. Later, when she'd stopped working there, she used to hold on to her great egg of a belly and scurry by the bookshop with her head bowed down in shame.

My father wanted to be some kind of artist. As a preliminary to this he worked behind the bar of a pub where poetry readings were held. He sometimes read the poems of the shyer writers, which was generally to the advantage of their work because he looked far more poetic than any of them.

According to my mother this pub was unusually full of wankers, bullshitters and piss-artists. (For a long time I thought these were technical terms.) When she grew weary of listening to Eugene reading other men's poetry, she began to look at ways in which he might pursue his vague vocation at someone else's expense. The someone she selected was an American by the name of Jack Fennessy. He'd come to Ireland, land of his forebears, for the horses and the dogs, and at first my mother thought he was just another tweedy bullshitter – groping around in the never ending Celtic Twilight. But she soon found out that Jack Fennessy was a real film director, that very important people regularly paid him good money to exercise his cinematic fantasies and that one of these fantasies concerned Saint Patrick.

From this American's point of view, the Apostle of Ireland had an adventurous, even a sexy career. As a boy, Patricius had been snatched off the British coast by Irish pirates and sold into slavery. For six years he tended sheep for his pagan master, consoling himself on the bare mountainside by saying prayers. In due course, God told him to walk for two hundred miles where a ship would be waiting to take him back to sense and civilization. All this happened, but not before Patrick had been bitten by the missionary bug. After a series of setbacks, he returned to Ireland as a Christian evangelist. So many miracles and spectacular conversions later, Patrick had done the trick for the whole island, incidentally ridding it of snakes.

What better way, Jack Fennessy was thinking, to honour his ancestors than to do the definitive film life of Saint Patrick. Even while he was confiding in Maria, the Ancient Order of Hibernians were putting up the money. Jack Fennessy was a feudal, seigneurial sort of film director. He didn't like messing with big stars – he'd had it up to here with them – he preferred horses, and 'unknowns'. Unknowns would swim in shit for the chance to be shouted at by Jack Fennessy and in Ireland, where so many people were unknown, whole communities were willing to act a part.

With a nudge from Maria, Jack Fennessy looked over the bar of this public house and into the paddock where the thorough-bred Eugene was pulling pints. As a gesture to his saintly future, Eugene found a nice new vowel for himself. Saint Patrick was Eugene Morphy. It was okay for my mother, and the newborn me, to stick with the second most common surname in Ireland.

A townland in Mayo became a fifth-century stockade. A bou-tique in Dublin supplied hundreds of furry bikinis for the females, knee-length saffron-coloured tunics for the males. Two blacksmiths and any number of grooms mustered the horses, a French dog-handler kept a pack of wolfhounds at bay and the Chieftains composed 'pagan' music. There was a certain amount of national outrage when the set for royal Tara, where Patrick bested the druids with his miracles, was built at Pinewood Stu-dios in London. The whole cast, minus the horses, had to migrate, and the townland in Mayo settled for permanent status as a tourist attraction.

When Tara was up, Maria packed St Patrick Morphy's bags. She might, though she never said, have been hoping that he'd resist, take some sort of initiative against the parting, but Eugene never once protested, not even about leaving me.

That was how Mrs Duggan came to have Saint Patrick living in her house in London. Above a mantelpiece littered with bills and recipes she displayed a curling black and white still photo-graph from the film. Eugene Morphy looked ever so beatific in a flowing woolly cape, leaning on a shepherd's crook and gazing wistfully out over the Irish Sea. My father was always great as a wistful man in black and white.

A week couldn't pass without Mrs Duggan lamenting the dispute between Jack Fennessy and his financiers, which had dogged *Patrick*'s production and frustrated its release. The Ancient Hibernians didn't like what they eventually got to see, a rough cut so steamy it made their eyes sting. Jack Fennessy's Saint Patrick had a thing about chests and nipples, but it wasn't a mother fixation. It derived from one reference in the real Patrick's *Confession*, the point where, on his voyage of escape, he's hard put not to suck the nipples of his saviours. The historians on the pay roll tried to be nonchalant. This incident had a routine context. Some people shake hands, some people rub noses and the ancient Celts sucked each other's tits. But Jack Fennessy ignored them. His Saint Patrick, my father, was an evangelical nuzzler of men, women, horses and dogs, great big wolfhounds.

The Ancient Hibernians said the film was dirty; Jack Fennessy said his conscience as an artist wouldn't allow him to clean it up. But while Jack and the Ancient Hibernians were arguing, Eugene and the rest of the cast were paid to stay in character, to keep their hairstyles and their costumes, so that, in the event of a compromise, they could lead the Manhattan St Patrick's Day parade.

It was not to be. After a while Jack Fennessy's Georgian mansion needed a new roof and his fourth wife was wanting alimony, so he had to go back to Hollywood. Ten years later, at the untender age of sixty-eight, he fell off a horse and died on his ranch in Arizona, surrounded by his sorrowing children. The wives all stayed away.

That was the end of *Patrick* and of Mrs Duggan's plan to go to America. She wanted to stand in some exalted spot along the parade route, to watch Eugene cantering by with his golden crozier and the slavering wolfhounds. But her disappointment didn't affect his status in her house. Eugene was always her favourite lodger, a political prisoner among ordinary criminals. He was allowed to keep an electric kettle in his room; his quota of baths was higher than anyone else's; he didn't have to report in for his tea every evening and I was allowed to stay in the spare room for weeks on end.

There were three principal reasons for my father's status in Mrs Duggan's house. First, of course, there was his charisma as the man who had impersonated Saint Patrick. Second, there was the fact that, just a few months before he died, Mrs Duggan's late and unlamented husband, Bill Duggan, had called Eugene Morphy a 'miserable misbegotten pansy'. Third, there was Mrs Duggan's belief that so long as a man was either useful or beautiful, he was entitled to the loving support of at least one woman.

Eugene wasn't very useful but he was certainly beautiful, and he had the loveliest of manners. Just as subsistence peasant communities are proud to support parasitic mystics and priests, so Mrs Duggan felt that it was her privilege to harbour a man like my father.

They lived in Camden Town, on a dark and dirty street where no birds sang. Mrs Duggan's sliver of Hebden Street reeked of the smells of work and thrift – beeswax, bleach and chicken stock – and the women who fancied my father resented it. Just when they were getting close, this stinking, gloomy house seemed to clap itself over him like a tumbler over a dice. In hope of meeting Eugene Morphy these women washed their hair every morning and they bought things they didn't want in shops he was known to frequent. But even when he'd smelled their hair and drunk the wine they'd chilled, he never stayed the whole night long. He went home to Mrs Duggan's.

She pretended great compassion for these importunate women and my own mother got counted as one of them. That was because I came to stay with my father in London whenever my mother in Dublin was fluttering for another man.

Far from compensating herself with more beautiful men or even useful ones, Ma made up for her deprivation by courting political men of conscience. She had her own version of what the matter with Eugene had been. She'd decided that he had no conscience. A conscience was like an organ of the body. You could be born without one, as Eugene Morphy, né Murphy, surely was. This lack meant that he couldn't help being amoral. Indeed he was innocent in his own depraved way.

My mother met the sort of men who moved her on Saturday afternoons at exclusive political demonstrations on global issues. Then it was off home for a roasted battery chicken and a bit of intimate class struggle. If a particularly sympathetic Saturday man showed signs of wanting to stay beyond the weekends, she would arrange for me to visit Hebden Street.

Mrs Duggan was not impressed. My mother did not have a proper scientific approach. She was a truly pathetic romantic, a sort of sexual banshee, too good for hell, too bad for heaven and condemned to wander this Earth in search of a nice progressive man. But there was no need for me to be contaminated. I was young enough to be saved. St Patrick's landlady was even prepared to take on this great work herself.

The mission began on a cold summer morning, soon after the respectable, fully-employed lodgers had left the house. My father was still getting his beauty sleep and so Mrs Duggan and I were together in her basement kitchen. Because it had rained heavily during the night each of the lodgers had been given a boiled egg for his breakfast. While she cleared away the dirty dishes I was asked to gather up the gutted eggshells. She spread newspaper on the kitchen table and the sticky shells were decanted on to it.

'Now take the rolling pin Jacinta and mash them up, not too finely mind. No, stop!' She took the pin from me. 'Better just break them up with your fingers. That's a good girl.'

She sat back in her upholstered chair and watched me shredding the sticky shells. 'Tell me Jacinta, what do you know about Hannibal Barca?'

'He took elephants over the Alps.'

'He did right enough, but do you know that when he was a little boy his daddy took him to a temple where a lamb was slaughtered and sacrificed to one of the gods of Carthage city. And then, do you know what?'

'What?'

'That's enough shredding, leave them nice and prickly. Then Hannibal's dad got him to put his hand on the slaughtered lamb and swear never to be a friend of Rome.' She told me this as though it had been an item on the early news.

'I suppose you're wondering what that's got to do with you?' I was.

'Well, it's only that I've been thinking what a pity it is that I can't be taking you off somewhere so that you could swear not to be expecting very much of men.'

Hoping that my father would soon rouse himself and come

downstairs, I mumbled something to the effect that I'd never expect very much of men.

'What's that?'

'I said I don't think I'll ever be terribly interested in men.'

'That's only as well as maybe.' Mrs Duggan hoisted herself up out of the chair and peered out through the grimy kitchen window into the backyard. 'The rain's eased up now. The slugs will be out for a feast.' She turned to fix me with her boiled blue eyes. 'Put the shells in a bowl and we'll go and deal with them.'

In those days I always did as I was told. There was a lot of creaking and heavy breathing as the bolts at each end of the kitchen door were pulled back.

Gutters dripped into this walled backyard, which smelled mysteriously foul. It was a yard with halitosis, about twenty square feet, just big enough for a line of washing, a desolate dog or an alfresco fit. It seemed to me that these London yards were places for demented people to rush out into screaming. Later, as even Mrs Duggan's bit of Hebden Street got gentrified, the yards were used by smokers. Except for a narrow perimeter of clay, her rhubarb bed, Mrs Duggan's yard was paved. She grew the rhubarb for jam and tarts, and it was probably her household's main source of vitamin C.

With an old toasting fork in one hand Mrs Duggan advanced towards her plants. Slowly she bent down to pull back skirts of foliage.

'Now, quickly! I don't want to be bent double any longer than I have to. Make a little wall of shells around the youngest stalks.'

On my knees, I started to build egg-shell cairns around the stalks she had exposed. Then, high above me, the flat Duggan voice explained that I was making anti-slug minefields. For fear of lacerating themselves on the spiteful debris, slugs would keep well away from the rhubarb. I was still fingering the sticky clay, mounding up my little walls when she got on to my wretchedly optimistic mother's latest adventure.

'So what do you think of this fellah your poor mother's gone off camping with?'

I stayed on my knees. The question confused and embarrassed me.

'What's he like?'

I stood up and saw that the curtains of my father's room had been pulled back. With any luck he'd soon be down to rescue me.

'He's very nice. He can do cartwheels.'

'Is he old or young, rich or poor, dark or fair, or what?'

'Dark. He's from East Timor. Ma says he knows about crop rotation.'

'Does he indeed.' Quite suddenly, Mrs Duggan was diverted by a pair of juicy black slugs, which I had already seen and whose progress towards the eggshells I'd been hoping to observe. They might have been a couple, about to start a family. But just like her Hannibal, Mrs Duggan didn't believe in taking prisoners. She plunged the toasting fork into the ground, spearing a slug on each of its prongs. The oozing, punctured medallions of slug made no sound, and there was no blood, but Mrs Duggan was a monstrous sight as she held up her rusting trident and told me how my mother should know better.

'Isn't that just what she needs, an orphan man who misses his real mammy. I hope you won't be such a fool when you grow up. Get up on that chair now.' I scampered up on to the backless chair against one of the yard's side walls, and she passed the fork to me. 'Chuck them over the wall.'

I couldn't. The dead slugs were so well kebabed that they wouldn't flop off the fork, and I was reluctant to finger them. For a minute I let one hand, with the fork dangling from it, hang over the neighbour's wall. I wanted to turn round and push them into Mrs Duggan's big moon of a face, to tell her there was something she took no account of. Even then I knew it had to do with bodies. For all my mother's talk of morality and political conscience, these orphan men who aroused her had sex appeal. They cleared up the spotty rash she sometimes had on her chin and made her lose pounds, effortlessly.

I said nothing of this. Instead I scraped the prongs clean against the spongey brick on the far side of the wall and then I climbed down off the chair and handed back the toasting fork. My eyes were smarting and my nose was running. Mrs Duggan had pulled a hanky from her apron pocket when my father, in a ragged silk dressing-gown, picked his way into the greasy yard.

'Ghastly morning, but I can see that you and Jassie are making the most of it.'

Mrs Duggan gave him her most unctuous smile. 'She's been helping me with the rhubarb.'

'Slaughtering slugs,' I yelped.

'Oh yes, well, nature red in tooth and claw.'

'Jacinta thinks I'm a bit hard on them.' Mrs Duggan gently touched the back of my neck but I jerked my head away. 'Come in and get some breakfast Eugene. We're due for some elevenses anyway, aren't we Jacinta?'

While he was tucking into a pair of best back rashers, which the other lodgers only got on Sundays, Mrs Duggan urged him to take me to the Natural History Museum.


From that day forward I was allergic to rhubarb, but I didn't keep up any other show of integrity. Treachery can be a mark of maturity. On my next visit to London I was an obliging Delilah among the Philistines, barely in Hebden Street before I was volunteering the critical information.

'He's a beery American who came over first on account of the draft. He plays Flamenco guitar in an Italian restaurant in Dawson Street.'

Mrs Duggan was gratified by my obvious distaste. 'Ah your poor mother! She'll never learn, will she? Students and trade unionists and banjo players, there's too many more where this one's come from. We can only live in hope for her.'

Mrs Duggan didn't see herself in Old Testament terms. Instead she often compared her position as the landlady of an all-male lodging house with that of those French café owners who wined and dined the Gestapo, just so they could be passing on useful information to the Resistance. On this honourably compromised, almost treacherous basis my mother owed her a hearing: 'She'd learn more about men from me in one hour than she'll find out in a year of tangos.' But since my mother wouldn't pay any attention to her, it was up to me to listen and learn.

## *Incarnation*

Homes round the kirk are its harled
Acoustic community, thirled to the dialect Word

Thrawn at the roots of platinum blondes, inveigling
Between hinge and door-jamb, an insidious Christ of
                                                    petrol,

Scuffed shoes and farmdogs, his rich kenotic bread
Wrapped on the shelves of rural supermarkets,

His frogspawn jamjarred from ponds:
Til him at hes mair will be gien,

Christ of 'The Cottar's Saturday Night',
*Doctor Who* and CDs,

Out there at the edge of the snowfields
In his overalls, sniffing, listening for something,

Then scliffing back into the village,
Dry-eyed, ready to eat.

# The Afternoon Despatch and Courier

The fourth chapter of a novel, *An Afternoon Raag*, to be published by Heinemann in June 1993.

Early mornings, my mother is about, drifting in her pale nightie, making herself a cup of tea in the kitchen. Water begins to boil in the kettle; it starts as a private, secluded sound, pure as rain, and grows to a steady, solipsistic bubbling. Not till she has had one cup of tea, so weak that it has a colour accidentally golden, can she begin her day. She is an insomniac. Her nights are wide-eyed and excited with worry. Even at three o'clock in the morning one might hear her eating a Marie biscuit in the kitchen. At such times, she moves gently as a mouse; we know it is her, and feel no danger. In the afternoons, she sleeps as a maidservant rubs cream on the soles of her feet. 'My feet are burning,' she says. At the base of her ankle is a deep, ugly scar she got when a car ran over her foot when she was six years old. That was in a small town which is now in Bangladesh. Thus, even today, she hesitates superstitiously before crossing the road, and is painfully shy of walking distances. Her fears make her laughable. The scar is printed on her skin like a radiant star.

Her hair is troublesome and curly; when she was young, it was even thicker than it is now. It falls in long, black strands, but each strand has a gentle, complicated undulation travelling through it, like a mild electric shock or a thrill, that gives it a life of its own; it is visually analogous to a tremolo on a musical note. It is this tremolo that makes her hair curly and unmanageable and has caused her such lifelong displeasure. The easiest way she disposes of it is by gathering it compassionately into a humble, medium-sized bun, rendering it graceful with a final plastic hair-clip, or by thoughtfully metamorphosing it into a single serpent-like plait that looks paradoxically innocent. When the maidservant cleans the room and sweeps the dust to one corner, one may notice there, among other things, a few black strands with delicate, questioning curves that always float away with the merest breeze.

In the bedroom there is a weighing-machine with a flat, featureless face. Solemnly, in the morning, when my father is still asleep, my mother slips off her nightie, which weighs no more than a feather, and, quite naked, embarks upon the machine; for she will leave nothing to chance, let no extraneous factor prejudice its judicious needle. When she is satisfied with what she has seen, appalled or happy, she will alight on to earth again, and slip on her nightie. Then with short steps (for she is no more than five feet and one and a half inches) she will cross all the way from the bedroom to the corridor to the hall to the verandah, making this long and lonely journey in the still hours of first light; there (in the verandah) she stands with the teacup balanced in one hand, pausing now and then in her thoughts (for she is always thinking) to sip her weak tea politely, watching the lane, in which Christian men in shorts walk their Alsatians, with a genuine curiosity. Sometimes the famous music director, Naushad Ali, whose film songs we still hum in our solitary moments, can be seen walking down this lane with a cane in his hand and a companion by his side, his face wizened, almost Chinese, but humorous, gesticulating furiously with the hand that has waved at a thousand musical instruments, bringing a loud melody to life as he passes the sleepy lane. He is old now, in his eighties, and has suffered a few heart attacks. 'So he is still alive,' my mother thinks as she watches him. Meanwhile my father is sleeping in a most gentlemanly manner, taking care not to spill over into ungainly postures, his repose both stern and considerate as he lies on the bed with the quilt up to his chin.

After my father retired, we moved to this lane in the suburbs. Ours is the only apartment building in the lane; the rest are bungalows or cottages that belong to Christians. This is a Christian area; Portuguese names – Pedro, D'Silva and Gonsalves – twang in the air like plucked silvery guitar-strings. The

Christian men are dark-complexioned and have maternal pot-bellies, because they like drinking. The women wear unfashionable dresses, flowery purple skirts that resemble old English wallpaper, exposing polished, maroon ankles and dark knees which they cover by pulling at the skirt-ends with chaste, dutiful fingers. These women and men eat pork, and sing and dance in cottages lit with cobwebs and dim bulbs, some of which have dates upon their façades (1923), and some of which are named after some beloved great-aunt (Helen Villa), no doubt a comical figure in her time. The Christians enjoy jokes and swear-words, and the women, when they are not sullen, are gently earthquaking with laughter at what John has just said with a straight face. They are in turn friendly, talking to you in queues at banks and post-offices, and short, taking offence when you innocently ask them for street-directions. Most of them are Roman Catholic; when asked, they pronounce themselves 'katlick', a word that sounds both childishly mischievous and appropriately rude.

When my mother finishes her tea, she walks to the harmonium, which is resting in the hall upon a carpet, covered by a tranquil garment. But if it is not in the hall, she will ask Ponchoo, the cook, who is now awake, to bring it to the hall, and this he will do, holding it by the two metal rings on either side, anxious not to bump it against a door or a wall, transporting its heaviness with a pregnant woman's delicacy that dares not pause for breath, and with deep suspicion he will veer its precious body through the ins and outs of the corridor, and bending humbly, lay it in its place on the carpet. Then my mother will settle on the rug and unclip the bellows, pulling and pushing them with a mild aquatic motion with her left hand, the fingers of the right hand flowering upon the keys, the wedding-bangle suspended around her wrist. Each time the bellows are pushed, the round holes on the back open and close like eyes. Without the body music is not possible; it provides the hollow space for resonance as does the curved wooden box of the violin or the round urn of the sitar. At the moment of singing, breath tips in the swelling diaphragm as water does in a pitcher. The voice-box itself is a microscopic harp, its cords tautening and relaxing with each inflection. My mother begins to practise scales in the raag Todi.

Morning passes. When my father used to work in the city, and we lived in a flat in Malabar Hill overlooking the Arabian Sea, my mother would sometimes go to the Bombay Gym-khana in the afternoon and settle upon one of its spacious, boat-like wicker sofas, sinking into its oceanic cushions and dozing off till my father arrived for tea. Coming back from school, which was nearby, I would see her there as a silent composition of loved details: the deliberate, floral creases of her sari, the pale orange-brown glow of her skin, the mild ember-darkening of her lipsticked mouth, the patient, round fruition of her bun of hair, and the irrelevant red dot on her forehead. Seeing her was like roaming alone in a familiar garden. In cool, strategic cor-ners, waiters stood in coloured waistcoats with numbered badges pinned to them; never did a name seem more apposite than then, in the afternoon, before people started coming in, when these waiters impassionedly *waited*, dark Goan men in neat clothes, inhaling and exhaling and lightly chattering among themselves. The most invigorating fact about the club was its long corridor, an avenue of light reflected off a polished floor and protected by arches. It was frequented mainly by company executives: general managers and directors. Dressed alike in tie and white pinstriped shirt and dark suit, they looked to me like angels. In the club, these managers would sit on chairs and childishly ring little brass bells to summon the waiters. With the waiters they shared a marital relationship of trust and suspicion, and an order wrongly taken could precipitate a storm and a crisis, a sudden display of emotions, shouts and insults. Food was in abundance, from the American hamburger to chop-suey to the local bhelpuri with its subversive smells of the narrow, spice-selling streets of west Bombay. My mother was always much amused by the sight of people eating around her, moving their mouths in a slow, moral way; human beings are the only creatures, she says, who eat habitually without hunger. Long-nosed Parsi lawyers stabbed their food, using knives and forks with jurisprudential elegance. Gujarati businessmen, educated in the school of life, employed fingers, holding the crispy wafer of the bhelpuri and biting it competitively, as if they were afraid it might bite them first.

Though we live now in the suburbs, habit still drives us to the city, from where my parents return at evening. My father falls asleep in the backseat of the Ambassador, this car which is now ours after his retirement, and my mother too dozes upon his shoulder. In a place near the rear-window are laid out the day's shopping, curved, inanimate objects my mother loves, such as spatulas and spoons, and little oases of food. The Ambassador is a spacious, box-like vehicle with a Taurean single-mindedness and a rickshaw's tenacity. It is known as a 'family car'; on Sundays, cousins and aunts on outings will sit, perspiring, inside it; I myself associate its hot floorboards, its aching gear-pulley, its recalcitrant pedals, with domesticity and the social events of childhood. Of all cars I know, it has perhaps the most uplifting name, as if its appointed office were to, wide-eyed, bring good news to the world. Meanwhile, our Ambassador joins the long, mournful crocodile of cars from Churchgate to Linking Road, and we know we are near home when we come to the Mahim Creek, where fishermen's boats are parked upon the sand; here, even if your eyes should be closed, or if you should be entering the city from the direction of the airport, you will be woken by the smell of dried or rotting fish, a strong but pure odour blown inland, bitter and sharply intimate as the scent of a woman's sex.

When it is evening in the lane, my parents go down and walk for half an hour. Their lonely parade, their quiet ambitiousness as they walk up and down the compound, sometimes conferring, is witnessed by a watchman in khaki, sitting on a steel chair beneath blue light. This is an exercise they have rediscovered from when my father was a student in London, and my mother his newly-married wife, introverted, with a red dot on her forehead and vermilion in the parting of her hair, awkward but warm in her huge green overcoat. Then, too, they would walk together the wet roads from Belsize Park to Swiss Cottage. Afterwards, they go upstairs, and my mother sits on the bed, reading *The Afternoon Despatch and Courier*. She turns first to the last page, where Busybee's 'Round and About' is printed. Thus she continues this daily column about Bombay, its Irani restaurants, its post offices, its buses, its cuisine, and this man's fictional wife and his dog. Years ago, my mother and I fell in love with Busybee's voice, its calm, even tone, and a smile which was always audible in the language. My father, meanwhile, is clipping his nails fastidiously, letting them fall on to an old, spread-out copy of *The Times of India*, till he sneezes explosively, as he customarily does, sending the crescent-shaped nail-clippings flying into the universe.

## Bits of Early Days

Still a shock to remember, facing
that attacking dog's fangs and eyes
at its gate;
seeing our slug-eating dog come in
the house, mouth gummed up, plastered!

Still a joy to remember, standing
at our palm-fringed beach
watching sunrise streak the sea;
finding a hen's nest in high grass
full of eggs;
riding a horse bareback, galloping.

Still a shock to remember, eating
with fingers and caught oily-handed
by my teacher;
seeing a dog like goat-hide flattened
there in the road.

Still a joy to remember, myself
a small boy milking a cow
in new sunlight;
smelling asafoetida
on a village baby I held;
sucking fresh honey from its comb
just robbed.

Still a shock to remember, watching
weighted kittens tossed in the sea's
white breakers;
seeing our village stream dried up

with rocks exposed
like dry guts and brains.

Still a joy to remember, walking
barefoot on a bed of dry leaves
there in deep woods;
finding my goat with all of three
new wobbly kids.

Still a shock to remember, facing
that youth-gang attack and all
the needless abuse;
holding my first identity card
stamped 'Negro'.

Still a joy to remember, walking
fourteen miles from four a.m.
into town market;
surrounded by sounds of church-bell
in sunlight and birdsong.

## Stopping at the Lights

I saw Scottie today. I was stopped at some traffic lights and I saw his little face, quite clearly. When he grinned, that's when I knew. But there were cars behind me, honking.

I've still got the bit of paper from his Dad. It's somewhere, I know it is. Tonight I'm going to have a really good look. Wigan, I think he's gone. I'm meeting this bloke tonight, 7 p.m. outside Garfunkels. He's from Computer Dateline, so I bet I'll be home early. I'll look then.

Off and on all day I've been thinking about him. Scottie, I mean. He was such a gorgeous kid. Ginger hair, freckly nose. Racing around going vroom-vroom. He arrived with his Mum four years ago and they moved into Trailer Four. They didn't have a car; they must have walked from the bus stop with their suit-cases, the wind blowing off the fens like knives. His mum, Janine, was very young but she always wore high heels. Mot-tled, bare legs, but always a pair of slingbacks. Ankle-chain, too. Looking at her face, you wouldn't think she was a goer. Mousy little thing, undernourished. It was like all the vibrancy had drained into her footwear. And into her son; he was bouncing with life.

I never knew where they came from, but that wasn't so unusual in those days. My husband, Jim, asked no questions. He didn't ask *me* many questions, either. To tell the truth, he didn't talk much at all, except to his budgies. He bred pieds and opal-ines; he played them Radio One. He stood in their aviary for hours, squirting his champion hens with plume spray.

Graceland, that's what our place was called. After The King, of course. It was a little bungalow outside Spalding. There were ploughed fields either side, as far as you could see. It was dead flat. The road outside ran straight as a ruler. We had half an acre out the back, conifers fencing it in, and it was there that the trailers were parked. Seven of them. At night you could see the seven blue glows from their TVs. Sometimes, when I was feeling fidgety, I'd walk around at night; I could follow the story in *Miami Vice*, the actors mouthing at me.

I could hear the sneezes, too; the walls were that thin. And the rows, of course. There were always people coming and going, cars starting up in the middle of the night. That's why Jim insisted on rent in advance, and deposits on the calor gas cylinders. Our tenants told me such stories about their lives and I always believed them. Mr Pilcher, who said he was just stopping for a week or so while a loan came through from the Chase Manhattan Bank. Mr Carling, who said the girl he was living with was his wife, though I heard her, quite clearly once, call him 'Dad'. The bloke who said he was a Yemeni prince before they took him back to the hospital. Sometimes the police arrived, Sheba barking, blue lights flashing around our lounge. When Mr Mason did a flit, for instance. He told me he owned a copper mine in the Cameroons but when they opened up his trailer it was full of these videos. I nicked one; I thought it might reactivate our sex life, but I just got the giggles and Jim was shocked. He was much older than me, you see; he liked to believe I was innocent. He wouldn't listen to those stories of Elvis getting bloated either. Who was I, to disenchant him? I was in a real mess when he took me in, he was ever so good to me. I loved Jim, I really did, though I did behave badly on occasion. But he always took me back, no questions asked. He didn't want to hear.

Janine was running away from something, I could tell, because she never got any letters. Nobody knew she was there. But then nobody knew that most of our tenants were there. It was as if we didn't exist.

'Know what we are?' I said to Jim one night. 'Lincolnshire's answer to the Bermuda Triangle. We're the place people disappear to.'

We were playing Travel Scrabble; he was trying to enlarge his vocabulary. 'FYRED', he put down, smoke wreathing up between his fingers. He had been a heavy smoker since he was fourteen, and ran away to join the Wall of Death.

'It's not Y' I chortled, 'it's I.'

'I know it's you' he said fondly, stroking my cheek with his nicotine-stained finger. 'Every morning, I can't believe my luck.'

After that, I hadn't the heart to correct him.


Janine was a hopeless mother. At that period there happened to be no other kids around; Scottie was bored, but I never saw her playing with him. She sat on the steps of her trailer, painting her toe-nails and reading the fiction pull-outs in women's magazines. Sometimes she tottered up the road in her high heels and stopped at the phone box. Once she dyed a whole load of clothes mulberry and hung them up to dry; they flapped in the wind like whale skins. She hadn't a clue about cooking; then neither had I. Sometimes, suddenly, she decided to make something impossible like angel cakes. 'Can I borrow a recipe book?' she'd say, but I only had the manual that came with my microwave. Domesticity wasn't our forte. But surely, I thought, if *I* had a kid I'd be better at it?

Scottie liked wandering into our bungalow. He liked tapping on the aquarium and making the guppies jump. He liked inspecting Jim's trophies from the Cage Bird Society. He liked sitting on my knee, pulling bits of fluff out of my sweater and telling me stories. 'My Dad's an airline pilot' he said one day. The next time his Dad would be a champion boxer. I'd be lying under my sun lamp and there he would be, staring at me with that clear, frank look kids have.

'Why're you doing that?' he said.

'Got to be ready for when the limo arrives' I said, my eyes closed behind my goggles. 'It's a stretch, see. Cocktail cabinet and all. Got to be ready for Tom Cruise.'

One day he came in when Jim had got dressed up in his Elvis gear. It was the white satin outfit – slashed shirt, rhinestones, the works. Jim was going to the Elvis Convention in Coventry. I was embarrassed – I was always embarrassed when Jim looked like that – but Scottie didn't mind. Besides, he was togged up too, in his cowboy suit. I looked at them in their fancy dress: the six-year-old Lone Ranger and the fifty-year-old Elvis with his wizened, gypsy face and bow legs.

'My Dad's a famous pop singer' said Scottie.

'Is he now?' asked Jim, inspecting himself in the mirror. He combed back his hair to cover his bald patch.

'He's so famous I'm not allowed to say his name' said Scottie. 'My Dad's got a Gold Disc.'

'Know how many he's got?' Jim pointed to the Elvis medallion on the wall. 'Fifty-one. The most awards to an individual in history. Fifty-one Gold Discs.'

I laughed. 'Know what Jim's got? A slipped disc.'

They both swung round and stared at me. I blushed. I hadn't meant to say that; it had just popped out. Jim turned away. He knelt down and adjusted Scottie's bootlace tie.

I tried to make it better. 'He got it on the Wall of Death' I said. 'Riding the motorbikes. You know he worked on it? He was the champion for years. They went all over – Strathclyde, Farnham. Till he did his back in.'

Neither of them replied. Jim was kneeling beside Scottie, rebuckling his holster belt. 'Wrong way round, mate' he said.

Eight months passed. Scottie didn't go to school. Sooner or later, I thought, somebody in authority was going to catch up with him and his mother. She looked restless, laying out Tarot cards on her steps and then suddenly sweeping them all into a pile. Sometimes she tottered up the road and just stood there at the bus stop, looking at the timetable. I dreaded Scottie going. I loved having him around, even though he got up to all sorts of mischief. One day I caught him opening the aviary door. Luckily the budgies just sat there on their perches, the dozy buggers. They were that dim. God knows what Jim used to find to say to them.

At our place, see, people came and went; they never stayed for long. Eight months was about the limit, for us. I remember one evening, when I was waiting for my highlights to take – I was

wearing one of those hedgehog caps – I remember saying to Jim:
'It's like, this place, we're like traffic lights. People just stop here
for a while, you never know where they've been or where
they're going. The lights turn green and whoosh! They fuck
off.'

I think he replied but I couldn't hear, the rubber cap was over
my ears, but it was true. We were just a stopping place at some
dodgy moment in people's lives, people who were trying to
make it to London one day, when their luck changed. Or maybe
they were escaping from London, from something in their past,
and they fetched up with us. I had a friend in London, Mandie;
she and I had this dream of setting up our own little hairdressing
business one day.

People came and went, and there Jim and I were, grounded on
East Fen Road with our broken cars. Jim had these cars out in
the front yard, you see – Cadillacs and things, Pontiacs, American cars, the sort you saw in films with Sandra Dee in them, and
despite his arthritis he spent all day underneath them, tinkering
with their innards, while his beloved Country and Western
songs played on his portable cassette recorder.

Scottie liked to sit in the cars too. He would sit there for
hours, waggling the steering wheel and making humming
noises through his lips. He was in a world of his own, he was
going anywhere in the world. When he climbed out he wiped
his hands on his jeans, like Jim wiped his hands on his overalls
when they were greasy; his face had that set, important look
blokes have when it's a job well done, that nobody else would
understand.

In July there was a heatwave. Janine grew jittery, like a horse
smelling a thunderstorm. I woke up one night and saw her
standing in the dark, ghostly in her white nightie against the
solid black of the cypress trees. The moon shone on her
upturned face.

The next morning it was very hot. There was a tap on my
back door and there she stood, thin and pale in her halter-neck
top. She never got tanned, even in that heat, and even though I

had offered her unlimited sessions under my lamp. Her face was tight; just for a moment I thought that something terrible had happened.

She said: 'It's Scottie's birthday today and he's set his little heart on meringues.'

'Why didn't you tell me? I want to get him a present!'

'Is Jim going into Spalding? He could give me a lift and I'll buy some.'

But Jim had removed the carburettor from the Capri, our only roadworthy car; bits of dismembered metal lay all over the yard. We were marooned.

So we decided to have a go at cooking the meringues ourselves. I phoned up my friend Gloria, who was trained in catering, she did the lunches at the King's Head, and she told me the recipe. Egg whites, icing sugar, easy-peasy but keep the oven really low, Mark One.

Easy-peasy it wasn't. Janine had run out of calor gas, see, so we whisked up the egg whites and put them on a baking tray in my own oven. Just then we heard a bellow from Trailer One. Mr Parker's TV had gone dead. He used to sit in there all day watching TV, and it was in the middle of Gloria Hunniford when the electricity went off. We were always having power cuts.

Nobody else was home that day except Mr Parker. We couldn't use his calor gas cooker. I'd only been in his trailer the once and, to put it mildly, hygienic wasn't the first word that sprang to mind. Besides, he was always trying to lift my skirt with his walking-stick.

So know what I did? I put the tray of meringues into the Ford Capri. It was at least 120 degrees in there. I put the baking tray on the back seat and closed the door. 'Aren't I a genius?' I said, polishing an imaginary lapel. 'I'm wasted here.'

We suddenly got the giggles. Even Jim joined in.

'One oven, fully MOT'd' I said.

'It's Meals on Wheels' said Jim.

'Change into fourth' said Janine 'to brown it nicely on top.'

Jim was chuckling so much that he started one of his coughing fits. Scottie jumped up and down. Sheba's chain rattled as she ran this way and that, suddenly sitting down and thumping her tail.

While the meringues were cooking in the car I went indoors, to find Scottie a present. I went into the bedroom. All my soft toys were there, heaped up on the bed – teddies, rabbits, the giraffe from my twenty-first. I liked to cuddle them at night. I picked up Blinge, my koala bear, and paused. It was as if I was seeing them for the first time. They made me feel awkward, as if I was intruding on myself. They were too babyish for Scottie.

Just then Jim came in. He had recovered from his coughing fit and he was mopping his forehead. He opened the wardrobe and looked in. He always took his time. Then he took out his cowboy hat.

It was still wrapped in plastic. You should have seen it: palest tan, with a woven suede band around the brim. The genuine article. He had bought it at a Country and Western event in Huddersfield and it had cost a fortune.

'Oh Jim' I breathed.

'Got any wrapping paper?' he asked.

We had a wonderful party, the four of us. Looking back, maybe we all felt that something was about to happen. At the time I just thought it was the rush you get with a birthday, the jolt it gives you. The fridge had rumbled back to life and we drank cans of Budweiser and a bottle of German wine. Janine and Jim, who had hardly spoken all those months, even danced together to Tammy Wynette, crooning the soppy lyrics. Jim was supposed to be off the booze, but to tell the truth it improved him. Janine's sallow face was flushed. I danced with Scottie, the cowboy hat slipping over his nose. In the middle we suddenly remembered our meringues. We rushed out and opened the back door of the Capri. They hadn't cooked; they had just sort of subsided. It didn't matter. We gave them to Sheba, our canine dustbin.

When the sun went down we sat on the back porch. Janine put her arm around her son and squeezed him. She wasn't usually demonstrative.

'You're a big boy now' she said, 'you're the man of the family.'

'He's not big' I said. 'He's only a kid.'

She squeezed him tighter. 'You'll look after me. You'll see it's all OK.'

'At seven?' I asked. 'Give him a chance!'

There was a silence. From the trailers came the murmur of TVs, the rising laughter of a canned audience. Beyond the bungalow, we heard cars whizzing past on the road. Where were they going?

Jim spoke. He said: 'I wish to God I'd had a son.'

That was the first and last time he ever spoke of it.


The next morning I was standing in the kitchen, looking at the bowl of egg yolks. Six egg yolks; what was I supposed to do with them? I was standing there when the phone rang.

A woman's voice asked: 'Is there a J. Maddox at that address please?'

'Nobody of that name,' I replied. It was so hot that the receiver stuck to my hand.

'Are you sure about that? Janine Maddox?'

I paused. Janine's surname was Smith. That's what she had told us, anyway. We got a lot of Smiths.

Something in the woman's voice made me wary. 'Sorry,' I said, 'nobody of that name here.'

A fly buzzed against the window pane. Outside, in the yard, Scottie was sitting in the Chevrolet. It was his favourite. I could just see the top of his head, at the wheel. Jim had managed to get the electrics working and Scottie was trying out the indicators. First the left one winked: that way it was London. Then the right one: that meant somewhere else, somewhere beyond my calculations. Somewhere only Scottie knew.

I suddenly felt sad. I went out the back. Janine had washed her hair. She sat on the steps of her trailer, her hair wrapped in a towelling turban, smoking. For once there was no sign of a magazine. I realized for the first time that she was ever so young

– twenty-two, maybe. Twenty-three. Younger than me. I realized that I hardly knew anything about her.

'Someone just phoned,' I said, 'asking about you.'

Her head jerked up. 'Who was it?'

'A woman' I replied. 'It's all right. I said I didn't know you.'

She looked down at her feet. They were bare today, but her scuffed white slingbacks were lying on the grass nearby. When her toes were squashed into them, Scottie said they looked like little maggots.

She blew out smoke, shrugging her bony shoulders. 'Thanks' she said.


There was a thunderstorm that night. I lay next to Jim, listening to his wheezing breaths. His lungs creaked like a door, opening and closing. My koala, Blinge, was pressed between us; my giraffe, Estelle, lay on the other side. She took up as much room as another person. I could feel her plush hoof resting against my thigh.

Outside, the sky rumbled. It sounded like furniture being shifted. It sounded like bulky objects being dragged across tarmac. I lay there drowsily. I've always loved thunderstorms; when I was little I used to crawl into bed with my Mum and smell her warm body smells.

Maybe, in fact, that noise *was* something being moved. At our place, things were often shifted at night. The thunder cracked. I touched Blinge's leather nose. 'It's all right' I whispered, 'it's nothing.' I ran my finger over his glass eye; there was only one left. 'I'm here.'

Jim stirred in his sleep. He wheezed, and then there was a silence. It went on for an alarmingly long time. I held my breath, willing the noises to start again.

Finally they did; the creaking wheezes. I wrapped my arm around his gaunt chest. He muttered something in his sleep; I couldn't catch the words. Then he said, quite distinctly: 'You've got your life waiting.'

The next morning Janine and Scottie had gone. Cleared out. Their trailer was empty. We never knew who had come to collect them, moving their belongings in the night, or where they had gone. All that remained were small mementoes of Scottie: his sweet wrappers, swept into a corner of the trailer – Janine was surprisingly tidy, she wasn't like me in that respect. A criss-cross of knife marks in the trunk of one of the cypress trees, as if he were going to start a game of noughts and crosses, and hadn't found anybody to play them with.

Not long after that, a few months in fact, they demolished our place to build an out-of-town shopping mall. A socking great thing, with an atrium – they're all the rage. It was called the Rushy Dyke Shopping Experience. Rushy Dyke made me giggle; it sounded like a lesbian in a hurry. Despite my sojourn in the fens I hardly knew that dyke meant ditch. To tell the truth, I'd hardly stepped a hundred yards up the road. If you had seen our locality you would understand. No point walking somewhere when you can see exactly where you're going, is there?

Our property, where we lived, that's where the access road is now. They've put up traffic lights, too, it's that congested. So I was proved right. Graceland, and its accompanying trailer park, was just a brief stopping place for all concerned.

I got a job at the Rushy Dyke Shopping Experience. Jim was in hospital by then, and I visited him in the evenings, en route to my flat above one of Spalding's hot spots, Paradise Video Rentals. Sitting beside my storage heater I grieved for my husband, whilst the local ravers visited the premises below, hiring videos with Bruce Willis in them. The manager, Keith, watched the latest releases all evening, gunfire erupting through my carpet. It was as if Scottie was downstairs, shooting everything in sight. Then the shop went quiet, and I was alone. I thought of Jim, wheezing beside me in the night. I thought of him more than he ever believed.

I'll tell you about my job. I stood under the atrium bit, glass arches above me as high as a cathedral. One side of me there was a Next; the other side there was a Body Shop. It was nice and warm, that was something. Canned music played, to put people into the mood. It never rained there, and the wind never blew like knives. They had invented new street names and put up the signs: Tulip Walk, Daffodil Way. That was because Spalding is famous for bulbs.

I had to wear: Item One – a mob cap; Item Two – a gingham apron. The first day I felt a right prat. I stood at a farm cart in the middle of the mall, selling Old Ma Hodge's Butterscotch Bonbons. They were packaged in little cardboard cottages, with flowers printed on them. Actually the bonbons were made in a factory in Walsall but who was I to tell? Maureen, who became my friend, she stood at an adjacent cart selling Country Fayre Pot Pourris. Know them? Those things full of dead petals nobody knows what to do with. Both enterprises were leased on a franchise basis to a man we never saw, called Mr Ranesh.

I only worked there for a year, while Jim was holding on for longer than anyone had expected. He had always been stubborn. Now he couldn't speak so well, he suddenly seemed to have a lot to say. On my evening visits he told me more than I had heard in five years of marriage to him. It was mostly about his early days in children's homes. He spoke in a rush, kneading my fingers.

At work I rearranged my wares, stacking up my fudge and toffee cottages and signalling by semaphore to Maureen, who was going through a divorce. She crouched behind her cart reading a book called *Life Changes – a User's Guide*. She said we were in the same boat, but I didn't agree.

I never knew what the weather was like, outside, so I can't recall what season it was when the man came in. He wore a two-tone turquoise anorak, so maybe it was winter. He looked lost; he didn't look as if he had come in to do any shopping. We didn't get many single blokes there, except at Discount Digital Tectonics; most blokes were simply being towed along by their wife and kids.

I saw him approaching Maureen, at the next cart. She flirted with him and flashed me a glance. A man! He spoke to her for a moment, then she pointed to me. He came over.

'Douglas McLaughlan' he said, extending his hand. He was a beefy bloke, not unattractive. Ginger hair and twinkly eyes. Sort of jaunty. Despite the name, he had a London accent. 'The charming young lady over there thought you might be able to help me.' He cleared his throat. 'I believe you have connections with a caravan park hereabouts.'

'Me and my husband ran it' I said. 'It was right here, where you're standing. But they knocked it down to build this.'

He paused, taking this in. 'Ah' he said. He offered me a small cheroot. A woman passed, pushing a pair of twins in a double buggy. A group of schoolgirls came out of the Body Shop, linking arms. 'I'm looking for a young lady called Janine,' he said. Then he added casually: 'And her little lad.'

It was then that I realized. I looked at him, recognizing the likeness. The ginger hair, of course. He had Scottie's freckles, too, and his jutting lower lip. Scottie's lip had that determined look when he was concentrating on his driving.

'I'm sorry' I said, 'I haven't a clue where they've gone.'

He smoked in silence for a moment.

'I'm sorry' I said again. I felt awkward, and rearranged the fudge cottages.

'Had to do a bit of travelling,' he said, 'what with one thing and another. Thought I'd found them this time. Thought I'd hit the jackpot.'

I looked up. 'He was a gorgeous kid.'

'He was?'

I nodded. The man took out a piece of paper and wrote something down. 'If you hear anything . . .' He said something about going to Wigan. Then he handed the paper to me. 'Funny old business, isn't it.'

We stood there for a moment. Then he pointed, with his thumb, at the little cardboard cottages. Sometimes, when I was bored, I arranged them into streets like a real village. He pointed at the display trays featuring the smiling face of Old Ma Hodge in her broderie anglaise bonnet.

'Don't believe a word of it myself' he said. 'Do you?'

I drive a Sunbeam Alpine now; it's a collector's item. First thing I did, when I came to London, was learn to drive. I whizz all

over London, fixing people's hair in their own homes. I started
on my friend Mandie's hair, and some of the blokes at the club
where she works, and the word got round. I'm quite good, you
see. I tell my new clients that I trained at Michaeljohn's and I
believe it myself now. Jim believed he worked on the Wall of
Death even though he only drove the equipment lorry. His real
name was Arnold, in fact, but he re-christened himself after Jim
Reeves, another of his heroes. I only learnt this near the end.
With all the harm in the world, what's the harm in that? Scottie
never knew his father; he can believe anything.

I was thinking this today, because I saw him. I told you,
didn't I? I saw Scottie when I was sitting at the lights.

It was at a junction leading into the Euston Road. These two
boys were there, teenagers really, washing windscreens. They
started on mine before I could stop them. There was a lot of
splashing and lather. I think they liked the car; you don't see
many Sunbeams around nowadays. Anyway I sat there, flus-
tered, rooting around for a 50p piece.

They did it really thoroughly, there was foam all over the
place. Then suddenly, as the lights changed, the windscreen was
wiped clear and I saw his face. He was wearing a denim jacket
and a red teeshirt; there were pimples on his chin, as well as
freckles. I only realized who he was after I had wound down the
window and passed him the coin. 'Cheers,' he said. His piping
voice had broken.

The cars behind me were blaring their horns. I had to move
on. I was helpless in the three lanes of traffic, like a stick in a
rushing current, there was a socking great lorry thundering
behind me.

It took me a while to get back to where I'd begun. It was the
same place, I know it was – big office block one side, church the
other, covered with plastic sheets and scaffolding. It was the
same place, all right. But the boys had gone.

Not a trace. Nothing. They must have picked up their bucket
and gone. There was nothing left except some damp patches on
the tarmac.

*Gentlemen always sleep on the damp patch.* I suddenly thought of

Jim, and how he winced when I said something crude like that. I thought of how he had been a gentleman all his life, with nobody to tell him how.

The lights changed to green. I thought of how he never blamed me for the one thing I couldn't give him. Then the chorus of horns started up behind me, and I had to move on.

# To Poverty
## after Laycock

You are near again, and have been there
or thereabouts for years. Pull up a chair.
I'd know that shadow anywhere, that silhouette
without a face, that shape. Well, be my guest.
We'll live like sidekicks – hip to hip,
like Siamese twins, joined at the pocket.

I've tried too long to see the back of you.
Last winter when you came down with the flu
I should have split, cut loose, but
let you pass the buck, the bug. Bad blood.
It's cold again; come closer to the fire, the light,
and let me make you out.

How have you hurt me, let me count the ways:
the months of Sundays
when you left me in the damp, the dark,
the red, or down and out, or out of work.
The weeks on end of bread without butter,
bed without supper.

That time I fell through Schofield's shed
and broke both legs,
and Schofield couldn't spare to split
one stick of furniture to make a splint.
Thirteen weeks I sat there till they set.
What can the poor do but wait. And wait.

How come you're struck with me? Go see the Queen,
lean on the doctor or the dean,

breathe on the major,
squeeze the mason or the manager,
go down to London, find a novelist at least
to bother with, to bleed, to leech.

On second thoughts, stay put.
A person needs to get a person close enough
to stab him in the back.
Robert Frost said that. Besides,
I'd rather keep you in the corner of my eye
than wait for you to join me side by side
at every turn, on every street, in every town.
Sit down. I said sit down.

## Map Reference

Not that it was the first peak in the range,
or the furthest.
It didn't have the swankiest name
and wasn't the highest even, or the finest.

In fact, if those in the know
ever had their say about sea-level or cross-sections,
or had their way with angles and vectors,
or went there with their instruments about them,
it might have been more of a hill than a mountain.

As for its features,
walls fell into stones along its lower reaches,
fields ran up against its footslopes, scree had loosened
from around its shoulders. Incidentally, pine trees
pitched about its south and west approaches.

We could have guessed, I think, had we taken to it,
the view, straightforward, from its summit.

So,
as we rounded on it from the road that day,
how very smart of me to say or not to say
what we both knew:
that it stood where it stood, so absolutely, for you.

## Wonder

For all the years of my growing up my elder sister – a solid child with red cheeks and small but glistening brown eyes – talked of nothing but birds. She won prizes for her bird drawings. They were done in a firm outline, head pointing to the left, then filled in with watercolour. Beneath, she printed their names, the season and a sign for male or female. The drawings went on the walls of her room, turning them into sky as over-populated as a summer beach. Once she stuck her head between the railings of Palmerstone Park to look at mandarin ducks and the fire brigade had to saw her free. When my sister wasn't talking about birds, she was silent. We lived in the suburbs; she would sit watching for hours in the garden, her ears, tuned to their calls, filtering out our voices. She would not eat chicken and she wanted binoculars; when she grew up she would be an ornithologist.

My sister loved birds. I understood that love could not be done by halves. Nor was it rational. It demanded dedication, as did its opposite, hate. My mother hated germs. She fought them daylong: they had to be prevented from getting in our mouths or noses. The easiest way was not to touch either of these places, but in case we forgot we had to wash our hands with amber see-through soap to kill them. Germs came out of your bottom and crept through the paper as you wiped yourself. All of us were chronically constipated. And germs were in the grass, so we always wore shoes. By the back step stood a little bowl of milky disinfectant and a scrubbing brush for us to clean the soles. Anything new that came indoors was washed straight away, even if it was sealed in plastic. Twice daily my mother scoured the kitchen with bleach, including the walls. Animals were prime carriers of germs, due to sniffing themselves, and so naturally none were allowed in. In our house things you touched were nearly always damp from just having been wiped.

When my sister went to the secondary school I learned that germs were also what made you have a baby; they came from the man and got in the woman if she wasn't careful. Also, she said, I was an accident, by which I understood some failure on the cleaning front. She was getting top marks. Mr Leaper said she was a born scientist and could easily go to university.

My father was for years designing my sister a cat-proof bird table, though he never actually completed it. He habitually didn't finish things. But in this case it was also because in his heart he felt creatures should be kept in their place – which was the farmyard or on the dinner plate – and because he loved the garden and as a result hated both pigeons – which might use the bird table if he actually finished it – and cats and dogs. One passion necessitates or modifies another: he covered shrubs and vegetables alike in fine green net, and the garden was kept dog-proof by tall fences and barbed wire threaded through the hedges. But there was nothing to do about cats except chase them.

From his seat at the dining-room table my father commanded a view of the whole garden. As we ate, his eyes raked it like searchlights. My mother's flicked anxiously between him and her plate, waiting. Most mealtimes we'd have to go out for a cat at least once, waving our arms and shouting 'shoo! shoo!': indigestion was another family complaint. My mother didn't join in: her part was to wait by the back step to make sure we removed our shoes and wiped them properly when we came back indoors.

My sister hated the disturbance. Her eyes would also be fixed beadily on the garden. She had a notepad by her plate to record in dated columns the incidence of common birds like robins, woodpigeons, bluetits, bullfinches, and jays. I in turn watched her as she ate and counted and marked. I sometimes thought that when she grew up she would become not an ornithologist but a bird – something bold and a little greedy, like a thrush. I was already jealous, something else that can't be done by halves.

The green woodpecker was a rare and beautiful bird, with

ringed eyes and a red patch on its head, like a skull cap. It was shivering: it had a broken wing and my sister had found it in a hedge, wrapped it in her cardigan and carried it home. She wanted to bring it *in*. I stood beside my mother on the threshold, and waited to see what would happen. Mother's face was tight: her lips sealed, her breath held against the germ-laden air. She wiped her hands up and down on her apron. My sister's beady eyes sought my mother's pale grey ones and tugged at them, half pleading, half imperious.

'*Picus Viridus*' she announced, 'I want to keep it in my room – ' adding 'I can make it better. A scientific experiment.' There was a long pause, and then my mother's hands fell still. She replied: 'I suppose so, if you wipe it down.'

I watched, amazed, as my sister wiped the green woodpecker gently with disinfectant, and then carried it up to her room. It was suddenly clear that my mother loved her, even more than she hated germs.

When I won two goldfish in a fair I brought them home in a plastic bag, my heart pounding, my stomach brimful and fragile like the bag. It was, I suppose, some kind of test. But as I stood on the tiled doorstep, I felt my eyes sliding away from my mother's, even as I tried to magic her the way my sister had. Fish were not animals, I insisted; besides, it was only *fair*. I wanted to have a tank in my bedroom, like my sister and her green woodpecker. But, she insisted in return, it was not the same: the fish were not sick; no one said I was a born scientist. Also, it was difficult to see how to wipe them.

'I'll ask your father if you can keep them in the garden,' she decided.

Underneath the tree my father called *Prunus* a tank was covered with wire that went right over the top and down the sides and was then tucked in under some old bricks, to stop the cats and foxes. The foxes came at night. You heard them call and you could catch a sight of them if the moon was out. Sometimes I dreamed of them, pawing and nosing at the bricks that held the mesh in place; I dreamed of finding an empty tank and two white skeletons, sucked clean, on the bright green lawn. I loved my fish, but I didn't draw them, I just looked.

My sister's room became a bird hospital. It had a sign on the door: 'Birds: Do not Disturb' and a very big bowl of disinfectant outside. The patients: finches and thrushes, blackbirds, even storm gulls, were arranged in shoebox rows. Broken limbs were set with splints and elastoplast. Diets were prescribed and administered: pipettes of milk-soaked bread, live worms. Some birds lived. Those that died were buried in their shoebox in the back right-hand corner of the garden, a shady corner where nothing but ground ivy would grow.

Now and then I was allowed to enter the bird hospital, leaving behind me the dust-free carpets, gleaming skirtings and wiped lightflexes of the house. Inside the sills were dull with dust, the carpet peppered with crumbs; rimed saucers and jars of desiccated worms stood on the bedside table; the counterpane was blobbed and streaked with droppings. I held the birds, wrapped in cloth, while my sister bathed their eyes or tapped at their beaks with the pipette until they opened wide. She still drew. The pictures now showed birds in all sorts of positions – preening, nestled together, poised at take-off or landing, pointing both right and left.

The room was dark, to keep the birds calm and help them to forget about flying. But when they began to eat better, to peck and flap and flutter about, the curtains would be opened and the windows flung wide. Perhaps immediately, perhaps days later, the bird would suddenly soar into the sky. You could tell when it had happened because afterwards my sister's eyes glistened with satisfaction, as if, I thought to myself, she had laid an egg. She was doing biology at school by then, and did indeed eventually go on to university – an education that finally enabled her to refute my mother's belief that all germs were necessarily bad.

I still went to see my fish in the garden every day – just lay on my stomach and stared at them as they wove between the weeds, sucked their food from the water's skin or simply hung suspended in a kind of fishy sleep. Time stretched and shrunk and passed. Inside, in a row on my bed, I had animal toys. A panda bear, an owl, a kangaroo, a lion, all with button eyes. I almost loved them but I knew there was a difference between the living and the stuffed, between wonder and comfort. Between humans and animals, animals and birds, between birds and fish, which lived where people couldn't even breathe. They had only glass to hold them from a poisonous world. Maybe it was cruel to keep them, but now I could not be without their swimming gold and their suddenly swivelling eyes. Looking at them was somehow looking inside me, at a part I didn't understand, a secret and a miracle. It must, I thought, be the same for my sister with her birds; I forgave her slightly. I reasoned that if she was right about my mother's accident with the germs, then she was one as well.

That winter, it snowed and my fishtank froze overnight to a solid block of white ice. I trudged through the snow to visit it every day, as people visit graves. Dumb with reproach, I refused to allow it to be disposed of. When the thaw came, I watched the ice melt day by day, revealing a small golden glow at the very heart. I felt sadder and sadder, as if I was melting too. And then, as I watched, the two fish moved, slowly at first, as if waking from a long, cold dream.

## *Boat Dresses*
*(for Steve and Joan Dilworth)*

whiskey & flakes of green leaf,
fish oil, pink stone-meat
spilling its fat

               a lung-feather from the throat
               breaks the thoracic tarpaulin,
               the sorrow of a buried wing

death is an easier thing,
black water nights
pressing heat on the moor's bones

               leave now, left ticking
               beyond the graveyard's sand,
               a chest of swords

a dying tree,
a spear-cage,
the vertical narrative of unchanging names

## Camera Obscura
(*for the author of* The Stumbling Block)

Lepidopterist of memory of ice. Erasure. The road.
Bone chants, moustaches wet with yak butter. Glacial
                                debris
in your slack mouth. A'lost section of tooth recurs.

Pink susurration of blood upon the outhouse wall,
passes childhood. Dread to hear yourself, truth's lure.
Or, wire slices her lip with heavy duty blade.

We live in sound, retrace the rasp of curses:
carbon breath lifting paper from a dying eye.
Things happen, and again.

As milk to mercy runs, the disks you name are ankle-
                                bones.
Skeleton fate swung as a pendulum of hazard. Scarlet
                                insects
shrieking in the clock. Sheathed fingers tapping final
                                storms.

Now lightning memory speaks, approaching core.
Bruises in translation spit, venom at an angle, lily-pads.
A whiskey bottle becomes a swallowed telescope.

Father's throat is opened to surgical intervention.
Essence of brass. Gold-watch gobbed against the lid.
We are the abused collar of an Hasidic trilby.

Tabled upon microphone altar, a painted revelation of the
                                city.
Broadcasting silent breath. Taboo of candlefat sweat-
                                blessed.
Dew of sexual transformation. The bench of paradox.

## Olive Invites You To See Her Change Colour

At the end of the night the clock does not stop. There is no change in the tone of the tick and tock. At the end of the night the dressing-table still stands still. Without moving its three mirrors reflect four olive walls. Without moving the walls surround a bed, stiff and strangled with olive blankets. In the bed is a body. This is Olive too. She is ninety-one and, like the clock, her ticking outlives the night. But, like the room, she does not stir until

At the end of the night, a nurse arrives with a cup of tea. This is Nurse Reme whose loud white Good Mornings drop in like sugar lumps daily except Sundays. The tea is for Olive, but Nurse Reme wafts its reviving perfume under her own nose while she struggles to open a window in the suffocating room. Daily except Sundays the window gives way with a gasp, the room gulps shocks of air and the dressing-table mirrors crash off the brackets on which they have been balancing since this time yesterday. The tea grows tepid as Nurse Reme puts the mirrors back in brackets (taking the opportunity to examine herself in profile, and from behind). From the bed, Olive watches without reflection as Nurse Reme fingers the sag of her underchin and the sad bags of her eyes. And then Nurse Reme gets Olive out of bed.

First she has to peel back the blankets and sheets without peeling back Olive who clings to them as closely as the imprint on the Turin Shroud. Brittle as parchment Olive scrolls herself up to slip through Nurse Reme's restraining hands. Having separated Olive from her bedclothes Nurse Reme's next task is to prise her off the mattress to which she now sticks like a burr. It is as impossible to pick or trick Olive off as it is to reason with her; instead she must be rolled to the edge of the bed and gradually worked loose. At this point Nurse Reme normally says something about the weather, and Olive's expression implies that she's never heard of it and certainly doesn't want to be doing with it now. Further animosity is extended toward the dressing-gown and slippers that Nurse Reme introduces next. But it is the vertical movement through space to the cruel anti-mealtime of the commode which Olive will simply not tolerate: she threatens immediate demise and Nurse Reme threatens Matron.

Nurse leaves and Olive falls, easier prey to the gravity which lets her bowels be, back under the warm slopes and shadowy groves of the olive blanketscape. Now in the room all is olive. Now and now the room breathes regular life-supporting air in and out of the window, in and out of Olive. She and the clock tick in the eye of time, still save for the involuntary twitch or tock of each new now. Dementia has altered her dimensions. Detached from her past, this here and now will be Olive's future, unless her memory catches up with her. Waiting in bed Olive flaps her hands like urgent assignments, but her eyes are clouded with certificates of absence.

The door opens and Matron appears to fill the gap. It might be another day but it is still now. And the window, to Matron Mber's pet dismay, is still ajar. Pausing only to wedge the mirror in place with some crocheted dressing-table animals, she pounces to shut it. Its cushioned closure restores the olive room to equilibrium. Matron Mber smiles at Olive, whom she may equally restore with Librium, and then at herself in the mirror as she rearranges the dressing-table, with the worn woollen creatures which double as tissue and trinket receptacles lined up in their correct evolutionary order. Matron Mber is older than she appears (both in profile and from behind). She is old enough to pretend to be Olive's mother.

Matron Mber sits on the edge of Olive's bed and squeezes Olive's hand. She whispers, at volume, that Olive has been a naughty girl but Matron isn't cross because she knows Olive is a little bit confused. She wonders, slowly as she's loud, if Olive might try and remember how to be a good girl. She wipes

Olive's face with a handkerchief moistened by her own spittle and says that although there will always be a caring home here for Olive, Matron has recently become aware of one on the Isle of Wight where a very special sort of therapy is practised. Known as Reminiscence, it helps you to remember how to be good, and sounds like just the ticket, doesn't it dear? Brushing bone-yellow hair out of Olive's eyes, Matron Mber concludes by suggesting that if it helps Olive to remember anything at all it'll be more of a miracle than Matron's own immaculate motherhood. Matron clasps Olive to her bosom and Olive bites it and Matron slaps Olive. But quick as a fish to forget a fracas Olive leaves it at that. And abrupt as an administrator, Matron Mber puts Olive down and arranges to send Nurse Reme to pack Olive's things. Then, forwarding her goodbyes, Matron Mber is gone

And two nice young men with a casual ambulance ferry Olive to the Isle of Wight. It is a dreadful day for a boat trip, but only dogs and dead people are allowed to remain down in the dark and dirt of the car decks, so squalling at every step Olive is bounced in a wheelchair up a steep stairway to a wet leisure deck. There the wind blows fit to whisk her screaming over the edge and out of sight as fast as a page of newspaper or an empty plastic bag. The nicer young man kneels at Olive's feet and gropes for some straps to fasten her into the chair. Made firm, Olive has to face up to the wind. The nicer young man holds her hands and reminds her of the old paddle-steamers which sailed this route, but Olive is too concerned with the current difficulty of breathing to be distracted by maritime history. Uprooted from her regulated room she has no rhythm to beat against the irregular buffeting of the breeze. Olive is never so much breathing as being breathed, but on this boat there is so much air that she is in danger of hyperventilating. Her eyes bulge a warning to this effect at the young man but he doesn't understand until the torrent that runs down her legs reaches his feet. The not so nice young man laughs and lights a cigarette. Olive swoons sideways and slams into him, sending his cigarette spinning into the water.

The boat stops at the Isle of Wight and all England's casualties disembark. Holidaymakers too poor or too xenophobic to make it any further stride on to this tiny parody of their nation and feel as big as giants. And it is a haven for the little folk too; for the elderly who, where time stands still, can catch their breaths and wear their hats without fear of the fashion changing. Only the smallest people, children and convicts, might prefer to be on another island; but they have no choice. All England's casualties arrive by ferry at the Isle of Wight but Olive is the only one driven off in an ambulance.

Overcome by the fresh air Olive sleeps like a branch. All at sea. Floating in dim greenness. Life-saved in the laps of waves, lulled by friendly faces in the mist, disturbed by flashes of light in the night. Restless toward morning, wet and almost drowning; then diving down at the last minute, deep down to safety, too deep to see the dreams. With such Olympic skill Olive swims to the end of the night. Exhausted by the effort she lies stranded, washed up on the shore of a new morning. Dozing, until

A Nurse arrives with a cup of tea and some Reality Orientation Therapy.

'Good day to you Olive, and how did you sleep? My name is Nurse Naughtie-Knight, if you recall. We met last night but it was rather late and you had had quite an adventure.'

She shakes Olive warmly by the hand and tips the tea between her teeth. Olive looks right through her.

'And here we are again in, as you will no doubt remember, room ninety-one of Allover House on the wonderful Isle of Wight. If the weather holds, you may like to take a stroll later. You will see that we have the good fortune to be situated on a clifftop.'

Still looking nowhere, Olive begins to look worried. Nurse Naughtie-Knight carries on.

'Now you get yourself dressed, and I will show you the way to the dining-room. Are you hungry?'

Olive has no idea. Nurse Naughtie-Knight pretends it doesn't matter;

'Don't fret, sweetheart. I'll bet my best nurse's badge that in three weeks you'll remember every meal you've ever eaten. And every lover you've ever cooked one for. Come along then, up you get, it's gone half past eight.'

Olive appears to dislike Nurse Naughtie-Knight's Reality Orientation Therapy. Olive appears to think that in all her days she's never heard such ROT. She stretches a sinewy tongue to the very bottom of the institutional cup of tea and splashes the unsatisfying liquid all over Nurse Naughtie-Knight's starchy nurse's apron. Nurse Naughtie-Knight misses the point.

'We're going to have fun and games with you,' she says.

The fun and games begin immediately after breakfast. When no one arrives to collect her, Olive attempts to assist herself back to bed. She leaves the dining-room with a dignity which, seconds later, dies with embarrassment as she backs out of a cleaners' cupboard. But no one notices her mistake and, walking unaided for the first time in ages, she sets off in another direction. All directions are corridors and they all look the same. There are no windows, no clocks, no mirrors to keep a body alive in these disoriented corridors dead from having their doors shut, dead from whiteness and disinfection. On the walls, wooden handrails tramlining away into the distance give just enough perspective for Olive to make her way forward inch by inch by inch by. But even if Olive locates room ninety-one, even if she remembers that room ninety-one is what she's looking for, she won't be able to get in. Residents' rooms are locked during the day, in the name of Reality. Too many residents demonstrate an unhealthy tendency to spend their waking hours withdrawing from the rigours of the real. Therefore, the too many residents of Allover House are encouraged to assemble in a day centre, a site of knitting and undoing, approximating to reality. Forced out to play, Olive inches unwittingly in its direction.

Before long she stops in her tracks. An elderly gentleman comes spinning through an open doorway right in front of her. He is knocked to the floor by the zimmer-frame which skids out after him. Then comes a voice, cross and tearful, warning him against ever making so bold again, and her a married woman too. The door bangs shut. The man heaves himself back up by the zimmer-frame: all that holds him off the ground is its armour, and his ardour. Olive is about to move off again when the door reopens and a smartly-dressed old woman steps quietly out of the room. She seems surprised to see the man in the corridor although she has obviously been seeking him; she is holding a pipe and a well-worn cap which she hands to him with a sense of fulfilled duty. He offers her his arm and they zimmer-frame away slowly down the corridor together. Olive follows.

Before long she stops in her tracks. There is an enormous crowd of people milling about in a small foyer. Hundreds of hats cast shadows of a bygone era over their withered wearers. The lady and gentleman whom Olive has followed can be spotted in the bustle, smiling and spitting at each other. Olive stays on the outskirts as a door opens and the crowd tucks and gathers itself through it. The door closes with Olive left alone in the small foyer. She inches onward. Suddenly, the small foyer unfolds into a larger one. The large foyer has no doors to crowd through; its walls are lined with armchairs and fishtanks. In the armchairs are people so pale and damp they look like they are in fishtanks. On their heads are hats which recollect no age but old age. Undigested reading materials and neglected needlework lie idle in their laps. A television mutters modern messages, but they can't hear it. Olive heads back toward the small foyer. There is something louder than the television behind that closed door. She stands outside it and listens. But she stands for longer than she ought and folds up against the wall like an ironing-board in a faint.

Olive can't imagine how she comes to be strolling in a clifftop shrubbery with the lady and gentleman of the zimmer-frame incident. The whip of wet grass around her ankles alerts her to the situation. She clutches her legs. No wheelchair! Whatever next!

Olive finds herself sharing a dining-table with the lady and gentleman of the shrubbery scandal. The gentleman blows bubbly kisses at the lady, and the lady calls the gentleman a nephew. Whatever next.

Olive notices that she is knitting a mitten for the gentleman of the kissing episode. Next to her in flowery armchair a lady she's never seen before is knitting an identical mitten. Olive and the lady have their feet on the same pouffe. Whatever next.

A strange man in smart mittens calls at room ninety-one. He offers Olive a lift in his zimmer-frame and they drive to a small foyer where she meets his aunt. During the introductions all three are swept off their feet by the glamorous wind which whirls through the door in the foyer. Olive's friend, and his aunt, are sucked into the room. Olive sees them go in the flurry of frills and furbelows. The door blows shut behind them. Standing alone outside the door Olive listens. And for what could be, for all she knows, the first time in her life, Olive experiences a shock of recognition. And folds up against the wall like an ironing-board in a faint.

There is music.

Olive hears the music. In 1962. And 1927. And 1944. And 1910. Olive hears the music . . . before she strolls in the shrubbery. So much music. So many Olives.

But listen,
the melody
is the same
every time.

It is the same melody. Heard at different moments during the twentieth century. By the same Olive.

Thus with a shock, Olive's ears and Olive's I's are reconnected. I recognise this music. I heard it as a child.

Olive opens the door and looks into the Reminiscence Room. Bright sunlight falls through leaded windows in diamond patterns on to jewel-coloured carpets and couches. Gold and glass glint on every surface, from glittering art works on velvet walls to gleaming decanters and cigarette cases on great mahogany tables. A fire dances beneath a marble mantelpiece laden with sepia photographs and gilt-edged invitations. A grand piano sings loudly, swelling the room with song: a song to make instruments of its audience; strumming their nerve-ends like harp strings, tonguing their organs like pipes. Between ornamented screens air moves stately with chords, heady with perfume of violets, heavy with flavour of crumpets. Olive stands on the threshold of the Reminiscence Room and looks for the crumpets.

Olive is too polite to venture uninvited into a room full of grown-ups deep in a conversation way over her head. But if they've got crumpets hidden behind a screen . . . After less than a second of indecision she gives the door a sly shove and some of the grown-up hats turn ominously in her direction. Olive is about to run away to the kitchen and obtain some crumpets at source, when she is arrested by the sight of her mother bearing down on her in a livid purple bonnet. Olive's stomach sinks and her heart pops into her mouth in preparation for corporal punishment. But her mother, intoxicated or immobilised by the company of her fashionable guests, is not the least bit vexed by Olive's rude entrance. On the contrary, she takes Olive gently by the bony elbow and steers her into the room, whispering:

'Welcome, Olive, to our little circle. Here in the Reminiscence Room at Allover House we regain awareness of who we are by reminding ourselves who we were. We do this on the premise of Ribot's Law: the tendency of the elderly to recall the past more clearly than the present, to retain long-term but not short-term memories. In this room you will hear the sounds, sniff the smells and see the sights of your youth. Here, you notice,' she indicates a couple giggling over a glossy gilt-edged invitation, 'how the music has brought back significant memories for your friends Mr and Mrs Mendelssohn. You see, Olive, Mr and Mrs Mendelssohn sometimes forget that they are married which leads to no end of upsets.'

The male Mendelssohn beams over his zimmer-frame and flashes something at Olive.

'Look here dear!' he says, 'This is the announcement of our engagement. We are man and wife.'

Olive looks unwell.

'And a finer couple I've never seen!' says Mrs Mendelssohn,

reaching with a pale claw to draw Olive on to the couch beside them.

Olive's mother summons everyone to shuffle round and hear the story of Mr and Mrs Mendelssohn's courtship and engagement. When all are still Mrs Mendelssohn, pink and twinkling and addressing herself to her husband for validation, begins:

'Was there a war on, dear? Was there a war? We had to get married because we weren't allowed to have any lights on. We had to get married quick before you went back to the front. No one minded though, not when it turned out to be a boy. We had lots of children for our country, didn't we dear?'

Mr Mendelssohn pats her hand proudly.

'I shouldn't wonder if we had five or six,' he chuckles. 'But you have jumped the gun, my love. It's the romantic side of things Nurse wants; let me have a go, before I forget again. A chap in the trenches has to have a dream and you were mine, Mrs M. I would see myself rescuing your swollen-bellied body from the evil arms of the enemy. I'd have to hack the bleeder's . . .'

'Now, now, nice memories only!' says the nurse in Olive's mother's hat.

Mr Mendelssohn grins an apology and tries again.

'And I'd win but it'd be a jolly close shave what with all your crying and carrying on, so I'd have to knock you about a bit too, show you who's boss . . . All right, all right,' he smirks in anticipation of the next interruption, 'but it's a rum do if a chap isn't allowed to remember what he remembers.'

The music has stopped. The nurse nudges the congregation into a smattering of applause and appreciative murmurs. Mrs Mendelssohn, flushed with her feat of memory, waves the white and gold engagement announcement in acknowledgement.

'All right,' says the nurse, 'some significant progress has been made today. This couple have realised the crucial part they played in their nation's greatness. Defeating the enemy and producing children are achievements to be much admired. What is more their marriage has survived, and how many of today's generation can we say that about? So, it's time for tea now but I will see you all same time same place tomorrow for more sights, sounds and smells of your youth.'

The room empties in an eager procession which narrows to negotiate a polite hand-shaking ritual in the doorway. Straying from its ranks Olive slips behind a screen to see if this will satisfy her craving for crumpets, and trips over the chaise-longue which stands silently behind it. She slumps on to its generous curves, and stays. The moon rises over the top of the screen. Its gentle beam illuminates the dark corner of the room and points out a crucifix with a gruesome Jesus hanging on the wall above Olive's feet. And without being particularly enamoured of each other's company Olive and Jesus sleep together, until

It is the next day. The Nurse who yesterday was mistaken for Olive's mother pops into the Reminiscence Room to put on the light, heat and smell in preparation for today's session. She nearly pops out of her skin when she sees Olive emerging from behind the screen. The nurse, who despite her shock remembers this time to introduce herself as Nurse Nancy with a special responsibility for Reminiscence Therapy, checks Olive for damage and bleeps for the doctor. For the life of her, Nurse Nancy cannot credit how Olive has been sat there all night with a search party scouring the house and grounds. Is the poor old dear invisible? Olive is taken away to her own room where the doctor sees her but she doesn't see him. This is quite the opposite of invisibility and the doctor pronounces her as fit and well as can be expected. Having enjoyed her best night's sleep for years

Olive is washed and brushed and breakfasted and back in the Reminiscence Room in the blink of an eye. Nurse Nancy, unable to discover whether Olive has a hat to wear in the sessions, fetches a spare one from the staff-only cupboard concealed in an antique oak bureau. Olive sits and twitches in her new old hat as her colleagues come in regal and rusty to the strains of Chopin and the smell of the steam railway. When everyone is settled in what Nurse Nancy thinks of as period poses she puts a gilt-edged invitation in Olive's fidgety fingers. The eyes of all the other reminiscees reflect the gold on the card as greedily as children's eyes reflect the glow of a Christmas tree. Nurse Nancy waits to see if it will do anything for Olive.

For Olive,

There was always something seductive about the touch of high-class paper.

There was always something repulsive about middle-class ostentation.

Olive snorts.

Nurse Nancy seizes her chance.

'Ladies and gentlemen,' she shouts, 'We are fortunate enough to have uncovered an exciting artefact from Olive's past. It is an invitation. An invitation to the engagement of Olive and . . . well, all will be revealed, if Olive will be so good as to tell us the tale of the assignation!'

There was always some fun to be had in answering an unreasonable demand; but Olive is out of practice. She shakes her head.

'Come on dearie, remember, do. Remember for that lovely hubby!'

For Olive,

There was never anything to be said for silence. Especially in the face of this sort of silliness.

She stops shaking her head and stares at Nurse Nancy.

Nurse Nancy looks into Olive's eyes and has to look away again at once. They are very strange. They are rolling. Through time. But they are staring.

And Olive does at least, does at last, speak. And makes a present of her past. Saying:

'I had known — for two years when our eyes first met. They were acquainted before: we sat on some committee together, or we stood within the same circle of friends; and — was often in my line of vision, in my line of fire too! I was considered a very opinionated young woman then, and I discharged my opinions at anyone who considered me. But . . .'

'Can you not remember his name, dear?' Nurse Nancy interrupts.

'No I can't' admits Olive.

'I suppose it was a man's name.'

'Well, make one up,' urges Nurse Nancy, 'because the blanks are very distracting.'

'If you insist,' says Olive. 'I'll call him Axel. Scorchingly beautiful and not at all English. A Greek, I believe, or perhaps a Turk. Whatever he was he dazzled my pale compatriots like sunshine on a snowy day. It was charismatic enough, in those times, to have but sniffed the air of foreign parts: how much more, then, was a man permanently abroad, a man in regular translation.

'And as if I wasn't melting already, I was always more than interested in people who spoke more than one language. I would, when the opportunity presented itself, ply bilingual specimens with what I perceived to be the profoundest of questions. Which is the language of your thoughts, I would ask, which is the language of your dreams? Are there things you can say in one language but not in the other; are you the same you in both? My subjects often found these questions an affront to common sense and sometimes condemned them for their profanity. I could not disagree. For certainly my queries reached a crescendo when I was stuck in a tight pew of a suffocating Sunday: if God is the word, I would wonder then, who is speaking?

If language led me to God it would take me to the Devil too, on the day, years after I became acquainted with Axel, that our eyes first met. On this day we were in someone's sitting-room somewhere and the air was stale with conversations that everyone had already had. I was so busy trying to be fresh with words that I'd heard a hundred times before, that I almost missed hearing some that I hadn't. But they were so different, these new words, that I would have to have been the same as everyone else in the room to have missed them altogether. I looked to see where they were coming from and there was Axel with his native language unleashed upon a struggling schoolmaster. And because I couldn't understand what he was saying, it seemed that he must be really saying something.

While I was looking, while Axel was talking, his eyes traversed my face with the indiscriminate politeness of the sun. And my rude eyes seized his and dove into them, fathoming their depth, as if it might translate his tongue. For several slow seconds we held each other's gaze, or rather his held still while mine slid in and out. This was in the days before the electric shock so I can't pretend those moments were quite that powerful; but these were also the days when eye contact was tantamount to oral sex and I was flushed from cheek to cheek. The perfection which I contemplated in Axel was doubled by the impossibility of my desire for him. He was deeply married, you see, and held a high position of international responsibility. He looked back at me as he left with his wife that day, and he looked as if he had been raped. As if he would never look the same again.

The next time it was better. Less ambiguous, less abrupt. I was excited and my eyes were wet with it. Lubricated, they penetrated deeper than the initial glancing blow. They turned him inside out. The next time I could tell he wanted it. Because he took it. Because his wife was sitting next to him and he didn't turn and tell her. But what could he have said?

It was a sign of consent that he let me look at him for longer, and with more intensity, than would have been acceptable in any other circumstance; that he would wait while I tried to see right through him. This was my justification for continuing to do something which was probably nothing but which felt wrong. As wrong as Eve, to fancy the apple. But I had nothing to lose, my world of sitting-rooms was no Eden; and I felt powerful enough to play the serpent too. And I would have continued to worm my way into Axel's very core had that gentleman not taken it upon himself one day to forbid me to go any further. He blocked my look with enquiring eyebrows and a public smile designed to deflect my gaze. The openness of him was, by this smirk, closed. That which had been silent had made a sound like a fart.

I banished myself from his presence or else I would have created a scene and caused no end of trouble. I dwelt mournfully on the possibility that our secret was merely a figment of my imagination or else I would have called him a coward. And then I saw him again, with all the significance that seeing has when it's all you ever do, across a round committee table and under its auspices. He glanced, but it was sour and made me sick to the stomach.'

'So?' says Nurse Nancy, hard after a softish pause.

'So what?' asks Olive.

'Did you get someone else, dear, did you get another one?' Nurse Nancy hopes there is method in Olive's madness. All good stories should conclude with a gilt-edged invitation. But the chances of that seem grim. And Olive's story has not been a good one; it has been going on for hours and nothing has happened.

'I think not,' says Olive, without guilt. 'The ones I could understand I didn't want. The one I couldn't understand I did want. Until I realised that even though he knew twice as many words as me he had nothing to say. So I abandoned the attempt to pluck Axel from the tree of knowledge. All I wanted was to know him, all I wanted was to pluck him.'

The room reacts as to a slap in the face. Its breath is sucked, in gasps and gulps, into the mouths of stunned spectators. Nurse Nancy pulls her lips tight to prevent more promiscuity, swallows hard in defiance of another tasteless torrent. Her group of die-hards strive to follow her example but their sad state of atrophy gives rise to small belches of 'Shocking!' and 'Shouldn't be allowed!' Antique handkerchiefs flutter in the gaseous atmosphere.

Olive leaves the Reminiscence Room and forgets it at once. She is lost in a small foyer. There are no landmarks and no signposts; but only the memory of where one has come from reminds one where one is going and Olive, coming from nowhere, can go anywhere. She heads off down one corridor as good as another.

Down one corridor as good as another Olive gains slowly on a nurse who, white as the walls, goes from door to door, smacking them with a bunch of keys and pushing them away. The rooms are opening; it must be nearly the end of the day. Olive holds her course but it is obstructed by Nurse Naughtie-Knight, who says;

'Hello Olive, you're keen this evening. In you go then, steady on,' and Olive is channelled into a room where a clock ticks and dressing-table animals play tricks on her confusion. Olive gets under the olive blankets of her bed. She does nothing, until

In the middle of the night Olive leaps out of bed to answer the telephone. It is Axel's wife, checking on the numbers for her Christmas party. Olive says that she will be coming alone this year, if it's not inconvenient. Axel's wife replies that it does rather complicate the seating arrangements and would Olive be awfully cross if her hostess provided her with a gentleman to balance things out. Olive, smiling invisibly, replies that that would be most kind. Detecting the mischief bubbling beneath Olive's words, Axel's wife asks if Olive has anyone particular in mind. Yes, says Olive, I want your husband. There is silence at the other end of the line. Olive braces herself and grips the.

There is no telephone.

There is only shivering on linoleum; blind, barefoot and back-to-front. Olive's conversation is out of date and out of place. Without a time and without a place Olive must be dead. Or she must not be Olive. Back in bed she pulls the covers over her lack of self. Sleep: and let only the blankets be olive.

At the end of the night an old man in mittens calls at room ninety-one. He offers Olive a lift in his zimmer-frame and they drive to a small foyer where she is introduced to his aunt. Suddenly they are surrounded by people surging toward the door of the Reminiscence Room. The old man and his aunt are swept inside. In the confusion Olive fails to go with them. But

It is not safe to stay outside for long. There is an air-raid on. Olive is not so confused that she doesn't recognise the sound of the siren. She decides to battle it out. But as she stands there, fighting against the war, the real fighting is coming closer. The hum of planes, the whistle of bombs falling, the chorus of devastation on impact is reaching a crescendo. Olive cowers against the wall whispering, like a prayer; War, I Don't Subscribe To You So Please Don't Splat On My Doorstep. Not a bang, not a crash but her own imminent whimper finally sends Olive flying in fright through the door to her right. But this is the wrong way. On the other side of the door is a battle-field and the sounds of war are louder. Hostile faces in gas-masks stare at her. They are all unfamiliar: she must be behind enemy lines. Olive covers her ears and attempts to get back through the door but someone is running towards her, ripping the gas-mask from his face.

'Since you're here, Olive, we'll postpone the war. I'd like one more push at clearing up this sticky business of your marital status.' Nurse Nancy brings Olive back into a room rendered no less threatening by the substitution of Handel for the sound-effects of war. Then Nurse Nancy supervises the substitution of beautiful bonnets for horrible helmets on heads which, to Olive, seem no less threatening after the swap. Someone opens a window to clear the mortar fumes, someone else collects in the ration-books; and finally, Nurse Nancy sits Olive down on the couch, and seduces her with the aroma of wine and roses, and the whiff of a gentleman's tobacco.

With less ceremony than on the previous occasion Olive is handed a gilded rectangle of stiff paper. With less ambiguity she is invited to remember her wedding. A jubilant peal of church bells nudges her in the right direction.

'Last night,' she begins timidly, 'last night I remembered that I did want a husband.'

'Good. Good. Go on.' Nurse Nancy still has a machine-gun aimed at Olive's head.

But Olive is stuck. She turns the invitation over and over in her hands, trying to read the name which circumscribes hers, the name of the husband. Her eyesight is poor and the writing is tiny. She could write much bigger than that. And it is remembering how big and how brilliantly she used to be able to write that gives Olive the impetus to finish her sentence.

'I did want a husband. But he was already someone else's, and would never have been anything but a man to me.'

War breaks out again. Everyone on Nurse Nancy's side tuts like pistols being cocked. In front of the firing-squad, Olive ought to take things a little more seriously. It is, after all, a matter of life and death; if she can't prove to these people that she's lived properly they might be a bit reluctant to let her die. Olive racks her brain and, mercifully, manages to cobble together something old, something new, something borrowed and something blue. This must be her wedding story. She plunges into the middle of it, because it doesn't seem to have a beginning. She says:

'I stood at the window of the biggest bridal shop in town and blushed to behold the overblown gowns and distended dresses on display. But they were not so shy; they did not shrink before my stare. No, they out-stared me with their evangelical whiteness, their cold confidence, their schizoid sexuality. I would have walked away, indeed I would never have dared to stop and look at all, had I not been wondering what it must feel like to step willingly into this high security prison for women, as if life goes on inside. Better dead than wed was my belief, yet, much as one toys with the idea of suicide, I flirted with the notion of doing the other thing. The decent thing. And so I went into the shop; and challenged my indecent self to survive the experience – to come back from the wed.

'A mature manageress, well-preserved in wedding-gown starch, swept stiffly to attend to me. I began to sweat. She was bound to require me to lisp coyly and peek from under lowered lashes, and I would be instantly unmasked as an imposter.

"When is the happy day, dear?" the fearsome matriarch asked.

"Not till next spring," I lisped coyly, "but I'm having a peek now." She obviously didn't realise that I had taken "the happy day" to mean the date for submission of a thesis I was writing, for she invited me to browse at leisure through the euphoric haze and whispering virginity of her exquisite collection of bridal-wear. And browse I did, and were it not for the sinister under-skirts of ropes and chains of husband-power, I would have crept into a cradle of embroidered silk and beaded tulle and slept until I became a princess.

'After a hundred years of whiteness had weakened my vision, the perfumed-breasted manageress appeared again before my eyes and suggested that I might like to try one on. And O yes, how I wanted to. I knew which was my favourite; it was one whose skirts billowed and foamed like an ocean, whose precarious bodice was encrusted with pearls. Together we sailed it to a deserted dressing-room. She shut me inside. Smiling at how I trembled I saw myself reflected fifty times in the watery mirrors which surrounded me as I took off my clothes. I stripped until I was bare as a shipwreck. And then I saw myself again. My body was white, but it would never be as white as this dress. In awe I stepped into it, in agony I fastened it onto me. I often wasn't comfortable in my body, but it would never be as uncomfortable as this dress. Vicious metal fittings caught my flesh, sharp fixtures gouged it, sheer weight bruised it. The gown was so rough with me; my breasts were forced upwards to frame my face, thrust forward to meet my fate; my belly was dragged down and down till it reached and rubbed between my legs. I could not breathe. I could not breathe. Wedlock is a deadlock. There is no way out. There is only way inside me the stretching and straining and screaming of sexual excitement.

'Caught in a taut and tightening trap, I could either tear the dress or tear myself. But I was already torn almost in two. Part of me was willing to comply with the frock, to be punished for not being a proper woman and doing the decent thing. This part was aching to accept the proposal and the pain of the dress as the only sensible solution to my unmarried madness. But the other half of me would never take such abuse, knowing that the dress was just a fabrication, fashioned from a tissue of lies. The other half was no masochist. In turmoil I turned to the mirrors to see which of my parts was telling the truth but there *was* only one: one enormous dress, one marquee, one bridal bed, one tablecloth, one net curtain and one of me who will suffocate unless she gets it off, gets it off, Gets. It. Off. O Yes! And just as I was doing so the majestic manageress burst in and offered to help me.

"My goodness, how I envy you rosy-cheeked young brides. When I see you looking so flushed and breathless I wish I could do it all over again."

'I reached my conclusion without her assistance, though she did unhook the gown for me:

"I've just done everything I'm ever going to do in a wedding-dress, thank you very much," I said. 'And . . .' Whatever else Olive says is lost, as

A silver-haired lady stands stiffly and stalks out of the Reminiscence Room, slamming the door behind her. A second storms sobbing behind the couch, shaking a fist at Olive as she goes. Two more scurry to the door, sparse eyebrows raising folds of forehead. As the room becomes vacant, so does Olive. As the room grows chill, so does Olive. Nurse Nancy watches her eyes ice over and blinding snow snuff out the fire. Olive shivers and for a moment Nurse Nancy feels sad that so hot-headed a woman should fall into the freezing hands of senility. But as Mr and Mrs Mendelssohn shuffle past in painstaking protest and go through the door separately so as to slam it twice, Nurse Nancy comes to the boil. Olive's memories are simply not nice, they begin nastily and they end nastily; and far from calling for celebrations and cheerful gilt-edged invitations they sulkily refuse to participate in society's most sacred rituals. Nurse Nancy thinks that, for the good of the group, Olive would do best to stay out in the cold.

Olive doesn't thaw out until a cup of tea sends a mild stimulant snaking around her nervous system. The jangling stirs her and a dining-room jiggles into view, as if through dispersing steam. Olive apprehends the dining-room with a sinking feeling which intensifies as it becomes clear that the dining-room is no fleeting flashback.

Olive isn't sure how much later it is that she stands in the doorway of the Reminiscence Room and watches everyone exchanging christening invitations and boasting about their babies, but the sinking feeling hasn't gone away. As a therapeutic space the Reminiscence Room is supposedly out of bounds to prejudice and victimization but Olive is not sure how far she trusts Nurse Nancy to uphold this law. Indeed it seems rather that the room is out of bounds to Olive if the fence of barbed stares and electrified hisses, erected every time she sets foot over the threshold, is anything to judge by.

But how they expect to raise healthy children behind such a barricade Olive simply can't imagine. There is grave over-crowding; Olive can hear six or seven babies at once, their screams distorted by feedback. There is inadequate sanitation; the smell of incontinence billows from the room on choking clouds of talcum powder. And the grown-ups only make things worse; shitting on their neighbours' babies in the struggle for supremacy of their own, shitting on their own in the attempt . . .

'Assuming that you are childless, Olive, it is inappropriate for you to join us during today's session. The group are very easily disrupted by difference,' says Nurse Nancy, demonstrating how much shit there really is in the Reminiscence Room. It is no place for children and Olive doesn't linger any longer.

But Olive hears a baby crying all night long. It seems that something in her peaceful tick tock window lock door clock room is out of place and calling Mummy! Mum! Mummy!

It has the wrong person. Olive, lying in nappies on a rubber-sheeted bed, can do nothing to help it. Olive wants her mother too. And

Olive wants it to be the end; the end of the clock, the end of the crying.

The end of the demands for Mummy! Mum! Mummy! Mum!

Because the longer they go on, the stronger her urge to answer becomes.

Until, in the middle of the night, there is a positive yearning. Yes.

There is a yearning in a part of her long since dried up and fallen out but there is still a yearning. There is such a gap, such an irregularity that Olive gets out of bed and looks at herself in the mirror. The room is dark and the mirror is darker but the face that Olive sees in it is bright and beautiful and ten years old. How could she have forgotten the child? Was the child so illegitimate that it didn't count? Was the child so improper that it simply slipped her memory?

This would explain the lack of christening invitations in Olive's life. But how is Olive going to explain it to Nurse Nancy? A child without a christening invitation, like a lover without an engagement announcement, is a memory to attack the heart of the Reminiscence Room. Nurse Nancy will hit the roof. But. What should it matter to Nurse Nancy that Olive has lived a life of uncontained lust, illegal love, invalid procreation. Olive wouldn't have missed any of it for all the tea and conformity in China. And Nurse Nancy, using the Reminiscence Room as an earthly annexe to the Day of Judgement, has only herself to blame. Does she seriously expect Olive to spend her old age cherishing the thought that she never stooped to sex, and perishing the thought that she stooped at least once and there was no gilt-edged documentation saying that she was allowed to. Nurse Nancy, you reactionary old bitch; I found myself the first time by forgetting those who tried to tell me what I should remember, and now I am found again.

At the end of the night Olive finds herself breaking and entering the bureau in the Reminiscence Room; the bureau from which the gilt-edged invitations are issued with security as strict as passport control. Olive plucks one from the pile and steals to the window to read it. What Olive sees could knock her down with a feather, but doesn't surprise her in the slightest. This invitation is not in itself an invitation. It is merely an invitation to invite. It leaves things wide open to interpretation. All it says is:

. . . . . . . INVITES YOU TO . . . . . . .

and they are all exactly the same. Some reactionary old bitch has bulk-bought blank cards and filled in the gaps herself. Some reactionary old bitch has ghost-written her patients' ghosts, impatient to exorcise the restlessness and wandering from their lives. Censor of memories, Nurse Nancy

Pops into the Reminiscence Room to put on the light, heat and smell in preparation for today's session. She nearly pops out of her skin when she sees Olive beside the broken bureau, brandishing a blank invitation.

'Let's try it another way, shall we?' says Olive. 'I'll tell my story first, and you fill in the card when I've finished.' Nurse Nancy's mouth falls open. This proves the powers of Reminiscence Therapy. This proves that Olive is a wicked woman. Nurse Nancy waits with bated breath as the rest of the old dears hurry slowly in and rumour that something different is happening spreads, misquoted as a Chinese Whisper.

Olive waits with bated breath. She supposes that when she opens her mouth the story will be there; but she doesn't know what the story is going to be and is worried where it might take her. But when the waiting and the whispering stop, Olive puts her old-fashioned hat on and starts with the only fact she is sure of.

'I had a bastard child. No, that's not absolutely right. The child was quite legitimate; I was a bastard mother. But my memory of this child begins before she was born. It begins in the late summer, at the top of a hill, in a tall slim house with high ceilings and sunlight on its floors. Mine were the rooms in the roof, irregular-shaped rooms which fitted me perfectly. And since the spring, the house beneath my heavenly apartment had been empty but for cobwebs and creaking. I had spent all summer standing in its wide open spaces, dancing down its dark passages and inviting my friends round to make believe we owned it. Thus it was with a suspicious scowl that I retreated to my rented attic in September and spied on the family moving in under me.

'There was a child. I didn't want a child. I was grown-up, but I didn't want a child. I was content to be the naughtiest person in the house. And the prettiest. And the one who bombs screaming down the steepest hill in the suburbs on a bicycle. I was content to be the person who cries in the night. But there was a child. And woken nightly by the child's crying I had to admit that she was smaller and scareder than me. Woken nightly I reached the nursery before the child's mother, half asleep and called, as if by a mermaid, to see. Embarrassed at my forwardness I would mutter some untenable excuse about having been passing the nursery anyway, and climb back up two obvious flights of stairs and into the confusion of my bed. In a dream I devised a way to build a baby seat on my bicycle.

'Over the next few years the baby seats grew bigger and bigger and we cycled faster and faster down the hill. I could go twice as fast on my own but when we were together I kept the brakes on all the time. She sat behind me like an invaluable back-pack; for the duration of the screaming downward hurtle I had absolute responsibility for her. I thought I should play her mother. I thought I ought to be good, so that she would be; I thought I ought to be safe, so that she would be. I shouted over my shoulder that she must never do this on her own.

'But before she had even learnt to speak she taught me that I didn't know what I was talking about. She wanted to bomb like I did, scream like I did, hurtle like I did. She wanted to live with the brakes off. And she wanted to be loved while she did it; loved without possessiveness, anger and fear. Love first, safety second. I knew what she meant. It was what I had always wanted from those who purported to love me. And she was doing it for me, so I did it for her. I released my possessiveness, anger and fear. I let go of the secret mother who held me captive from the inside, and who threatened to contain this separate little being too. This was as atomically disruptive as I imagined giving birth to be; I forgot myself in the process. I let go of the brakes and she lived dangerously, bombing screaming and hurtling down the steepest hill in suburbia on the back of my bike. Her name was Cicely, but I called her Nicely because that was how she did me. She was the perfect daughter because we both knew that her life didn't depend on me. We thought we knew. But we knew nothing . . .'

Olive pauses and is paused for so long that the more absent-minded members of her audience think she's stopped. Nurse Nancy likes Olive better now she's not so bloody sure of herself. She picks up on the ominous down-beat of Olive's last words and asks her to continue.

'I don't know how to tell you.' Olive's eyes are too distressed to meet the nurse's. 'She died, she. Died, she was just ten years old. I thought she was going to save the world but she was obliterated in an instant by a birthday, a bicycle, a brick wall.' Olive's fingers pluck at Olive's throat in panic. 'It was, it was a, it was a birthday bicycle and I bought it for Nicely because I loved her with the brakes off. I loved her and I let her bomb, brakeless, down the hill on her own. Standing at the window of the highest house on the hill, I watched as she hurtled screaming toward the wall of the house at the bottom and I wondered if it was still what she wanted. I think she didn't want to stop. I think she didn't want to hit the bricks, I think she didn't want to die. I stood at the window of the house at the top of the hill and I watched until her brand new bicycle bounced broken on to the roof of the house at the bottom.

'They said, they. Said, I should have taught her how to stop. Jesus, She. Knew where the brakes were, She. Knew what a wall was. I think they meant I should have frightened her. But, she. Must have seen the end, wasn't that.Frightening enough?'

Because Olive is reliving rather than reminiscing Nurse Nancy takes her hands and tells her to get a grip on herself. The rest of the group are completely gripped and hang heavily on Olive's every word.

'I stood at Cicely's grave – I couldn't call her Nicely when she was dead because she wasn't – and it was such a monstrous silence, such an outrageous breach, that the me she had set free almost died too. I wanted her back, but she had never been mine. I didn't want to be alive without her, but I had no right to grieve for her. Because what is grief if not anger, possessiveness and fear; and what do the dead deserve if not a little respect. That's the end, it's finished.' Olive breaks off abruptly.

'You must have been mad, Olive, to let that child ride that bike down that hill,' says Nurse Nancy, and when a trained nurse calls you mad there is no point arguing any further. But as mad Olive leaves the Reminiscence Room Nurse Nancy hands her a whole wad of blank invitation cards. Like the cards Nurse Nancy doesn't say anything. Like the cards she is tinged with guilt.

Mad Olive stands in the small foyer and knows where she is. It is lunchtime, and she knows where to go. Now that she knows where she is, she doesn't want to be Olive.

At the end of the day, she decides it is time to get lost again. But unlike last time, when everyone except Olive knew where Olive was, this time no one except Olive will know where Olive is. In the small grey morning her plan is large and black as the shadows which pad the cells of Allover House, where sanity volunteers to chain itself to the beds. Olive, out of bed, would rather be mad. She stays up all night writing invitations to her strait-jacketed housemates and the jack-booted Nurse Nancy, in case they want to try and find her. Then in the early hours she storms the strangled corridors, stopping to slide a gilt-edged card under each door. Finally, just before dawn, she hurries away to hide.

At the end of the night a hundred nurses open a hundred doors and step with sensible shoes on a hundred of Olive's clues. All over Allover morning tea goes cold while old bodies stir to the hot gossip of mad Olive's latest escapade. Wilder than a wedding, funnier than a funeral, Olive's invitation is in everyone's hands and her words are on everyone's lips. They are difficult words for mouths dry with excitement and undrunk tea.

A huge shrunken crowd thunders toward room ninety-one. People with walking-sticks beat people without walking-sticks to the prime positions. Mr Mendelssohn uses his zimmer-frame as a riot shield and gets the best view of all. He is half in and half out of the room and in the way of the door, on which is stapled an enlarged reproduction of the cause of all the excitement. Mr Mendelssohn performs a valuable public service by reading aloud, at regular intervals, its enigmatic contents:

Olive
### INVITES YOU TO
see her change colour

His every rendition is punctuated by frail howls of derision and faint roars of dissent. These fuel the fury of those in charge of getting to the bottom of something which is rapidly proving bottomless.

In room ninety-one Nurses Naughtie-Knight and Nancy, together with two of the management men who care less but gain more from their retired charges, are trying to locate Olive. They had come the moment they were invited, expecting to find her crazed or confused, but expecting to find her. Confronted with a vacant room they launched an angry search party around the home and its clifftop gardens. The search party returned angrier, having found nothing even vaguely olive. They are forced, finally, to take Olive seriously. Nurse Naughtie-Knight points out that changing colour makes it possible to become invisible against any number of backgrounds. For several minutes the four stand with hairs prickling on the backs of their necks and scrutinize every aspect of the room as if they might catch the carpet or the armchair breathing and just be able to make out the bare outline of a beige or a black Olive. Then Nurse Nancy reminds everyone that it is Olive who is demented not themselves, but that no one, no matter how mad, can simply disappear into thin air.

New and improved search parties, including real police, spend weeks attempting to prove it. The Isle of Wight scours itself for an elderly lady wearing a dull green nightie. There is so much green, however, that from a helicopter almost anything could be Olive. The able-bodied residents of Allover House conceal their disapproval of Olive and are photographed, combing the shrubbery for clues, by the national press. Mr Mendelssohn, zimmer-framing the shrubbery, even manages to find some fond tears. The literal-minded residents remain convinced that Olive is still in the building. Invisible, she creates more chaos than when she was merely indistinguishable from the olive blankets on her bed. Unseen, she incites more unrest than when she was simply obscene. The House is haunted, and Nurse Nancy in particular cannot sleep. Night after night she climbs the walls of the Reminiscence Room, expecting at every moment to find herself face to face with the foul mouth and rude eyes of her tormentor. Olive lurks indefinitely on the couch; if Nurse Nancy should forget and sink into its depths something both older and younger than she, something that ignores the laws of time, will embrace Nurse Nancy and cause her to orgasm fit to rupture her one-way-only middle-age.

Fortunately there is no one to witness Nurse Nancy's crisis. Now that the present is more exciting than the past, the Reminiscence Room is redundant. It is, instead, the large foyer which pulsates with people who are so alive that they don't care whether they are wearing hats or wicker baskets on their heads. People who had resigned themselves to pretending to be dead until they really were, come out of retirement to join the Olive debate: this House believes that Olive is better off out of it. And this House wonders if the rest of us wouldn't be too.

At the end of the day a body turns up in a fishing net, caught in the black waters below the clifftop gardens of Allover House. It is officially identified as Olive, but it is actually blue.

## *Last Crossing of Isolde, Act I, scene ii.*

The dying Tristan has sent his friend Cardin to Cornwall, there to kidnap Isolde and bring her – in the disguise of a healing-woman – back to him in Brittany. The ship employed on this dangerous mission is manned by French troubadours disguised as merchants, and skippered by a sinister mariner named Captain Clement, who appears to know more than he should about the 'healing-woman's' true identity. As he waits on the quay for Cardin to return with the disguised Isolde, he orders his cabin-boy, Valentin, to ready the ship for departure. But there is a surprise in store . . .

[CAPTAIN CLEMENT looks towards the cliffs, at the approach of CARDIN, ISOLDE and BRANWEN]

CAPTAIN  Everything I have ever expected happened.
     And this, as they clamber down that Cornish wall
     Towards the ship I captain is the one
     Of which I am most sure. The blood they spill
     In stumbling over the rocks is bound to be blue.
     I know you, I know you.
     They've helped each other down: they see the ship.
     They'll need a boat to get 'em across the bay,
     And there it is. The man
     Is happy things have gone as planned, whatever
     Things, whatever plan. He pushes away.

[Enter VALENTIN from the ship]

     Exhausted the possible work, or just exhausted?
     Check those cabins again.
VALENTIN        The landing-boat!

| | |
|---|---|
| **CAPTAIN** | What of the landing-boat? You can't have found<br>Yourself in it again, Valentin: you can't<br>Stow away on a boat you have a job on.<br>You are a cabin boy. You have a cabin. |
| **VALENTIN** | I looked in the landing-boat – |
| **CAPTAIN** | The skimmy |
| **VALENTIN** | – The skimmy,<br>And there I found – I found it's full of a family! |
| **CAPTAIN** | It's what? |
| **VALENTIN**<br>[to offstage] | You must come down and see the Captain! |

[Enter an English Family: MR HENRY ORMOND, MRS
MARGARET ORMOND, ELINOR, KARA and their
friend DR VOGEL]

| | |
|---|---|
| | Here, sir, you must come! |
| **CAPTAIN** | What on earth is this. |
| **ORMOND:** | Ormond. Ormond H. Ormond M.<br>Ormond E. Ormond K. And Vogel. |
| **VALENTIN** | He says his name is Ormond. |
| **CAPTAIN** | Valentin,<br>Go and check the cabins eleven times. |

[Exit VALENTIN]

| | |
|---|---|
| | My stowaway discovers an entire<br>Clan of stowaways. Did you expect<br>To last these six or seven days at sea<br>In that? |
| **ORMOND** | We were rather hoping to come to some<br>Arrangement, vis-à-vis, anon, monsieur. |
| **CAPTAIN** | I'm not a Frenchman. |
| **ORMOND** | Ah, an Englishman! |
| **CAPTAIN** | Nor that: I am a mariner. |
| **MRS ORMOND** | How super! |

ORMOND      Margaret, quiet.

MRS ORMOND             Girls, that's a mariner.

ELINOR      Kara, that's a mariner.

KARA                    Uh-huh.

ELINOR      That means he's been at sea.

KARA                    How super for him.

CAPTAIN      What are you, Mister Ormond, that you cram
Your brood into my landing-boat? Escaped?

ORMOND      Escaping, Captain Sir, but not the Law.
Escaping an old way of life for a new.

MRS ORMOND      But just for a little while.

KARA                Already too long.

ORMOND      We are an ordinary cultural family,
Tolerably wealthy, not unlike
The neighbours or the neighbours' neighbours.
     But
With one extraordinary exception. Me.

MRS ORMOND      Mr Ormond's a playwright, and we act.

ORMOND      Tell him, Margaret.

MRS ORMOND             We do the Tales of Arthur.

ORMOND      We *did* the Tales of Arthur.

CAPTAIN             Arthur the King?

ORMOND      A tolerable title, but not ours.
We've kept the entire town on the edge of its seat
With 'The Beautiful Tale of the Love of Arthur
(King) and Guinevere (Queen)' – that's Mrs
                  Ormond –
'Including the Huge Exploits of the Loyal
Lancelot, a Knight', a play by Ormond,
H. H is for Henry. And that's what we did.

CAPTAIN      You're strolling players.

ORMOND             No. Not strolling.
Players, yes, but up until now immobile.
Known and loved in our town.

CAPTAIN             Then a small town.

ORMOND      A tolerable size.

KARA             A tiny dump.

ORMOND      Finally, and not without regrettings,
I plucked the best idea out of the air,
The ripe idea, and here we are: travelling.
We heard of a giant festival in the hills
Of France, for many actors, many playwrights, –
Not your clever-clever, when-will-you-pay-me,
Juggling prancing troubadours, but serious
Actors, writers, lovers of the Arts.

CAPTAIN      You mean you are not paid. Not at a court.

ORMOND      How do you know that, sir?

CAPTAIN                For one thing,
You stowed, or tried to stow, across on my ship.
And for another, I know some troubadours.

ORMOND      I trust we have not offended.

KARA                    'We'?

CAPTAIN                    No.
I've never seen an 'act', nor care remotely
Whether such stuff is paid-for or indulged.
As to your stowing away, you tried and failed
And there's an end, there's a – curtain on that.
. . . So this is all of you.

ORMOND                  I'm afraid yes.
Dr Vogel and I – not a medical doctor –
We are our only men now, hardly enough
To mount my latest spectacle of Love.
If I am to do Tristan, and he the King, –

CAPTAIN      What?

ORMOND           We will need a Rivalin, and a Gandin.

CAPTAIN      You're making a play of people who are *alive*?

ORMOND      A risk, I know, but Art, Sir Mariner, Art!

CAPTAIN      Art be quartered! Now I can see the thing.
That's why you stowed away: you're scarpering.

ORMOND      No, not at all. How could our play insult?
'The Beautiful Tale of the Love of Mark (King)
And Beautiful Irish Isolde' – that's my Elinor –
'Including the Huge Exploits of the Loyal
Tristan, a Knight', a play by Henry J. Ormond.

It's a similar play to the first but contemporary.
It deals with the great love-tale of our times.

CAPTAIN    What if the tale was still unfolding?

ORMOND                             No,
This is the tale of the Irish War, and the peace
Engendered by the marriage, plus a few
Incidents of the Hero slaying the giants,
Irishmen, dwarfs and what have you.
There are limits to how topical one can be.
Even for a modern writer like me.

CAPTAIN    Rumours cross the oceans.
Why did your Tristan leave for France so quickly?
Is that in your happy act?

ORMOND                   He *came* from France,
Did Tristan, out of Parmeny. We do not –
I am sorry, sir – believe the rumourmongers.
Those, there always are. We came through
   Cornwall
Researching our new work and we ignored them.

CAPTAIN    Valentin!

MRS ORMOND    It's a nice ship, isn't it, girls?

ELINOR    Looks good and strong.

KARA                 Wet, dark, creaking.

CAPTAIN    Playwright, you make ready. Valentin!
[to ORMOND]    Can the women cook and you pull a rope?

ORMOND                      Of course!
We are an ordinary modern family.
Not afraid of work, are we, Ormonds?

ELINOR    We're not!

KARA         *We're* not, no.

VOGEL             And nor's the Vogel.


[Enter VALENTIN]


CAPTAIN    Good. Valentin, that landing-boat is a charm.
It brought me you, and now it brings me these

|                |                                                    |
|----------------|----------------------------------------------------|
|                | Ordinary Ormonds. They are players.                |
|                | They played in a town but now they'll cross the sea |
|                | With us to France, and not in the skimmy. Show     |
|                |    them,                             |
|                | – Show them to the hull. You can sleep among       |
|                | The silk and china plates and the caged birds.     |
|                | The wine'll be down the trouba – the merchants.    |
| **ORMOND**     | Troubadors?                                         |
| **CAPTAIN**    |         This is a merchant ship, |
|                | Master Ormond. So, it is full of merchants.        |
|                | Take your chance. I am ordinary. I want            |
|                | A playwright on my ship.                           |
| **ORMOND**     | The immensity of our gratitude –                   |
| **CAPTAIN**    |                   Is big. |
|                | Go up before I change my mind. Aboard.             |
| **ORMOND**     | Thank you!                                          |
| **MRS ORMOND** |    Thank you!                        |
| **KARA**       |                 And the nightmare went ahead. |
| **CAPTAIN**    | Show them, Valentin, quickly. Go, go!              |

[VALENTIN leads the ORMONDS and VOGEL off,
on to the ship]

Too much has happened now for this to be
                      Chance.
Actors are everywhere on the *Esperance*,
The flagship of a hero unseen
For many months in Brittany. Then there's him,
Cardin, the desperate oarsman: it is clearly
Him, and the ladies hooded. That was likely.
But I need a wind to catch the hoods – there,
The blondest banners! Cardin, better be quick
To cover their heads! Now, now, I know them.
He knows I know him, Cardin,
But thinks I have been at sea forever, as if
That would make a trusting

Infant of me in an adult world of scandal.
As if there were no love in the sea.

[Lights down on CAPTAIN]

## *Thucydidean*

Continents then were affected by violent
    earthquakes, eclipses,
withering droughts and subsequent famines,
    pestilent outbreaks . . .
Faced with the Plague, the ignorant Faculty
    shewed itself impotent;
equally useless were all of our sciences,
    oracles, arts, prayers . . .
Burning sensations occurred in our heads, our
    eyes became bloodshot,
inside our mouths there was bleeding from throat and
    tongue, we grew breathless,
coughing and retching ensued, producing
    bile of all species,
genitals, fingers and toes became festered,
    diarrhoea burgeoned . . .

Terrible was the despair into which all
    fell when they realized
fully the weight and the magnitude of their
    diresome affliction . . .
Not enough living to bury the dead or
    cover the corpses . . .
Seeing how swift and abrupt were the changes
    Fortune allotted
(money and life alike being transient
    under the Pestilence),
profligate wretched citizens turned to
    lawless dishonour,

heedless of gods and of law for they thought themselves
    already sentenced –
then was there bloody and slaughterous civil
    mass insurrection.


## *Euripidean*


What we have long foretold will before long be
    fully accomplished, the theme of dirges.

Low, low it lies, imperial majesty,
vanished the pomp, the high-vaunted vanities,
    nothing remains, no name, no issue.

Mothers, expire with grief on beholding your
progeny thus deformed and your lovely ones
    now become loathsome, pallid, death-waxed.

    Hostile manipulator, Cronus,
    what need had I of sons or daughters?
This grievous fate should not have befallen me:
    children from these arms wrenched for ever.

    Not to be borne, such weight of anguish.

See, the audacious miscreants suffering.

'Wretch that I am! What cause is assignable
for such a chain of diresome calamities?'
Folly, towards which untutored man inclines;
    Sunk City's scum and pestilential
terrors, ascribe to gods unassuageable.

Nor may we now reach forth with our impotent
   hands to forestall our headlong downrush,
   having irrevocably acted.

     Some, there are, hold that the ills attending
   mankind exceed his joys; per contra,
others opine that his frail life encompasses
more bliss than woe – for how could he, otherwise,
   bear to endure each grief-racked orbit?

## *Deceptively Spacious*

When I was house-hunting prices were still shooting up, or I probably wouldn't have bought where I did. I'd been looking for months already, sifting through new estate agents' leaflets every weekend and trekking round darkest Hackney every evening to inspect the compact, the carefully modernised, the deceptively spacious.

Deceptively spacious was my favourite, because it doesn't really translate. My secretary Jill pointed it out over coffee one morning.

'Does it mean that although it looks small it's really quite big, or that it looks big despite being small? And how long's it supposed to go on for. I mean you'd have to find out for sure sooner or later – '

We laughed, and I said that it was only when you thought about it that you couldn't see what it meant, and Jill said How Like Life. She used to be an actress, well, she still was then, she'd only been temping for a year or so, off and on. I remember I thought, Well, you look like a secretary despite being an actress; deceptively thespian, that's you. I only thought it, though.

The next day I found my house. It looked straightforwardly small to me. And it wasn't exactly Close To All Amenities, but then if the Tube had been any nearer the price would've been higher. It was such a pretty little house, just what I wanted. I should never have bought it.

Because I felt uneasy as soon as I crossed the threshold. I refused to notice this properly though, as it didn't make sense. The house looked so nice.

'The street's amazingly quiet as well,' said the woman who was showing me round. Her name was Frances. She was a solicitor, 'Part-time at the moment.' She made us some coffee, using proper beans. I knew estate agents advise this on account of the elegant cosy smell, but looking at Frances curled on her pale striped sofa I suspected her of never ever using instant, nor teabags either, and I felt the beginnings of something, an emotion I couldn't recognise.

She was very good-looking, this Frances. Though in some ways she looked a bit like me, same colouring, similar bone structure, same age. But she was slim. She was about six months pregnant as well.

'Or we wouldn't be moving,' she laughed, patting her neat round stomach. 'We'd be staying put.' She had a pretty laugh.

I sat there sipping coffee while she went on about shops and swimming pools and I thought to myself, quite clearly: she's got my life. She's got it. The child, the husband, the house, the job, she's got all of it, no wonder there's nothing left for me.

I still couldn't identify what I felt, I was home again, hours later, before I recognised it, like one of those close-up photographs so magnified that you can't imagine what it's an actual picture of, and then the camera pulls back and it turns out to be a toothbrush or something.

Of course I'd been jealous before. If you're fat you can hardly avoid it, you live with it every day the way some people live with volcanoes. I'd come close to a minor eruption the day before, when I'd nearly made that crack about Jill being deceptively thespian, Jill's very slim as well and has sometimes made roguish or coaxing faces when she's come across me eating a doughnut or ringing out for a pizza.

But what I felt for Frances was different, not so much a major eruption as something final and complete. As if I were no longer there at all: not a fattish thirtyish not-quite-made-it female executive sitting on a sofa being jealous, but Jealousy itself, in whatever monstrous form you care to imagine a sin incarnate. Or like one of those 1950s Sci-Fi films where someone's taken over by aliens and still looks the same, but there's nothing of the original person left inside. Except there was a bit of me left inside. My appetite; that was intact. Jealousy incarnate was furiously hungry when she got home, she emptied the fridge and the breadbin and nipped out later on for a takeaway, though by then the camera, as it were, had pulled back enough for me to see what it was that had engulfed me.

The sale went through very quickly. I went round twice, measuring up. Frances was anxious to help.

'I do so admire you, doing all this on your own,' she said to me once.

I remember how my heart pounded as I rang the doorbell. It was a lot like being in love.

The second time, her husband was there too, John, the same age as her, another nice-looking intelligent face. From the photograph on the mantelpiece they'd clearly been together ages. It seemed to me then a sort of generosity, to love so young, to risk marriage early; I'd been too scared to chance it when I was young, though it had felt like being free and independent at the time. And all the good ones have been snapped up by now, I told myself, leaving late-starters like me just the various hopelessly ineligible unmarryable dross.

It wasn't as if my job was any great shakes either, it was looking like a fairly well-paid dead-end. I kept thinking, All my life's been one haphazard cowardly mistake after another, I can see it now, Frances has shown it me. Then I thought, Soon I will never have to see her again, and everything will be as it was, or at least seem so, which was good enough for me.

I moved in in early August. The house was perfectly clean. There was a bottle of milk in the fridge, and (I snorted) a packet of loose tea, and a little welcoming note beside the fresh flowers on the kitchen windowsill. There was another note stuck to the central heating controls, in case I'd forgotten her careful instructions (and I had).

Of course it didn't take me long to dispose of all this unbearable pleasantness. But the place still felt completely alien. Once or twice I found myself imagining that the house missed her, that she had suited it better.

And then there was the mail. They'd paid for it to be redirected for a month, but after that I started getting piles of it, nearly all for Frances. A lot of it looked like circulars but there were plenty of real letters as well, far more than I ever had. I used to imagine they were all warm loving notes from friends in the country asking her down for the weekend, or wedding invitations. The circulars were all for charities, she'd obviously been contributing to them all in some major way, Oxfam, War on Want, Mencap, World Family, Organic Farming, Save the Whales. You can see the mail was no help at all. Not just slim and pregnant and well-loved and successful and good-looking but concerned as well, caring.

'Why don't you redecorate?' suggested Jill. I'd hinted something about not feeling quite at home yet. We were having a drink after work. 'It'd make the place seem more like yours.'

'I can't face it,' I said. 'It's just what I would have chosen anyway.' I told her about the frieze of grapes and vineleaves curling round the kitchen ceiling, hand-painted by Frances.

'Have a party, then, a house-warming!'

'No, I'm too fat.'

There. Said out loud. And of course she couldn't really say anything to that, clearly I'd put on quite a bit lately and she knew she was too slim to urge me to be sensible, what do appearances matter, don't talk nonsense anyway you're just rounded, all that stuff.

'It'll get better,' I said. I certainly hoped it would, because what I felt was no fun. I suppose of all the sins Jealousy is the one that doesn't actually look much fun from the outside. It was hard work in fact. I was very busy being Jealous, what with eating and redirecting mail I had hardly any time for anything else. I was worn out.

At the end of October Frances wrote to me, a plain postcard, black ink. She thanked me very much for being so kind about the mail. Would I accept her apologies for having put me to so much trouble? She couldn't understand it, she'd written to everyone at least twice. Would I please stop worrying about any fresh arrivals, and just throw them out? She hoped I was settling in, and Sophie Louise had arrived 19 August, 7lbs 6ozs, and was keeping her very busy!

My leather jacket was too tight by then, and last year's winter boots wouldn't go on at all. My weight was a record, positively a personal best. I threw her letters away all right. But I started to open them first. Well, she'd given me permission, hadn't she? It was like taking something out of a skip. And it felt like getting a bit of my own back somehow. Though it made me feel worse as well, Jealousy with warts on, secretly prying. It was all circulars by then anyway. I remember how tired I felt slitting open another catalogue from Greenpeace. I felt tired all the time.

'I think you ought to see someone,' said Jill to me that autumn. None too friendly. 'Honestly, I think you need help.'

I just gave her back the letter she'd handed me to sign, pointed out a typo and asked her whether she'd heard from her agent recently. That shut her up.

Then one evening in November I came home to find a real letter for Frances. White envelope, wonky typing. I picked it up. It was marked 'Private'. I understood that if I delayed for a second I would have to redirect it and send it off, so I just tore it open immediately. I was still standing in the hallway with my coat on. I thought, It's her auntie saying glad you liked the cardigan and is John a 40 or a 42-inch chest?

There was a letter, and two photographs. The first was of a little blond boy holding up a blue teddy bear, the second a baby, caught just in the instant of smiling, a big unfocused sozzled grin.

Then I read the letter.

Frances, here are Matthew, 2½, and Rachel, 8 months, whose lives you are destroying. For God's sake realize what you are doing. These are his children, he is not free and never will be. Please, please, leave him alone.

That was all. It was unsigned. I read it again, I read it several times before I understood what it was about. Then I went into the kitchen and walked up and down beneath Frances's pretty painted frieze.

An anonymous letter. Not exactly a poisoned pen, more pleading and reproachful. Who on earth could have sent it? The children's mother? No, it didn't sound like a wronged wife somehow. Wouldn't a wife have made claims of her own? Not, he is not free, but he is mine.

Has to be grandma, I told myself. Elementary. Who else would care so much about the children, or have photographs to send? And no blame attached to the faithless man: Oh Frances, I thought, holding the letter up to my grinning mouth, oh Frances, his mum's written to you, telling you to lay off!

I saw her smiling and patting her stomach. Perhaps it was the lover's baby, perhaps she hadn't known for sure, perhaps she'd been in dreadful anxiety in case it looked like the wrong one, Sophie Louise 7lbs 6ozs with unmistakeable jug ears or pale ginger ringlets!

I decided I had to go for a walk, although it was raining. I felt like Gene Kelly, I could've danced in the flooding gutters, all thirteen stone of me gigantic in my flapping raincoat, singing in the rain. Because it happens that I'd never gone out with a married man myself, I'd never tried to make off with any little kid's daddy or endlessly lied, as adulterers must, to someone who loved me. And it occurred to me that as I had seen her so Frances might have seen me; a fatter, lonelier, less successful version of herself. Had she underlined the differences a little, to reassure herself? Perhaps she had even envied me my neater self-reliant life.

'I do so admire you, doing all this on your own.'

Had she held up the idealized portrait I'd been so unable to see round? All those notes and flowers and all the time there was Matthew, and the baby, and your Sophie Louise, you greedy selfish lying Frankie! I'd been depressed, I thought, and the diagnosis was an instant comfort. I'd been depressed, probably on account of moving as much as anything else. Everyone knows how stressful moving house is.

But everything will be all right now, I thought, and I marched along twirling my umbrella. I felt better already. In fact I felt terrific. And I might have looked enormous but I felt thin. Deceptively spacious, that was me.

Of course all this happened a few years ago now. So I can tell you that I lost all that weight. Not from any new diet or sudden access of willpower but because I had discovered one of the secrets of weight control, which is that if a diet is to work you need to feel thin first. If you feel fat you're too hungry to diet, you might as well not bother.

Discovering I'd made Frances up kept me feeling thin for ages. I just wasn't hungry; I'd never been so slim. Would I have been taken on to the board the following autumn, if I hadn't lost five stone? I think not. Would Michael have looked at me twice? Absolutely not. Would I have gone bankrupt the spring afterwards, if he hadn't moved in and helped with the mortgage? Probably.

These things happened. The real postscript is that their cause didn't. It still feels rather strange when I think about it, not that I think about it that much. But four or five months after the anonymous letter I had another one. Or rather Frances did. I threw it away after I'd read it but I can remember every word.

Dear Frances,

I'm so sorry. I've made a terrible mistake. It's too complicated to explain. I thought it was you. You must have been so bewildered and upset. I was wrong. I'm sorry.

Still no signature, silly old woman, I ask you, fancy getting a thing like that wrong, what a tick!

I was a bit surprised that I didn't care about it not being Frances. It didn't make any difference, I went on getting slimmer and easier to work with. I wallpapered the front room as well, very pale regency stripes, very nice, for my belated housewarming.

And I've thought, who knows, perhaps the poor old grandma got it right the first time. I feel a sort of affection for Frances, who has played such a strange undercover part in my life. Were you faithful, Frances, though you looked adulterous? Or adulterous though you seemed faithful?

Deceptively virtuous?

That might fit.

## The Villa

His famous cock
that he goes on about's
about as much fun
as a frozen lamb,
and I just ran away
across the heath
one night;
I left the moonlit villa
far behind,
the helicopters, chainsaws,
parrots, knives,
and little maids who specialize
(he gives them sweets)
in screaming
at the parrots;
I slipped away,
and came back
here,
to you:
breathing gently
like a giant flower
smelling of custard
being stirred,
and licked –
custard
made of eggs
and warm vanilla pods,
where egg-white isles
float
to Paradise.

## Marguerite

Because of the execution or suicide
of so many of his intimates,

they are looking with mounting desperation
for someone who really knew him –

someone who knew the place
where he held the meetings,

who had seen his face;
someone who fed him,

mashed the flesh of his apples;
replaced his warm lilies;

who tiptoed across the bright fence
in her checked dress

with a convoy of lorries
rumbling through her heart.

That person is me.
But nothing will induce me to come forward.

I will stay here in the ruins of the hospital
with Marguerite, the one I love,

who has not forgiven me for going away before,
and will not forgive me again. Not a day passes

Without my sitting quietly by her cage
as if to apologize.

The people on the island bring her meat
caught in the woods for her.

These are the men with disabilities,
who feel respect for such a proud creature.

And those confined to wheelchairs can sing
praises to her streamlined silhouette.

# Revelations

Dead stories had never been hard to find when the trade winds blew. The islanders would always discover something in the days that followed. Tales were trawled from the jaded depths beyond the harbour walls or thrown up by the surf to be dragged from the shore, rubbed down and cherished by beachcombers. Young Ike knew all about the stories from years gone by. He had heard them from his father, who had heard them before from his own father, whose forefathers were said to have died from a plague of nostalgia.

Now Ike, in his youth, suffered a deep sense of insecurity, for every islander had a story to show, and he had not. To simply recite a tale, embellished with the hearsay of generations, was no antidote for his troubles.

'If I have no story, I am nobody,' he would sigh, before snuffing the candle at bedtime. Only his dreams revealed the tales that he most desired, but he could never remember them come the cockerel's morning call. His nightmares, however, remained with him during the daylight hours. Ike feared that when he grew older and had children of his own, he would be forced to explain that he was always in the wrong place whenever a story washed on to the island shores.

Once, while Ike was kneeling in a distant rose-garden that flourished upon the bones of his dead mother, the winds began to whistle and the ocean relinquished her grip on a fine tale. It was only when Ike returned home that he heard about the old drowned Negro, found beached upon the shingle when the tide was at its lowest.

The children responsible for the discovery told Ike how they had stood over the careened corpse and convinced each other that the chill, hollow eyes of the poor man withheld stories of loneliness and desertion. With the sun dipping low to kiss the evening water, they had dragged his bloated carcass into the harbour village to prepare him for a mariner's burial. After stripping him bare and scrubbing the barnacles from his body, they discovered that the flesh on his back wore the mark of the lash, while tattooed along the length of his hidden joy was a faded inscription, bearing the word: F R I D A Y, which everybody assumed had been his favourite day of the week.

Ike's father owned many glorious stories. With his skill for creating something new from anything old, he favoured the washed-up tales that could provide him with material for the inventions that he built. His proudest creation was the impenetrable suit of armour that could never rust. This, he had woven from the scales of the little drowned mermaid and sealed with a coat of oil, drained from the beached whale that was thought to have once housed a man, judging by the furniture discovered inside its belly.

It was the tale of the little mermaid that kindled Ike's curiosity. Although her discovery was no mystery, for everybody knew that she had been found sprawled upon the sun-baked mud-flats, it was her demise that puzzled Ike. He could not understand why there had also been an elegant line of footprints found at the scene that led up from the surf, trailed across the sands and halted underneath her parched body. Officially, Ike's father recalled, the poor fish was assumed to have been hauled from the waters as the victim of a homegoing pirate and probably dumped after he had slaked his salacious thirst. Secretly, he believed that she had made it from the sea by her own accord. There had been no evidence of a struggle and her lips, unusually for a mermaid, were said to have been dressed for the kiss of a lover. After his father had explained his own hunches about her story, Ike would always ask the same question.

'Why trade her beautiful tail to walk from the waters and drown in the air?'

His father would tug at his silver beard and gaze up at the skies for an answer.

'Only dreamers and the dead love that which can't be touched,' he would reply.

Some day, Ike was sure he would have his very own story. He would go to any length to make it his own, for he refused to believe that anybody might perish in the pursuit of their dreams.

Although Ike occasionally found tiny tales along the shoreline, they would never be sufficient for his needs. He had once spotted a tiny green boat drifting just off the shore and waded in to retrieve it. After towing it from the chilly waters, Ike found that the vessel contained only the decayed feathers of an owl and a cracked feline claw, embedded in one of the oars. He had studied the story for a while, failed to make any sense of such nonsense and abandoned it for the surf to reclaim.

Leaving the scarlet blushes of the evening sun behind, Ike would saunter home from the beach at the end of every unlucky day. He would spot his father watching anxiously from the workshop window and shake his head in despair.

'It must hurt so much to have nothing to tell,' Ike's father would think.

He would always endeavour to cheer Ike up by telling him about a tale that was rumoured to exist but had never actually been found.

The boy's father would explain how he was certain that the lifeless yarns passed down through the generations were only decaying fragments of a much larger story. The bottle filled with soggy footprints that had been scooped from the very surface of the ocean? The persistent netting of mouldy loaves of bread, rancid bottles of wine and even the washed-up shawl that bore the shadow of a withered man?

'These are not stories,' the inventor would declare. 'They are mere chapters!'

Ike was thrilled by the accounts of each episode. He would hop swiftly to bed after his father had finished, convinced that his story-searching was not as futile as it sometimes seemed. Perhaps one day, Ike thought, the waters would reveal something epic, just for him.

His father would remain awake deep into the night, pondering the elusive clue that might bind all the yarns together. If it was ever discovered, he believed the tale could be the greatest story ever told.

One evening, Ike returned from the harbour mouth and marched into the workshop. His clothes were so drenched with trawler fumes that the great inventor was instantly drawn away from his work.

'Will this be the beginning of my story?' asked Ike, grinning broadly.

His father's half-moon spectacles slipped to the tip of his nose in surprise when he saw what Ike clutched in his hands. The boy explained how he had been given the tale by one of the elder fishermen, having unravelled his nets for him upon the harbour walls. As a reward, the fisherman had told Ike a tale about how his own great-grandfather's nets had once snagged a catch of drowned animals.

A pair of giraffes were the first to become entangled in the lines, followed by the discovery of two young tigers, trapped in the lobster cage, which, after it had been reset, bagged first one peacock, then another. After that came the storks, the stags and the dodos, all fished from out of the blue and buried in the largest grave with the prettiest flowers, for the islanders had been touched by their lonely faces, as if each creature had witnessed its own family fall victim to the waters. It was not until springtime, when the currents had swung around to the warmth of the west, that the wooden keel of a boat poked its snout from the crest of the surf. According to the fisherman, it had taken a gang of the strongest islanders the length of a week to haul the ark from the grip of the undertow.

When Ike had asked him if he could be taken to see the shipwreck, the maudlin tones of the old fisherman sunk deep into sadness, croaking that the ravage of time and the salt-lick of the sea had rotted the hull until nothing remained but a pile of damp wood. With the approach of the summer months, the heap had dried to dust, releasing a musty scent across the harbour which made the islanders talk of a lost and darkened age. The story of the ark had soon been forgotten, however, when the trade winds carried the dust into the expanse of the skies and scattered it over distant lands, too far away for their own small boats to reach.

Ike never fully believed a story unless he saw it with his own eyes. To prove the tale was not a myth, the fisherman had gone below deck, where Ike heard him rummaging among the oily swabs, the broken compasses and the whiskey kegs. Eventually, as the waves that lapped at the wall of the jetty had begun to sparkle under the moonlight, the fisherman clambered back up the ladder. He had then shown Ike a spherical curiosity, no bigger than the palm of his calloused hand, red as the blood in his veins and crowned with two sprouting green leaves. The fisherman had twisted the globe around to reveal a deep scar, the shape of a sickle moon and the size of a hungry mouth.

The fisherman had been stumped as to what the soft trinket might be. It had been handed down to him by his father who had kept it in a jar of pickling water, in fear that it might disintegrate. The globe, he had explained, was discovered deep inside the hold of the ark, contained in a silver casket encrusted with the filth of ages that had taken three days and a mallet to remove. The old fisherman, having pushed the globe into the boy's eager grip, then told him he could keep it, for the casket was all the pawn shop had accepted.

Thrilled by the tale, Ike had dashed home to show his father.

Listening to his son's account, Ike's father had been seized by the thought that the scarlet curiosity was so very ancient and of such a simple shape, perfume, colouring and texture, it might possibly be the tale that spawned the roots of all stories.

Days and nights dissolved into one as the great inventor made copious measurements and diagrams to decipher exactly what story the sphere could tell. According to his equations, he hoped to reduce the different meaning of each and every dead story that had ever been found, until only one common element remained: the key to all tales.

And what, Ike would ask, did he think the tale might be? To which his father would reassure him with one almighty claim.

'From this small seed will grow the mother and jewel of all stories!'

As he continued his experiments, however, Ike's father became obsessed with the hidden tale. With his judgement blinkered by excitement and his wisdom befuddled by his dreams, he soon confused other tales with the one that hypnotised his gaze.

Watching his father sweat so hard over his work, Ike began to worry that the tale would never reveal itself. He stood by the window and gazed wistfully across the sand spits and the barren shore.

'Somewhere,' he thought, 'the best story is waiting for me to find.'

Had he only turned his attention to the skies, he might have seen that not all tales drifted listlessly over the waters, for some were still being told.

*Contr'y to the evil slander put round by some folk, I took great heed of Pa's wise words and should never have tumbled into them waters. So what did I do wrong? Standin upon the very tip of that accursed cliff, looken down at the tall ships as they chases the breeze, I did listen to my old man very fucken carefully.*

*Pa says to me, 'Icarus, (I despises my dead mother for that name, though I never did know who she was), just steer a course midway between the seas and the heavens so the sun don't burn yer back and yer wings don't get weighty with water.'*

*'Swimmen and sunburn is fer fools alone!' I waxes, catchin his fine daddyeye. I sees Pa is looken pretty tearful when he straps the wings to my mighty shoulderarms. I grins at him. Everything is just fine and he kisses me on the cheek. Then, with enough courage to poke the eyes from an eagle, Pa raises his wings and steps forward into nothin at all. I feels a sharp tightenen in my balls and my belly and I yells, 'Daedy, (the occasion affords my lyrical licence), you sure is a mad bastard!' But I follows him gracefully into the air, like a tender fledglin, chasen the mother bird.*

*I feels mighty sure of myself.*

Days flew into weeks without any sighting of Ike and his father. Although nobody knew of the existence of the scarlet sphere, the boy had last been seen scuttling from the harbour to the workshop, clutching something round in his dirty handkerchief. Excited whispering could soon be heard across the harbour as rumours and speculation were spawned by the islanders.

Might it be a cannonball for a great ship that could sail many leagues under the surface of the water? Could it be a doorknob for a wardrobe that contained a magical land? Perhaps it was another mouthpiece for the flute found lying under the jetty that when played, drew the vermin from the cellars and even made the children dance a jig. No one knew for sure and when the door of the workshop did eventually swing open, both Ike and his father were met by an anxious crowd of story-mongers. Ike, who had cheered up now that the mystery had been solved, stood proudly beside his father, who held the sphere up for all to see.

'This,' he announced, 'is a magic bean!'

Everybody gasped.

'A bean that belongs to a lost set, each one a different colour.' A few mutters of disbelief welled up from the back of the crowd.

'These sprouts,' he boomed, ignoring the jibes and pointing at the leaves, 'are the beginnings of a great beanstalk that will touch the underbelly of the clouds and allow us all to climb up and see the castles in the sky!'

The islanders stared at the inventor, fearing madness had beset him.

'What proof does you have?' they asked, peering intently at the globe.

To the sparkling hush of the undertow as it scraped over the distant shoreline, Ike's father urged the islanders to recall the washed-up tale of the boy with the broken neck. Did they not remember how the fingers of the corpse were said to have been locked firmly around an axe? And his eyelids; how they failed to shut for more than an instant, without springing wide open to fix a dead gaze upon the clouds above. They might also recall that the body was said to have been wrapped in a shroud of supple green branches that had sprouted leaves and continued to

grow longer, even as their forebears had buried the body. The
tale, Ike's father proclaimed, was the oldest yarn ever plucked
from the shores of the island; the story that bred all others.

'Just look at the leaves that spring from the bean! It's ready to
grow again!'

That afternoon, the excited crowd witnessed the ceremonial
planting of the seed of the story. The honour was bestowed
upon young Ike, for it was to be his tale. With great pride, he
buried the bean under a tangle of thorn bushes that encroached
upon the workshop, as everybody thought the stalk would need
a little shelter from the trade winds.

Despite the chatter of excitement that flourished in the harbour, the beanstalk failed to reveal itself. Ike would rush outside
each morning, only to discover that nothing had changed overnight. He would glance up at the clouds and wonder how it was
possible for such a small story ever to reach such a gigantic
height.

'Tales can grow tall. Very tall indeed,' his father had said
when the bean was planted. Ike was certain that he had never
been wrong before.

Days sprouted into weeks and the numbers that ventured to
the workshop soon dwindled to nothing. Ike did not give up
hope, spending his time pacing the path outside the workshop.
His father could see how much the story meant to the boy and
began to dread the possibility that the tale would never push
through the earth.

The month exhausted its final day and the great inventor
shrugged, apologised to the islanders for his folly and admitted
failure. Word swiftly spread that the sphere was useless. The
interest that had taken root after its discovery soon withered
when the tides brought more tales for the islanders to chatter
about. The possibility that a story might ever be found alive
soon fell entirely from their thoughts.

*After leapen like a spring chicken from a nest of burnen coals, I did*
*plummet towards the seas. My balls shot into my mouth I did drop so*
*speedily. So with one God-fearen flap and a prayer to my dead mother,*

*I saved myself a swim. I must look like elegance itself right now, as I wheel upwards to join my old man, but not so high as to cinder my fine fucken feathers, no sir! Together, we soar along the flanks of the crusty land below, leavin behind its bloodchillen bull-man and bottomless labyrinth to rot in its own sorry history. From up here in the skies, the shepherd, the fisherman and the plough-pusher be no bigger than my baby toe-nail. From down there, I reckons we sure is looken like a couple of fine young gods. Especially me.*

*I keeps mighty close to Pa and I sees he is smilen and laughin. He shimmers close to my side and yells: 'Son, yer doing so well, I never expected to see yer get this far!' And I looks at my old man in confusion and replies 'What the fuck are yer talkin about? I'm so fine, I was born to fly!'*

*Now Pa, being older and weaker than my handsome self, soon starts laggin a touch. I shouts 'Daedy, you flap yer fucken wings and keep up!' (I uses my words harshly. My deviltongue always makes him real mad and determined.) Sure 'nuff, Pa makes for much huffin and panten 'til he races ahead as we soar on over the waters. I trusts dry land comes swiftly or I sure will be knackered.*

Ike could not bear to think that the bean he had been given, his very own story, had failed to come alive. Even the youngest child on the island now had her own tale. The lighthouse-keeper had found her wailing on the beach, her foot cut open on a shard of broken glass that appeared to be the heel of a fragile slipper. He felt very left out indeed and blamed his father for his unhappiness.

His father could not bear to watch Ike brooding any longer. No amount of apologies could rid him of the guilt he suffered for scuppering the boy's hopes. If Ike could not find a tale, he thought, then a story would have to come to him.

One morning, Ike awoke to discover a note from his father. It explained that he had taken his axe and set off for the far side of the island, where the tall trees on the cliff-edge were famous for snagging stories carried by the trade winds. The note finished with an assurance that Ike would receive a surprise come nightfall. Ike, however, had lost faith in his father's promises and left the workshop to scuttle over the sands and plunder the rock-pools. All day he searched, until long after the waters had been bleached silver by the glare of the moon. Once again, though, Ike returned home empty-handed and broken-hearted.

As he rounded the spit that led to the workshop, Ike's tearful eyes fell upon a sight ahead that instantly cast a sparkle of delight across his face. Beneath the night sky, towering high above the thorn bushes and surrounded by a cluster of white hemlock, stood a great tree. .

Giant boughs swayed in the moonlight, glittering with a flourish of leaves and a thousand and one scarlet spheres, just like the one that his father had planted.

'My beanstalk!' he cried. 'My story!'

Although it was not as tall as his father had promised, Ike dashed towards the tale, certain that it would not be long before it grew to its full height. He stood in awe under the dark canopy of branches, his arms stretched up to the skies. The moonlight sifted sharply between the leaves, casting thin white shards upon the boy and the surrounding earth.

Ike took a step back to see if the tip of the tree was still growing. As he did so, his heel caught on a root that sent him sprawling to the ground. He lay where he fell, gazing at the sea of stars above him until his head stopped spinning and the ache in his ribs subsided.

'Are you hurt?'

The soft voice came from behind him. Ike turned his head to see a tall figure in the shadows under the tree, silhouetted by the waning moon.

'Who are you?' he asked, sliding back from the visitor. Ike had not expected anyone else to find his story. She gave no reply, laughing instead as he tried to stand.

She sidled back to the foot of the tree. Resting her back against its trunk, she pressed her head to the smoky bark and smiled. A cold breeze snaked through the branches. The shadows beneath the tree shimmered gently in the moonlight, revealing to the boy a brief glimpse of her nakedness.

'I saw you fall,' she said, craning her neck to study the rustling canopy of leaves. 'Once is enough. I'll make sure you don't fall again.'

Then, just as Ike had pulled himself to his feet, a serpent lowered its head from the foliage, uncoiling a lithe body from a hidden branch. Ike's jaw dropped in horror. He tried to cry out but his lungs were smothered by fear. The creature dropped lower to stroke her hair with its sizzling tongue. She remained still for a moment with her eyes tightly shut, flinching slightly as the serpent slid down her neck to leave a glistening trail across her flesh.

'Stop it!' yelled Ike. The serpent paused, flicked its tongue across her skin and curved its head up to face the boy. Ike swallowed hard. Beads of oil dripped from its scarlet scales as the serpent rose higher, its tail still entwined in the overhanging branches. It blinked once and began to stretch towards the boy.

'Not him!' she cried, slipping away from the serpent and darting to Ike's side. She ran both hands around his waist to protect him. 'Just me! Won't that do?'

Ike threw his arms out and clung to her body as the serpent reached further to touch the boy's nose with its oily snout.

'Oh Father, help me!' screamed Ike, charging the skies with his plea.

Plodding slowly home from his fruitless quest, Ike's father froze when he heard the cry. He could not mistake the voice, nor the fear in its urgent tones and he was tearing towards its source before the echo had even subsided.

To the soft whispers of sliding flesh, the serpent began to coil around the couple, gently restricting all movement and drawing them closer together. They were squeezed so tightly that Ike saw nothing but his reflection in her frightened eyes.

Slowly, the serpent slithered up from between his legs, poked its diamond head between their pressed faces and glared at Ike. It caught the boy in its gaze, fixing him so sharply that Ike began to tingle under its spell. The snake flicked its marble eyes at a rosy globe hanging from a branch above. The early morning breeze began to swirl around the tree, blowing gentle whispers into the boy's ear.

'Take it, my sweet.'

The serpent loosened its grip on Ike's arm. Still the boy remained caught in its wicked gaze, oblivious to the thunder of footfalls drawing closer with every second and blind to the glint of his father's brandished axe.

'Just a bite . . .'

Ike raised his free hand to cup the fruit and plucked it from the branch. He pressed its flesh to his lips only a moment before the breeze turned to a bellowing scream.

His father lunged between the couple, knocking the woman to the ground and sending Ike spinning sideways. Before the boy could even draw breath, his father had grabbed the serpent with his free hand, driving the creature hard against the tree. The axe arced gracefully through the air. Ike's father, screaming with all the venom he could muster, drove the blade so forcefully home that it severed the snake's head and, as if the two were inseparable, sliced clean through the trunk of the tree. He dropped the twitching body of the serpent and staggered back as the tree fell among the thorns. A piercing shriek rent the air behind him. He turned to see the woman fall to the earth, as if she too had met with a blow from an axe. Ike rushed to her side to help, but scrambled back when she clawed madly at his feet. She thrashed and snarled, writhing upon the ground and driving the earth into the air to form a dusty shroud against the morning light. The dark veil only lifted when she lay still; trapped against the fallen tree, caught on the thorns of the bushes.

The boy staggered forward, his shadow falling over her body. In that black abyss of a moment, her skin had become gnarled as oak and her bluebell eyes had withered in their sockets.

Ike's father, overwhelmed by the outcome of his action, dropped the axe and covered his eyes in disbelief. He dragged his fingers from his face and saw the rotten fruit lying beside the body of the serpent. He could not bare to turn and face her corpse, for he realised that with just one blow of his axe, he had felled the entire story. He sensed dreadful words spill to his tongue, words that were not his own, for they were an echo of what had yet to come.

'The horror! The horror!' he cried, beholding the weeds of the paradise garden.

Ike thrust his face deep against his father's chest, weeping with grief and hiding his eyes from the ruined world around. His father could not find the strength to contain his son's distress, for his own eyes were turned to the rumbling skies above the ocean. A swirl of bruising clouds had begun to twist together, spiralling upwards from the horizon to point troubled fingers towards the island.

'This tree,' his father whispered, through the drone of the coiling winds, 'really was the story that sustained all living tales.'

*Merciful beggarbones, what is this that I sees! The skies ahead is stirren up mighty trouble and Pa is soarin right into its eye. Great coal-black clouds, thick as prison walls, are loomin up and twisten around before us. Even the sun that warms our backs is swamped in a bellychokin fog that very fucken quickly swallows Pa whole. I tries a nimble about-turn but Lordy, that storm gives me such a whippen. I fluster and flaps my bastard strong wings for balance but the winds starts to draggen me inside its belly. I thinks to myself, this is it Icarus son!*

*My sorry shadow gets to growen bigger on the frothin waters below. I shouts 'No. No. NO!' but the cloudwool fills my fine mouth and I gags on a terrible stench. I smells death. Now I knows that a storm tastes fresh, so I opens my eyes and sweet Lord, what did I see! Stories, fucken stories by the muleload, all bleeden and cut as they flail in the winds. They gets dragged up through the storm. I hears their bones crashen against the railings of the pearly gates above. I hears 'em hollerin, 'This is not what should happen!' I sees 'em begin to wither before their time is due. I listens to their cries on the lightnin strikes and I sees their tears lash the earth.*

*Who does this to us?*

*There be mighty hell to pay when I catches up with 'em!*

*This stormrage starts to liften me towards the sun. I feels flames lickin the flesh on my back but I refuses to go the way of my brothers and sisters. Not just yet. Let me be the one to sort out our sorry tale! I give*

*the winds one last heave, kickin my legs and slappen the wingflames dry
as I do. And I am puked out.*
  *I fall. I thrash about. I hit the furious waters.*
  *I am extinguished.*

Too frightened to remain in the open to bury the dead story,
Ike's father urged the boy across the spit towards the safety of
the harbour port. They tumbled around abandoned cottages; the
clatter of swinging shutters indicating that the occupants had
fled for their lives on sighting the furious cloud swirls. They
hurtled into the square, only to be engulfed by the panicking
townsfolk. Ike had to cling to his father's hand to stop himself
from being dragged under the stampede of feet. Everybody then
clamoured to gain entry to the cellar of the boathouse, for it was
built to withstand the most brutal tempests.

The maddened winds spluttered and roared with such force
that the weathercock perched on the top of the lighthouse buckled on its copper pivot. The frosty north swapped places with
the lush warmth of the south while bleak east and prosperous
west became one and the same. Utter confusion prevailed.

*Oh Lord, my bonyhard body has taken a terrible beatin. I holds my
breath as this infernal current pulls me down and starts to chewin me in
its toothless mouth. I tumbles through the battered shells of shipwrecks,
my throat fills with stinken fishbones and great sharks razor my legs.
Just as my lungs are yellin for air, I feels the sharp cut of shingle and I
knows I have been spat on to dry land. I raises my head from the surf. It
is very fucken dark here. Across the spits I sees a harbour where fishen
boats lie smashed against a jetty. I hurt so bad that I crawls from the
waters like a dyin lizard. Raisen onto my bleeding legflanks, I screams
my distress into the winds. Somebody will feel my sting. I will stay
alive to avenge my brothers and sisters. Even if it kills me!*

The very foundations of the boatyard were beginning to groan
as the winds bore down upon the port and howled at the bolted
door. As the islanders sat huddled, frightened and shivering in
the furthest corner of the basement, word began to spread of the

sighting of what was either a drowning mariner or a great sea bird. Those who had actually been drawn to the shoreline by the sound of the terrible snarling and roaring, all verified witnessing the same sight, though they had swiftly taken to their heels in fright. What was certain was that the beast who had dragged itself from the surf by its bruised haunches, bore two smouldering wings upon its back.

*I feels weak now, lyen flat out on the sand. My poor flesh is charred and my brittleburny bones are poken from my body. I am very fucken determined to get some retribution! Now I hears voices hollerin my name. Calm down brothers and sisters! I'll sees to it. I feels like I need to scream into that sorry harbour and tear great clods of flesh from the first scab that crosses my path. I got to rest though. I needs to hide out to get strong before I takes revenge.*

*I starts to scrapen along the shoreline like a crab come back from the seadead. I soon tires of crawlin so ghostyslow and I tries to launch into the air. I fails. Over and over I fails. I collapses into the water, crushen the tattered wingframes so bad that my feathers starts to rippen away and tossin in the surf behind. Lord, I can't get off my fucken back now! I sees yer up there and I'm ashamed. Turn around. Hide yer eyes! The undertow spins me onto my bellyflab and I swallows so much water that I sick up on my face. I nearly fucken chokes on my bitterness, bringen tears to my sorry eyes. When I wipes 'em, I sees a smokestack, peekin above the dunes. I gets to crawlen nearer and I sees a wooden hut. That'll do.*

The cowering islanders soon realised that many of their flock were missing. At least a dozen were reported to have been cut down dead by the fist of the storm. Great wails of widow-grief sung out in broken unison. Ike and his father, knowing the cause of the upheaval, stared helplessly at each other.

'I never wanted a story like this,' Ike whimpered, to which the howls and sobs that filled the cellar suddenly ceased. Ike looked around. Every face was upon him.

'Did you say your story?' the lighthouse-keeper demanded.

A splinter of lightning crackled down the chimneypot, betraying the guilt in the eyes of the boy and his father.

'What have you done!' they all cried, pulling themselves to their feet and bearing down upon the couple, who, with no other choice, blurted out their misadventure.

'Get out and die!' screamed the crowd, lashing out at the pair and hurling flintstones upon them as they scrambled to make their escape.

The storm unleashed a barrage of thunder to welcome the couple into its open lair. Ike's father forced the rusty key and locked the cellar door. The barrage of fists that hammered from within told him it would not be long before the mob broke free.

'We must fly from here!' he yelled, taking Ike's hand and pulling him across the square. Braving the onslaught that raged above, the couple darted from door to door, heading back to the workshop to build a means of escaping the stricken island.

*With yer fiery crack o'lightnin spit showen me the way, my brothers and sisters, I heaves myself to the path. Then, my eyes catches my wits and mercy me! I sees a tree, lyin besides a lifeless gardenserpent. Oh my! A fallen bride too. Now I knows why I was sucked from the air. Don't you worry my sister! We'll have our day once more! I pulls myself into the thorn bushes and I am torn so bad, my broken wings rip clean from my shoulderarms. I have to ditch 'em. I can't fly without rest. These apples sure taste good in the pit of my guts. I sits and waits. The Devil is twisten and writhin in my balls and my belly. I am really very mighty fucken angry!*

They staggered onto the beach. The lungs of the storm were inexhaustible and its fierce breath inescapable. Ahead of Ike and his father, beyond the shore and the sandspits, stood the workshop. Despite being so close to safety, they both came to a sudden halt when they saw what lay in their path. Before them, along the length of the shoreline, lay a trail of cindered feathers. Ike snatched one from the sands and turned to show his father, who had already grabbed as many as he could.

'A gift from the skies!' his father yelled under the winds. Ike

pulled the remnants of his shirt from his shoulders and began to
snatch the soggy down from the sands. As they braved on
towards the workshop, Ike failed to see an obstacle that lay
across the path. He tumbled to the ground, his head grazing
upon a splintered wooden frame that scraped the skin from his
cheek and made his father cry out in joy.

*My fine feathers! My busted wingframes too! Thieves! Fucken vul-
tures! I sees 'em comin my way and my bones are rattlen-ready to dish
out a thrashin. What shall I do my brothers and sisters? Are these the
fuckers that felled the provider of stories? Shall I leap from the bushes,
a'roarin and splutteren. Maybe rip their sorry heads from their necks?
What are yer thinken Pa? Yer wailin songs are sweepen low across the
waters and it pains my head. What a sorry opera it is yer singen. Can't
yer quit? I got to finish my story, just tell me what to do!*

Ike slammed the door shut against the storm. The winds could
no longer touch them and he sank to the floor in exhausted
thanks. Though his hands trembled, his father quickly heated
the remaining whale oil and splashed the sticky fluid across the
length of the frames. The storm had still to pass and Ike wondered whether it would ever leave them alone.

'I never dreamed it would come to this,' he croaked.

'If we fly,' Ike's father replied, lost in his work, 'we shall have
no need to dream.'

By the ebb of a dwindling candle, the couple weaved their
means of escape. His father instructed Ike to glue the longest,
sturdiest feathers at the base of each frame, lining the down in
diminishing length across the span.

They crafted first one pair of wings, then another, cobbled
together from the mermaid's armour and strengthened with a
length of whalebone. Just as they were finishing their work,
binding their looped belt straps to the base of each frame, a huge
thud crashed above them. They looked up. The roof remained
intact. The rafters still held strong and the light from the candle
invaded every dark shadow behind the wooden beams. It was
just the winds, thought Ike.

*I am perched like a hawk; my head squeezed between my tucked-up knees, my butt sticken out behind my legs and my fingers like talons: sharpened, stretched and ready. I had been thinken to myself, Icarus son, you really not in a position worthy of yer status, crouched down there in the muleshit and the prickthorns. Yer might have been a king had you flown to the end of yer tale. Get yerself a throne, quick fucken sharp. So I clambers on to their sorry roof, closer to my dead family of stories. Quit speaken all at once my brothers! One by one sisters, you'se all starten to confuse me with yer chatterin. I'll sees to them myself, I don't need you'se urgen me to speak in yer taletongues. Get out of me please, or I'll huff and puff and burn the hairs from my chinny-chin chin!*

*Quit putten wordystories in my fine mouth!!!!*
*I am lost fer words.*

'Now pay attention to every word I say,' his father began. As he instructed the boy in the rudiments of flight, his throat tightened, for he realised that he was exploring a science he had never dreamed of pursuing. Ike, however, was not listening. He was now entirely trapped within a story that he had never heard before and could do nothing to escape from.

*I sees ya! I sees ya! Guidin that poor waif from the door. It's so very fucken difficult movin against the lash of the storm with wings on yer back, don't yer think? But wait! I sees a shaft of sunlight splitten the skies. Maybe the heavens open so the angels too, can see yer folly. Are yer watchen dear Pa! Do yer rage? Does Mother weep? Fret no more. I should be so very fucken sorry if yer failed to see how I put an end to this chapter. Yer'd be so proud of me.*

Edging nearer to the cliff-edge, Ike felt the sunlight hit his naked back. The storm was passing and the curve of a pale rainbow began to forge across the waters. His father smiled, believing it to be a fine omen for their journey. The ocean, calmer now, drew nearer and extended away to meet the bloody tints of a sun-scorched horizon. As they pushed forward, their wings draped behind them and bounced over grassy ruts, wrenching the first of the feathers from their makeshift frames.

*Don't stop now, go straight over! What do they look like, Pa? Nobody can match yer craft and skill. I wants to sees 'em launch out, but my bones are achin so bad I feels my good self faden away. I am hurtin so very fucken much my brothers and sisters! I can see you'se all peeren over the edge of the partin clouds. Just one jump ahead and they'll fly into yer hands. But what's this? Oh shame, an audience come to watch. And look! They'se mighty angry, bayen for the blood of the birdmen. Go on. Jump! Make a slice o'history for me!*

The urge to leap was irresistible, yet altogether petrifying. The lynch mob charging towards the couple, armed with pitchforks and flaming torches, put to flight all thoughts of remaining upon land.

Ike braced himself. He spread his wings out wide; the soot-laden feathers rustling in the breeze. A solitary lapwing circled ahead, fixing a mocking gaze upon them as it rode the skies. Ike watched the bird. It soared down, plummeting below his line of vision to vanish behind the gorse that marked the boundary between the earth and the heavens. He leaned forward to follow its line of flight and saw nothing but the still waters.

'Burn the beggars! Toss them on to the rocks!'

The roar of the marauding crowd was so near they could feel the heat of the torch flames on their backs. Ike's father kissed the boy fully on the cheek, savouring the moment before his feet took him into the air. Their bodies had never felt heavier as they gave themselves over to the hideous abyss. But they were compelled to jump as the mob reached out to grab them, and they flew. They soared!

*Oh Pa! Oh heavens! They fucken fly. This isn't supposed to happen. I feels a dizzy sickness risin in my balls and my belly. This perch starts to shimmer in front of my eyes. Pa! Can't yer take me now? What am I to do, my brothers and sisters, have I failed yer all? Are yer hidin yer heads in shame behind the angels? Does they comfort yer? What's it like*

*up there? I want to be there! Pa! Pa! Pa! I am cryin so very fucken
loud. That's it! I feels yer gentle hand wrap around my neck. Let me
drop! Yes. Up! Further! Higher! Oh Pa! Oh Mother, my brothers and
sisters. I'm so very fucken glad to be with yer all.*

The islanders lined the cliff edge and gazed on, devastated by the
escape of their quarry, their torches cast into the waters. The
first to turn back were met with a dreadful sight. Hanging from
the spur of the workshop roof, by a noose of entwined feathers,
swung the charred body of the fallen angel spotted when the
storm had begun to roar. The yellow bones of his shoulder-
blades stuck out from his skin, forcing his arms out wide to grab
the air.

Nobody buried the deceased seraph for weeks, believing that
the haunting ebb of his eyes withheld another tale, not yet completed. If he were to be put to rest before his frightened face
drew peaceful, they thought, then his grieving ghost might torment them for years to come.

The ocean shimmered brightly below father and son. The
island had long since receded to a meaningless dot, leaving them
with just the sun on their backs, the limitless skies and their own
dark shadows that skipped across the surface of the waters. Ike
trailed his father by some length, but the vast emptiness around
them secured him in the faith that they would always be
together, no matter how far apart they became.

Lifting himself effortlessly towards the aching sun, in his
eagerness to explore the wonder of flight, Ike felt himself to be
so light as to be almost weightless. Then he sensed the acrid tang
of whale oil, as the first stray feathers fluttered across his horrified gaze to tumble into the surf below.

Even as the waters swallowed his flailing body, the boy called
out to his father, who, according to the tale, could do nothing to
save his wayward son. Instead, the inventor struck onwards,
forcing himself not to look below to see the charred flecks of
down as they drifted upon the surface of the ocean. Eventually,
they might wash ashore; to begin life again, as another dead
story.

## A Kind of Poetry

The first empties his pockets
and then builds towers
of the different denominations
to stand by his place at table
while he chews.

The next daydreams
of the death of an imagined relative,
a solicitor's letter the spell
which will change his life.

The third throws most of what he has
at women and flighty horses.

The fourth retains in his nostrils briefly
the faint, print smell
of new notes out of the machine.

Number five never fails to consult
the experts and the stargazers
before attempting
the timidest transaction.

While six, poor six, who must beg for it,
knows just which pitch is lucky,
and which not.

## *Marvin Gaye*

He added the final 'e'
to counteract the imputation of homosexuality.
His father was plain Revd Gay, his son Marvin III.

He slept with his first hooker
in the army, coming off saltpetre.
He thought there was another word for 'virgin' that
                                        wasn't 'eunuch'.

Including duets, he had fifty-five chart entries.
His life followed the rhythm of albums and tours.
He had a 'couple of periods of longevity with a woman'.

He preached sex to the cream suits,
the halter tops and the drug-induced personality dis-
                                        orders.
When his hair receded, he grew a woolly hat and beard.

Success was the mother of eccentricity and withdrawal.
In Ostend he felt the eyes of the Belgians on him,
in Topanga someone cut the throats of his two Great
                                        Danes.

At 44, back in his parents' house,
any one of a number of Marvins might come downstairs.
A dog collar shot a purple dressing-gown, twice.

# Moment of Downfall

I was caught off guard by the invitation to the class reunion. Fifteen years on. That was the first shock. I had swiftly torn up the invites to the fifth and tenth anniversaries without a second thought so why was this one different? Well, I'm getting older, that's part of it. I've noticed lately how charmed I am to discover that I have known what is obsolete. You know the sort of thing – the brand names of sweets long since cleared off the shelves, forgotten street games, the characters in teenage comics. It's like coming into an unexpected inheritance. But it wasn't nostalgia that made me pause before destroying this little missive from the past. It was the name at the bottom. It was signed Elizabeth Norton (Page). The double surname threw me at first. Like a disguise, it sat there taunting me. Guess who this is, it seemed to say. A roll of drums. Yes folks, the person you've been waiting for, Li-iz . . . Page!

Funny, isn't it, the power of names. They lodge with you long after their owners have disappeared. I can still remember the roll call from High Babies – see how that dates me – the list of girls who sang seconds in the school choir, the rota of supervisors at my first job. Just recently I came across a piece of paper among my things with the names of seventy people on it. I wondered for a moment why they were all gathered together like this (had I been making an inventory of my friends?) until I realised that this was the guest list for my wedding, the one that didn't happen. I chickened out at the last minute. But that's another story. Seeing our names there, Tony's and mine – this must have been when I was trying to sort out numbers for the hotel – comforted me, strangely. It spoke of a full life with a well-defined place for me at the centre of it. I read through the list aloud; it was like repeating a mantra, the low hum of the once

familiar. It reminded me of Mrs Bergin's kindergarten. A basement room with small-paned windows and pocked wooden
floorboards, small feet drumming on the planks and the glorious
discord of tables sung out by forty four-year-olds. We
seemed to have learned everything by chanting. Dick can run,
Mary can run, Spot can run. All eyes on the board, all together
now.

Of course, I know that part of my preoccupation with other
people's names is the anticipation of my own being celebrated. I
imagine, sometimes, that I am famous and a TV documentary
team is going through memorabilia seeking *my* name out from
the crowd, the camera scrolling down through lists of
unknowns or panning out across a group photograph before
settling finally on me. There I am, in grainy close-up, smiling
hopefully, giving no clue to the germ of greatness within. The
fantasy only goes this far, sadly. I have yet to decide how to
make a name for myself.

There was a time when my name had a magical power. When
I was a child I used it to hypnotise myself. I would sit in front of
the mirror in my room and call my name aloud several times,
rocking back and forth until I was no longer inside myself but
floating in some high corner of the room, watching myself far
below. It was a solitary pleasure, I must admit. I was always
afraid that I would crash down before I could smuggle myself
back inside again or that my mother or someone else would
come in, interrupting the process and leaving me dangling forever in mid-air. It was always a relief to be safely snug within
again but the knowledge that I had the password with which
I could spirit myself away at any time was both fearful and
exciting.

But where were we? Liz Page. Liz Page was a rangy, attractive
girl with the sort of looks which even then – we're talking
thirteen here – would bloom spectacularly but would age badly.
Oh, the dark eyes would survive, but wouldn't her straight nose
sharpen too much when she was older and her thin face become
horsey-looking? That was what my mother would say. She

meant well, of course, or rather, she meant well for me. She recognised the curious mixture of envy and disdain I felt for Liz Page, realising, I am sure, my secret and shameful craving to be liked by a girl I did not care for, and for whom my mother did not care out of loyalty to me.

Why was Liz Page so popular? (I feel I have to use both her names; they sit together as a unit. Liz, alone, would seem bereft, powerless.) Well, I suppose, she was good-looking, she was thin, she had a place on the hockey team – these things were important then. She had the knack of always being the centre of attention. The others seemed to gravitate towards her. I never saw her walking on the corridor alone; she was always with a gang that strode along four abreast forcing girls like me to hug the wall. On the tennis courts or in the classroom if there was a huddle of girls together, it was always around Liz Page. She was tall for her age. She had the coveted job of opening the sash windows and in school photographs she was always in the dead centre of the back row, the anchor around which the tableau was built. She misbehaved, but in a sly way – lots of face-pulling and note-passing – and she rarely got caught. In this way she neatly saved herself from being considered a goody-goody, not only by us, but by teachers too. They suspected consistent good behaviour as much as we did. They liked girls with spirit, they said, and Liz Page's capacity to bluff her way through questions (she skimped on homework) never failed to disarm them. She had, my mother asserted in her defence, a good manner. That was because she always had a bright hello for my mother on the street while I shuffled past *her* mother, resentful and defiantly shy.

Perhaps I was the enemy for Liz Page in the same way as she was for me. She must have distrusted my fat glumness and sensed the secret spite in my heart. My dogged brand of book-ishness might well have daunted her but it seemed to me then – and still does now – a poor substitute for her coltish grace, her long-limbed ease, her shallow but endearing charm. The truth is there have always been Liz Pages for me. They follow me, surround me. I look for them. Whereas she has doubtless shrugged me off; she would probably have to be prompted to remember my name.

I was curious, of course, about the reunion I wouldn't go to. I wondered what they would look like. All I could imagine were their little girl faces superimposed on women's bodies. They would get dressed up (their sense of competition would not have deserted them) but they wouldn't overdo it. The rules of teenage mating would still apply. You *never* wore your best. And now, as then, those who came too hopefully in clothes that advertised their newness would be silently despised. The evening's events would go something like this. First, there would be Mass in the oratory, then tea and sandwiches in the convent, where we would be expected to mingle with the few aged nuns who still remain and still remember us. There would be some polite oohing and aahing as we rediscovered one another. The sense of occasion would not allow us to descend into girlish shrieking (that would come later). Then Sister Xavier, still living, I believe, would clap her hands peremptorily and call for a short silence for those who could not be with us – surely death has claimed its youthful percentage? I toyed with the notion that my absence might be counted as a death of sorts. I imagined what they might say. Poor Della, that's what they would say, which is probably what they'd say about me anyway, dead or alive. Then we would be led through The Nuns' Corridor (the geography of the place, its names, they haunt me too) to the assembly hall. Liz Page would deliver a suitably chummy speech with just the right amount of sentiment so that we could stand surrounded by the props of our youth – the creaky stage, the battered piano, the vaulting horse – and sink into a brief, dreamy, manufactured sadness. And later, of course, there would be drinks in a pub, a meal, and the girls would let their hair down. At some stage in the night, late, probably just before she was about to leave, Liz Page would turn to me and with a jubilant insincerity would enquire: Well, Della, how's life been treating you?

That would be my moment, wouldn't it? Where would I

start? The moment of downfall is always good. The year is 1970.
We are in our first year of secondary school. It is early summer.
High blue skies and drowsy afternoons, a time when the world
seems to offer the gift of endless days. There is an air of levity
about – these days have forgotten the gravity of winter and the
solemn start to the school year. The nuns, overheated in their
dark habits, are red-faced and slightly comical. The lay teachers
– Mr Crawford for Latin, Miss Busby for French – resort to
jokiness or snap their books shut with ten minutes to go and
send us home early. In case she doesn't remember, I will remind
Liz Page that this was the year Sister Baptist was sent to the
missions and Mr Crawford taught her to drive on the playground. He had a low-powered motorbike which he used to ply
his trade between us and the boys' college three miles away. He
travelled, goggled and helmeted and swaddled in waterproofs.
A nervous Sister Baptist sat astride the machine – we thought
she might ride side-saddle – and chugged her way across the
forecourt of the school with Mr Crawford taking up the rear on
foot. We could hear the drone of the engine from our classroom
and during break-time we would watch the lessons mirthfully
from the upper windows. Sister Baptist, her veil fluttering under
a red globe and wearing Mr Crawford's outsized anorak, man-
fully revved at the controls and struck down on the kick pedal
with a polite foot. The machine would suddenly judder into life,
shooting forward like a sprinter from the blocks only to stall
moments later and come to a grinding standstill. Mr Crawford,
a big-boned, solid man, would mime the actions for her repeatedly, crouched ape-like, legs apart and knees bent, one foot
pawing the air, his thick fingers clenching and opening in dem-
onstration. There was much mounting and dismounting, which
we found hilarious, and once or twice she rode pillion, her hands
lightly clasping his burly waist as he did nifty figures-of-eight
across the tar. Liz Page will certainly remember this. She was the
one who led the raucous band of spectators.

The round of petty thieving started around that time. They
were trinkety things at first – hair slides, combs, a bracelet. Then
Esther Bailey's watch was taken during gym, followed quickly

by Denise Harding's fountain pen; within a week, Sheila Downey's purse was gone, Babs Riordan's hockey stick and Mary Ferry's ballet shoes had disappeared. The final straw was when someone – 'someone' was a character that would, in time, gain resonance for all of us – someone stole Cathy Butler's locket from her shoe cage. She had buried it in one of her runners during play rehearsal and when she came back it was gone. The locket belonged to Cathy's mother who had died when she was a baby and this was her only memento. How melodramatic it all sounds, but true, nevertheless. A tear-streaked Cathy and the ghost of her long-dead mother (the story was she died having Cathy) hovered magnificently in our midst. Something, Sister Xavier declared, would have to be done. We were, she went on, in the presence of a cruel and heartless thief.

I remember how excited this made me feel as if we were on the verge of a great adult discovery.

'Until the thief (enunciated with glamorous emphasis) owns up, all of you are under suspicion.'

Lessons were suspended. We were all to be punished, we were told, until the guilty one confessed. At first it did not seem like punishment. In fact, we couldn't believe our luck. For once it was perfectly acceptable to stare off into the blue mid-distance, or lapse into a lazy reverie unchecked. But, after a few hours, the enforced idleness made us twitchy. We sat in the classroom while Sister Xavier paced up and down between the rows, her large, age-spotted hands toying with the hems of her capacious sleeves. Sun streamed through the windows; from below we could hear the lazy pock of tennis balls and the desultory cries of 'love', 'love 15.' This, particularly, reinforced our sense of being stranded in the middle of our own drama; as in the midst of grief, life around us continued on as normal. The bell rang out to mark the change of classes, followed by the clattery hubbub of droves of girls in transit on the echoing corridors. For five minutes we relished the institutional clamour outside our door, then the bell would go again, doors would slam, and an eerie silence would descend.

I have to admit that there were parts of it I enjoyed. Our crime

– at that stage it belonged to all of us – made us gleam with danger. 'Are you in 1A?' girls would ask, rushing up, girls who would normally have ignored me. Or they would camp outside our door ready to pounce on any fresh news. Even Sarah Kinnell, a fifth year who was tipped to be the next head girl (alas, she never made it; she got pregnant that summer) took me aside on the corridor and whispered: 'Is it true that Laura Daly did it?' So this, I thought, is what it's like to be popular, to be in demand. It was like walking among magnets; I had to *do* nothing. I knew, of course, that it was the notoriety attached to the thieving that mesmerised them and made them envious, and that once the thief confessed *she* would replace me in the hypnotic glare of their attention. But while it lasted I savoured it.

Liz Page thought the whole thing was a hoot. That was one of her expressions. She didn't take it seriously, or at least, not in the way I did.

'You'd want to be nuts to steal things from around here. Shops would be much better,' she said as we filed out of class after our second day of confinement. 'Anyway, who on earth would want Mary Ferry's stinky ballet shoes?'

She hadn't been listening to a word Sister Xavier had said, I thought crossly. It wasn't the things themselves the thief was after. What kleptomaniacs crave is attention; they desperately want to be noticed.

On the third day I tried to get out of it. I told my mother I had a headache, which was true, but it was only the same thudding dread that accompanied most of my mornings before school.

'What's this in aid of?' she asked suspiciously as she pinned up her hair. I'd left it too late; she was ready to go to work. She used to dress on the run. I'd often seen her in her stockinged feet in front of the mirror in the kitchen wriggling into a skirt or pulling a sweater on while we had our breakfast. Similarly when she came in from work she would tear off her tights as if she were being let out of harness, or extricate her bra down the sleeves of her dress muttering 'God, this thing is killing me!' My mother had very few private moments.

'Well?' she asked.

I was already ashamed of this feeble attempt. My mother demanded physical evidence – a roaring temperature or a raw throat – before she'd keep me out of school. Any sickness threatened to topple the fragile routine of the household. She packed me off with two aspirins (in case it got worse later on) knowing that I wouldn't take them. I had difficulty swallowing tablets; they always ended up as gritty meal in my mouth. And I wouldn't admit at school that I needed a spoonful of jam to help the medicine go down.

'Wait till you grow up,' she said, 'then you'll know what headaches are.'

It was a scorching day. The room smelt of fresh sweat and stale fear. We had the jaded air of refugees or survivors of a shipwreck, nerves jangling but dull-eyed from the tedium of the flat, open sea. We had long since given up hope of catching sight of land. It was as if this was what our life had always been. The school sports were on that day. From the playing fields we could hear the rowdy baying of those let loose. Their freedom taunted us cooped up in our classroom. The school was deserted, the corridors tinged with the melancholy ache of an unpeopled public place. When we were let out to go to the toilet – always in twos – the emptiness forced us to whisper as if we were somewhere sacred and forbidden.

At noon Sister Xavier ordered Liz Page to open the windows as far as they would go – Susan Gilbert had fallen asleep at her desk and Frances Cahill was feeling faint and had to sit with her head between her knees. The waft of a breeze, the buzzing of summer, the distant roar of the crowd infused us with a new alertness.

Sister Xavier who had been sitting on the podium reading her office, her lips moving silently in prayer, rose and went to the open windows.

'There is,' she said finally, addressing the cloudless sky as if she were talking to God out there, 'someone among us who desperately needs help.' She paused, then turned around scanning our faces, until her gaze fell on me.

'Someone who does not feel loved.'

The word sent a titter of embarrassed glee through the room. I felt my cheeks colour. Yes, I thought fiercely, there is.

'Someone whom we overlook, perhaps, someone whom we do not notice,' she crooned softly. I remembered when my mother used to talk to me like this.

'Someone who isn't top of the class or captain of the team, whose gifts and talents we have failed to recognise . . .'

Yes, I thought, she knows, she understands.

'Someone who is calling out . . .'

I could feel my lip quiver and incriminating tears well in my eyes. If I didn't get out soon I would end up crying – in front of the whole class. I couldn't bear it; I had to stop her before it was too late. I rose to my feet.

'Yes, Della?'

I looked around me. For one intoxicating moment I felt the rapt stillness of their full attention. I saw in their faces, shock, awe, a grudging respect. I was going to save them all, and one in particular. I could feel them willing me to speak. Go on, they urged silently, go on, do it.

'Sister, I . . . ,' I faltered even then, 'I have something to confess.'

I have long ago worked out that it must have been Liz Page. I mean, it's obvious, isn't it? Who among us sought out attention more than she, always in a crowd, the teachers' pet, the classroom hero. She was bound to get drunk on all that popularity and it must have made her greedy for more. Think how it would have ruined her if she had been unmasked as a thief; some of her friends would never have got over it. Her mother would have been devastated. My mother used to say darkly that all was not well in the Page household. Liz, she would say, Liz has her problems too. How right she was.

'You, of all people, Della,' Sister Xavier said after she had dismissed the class. 'And your poor mother, it'll break her heart. First your father, and now this . . .'

My father had died the summer before. A drowning accident. A rip tide. My mother and I watched from the beach as he went down. We heard him call out but there was nothing we could do. He had ignored the red flag. It took them days to find the body. It had been swept out to sea. My mother and I went to the beach every day. She would scan the horizon as if somehow he might still be out there waving to us. She wouldn't let them remove his heap of clothes from the shoreline. As long as they were there, she felt he might come back for them. Anyway, she said to me, that's all we have of him now . . .

'And what did you do with Cathy Butler's locket?' Sister Xavier asked.

'I threw it away.'

That was when I had to *start* lying.

'But why, Della, why?'

I shrugged. What could I say?

She looked at me sorrowfully and shook her head.

'Poor Della,' she said. 'Poor Della.'

It was the making of me, really, you could say. The reputation of petty thievery dogged me long after the brief glory of confessing had faded away. And long-term notoriety, I found, was less spectacular. The others were wary of me; they shied away from talking to me. Nothing new in that except that it was accompanied now by a new watchfulness. They circled around me although it was they who were afraid that I might swoop, not the other way round. And *that* had its own power. Not unlike being able to hypnotise myself, a knack I subsequently lost. (I found my name could no longer render me light and invisible; it had become a heavy, grounded thing.) The only other difference was that they hid things from me, their bright, glittery things that is, as if I were a magpie unable to resist the dazzle.

I have Sharon to blame for the marriage that didn't happen.

Sharon at the hairdressers. I never knew her surname. They don't tell you the stylists' second names; that way it seems like they're friends of yours. Chatty Sharon cut my hair on the morning of the wedding.

'This lady's getting married today,' she announced to the salon, beaming. Several red-faced women trapped under the driers nodded stiffly and smiled.

'A white wedding,' she said, 'isn't that lovely!'

I sat in front of the mirror, dripping. I always feel at my plainest at this point. Slicked down hair and a splotchy face from the wash, or is it the lights in these places?

'I think it's wonderful,' Sharon confided, 'that people get married, I mean. Biggest day of your life, my mother says, a girl never forgets her wedding day. It's her day, really, isn't it, the bride's . . . ?'

She started to snip at the tails round my ears.

'I don't believe people should live together beforehand. I'm not a prude, mind you, but it's so much more romantic, I think, making your vows at the altar.'

I tried to tune out of the chatter. I wondered if it would be very rude to ask for a magazine.

'It makes it more real, doesn't it, going public like that. Standing up in front of all those people and saying "I do".'

I felt a sudden shiver.

'I mean to say it's easy to live in sin because nothing is expected of you. Nobody's to know what you've promised. But if you get married, now that's different.'

She was on my fringe. I could feel the jaws of the scissors near my temple though I had my eyes firmly shut.

'Then you're telling the world, aren't you?'

She tilted my head to the left. It made me look quizzical.

'You've said you'll love, honour and obey in front of everybody . . .'

She was working somewhere near the nape of my neck now. I always think of that part of me as being the most secret; so defenceless and untouched. I could feel the cold metallic click of

Sharon's scissors. She was concentrating, I could tell. Just as well, one slip and I could have been ruined.

'Now, my fella, Eddie, he just won't have it. Won't commit himself, know what I mean? You'd think I was asking him to admit to a crime the way he goes on.'

She sighed heavily, as she fluffed up the top of my hair with a bunched fist.

'Afraid of getting caught, that's him.'

She looked at me sourly in the mirror for a moment, then remembered herself.

'Now,' she said brightly, 'let's get you under the lights!'

As for Liz Page, she has thrived by all accounts. Not that I follow her career or anything but I hear about her on the grapevine. I know she worked for a bit in the bank and then she got married. I know they have three children, two sons and a daughter. A nice size for a family. That's what we would have had, Tony and I. First there would be Anthony (called after his father), then Colin, and Rachel for the girl. I've always liked that name. Rachel . . . it has a ring to it. I see a fair, willowy girl, full of grace and humour, a much-loved last child. In my dream I am standing in an airy house waiting for the sound of her step in the hallway, brimming with that secretive mother-love that displaces all others. I expect her home at any minute. I am filled with the promise of her arrival. How different things would have been if I'd been a Rachel . . .

## *Red Flag Down*

Who is going to praise those crowing
over the lowering? Almost everyone
it seems, forgetting snails, dimheads,
the lumpen with eyes like chuckies. Come now,
it's a red rag the bull has seen through,
saunters past. Any flared nostrils
breathe out a hubris of supersession,
nothing crude – anger, regret – no thanks.
*Sodruzhestvo* beats frankincense
into Boney Yeltsin's cocked hat,
heads on a salver are ten a penny,
let the hordes yell. Has he his arm
tucked into his tunic yet? No tunic?
A double-breasted suit will do.
We're democrats from Lisbon to—
to – Ulan Bator, where it's horses
currycombing the lower chamber,
throwing stirrups over khans—
oh yes, and you'll see stranger things,
winter's tales, tempests of hurry,
a suitcase with an old dog-
ma hurled into the willing Vol-
ga like an apple in a ha-
ha. Hah! A steamy, seamy time,
skew-whiff for *mesteremberek*,
brilliant for peddlers in shop-doorways,
deadly for grannies with ice-cracked bones.

What a jangling from the bell-tower.
Switch it off, let's hear the year
slipping through the bars of the moon
to thud and wail on our filthy snow.
Who will look after it? Someone. They stand,
the patient, in their queues, with nerves
of iron and will come through, right through.

## *Marmalade*

She had been reading her paper in the booth when she recognised the voice, the clipped inflected accent punching through the air.

Alice, he shouted, Alice! What a lovely surprising!

Alice looked up from her newspaper and nodded.

Well hello, she said, how are you?

He gestured to the seat beside her, was it free?

She moved across and put her newspaper away, of course.

Well, well. How *are* you, he balanced his cup and saucer as he sat, how *are* you?

Alice was fine, fine. And you?

He was okay, he frowned a bit and gestured to the table, had she eaten?

Alice was just having breakfast, she pointed at the pastry plates cheerfully, pigging out a bit, she laughed.

They sat in one of the deep red booths to the left of the café, a warm cushion of velvet between them, condensation rolling up in coils from their saturated coats. All around them the noise and clatter of cutlery and china, interrupted across the space by silent women who had left their fur hats on against the cold and were checking their make-up in the mirrors, patting their cheeks, checking their lips for smudges. Steam rose between greetings, men with gleaming umbrellas moved to one side, starched waitresses flitted along the matching tablecloths, pencils behind their ears, '*Gruetzi*' and '*Wie geht*'s', glissando, delivering shining silver jugs and trays of pastries, tiny white porcelain dumpling-pots of jam. Outside the snow was full of yellow puddles and footprints and men in heavy coats leaning like dancers into the wind.

He moved a casual elbow up on the tablecloth and looked in her eyes. Now, he said, settling down, I want to hear *all* about you. Alice began to butter a croissant and smiled, there was nothing to tell really, everything was the same.

You moved house, he said, I heard you moved.

She nodded and scooped up a spoonful of marmalade, that's right, I did.

Still this cravings for your funny orange jam he said, smiling towards her plate. Alice tipped a crumb from the corner of her mouth and laughed.

So where are you living now?

Oh, Alice ran her tongue across her teeth, not far.

Where are you living he persisted, tapping his finger slowly on the table, I want to know *everything*.

Alice smiled and heaped a spoon of blackberry jam on to her croissant. He wagged a conspiratorial finger at her and winked, I think you are exaggeratory with your hidings Alice, and he leaned forward lifting his finger from the table, and tapped her lightly on the nose.

Maybe, she said.

He begged her pardon, straining to hear, his face in a spout of steam.

I said maybe, she repeated, smiling, and turned the pastry plate around.

She suggested he eat something, pushing the plate towards him gingerly, dabbing her lips with the pink serviette. She offered some cheese, fruit. Croissant? Jam?

But he wasn't hungry really, his eyes stayed fixed on her face.

Really?

No, he wasn't hungry he said.

Oh I know I'm a glutton she said, it's just that it's all so delicious.

He laughed and kept his eyes on her.

You always had such lovely hairs, he said and reached a hand towards her, stroking her head. She swallowed a mouthful of coffee and said thank you, and a moment later, I do my best.

He sat back against the padded bench and smiled.

So, he took his hand away and spread it out over the table-cloth, how have you been?

And she had been fine, fine, just fine, she examined the pastries again while he watched her. Fine really, very busy, you know, here and there, this and that. She chose a Danish one, with three concentric swirls of nutmeg and cinnamon.

*Eat* something, please do, she said, I really can't finish it myself.

Fine, he repeated, fine, crinkling his deep grey eyes, fine?

Absolutely, she said, fine.

He pout-sulked against the corner of the booth, he made a pretend face with his eyes, he blew his cheeks out in mock exasperation, *fine*.

How have you been yourself, she wondered?

Actually, he lit a cigarette, searching the stucco work on the ceiling, the patterns on the floor, the faces locked together all around him, actually, he said, removing some tobacco from his tongue, I have been up a bit of a bad shape lately.

Really?

Well, yes, actually I have, he snapped his fingers lightly for more coffee.

And where, she ventured, exactly up the bad shape was he?

He leaned over and borrowed an ashtray from the next table, slipping back into his seat. After a moment he shrugged, looking up at her quickly and then casting his eyes around again.

Claudia has left me, he said.

Oh.

She raised her eyebrows and cleaned the edge of her knife against her plate, cutting another piece from her pastry.

Yes, he stubbed the cigarette out, she took her things away and said she was moving to Damascus.

A bit extreme surely, Alice said, the last word muffled by icing.

No. No. She is doing a researcher thesis for arabesques in Islamic architecturals.

Interesting.

Yes, but, my relations with her were faltered anyway, I think she makes this journey as an excuse.

An excuse for what?

She needed some breaks, he waved a listless hand.

Alice pronounced the pastry very delicious and licked her fingers.

You miss her?

He cocked his head to one side and pouted. He thought for a while, looking around and after a few moments he said that he did. Yes. He took some cheese.

Alice nodded.

Some time I am quite isolate in fact he said. The flat is empty. Yes, he rubbed his chin, his voice quiet, I miss her. Alice gathered the crumbs into a corner of her plate and rounded them into a ball, well, the flat *would* be empty if she's gone, she said brightly.

He looked away and shrugged.

After a moment Alice rolled her arm in an exaggerated arc, well goodness me she said laughing, and tapped the face of her watch, is that the time already? She collected her newspaper from the table and began to get ready to leave.

He leaned over the table, ignoring her, and took the tiny porcelain pot of marmalade between his hands. He tipped it over against the light, examining it.

Now *that*, he said, concentrating, is something that has always been a puzzle with me.

Hm? She was already standing up.

This marmalade, he said, holding it towards her, this word.

This is quite typical actually, his nostrils stiffened over the tablecloth, so unnecessary. Why does English have one word for marmalade, and then all the other confections are just jam?

She didn't know but thought the blackberry one was particularly tasty and opened her mouth wide, rolling out her blackened tongue. He waved a hand dismissively and put the marmalade pot back on the table.

Maybe we could have dinner one evening he said. He put his hands in his pockets, leaning back.

Maybe, she said, slipping her arms into her sleeves, fine.

I don't have your number he said, sitting forward again, wait, I'll get a pen and some paper.

Oh that's okay, she slipped the last button of her collar into place, smiling at him as she brushed past, I'll call you.

He watched her make her way to the till, standing in line while it chimed out, ornate, glinting, dappled under the light. She waited for a moment, apologising, searching her purse for change, the right notes, and the chignoned head of the cashier smiled back at her, bowing as she walked towards the door.

Suddenly she turned around and looked back at him, beaming from ear to ear. She walked over to the booth and leaned her face over the edge, tossing her scarf around her neck. Isn't it French, she said, tucking her hair into place, I think it's from French.

He looked up at her, puzzled.

It's after Marie Antoinette, she said. She got sick and they made her a special jam from oranges. She cocked her head to one side, 'Marie est malade', you see, marmalade.

She rubbed her fingers into her gloves and smiled at him again, then she was gone.

## *Whooper Swans*

They fly

    straight-necked and barely white
      above the bruised stitching of clouds
       above wind and the sound of storms
       above the creak of the tundra
        the howl of weather
         the scatter
          and wolfish gloom
           of sleet icing their wings,

they come

   on their strong-sheathed wings
     looking at nothing
       straight down a freezing current of light,
        they might
         astonish a sleepy pilot
          tunnelling his route above the Arctic,

his instruments darken and wink
    circling the swans
      and through his dull high window at sunrise
       he sees them
        ski their freezing current of light
         at 27,000 feet
          past grey-barrelled engines
           spitting out heat
            across the flight of the swans,

and they're gone

   the polar current sleeking them down
    as soon as he sees them.

# White Moon

White moon

> sheeted by cloud
> slurring the little fields,
> when will you press them
> with owl-soft heaviness
> so that they yield
> harvests of oak shadow,

> white moon

> the cloud-turreted sky
> hurries towards midnight,
> your flakes thicken and fall
> as we wait in the lane
> looking up and guessing
> where you will come.

## *Flight*

1962: Five

A first – the first? – memory of her, or the first that seems to count: dancing in a hailstorm in a navy and white polka dot dress. There is a cigarette between her teeth, which in your dreams will become a rose, there is a light like a lightning strike in her eyes, and her full skirt swings up around her knees as she holds it tight in her fists.

The Bowes Park Road isn't used to this. Car drivers honk and wave, or begin to swerve, and pull out of it just in time. Lorries slow down as they pass, prolonging their splashing of the four of you – the woman, and you, and Bridget Wilson, and plastic Jezebel. (You call all your dolls Jezebel, for the hell of it and to watch the eyes of surprised enquirers.) Bridget, fastened white-knuckled to the handlebar of Jezebel's pram, stares hotly in another direction. But you, summer dress plastered to your back and dripping between your legs, are mesmerised. Singing a rickety can-can, small hat lurching over an eyebrow, the dancing dervish takes your fingers and you splash together past the gas-works, giggling, because there's still so far to go before you're home, and because, before she started dancing, you were think-ing of crying. The rain is warm, as summer rain is; it slides between her fingers where they clasp yours, and when she bends to stroke her face along your cheek, you see the drops, like tiny mirrors, or beads of sweat, on her lips.

The next day, Bridget Wilson withdraws the marble she gave you, her cut-out Bunty doll, and her friendship. 'Your mother is mad.' She says it in the playground. Look at your thumb, which has blue ink on it, turn on your heel, and begin to walk away.

'And she's a criminal! She ignored that sign, Keep Off The Grass. She ignored it.'

You know better. Just keep walking.

1982: Twenty-five

On local rags in Croydon, Cromer and Cranleigh, you have conjured phrases out of nowhere to make the local news both engaging and entertaining, a pyrotechnic display of fun and philosophy. For five years you have done this. On nights of celebration – the local football team do well, the mayor's daughter marries brilliantly, a mother safely delivers quads – you have written like the wind, clattering on souped-up Olympias, a pencil, for good luck, stuck behind your ear. On days of tragedy – the team relegated, Sainsbury's razed by arsonists, horrific deaths in motorway pile-ups whose reporting leaves you shaking, drained and angry – you have struggled long over the right nuance. And, on days of no news whatsoever, you have made it up.

It turns out to be worth it. Your first job on Fleet Street, and in the features and not the news room. You write fillers, as yet, and do research. You are ecstatic.

After your first night, a long one, cross the scrubby hinterland of a darkened Fleet Street, where tumbleweed blows in bales toward Cambridge Circus, and enter a wine bar in which a woman has never before set foot, or not as a customer. Clear your throat in the sudden silence, but doggedly refuse to leave until you have been served.

1963: Six

Against the odds, you are a precocious reader. Teachers, finding the talent in you, sow you with words and watch them take seed and sprout. Encouraged, begin to scrawl laborious stories in blunt pencil on wide feint pages, but show them carefully to no one.

Home alone one cold afternoon, and searching for more words to consume, invade the clammy sanctum of your parents' bedroom and, beyond holding back, haul out the secret card-

board box which contains every theatre programme, every
Christmas card and birthday card and telegram your family have
given, bought or received. On Your Engagement. U2R1. Dear
little baby, bundle of joy, pink . . .

One huge, stricken Valentine, the heart a pumping bludgeon
of slick, red satin. Inside, like a tot's hieroglyphics, it says: 'To
ym dalling hubsand'. Mirror writing. The writing of confusion.
Puzzle hard, to check if that's the way the words are really
spelled.

1983: Twenty-six

Knowledge becomes your friend, the dictionary your bible. Get
distracted during office research by intriguing words, and disappear on their trail, wasting serious womanhours. Begin to
take a perverse pride in using esoteric phrases understood by
few, although these are generally removed from your copy by
sub-editors who have had it all before, in different ways, but all,
ultimately, as exhausting.

Find yourself elected to the paper's quiz team, and week after
week defeat your rivals, hacks from Marxist broadsheets and
right-wing old guard institutions, at game shows set up in dingy
pubs where the floor is muddy with beer and sawdust
(imported). Understand, eventually, that the team you're on is
winning because you swot. You're keeping them at the top of
the league table. Pride yourself on this, and pity their threadbare
brains.

Read all the way to work, and all the way back. Browse in
bookshops in your lunch hour, grazing through Socrates and
Simenon, Aeschylus and Atwood with ruminative application.
Slouching down Charing Cross Road one lunchtime, head
buried in *The Female Eunuch*, walk into a man with such a shock
of red hair, you really should have seen him coming. For brief
moments, both stand rooted to the spot, peering over the pages
at one another. Decide you like the eyes, at any rate.

His name is Len. He thinks you need to refocus, perhaps on
something further from your eyes than ten inches. He takes you

for coffee. He has never read Germaine Greer or, come to that, much of anything. Fight, but go under. Partially.

1964: Seven

Win the class prize for Effort, not as flattering as the one for Achievement, but you still get a book token. Hopscotch home, your shoebag hanging from your shoulder and nuzzling the backs of your knees. Pull up short at your front door; everyone can hear what's going on within. 'Bitch!' 'Bastard!' 'Moron! Thick-headed, brainless moron.' The words they know: a small and, at times like these, a dwindling vocabulary. Aware that your slide has worked loose, drag it savagely through the tress it holds, tearing out many hairs, and stare at the three white ducks smiling foolishly on a blue bar. Inside the house, a table resounds. 'Try to write letters, damn you. You *stupid* cow. Don't telephone everyone. How am I going to pay *this*?' There is the dull noise of something coming apart.

Hurl yourself inside, your mother's Sir Galahad. She'll need you now – she has no defence. What can she say? One thing she can't do, after all, is write letters, or not without endless effort. For you, words float and sing, plump and bright as schmaltzy Disney birds. For her, they're caterpillars that squirm defiantly on the page, then sprout wings and fly out of reach, misshapen butterflies that stick on her lips and tangle in her hair. Understand that there is no order in the world's chaos, and no way to begin to make it, unless you can name events and pin them down at intervals, preferably skewered on to paper by pen nibs, like tethering a flapping tent with pegs.

1984: Twenty-seven

Move in with Len. Wonder if this is entirely the best plan, since he expects nothing of you and is impressed by your slightest achievement. But know you can't resist; after all, he expects nothing and is impressed . . . He is tender, too. The fly, the

spider – probably the house dust mite, although he is allergic –
are his friends. He will soothe your corrugated brow.

At work, vacancies open up above you on the newspaper.
Pulling on seven league boots, begin to step into them.

1965: Eight

Tiny sobs, quiet now, bursting softly against her fist like dis-
solving doves. Get out of bed and, moving on muffled toes,
bring her a cold flannel to lie against her hot cheek; it drips too
much, leaking off her chin, your elbow, and she almost giggles.
Why is she so silly? Why is she such a silly thing? Even an
inexperienced, careless big sister wouldn't be laughing now.
Sensing your stern concern and with, in any case, her heart not
in it, she sobers, murmurs reassuringly, in the back of her
throat, and stills. Ssh.

Hitch up your pyjamas at the knees, the way you have seen
men do, and kneel between her legs where she sits on their
double bed. Billow of warmth. Reach up the flannel because
there is mascara, wet dustings like uncertain shadows, stuck
around her eyes. Dab fumblingly until she pulls a face, pushing
her nose sideways with a thumb and going, for two minutes,
cross-eyed, Harpo Marx right here for you. Dab again.
Annoyed at your clumsy work, wring the wet towelling into a
pot plant, stubby, eight-year-old fingers bumping together like
badly-rehearsed dancers. Whisper, leave him. But you don't
think she hears. She has turned and is looking, calmly, at her
face in the moonlit mirror. She's watching her jaw swell. 'My
head aches,' is all she'll tell you. Her head is always aching.

Say, run away with me. The two of us. I can look after you.
Feel wild with the thrill of it, desperate for the taste of it, the
crazy freedom of the dark that's outside. Take her finger, the
middle one. Begin to walk to the bedroom door, pulling at her
hand. Let me take you. C'mon, let's go.

From the sitting-room, just a door away, the wave of an
audience's laughter surges to break against the orange-flock

walls. 'Take the money or open the box? What's it to be? What should he do, ladies and gentlemen? We can't hear you . . .'

Four feet from the screen, he's sitting like the picture you once saw of Abraham Lincoln. Hands rock-like on the crimplene arms. Feet jutting out in his slippers, tug boats ready to steer. A faraway, indistinct look in his eyes.

When he feels you there, a diminutive and reproachful figure, he says, without turning, 'Just keep her out of my way, and keep her quiet.' He sighs like a giant; look down at his huge feet. There is a weight of responsibility on you, and you don't know if it can stop you growing.

## 1985: Twenty-eight

Split up with Len. Again. Finally, you tell yourself. 'Why?' he asks. 'What?'

Hurl about the room, fisting the air. 'I don't know. I don't know. It's just how it has to be.'

He strides to your side, holds your arms, which still try to flap like jerky chicken wings, and looks at you hard. 'What have I done?'

But there is nothing. He fixes things around the place – broken fridges, flapping blinds, the dinner, a drink when you need it. He talks, on subjects you want to discuss, and listens to your responses. He caresses you in the night, his hands planing like seals down the funnels of your back. His behaviour is beyond reproach. But he doesn't understand your passion, the lust for words, doesn't quite appreciate what you do. Begin to pack your things – photographs, books, a clockwork monkey, your postcard of the Chrysler building, typewriter, the kitten. You will all depart together, maybe tomorrow, maybe the day after.

And you do. Leave the flat, and walk into indeterminate space. Search for somewhere to pitch your flag.

1966: Nine

Finish mapping out the tributaries of the Hudson River. Blow
the last shreds of rubbing-out from your diagram, critically
squint at it, then pack away your day-glo felt-tip pens, biros and
ruler in your Arsenal Forever pencil case. Behind you, the TV
laps at the curtains, at the carpet. All that's visible of him, when
you glance back from the kitchen table, is a massive, furry arm –
like an orang-utan, from Borneo or Sumatra – resting a bottle
of Barley Wine on the carpet. The *Star Trek* theme reaches a
crescendo, luring you. Intend to watch it but, on the way to
dump your books in your room, pass theirs, where the baby has
her cot. On the bed, singing May to sleep, your mother. The
White Cliffs Of Dover. It's A Long, Long Way To Tipperary.
Pack Up Your Troubles. Songs from a dislocated childhood,
from a war zone and war years, your father's and your grandfather's time; songs to solace troops, soothing a baby to sleep.

Your mother sang these strange lullabies to her own little
sister – Aunt Laura, who could do the splits and walk on her
hands and wanted so badly to run off and join the circus. She
sang them most often when they both were lonely in their isolated, evacuee years. A Cornish farm, lost in rolling greenery,
where mum fed the pigs and milked the cows and no one
noticed she still wasn't reading or that, when she tried to write,
words came out backwards.

But now is now. Creep up on the bed, snuggle into a ball
behind the warm shape, and listen to her back resonate with the
songs. When May is asleep, get carried, a floppy, limby puppy,
to your own room. 'Let's see – a silver one-piece your gran
made Aunt Laura to wear in the children's gymnastic displays,'
she answers your drowsy question. 'She looked like a beautiful
fish.' Warm hand, rubbing your calf. Stretch your foot. She
holds it. 'I think your sister has the same shaped back, Ramona. I
think your sister will be double-jointed.'

Try to touch your nose with your tongue. Say, 'What about
me?'

'I don't think so, poppet.' She kisses your mouth goodnight.

'Just one set of joints for you. But that doesn't mean you have to keep your feet on the ground.'

Close your eyes. Float, and dream, and fly.

1986: Twenty-nine

Begin to hang around learned men, or men who have the wood-enness, captivating egotism and touch of the aloof the learned cultivate. Their pristine other-worldliness fascinates you. At a party in a gallery, backing out of a press-starved artist's clutches, bump into a coat whose tweed is the deep, shadowy blue of Scottish gloamings. Its occupant turns, regarding you with cocked eyebrow and questing grin. Both stare at his coat, which is soaking up your spilt wine like a glutton.

'Please,' he pre-empts your apology. 'A pleasure to have some light relief in this crypt.' His tone gives you Cary Grant, his expression is stage-woeful and, framing a face with this much youth left in it, the shameless streaks of grey at his temples look like go-faster stripes. He smiles at you more broadly. 'Or perhaps it's not such a crypt. But, if you intend to stay a while longer – and I hope you do – ' twinkle, twinkle go his eyes, 'you'll need some alcohol back in that glass. May I?'

Theodore, you will learn – from him and from people you later ask in uncharacteristically giggly late-night phone conver-sations – 'has a reputation'. He is a Writing Fellow at one of the lesser-known redbrick universities, a place which, during the obstreperous seventies, kicked up quite a rumpus, and which has consequently slipped, on the university top ten, to a position of faded indignity. You are not to know this last; your encounter with higher education has been brief. 'I went to Sussex.'

'To do what?' Dexterously, his tongue locates and removes a shred of red pepper from an incisor. Notice a small white hair curling from his left ear, and find it unaccountably charming.

'To research a feature on their experimental rabbit breeding.' Maintain a deeply studious expression, and twirl your glass reflectively. 'Unforeseen developments had occurred. Project too successful. Lots and lots of rabbits. Careless, overworked lab assistant – mass outbreak. Guerilla bunny colony rings the place. Dawn raids on the campus allotments. Decimated carrot crop. Boy almost breaks his neck tripping over a rabbit on the playing field. Interesting feature. Need I go on?'

Theodore – who claims to be a novelist and poet – loves it, and finds you refreshing, he says, magnetic. It's mutual. He holds you rapt with talk of narrative structure, reality base, plot and counter-plot, Derrida, Levi-Strauss and Woody Allen.

'I could talk to you all night,' he murmurs. But little talking is done back at your flat.


1967: Ten


In March, see *Lady And The Tramp* and every single episode of *The Monkees*. Fall in love with Davy Jones, but think about him often as a cartoon character, a scruffy dog yodelling to you across the rooftops. Spend three weeks' pocket money on a framed, tinted picture of the singer in Woolworth's, where the saleslady tells you she's his aunt, and you believe her.

This is the year you're into photography, anyway. When the funfair comes in June, snap away at everything with your new Kodak Instamatic. When you get the film back, the picture that stands out for sheer composition, the one you look at again and again, is one of your parents, lost in a kiss on the Ferris Wheel.

August. Floating laboriously, watch her from the sea as she paddles and laughs at the greedy foam's edge. Voluptuous, full as a fruit, in a pink and white candy-striped swimsuit, she seems as beautiful and as giddy as Marilyn Monroe. Not far from you, May gurgles and precociously vaults through the sea like a dolphin while, out where it's deep, he surfaces, spluttering, waves to the rosy woman, then plunges again, blue-black hair slick and shiny as an electric eel . . .

At the school open evening, her hair is like Snow White's, very long, very black, and her cheeks glow. People's fathers come across to talk to her, smiling into her eyes, until people's mothers pull them away. ('Why is that woman *alone*?') You and she stand, paired together in the middle of the room, like Bambi and Thumper on the ice, hesitant to step out. Drag her to your desk; it's like hauling a shopping trolley, okay once you get the momentum going. Sit her in your spindly chair and spread your paintings before her. She begins very slowly to turn the big, cracking and encrusted sheets, scrutinising every daub to its triumphant finale. Halfway through, she beams, and hugs you tight. And then her gaze goes' on to take in something past you, over your shoulder, and she smiles. Turn to see your father who, still grainy with cement dust, sheepishly slaps at the leg of his mildewed suit, then strolls across from the doorway and puts his hands gently on her shoulders.

'Ah. Mr and Mrs Price? We meet at last.' Mr Dawson grins at you, shepherds them toward his desk – 'Oh, leave the paint fiend where she is.' Pull out your jotter and scribble in it. After five minutes, glance across. He's showing them your stories (you trust him), and she's smiling, and looking at his finger as it points to interesting words, measuring from what he says the way she should organise her expression. No one would guess.

1987: Thirty

Theodore is an ungraspable lover, navigating the tangling reeds of commitment with the ease of a man greased for a cross-channel swim. He is evasive about his romantic history; perhaps a sunken galleon lies on the ocean floor, shifting painfully when the current eddies. In any case, your careers come first and, when you ask, he says he loves you. 'Of course I do, Ramona,' he murmurs, stirring his cappuccino and considering the shapes of trees through the window. 'You know it, why must you ask? Try to put your mind on something higher, dear, something other than yourself. For example, look at how sere, how skeletal that elm has become. Isn't there a strange, post-structuralist romance, in a way, to . . . ?'

Screw up your eyes, and try to see what he sees. Begin to doubt that it is in you. When Theodore discovered your new job – editing the women's section of a daily newspaper – his congratulations rattled hollowly, like peas in a bucket, and the scorn in his eyes was like a hail of poison-tipped quills. There is, of course, a shelf-life to novelty, but Theo, for all this, still keeps on coming round, drawn by your repartee and bedsocks. Say less and less about what you do and, at night, when he has been able to fit you in between the endless campus late nights, roll away from him after making love and admit silently to the dark that you resent him. And yet, his intelligence holds you in ghastly, ghostly thrall. It elevates him beyond his actions; it is his pillar of light.

One evening, drunk and fizzing with recklessness, gatecrash a literary party. Theodore is surprised to see you. He tells you the party is boring, a damp squib, that he's only here because he has to be, etcetera. 'Lucky old you,' he says. 'You could leave right now.'

In the ladies' room, as you brush your hair before calling a cab, overhear a woman crying, in a cubicle, into the arms of a friend. From the things that are sobbed, and moaned, and confided, discover that this is Theodore's wife, and that you are not his only liaison. 'A reputation.' Ah, so. Outside, squirt your fountain pen down Theodore's shirt, tell him his poetry stinks, and leave in tears.

Sink quickly, without bothering to clutch the couch grass on the bank. Convince yourself you are indeed, on many counts, rather slow. Slink away mentally to the hacks' graveyard and loiter there, amid the dried-up Tipp-Ex bottles and the expanding armbands and the green peaked visors. In your free time, stare stupidly at space. Abandon books, and the places where they are sold. There is nothing friendly there, nothing trustworthy either. Words are bastards, after all.

Concerned, your sister calls, in the night from many distant cities. She has an innovative high-wire act with an international circus of some renown. She takes death-defying risks, but only after learning how, by physical manoeuvre, to outwit her leaps, to diffuse their menace. Her lover is Alice, gravity-defying partner in their tumbling show. Together, they swing and leap and, gleaming with confidence, fall and catch and soar. They have a

net – it is the law – but, she proudly claims, they will never need
it.

'So what should *I* do?'

She says it's experience that gives her such grip. Knowing
how to handle it when you miss the bar, or the timing's off and
no one's there for the catch. Some grisly things can happen, she
says; but it's worth it for the feeling when it works: the know-
how can facilitate some really quite breathtaking stunts. 'Anything else, wise one?' you ask.

'Rosin.'

1968: Eleven

When they fight now, put on your record-player and dance to
Rolling Stones tracks, turned too loud. Spend a lot of time
dressed in her raincoat and his trilby, a piece of rolled-up card in
your mouth. Call yourself Ingrid and think about disappearing,
taking off to far distant places, Humphrey reading you his
favourite poetry during the flight.

Coming in from your evening paper round, hear her voice
from the bedroom. It is summer, and motes drift on spears of
warm light which finger between the drawn curtains. Her head's
bad again; she wants a cold flannel. Tell her she should see about
getting glasses, then squat beside her, and take one hand, with
its broken nails. Cold water from the cloth trickles into the
forests of black at her temples, losing itself on her scalp. She
wants you – you can barely hear – wants you to do something
about his tea. He'll be home soon. His tea should be ready.
'Bugger his tea,' you tell her, but you get up and walk toward
the kitchen anyway. She says something. What? Quietly: what
did you say, ma?

'He works very hard, your dad. Now then.'

Such tenderness.

1988: Thirty-one

Theodore calls. It has been a long day, you are tired, not prepared, although the two of you say lately that you are friends. Silent with shock at the sound of his voice, listen to the liturgy of his recent achievements, the crown, the pinnacle being his new book, on the brink of publication just in time for Christmas. Before you part, request the return of stories you wrote, things which he had begged to see, and then declined to mention. 'By all means,' he assures you evenly. 'They were all rather sentimental, anyway. Beneath you. I'm sure you can do better. Tell me,' you hear him draw on a cigarette and let it out, 'why are women so obsessed with their mothers?'

Realise, in horrified, exquisite pleasure, that although he has never been rumbled, Theodore is the stupidest person you know. Suddenly feel loosed, freed. In answer to his question, explain that you really can't say. Sign off. Cross the corridor to the paper's literary section, confess your secret desire to break into book reviewing and, browsing lazily through the batches on the desk, fish out Theodore's oeuvre and suggest, 'Why don't I try out with this one?'

Feed your machine some paper. Make coffee. For the first time in a while, relish a job.

1969: Twelve

When she dies, wilting in the shade of an unsuspected tumour – which you later imagine lurking like a spider behind her eyes – miss it, because you're on a hiking trip with the school. When you are brought home, and stand in her bedroom, condolence cards shuffle, like sad white sighs, like tourists, on the insides of the window ledges.

At the funeral, there is much whispering, it seems, when the three of you – he holds your hands, a child on each side – walk behind the coffin to the front pew. With the first hymn, he falters, sits suddenly when everyone else is standing, and begins to sob hard into his hand, then gently into your shoulder. Your brittle heart melts a little.

It's summer again. On the lawn outside the church, wreaths float like jazzy halos. Imagine her appearing, putting one on her head, and leading you over the grass in a waltz or a polka. 'I loved her so much,' he is whispering, kneeling before you, looking at you. 'So much.'

Stare away over his head. In the sun-soaked meadow that adjoins the cemetery May, not understanding what's happening, and also understanding, somersaults in crazy circles, her face strawberry-scarlet. The sky is cloudless, but for a stubble of white in the distance, like straggling birds flying somewhere.

An aunt wants to speak to him. He says, 'In a minute, love,' and leads you to a wooden seat. He takes your hands, jiggles them about in an awkward way. 'I'd say your mother had what she really wanted from life,' he gets out, eventually. 'In that way, she was one of the most intelligent people you'll ever know.' Keep your expression blank. 'Do you see?'

For your thirteenth birthday, three months later, he gives you a small party, which you don't want, but it happens, anyway. Refuse to come in from the garden when your friends arrive and then, when you do, watch his huge, clumsy hands shaking the jelly from its cat-shaped mould and say, 'You've broken it. The ear's come off.'

At Christmas, when you sing in the school production of Handel's Messiah, tell him parents aren't invited, a blatant lie.

In the school pool, practise holding your face underwater, listening to the way noise gets soft and blurry. Finally, learn to swim beneath the surface. Fin about slowly there, for long, lonely periods, eyes open and staring at everyone's legs, skinny white creepers with bruises.

1989: Thirty-two

Your review of Theodore's book, typed by fingers whose nails you paint a luscious, chip-resistant flame for the job, is one of the most incisive critiques you have written. It's a stormer.

Dispense entirely with the protective safety-net you usually employ for journalism and, the bit again between your teeth, surge back into the job with renewed vigour. Your first full-page feature in some time, about a woman who runs a Pestalozzi school, appears in a highbrow journal, and receives a huge post-bag. Len calls up, to congratulate you, and invites you for a celebratory meal.

'I thought you might hate me,' you say, your voice trailing a question mark.

'Ah, no. You were off on a word chase, in love with something that wasn't me. After the Knowledge, like some insane cab-driver.' It's his joke. But the tone's ironic. Least you deserve. Anyway, the meal is good.

Better than these things, your sister and her troupe of per-forming friends are in town. Beneath the big top's tarpaulin, in the criss-crossing beams, she drifts with Alice through enchanted plains of air; they seem to caress in flight. And, as you crane back to watch their dance in the sky, it comes to you at last that this is how your parents were. For them, everything was physical. It was all choreography, a wordless way they could react together. Something for only two people, a blazing kind of ardour of which you and May were a captive audience.

After the show, still half-dazed with the new thought, take May and her many sets of joints to a small but intimate bar. She looks good, you're happy to say, brown and muscular, quizzing the barman good-naturedly on the sugar content of his soft drinks before spiking her Appletize with gin. In an alcove seat, underneath a stuffed bear's head, talk about typewriters and trapezes, and now and then. She has made the effort to see your father this week; his message to you is to try Pan Am, 'obvi-ously a more frequent service than British Rail'.

'Oh, God.' Hold your glass, with its dribbles of condensation, against your forehead.

'No, it's okay,' she assures. She stirs her drink with a swizzle stick declaring that Waterloo is Southern Comfort country, then taps it on the side of her beaker. 'He's fine, spends most of his time looking at snaps from the old days.' She deepens her voice, rolls the phrase out with a midwestern twang. And she says something else, begins some wild yarn, only you don't hear it. You're busy watching scenes that reel through your mind, photographs that come to life, everything transposed into a Technicolor West Side Story scenario. Your mother's flailing skirts at a dance; your father serenading her once, in the evening garden (May giggling her head off under the covers); his voice, bellowing curses in the kitchen, your mother's hissed threats and her hand, cracking a slap across his cheek. Scenes flicker faster: Theodore's pale and effete digits contrasting with May and Alice, tender seraphs grappling for each other's fingers on a bed of empty space; and you, nails coloured red as roses, hurling and mixing words not just as instruments, but as objects of passion. That is where the real strength lies, and where it always did. That's what matters. Taking your toes off the ground, taking the leap and the risk, in a silver costume, with your blood pounding, and no net.

Leave the place when they start to lock up. The street seems somehow out of shape, things leaking, structureless, from their outlines into dazzling anarchic positions, letters and phrases on advertising hoardings flirting with your mind. White neon shining from a wall looks like a modernist bouquet, looks, if you squint, like a cluster of balloons. Think about grabbing it, then wonder exactly how drunk you are.

Your thoughts colliding, reach the end of the road in silence, just as a sudden rainstorm starts. And, without further consideration, and because walking is for those without wings, and because she's smiling and it seems the only thing to do, take May's hand and waltz her across the empty street.

## *Town World*

Buckled and tilted a few degrees
this way and that, a plane

that runs always
to an horizon of roofs;

tarmac tracks
stamped through roof-slates;

tree-heads, ornate school chimneys
pushed high enough up to imagine over

to the next hard skyline,
border to another brick dish

with another covered river;
then over again to almost the same valley,

and past that to places that might look
the same but where *you'd*

be different; places where rumours start up
then crawl here on names without images; alien

factory-odours drawn up by the sun
and slid our way. Districts

with ancient buses; black air;
roadways of girders; concrete

visions in sunset dust. You'd never get home.

## Contemporaries

It's pleasant to be a contemporary.
– It's the importance of people.

What courage they have
to build a Cathedral in a mess of slums,
to compose even one small tune
like a bird in a thorn bush,
even to say Hello to their neighbour,
and all within a few feet from a grave.

A huge world in space
explodes: What's that compared
with the first word spoken by a baby,
or the last word spoken by anybody?

## A Difference

Times were when, not thinking of what to
do,
I did it.
It was as easy and helpless
as walking into the future.

Migrant birds arrived
on the cliffs of Handa. I didn't think
of where they came from
and where they would go to.

Now I'm troubled by wanting to know

for, having spent most of my years,
that precious wealth, so few coins are left
they hardly jingle when I count them.

Sad to be a miser limping into the future,
consoled only by thinking
today was the future once – and look at it
giving me so many gifts
I envy myself.

# *Dancey*

A boy, William Ness of the croft of Eard, was on the hillside one day, walking into the tail of a blizzard, well muffled, to see that none of his father's sheep was in trouble, when he saw someone approaching slowly, rising and falling in the drifts. The blizzard had moved on southwards, and now the sky was clearing over the islands. William Ness saw that the stumbling lost one was a woman. He had never seen her before. He approached, cautiously. The boy asked her who she was, and where she was going. She only shook her head.

She was wearing a grey cloak with a hood, and it was soaked, more coldly and intensely than any hour-long blizzard could have penetrated. Her coat hung so heavy on her that she could hardly stand, much less walk.

After his faltering questions had got no answer, his first impulse was to turn and run home as fast as he could. Women from the sea still moved through the old men's winter stories, and that and a hundred other images were vivid and terrifying and beautiful in the boy's mind.

The young woman turned and pointed back towards the cliff and the open sea, whose cold blue brightness was beginning to be blurred and stained by another blizzard. Then, more insistently, she pointed to the sheep shelter further up the hill. She laid her cold wet hands on the boy, she said over and over again, urgently, a single syllable that he could not understand. Her whole body yearned towards the sheepfold, over which the first snow-flakes of the oncoming blizzard were now drifting.

William Ness shook his head. Words were useless. He pointed towards the valley below and the seven or eight crofts with smoke rising from the chimneys. There they might be able to help her. There were a few old sailormen in the valley. Perhaps they would understand her tongue.

She consented, with a weary shake of the head, to go with
him. Meantime the entire Sound, and the coast beyond, were
blotted out by the snow-cloud. Flakes swirled thickly round the
woman and the boy. A lamp had been lit in the croft of Eard. It
dimmed in the storm's onset. The further crofts were ghost
houses.

The nearness of help and warmth seemed to give the young
woman new strength. She walked alongside him. He could
smell the strong salt from her clothes. Once or twice she
stumbled on a rock or in a rut. The boy was familiar with the
ground. He held out his hand to her. The intense coldness of her
clutch put a shudder through his body that reached as far as his
heart. But he held on tight and led her down a sheep path.

Near a spring where some of the higher valley crofts got their
water the stranger stopped. She bent down and kissed the boy.
Then her knees gave and she collapsed.

'Come on!' said William Ness, shaking her. 'We're nearly
there.'

She did not stir. He touched her face. His fingers flinched
away from a still more bitter coldness. He turned and ran helter-
skelter through the thickening blizzard to his parents' croft.

The room was full of neighbours. It was one of the last days of
Yule, when the families trooped from croft to croft with little
gifts. William brought into the house a swirl of flakes. The flame
in the lamp leapt in the draught.

'Shut the door, boy,' said his father.

'You're that cold!' cried his mother. 'Come over and sit by the
fire.'

The stout brisk woman from the next croft, Madge, chafed
his hands till the bones ached.

A fisherman put a whisky glass to his mouth and bade him
drink. A fine fire kindled in his stomach and comforted all his
body. Two or three valley children came about him. They imi-
tated this old one and that. They plucked mimicry and laughter
from each other. William laughed too.

His mother carried round a board of cheese and oatcakes. His
father followed with the stone crock of ale.

Billo who had been a sailor began to sing a ballad but forgot the words. They rallied him with mockery and encouragement. He tried again, twice, and faltered. At last they latched his mouth with a glass of whisky. There was much laughter.

The door opened. The laird's gardener came in. They saw that the night was thick with stars. The newcomer opened his whisky bottle . . .

One by one the children began to yawn and rub their eyes. Two of them curled up in a corner beside the uneasy dog and went to sleep.

In a lull of the conversation, William said, 'I met a strange woman on the hillside. She fell down. She's still out there. Maybe we should go out and bring her in.'

But William had such a low voice that only his mother and Madge heard him.

'I declare,' said his mother, 'that boy sees things that nobody else sees.'

'A bairn's imagination,' said Madge. 'They grow out of it.'

Then Tommy the joiner, after much pleading, put his fiddle to his chin and began to play. Pair by pair the young folk circled each other in the middle of the floor. The old man Anders stuck a red-hot poker in his mug till the ale hissed and steamed; as if he didn't have enough of a flame in his face already.

Round and round the dance went. William drowsed with his head on Madge's great stony knee.

Near midnight the door was thrown open. The newcomer was so coated in snow they did not recognize him until he had wiped the grey mask off his face. The music stopped. The dance faltered and stilled. It was Mr Spence the general merchant from the north side of the island, five miles away. 'A good Yule to you all,' he said gravely.

'You're welcome,' said William's mother. 'We didn't expect a visitor from so far away on such a night.'

'I came to say, a ship struck on the reef of Hellyan in the snow-storm this afternoon, just before sunset. The shore's covered with bodies. They've all been taken into the kirk hall. Tommy Wilson, I came specially to see you, about coffins.

Thirty-two bodies so far. The minister and the schoolmaster think she might have been an emigrant ship out of the Baltic bound for America. There were a dozen women, most of them young. There were half-a-dozen bairns. God help them!

William's father poured out a large dram for the news bearer. Some of the whisky splashed on to the table.

There would be no more music or dancing that night . . .

There was silence. Then a small pure voice repeated his story of the young foreign woman on the hill. 'She's still there,' said William Ness. 'She fell and wouldn't get up again.'

His father raged at him, 'Why didn't you tell us this?' William hid his face in Madge's skirts.

Three young men were putting on their coats and caps. A lantern was brought from the cupboard and lit.

'Thirty-three coffins,' said Tommy. 'I'll have to send to Hamnavoe for wood.'

'There'll be wood in plenty from the ship,' said Billo the sailor. 'Staves and planks everywhere. They'll take their ship with them under the earth.'

'She fell beside the spring,' whispered William.

The searchers, going out, paused. 'Beside the spring . . .' There had been so much snow all night that if a woman was lying near the spring she would have the whole hillside for her shroud. They knew every contour; they must look for a long low hump.

The boy spoke again. 'The sheepfold,' William said. 'Look there too. The woman kept pointing at the sheepfold.'

An hour later, two of the searchers brought in the body of the young woman and laid it in the barn.

The third man returned half an hour later, carrying a child. It was still alive. The peat basket was emptied of peats, and blankets were laid in it and the child was set in a nest of blankets. A spoonful of watered whisky was tilted into the infant's mouth. The child opened its eyes and cried once – a sound new but older than all languages – then it drifted into sleep beside the hearth.

What should be done with it?

'There's bairns in every croft in this valley but mine,' said

Madge. 'I'll take it if nobody else wants it. I'll have the blessing of a bairn without the burden of a man.'

Nobody disputed the fostering; well after midnight Madge Selquoy carried the shipwrecked child to her croft across a field deep and blue-black under snow.

It looked like being a good harvest in the valley, nurtured all summer with bounteous sun and a sufficiency of rain.

A generation had passed since the shipwreck. A slow wave of time had gone over the valley, taking away some old ones and also, as sometimes happens, a few young fishermen were scattered and lost in a quick wave of the sea. But always there was a stirring of children in this croft or that: the generations rise and fall.

Particularly in the croft of Strom down at the shore there was rarely silence while the sun was up. The solid rooftree was shaken morning to night with cajolery, laughter, hectoring, rage, songs. The woman of the house, Dancey, had been ten years married to Andrew Crag who had the fishing boat *Hopeful*. They also had a few acres where they kept two cows and grew potatoes and cabbages and oats, and they had a score of sheep on the hill. But most of what nourished Andrew and Dancey Crag and their six children came out of the sea.

And Dancey would help push the boat *Hopeful*, loaded with creels or lines, into the sea in the morning, up to her thighs in the cold water. And then again, in the afternoon or early evening Dancey was there when *Hopeful* returned, sometimes heavy with fish, sometimes with only a thin scattering along the bottom-boards.

'What are you thinking about?' she would say tartly to Andrew whenever there was a poor catch. 'How am I going to feed your bairns on a few trashy haddocks like this?'

Andrew would remark mildly that he had no control over the vagrancies of fish. 'I do my best but I can't compel them.'

Plenitude or scarcity, Dancey would take the basket of fish on her back and hump it up to Strom, where several mewling cats waited for her, and gulls circled above waiting for the gutting to begin.

Inside, the youngest child might be wailing from its crib, and two little ones playing with water or wild flowers on the door step; the three eldest were safely folded in the school. Many a morning, that fine summer, while Dancey made butter or stoked the hearth for the baking of bannocks, she could hear the murmurs of multiplication, poetry, geography, drifting from the small school above.

'A few poor things of mackerel,' she said to Andrew one day. 'Go up to the hill, see if the sheep are all right. I think you're better with sheep than fish. If the weather holds, there might be a good harvest. There'd better be.'

Then she turned and gave the five-year-old boy Joe a ringing slap on the side of his head for putting his fingers in the butter. And Joe yelled as if the sky had fallen down on him. And Andrew went away up to the hill to see to the sheep.

Even in that exceptionally fine summer, there were a few anxious days in the valley when the eight fishing boats were out; after a golden morning the wind got up and the outer sea roughened like sackcloth, and the waves came crashing in over the shore stones, peal after peal.

Then there were the anxious women standing here and there on the sea-banks, alone or in small groups, shading their eyes westwards, dumbly willing their men to come back, even if they hadn't a fish to show for the venture and the hazard.

Dancey was never among those watchers. 'Fools!' she said. 'The fires'll be out when their men come in cold. What can they do about it? The sea will work as it wants to!'

And the boats came in from the claws of the storm, one after the other. As they passed the croft of Strom, going on home, the women would look askance at the door. What kind of a woman was she, who seemingly had no care or keeping of her man, and was so completely acquiescent in the will of the sea, whether it was benign or murderous . . . ? Then when Andrew came up, tired and soaked with salt, she would make room for him beside the hearth, and break the peat into yellow flames, and say, 'How many fish did you catch? Half a basket, it could be worse. You fool, could you not have seen the storm coming?' Then she would heat ale in a pot, and add sugar. While he drank, the bitter incense of sea rose slowly from his trousers and jersey and boots.

And Dancey, up to her elbows in oatmeal, bent and kissed little Willa who had nipped a finger in the jamb of the door.

In one or two of the crofts, a woman would be saying to her fisherman that she was similarly warming with hot ale and peat flames, 'What do you expect? She isn't one of us. A foreigner from who knows where. None of us will ever be able to understand her. Hard on her man and hard on her bairns. But she does keep them well-fed and well-clad, that's true . . . !' A generation, a slow ponderous wave of time, had gone over the island and the valley since the winter of the shipwreck, and it had taken away many of the older folk, including the old people of Eard, to whose end-of-Yule celebration the child of the sea had been carried with a small flicker of life in it.

Up at Eard now lived William Ness, a bachelor, who farmed his few acres and had little to do with the other folk of the valley. He lived by himself, a careful secretive man. Not even a tinker was suffered over his threshold; only the missionary, and the laird's factor when he came for the twice-yearly rent. Children were sent away gruffly. Young women, going up that way with buckets to the spring, had to go through the deep heather behind the house. William Ness looked after his few beasts and acres tolerably well. But he never went out fishing. After his father died, the boat *Swift* lay on the noust and began slowly to warp. Now she was a poor shrivelled husk beside the eight well-kept fish-seekers of the shore.

On a Sunday he would put on his dark suit and take his Bible and go to the kirk five miles away. But always alone, never one of the little groups of worshippers here and there on the road. Remote and stern, he listened to the sermon. During the prayers, he drooped his head a little. He did not open his mouth during the hymns and psalms. He would place one penny gravely in the collection plate, going in.

A strange, lonely man. Yet the valley people accepted him, as the valley had accepted all kinds of people for hundreds of years since the first ox had dragged a plough through the heather. Nature in individual men and women was as unpredictable as the sea.

And the wave of time had carried away Madge Selquoy, the foster-mother to the shipwrecked child, but not before the child had been reared and nurtured and instructed in all the ways needful for an island girl to know.

There had been a few initial difficulties. What name was Madge to call the child? The child was about a year old, she must have a name, but there was no means of knowing what name she had been given. The ship was so broken up that only her port of registration, Danzig, was found carved on a timber. Danzig the child was called too, when the minister came to christen her. And there was another complication, for nobody could tell whether the bairn from the sea was Catholic, Lutheran, Orthodox, or Jewish. Drops of water were sprinkled on its head, and Mary Danzig cried a little, then slept.

'And mercy me,' said old Philip of Graybigging, 'once the bairn comes to the age of speaking, what way will we know what she's saying, and her with a foreign tongue in her head?'

But when Dancey was two years old or thereby – her birthday would forever be a mystery too – she spoke the slow lilting cadences of the other valley children, a language touched with a slight melancholy, Scots-English words thrown upon a loom of ancient Norn.

And Dancey mingled freely with the children of the valley, and all went well in their work and play. But always this aura of mystery clung to her.

An upsurge of time brought together the girl Dancey and Andrew Crag, the crofter-fisherman, whose father had fallen from the crag to his death going after gull eggs five years since, and whose mother was 'wearing away' in the deep chair beside the hearth-fire. The old woman put bitter looks on Dancey when Andrew first took her to Strom, in the way of courtship. She had been kind to Dancey when Dancey was a child and a

young girl. But to have another woman sharing her little king-
dom! It was a hurtful thing. 'That foreign slut!' she would
mumble, but loud enough for the girl to hear. Once the old
woman opened her eyes and there was Andrew kissing the girl
goodnight in the open door, with a star out beyond them, cold
and brilliant. 'Andrew Crag!' she said harshly, 'this was a decent
house always. It is my house – Strom belongs to me. You leave
here this very night. Go and live with that creature, whoever she
is . . .'

But in the morning she had no memory of what she had seen
or said. She knew that her thread was fraying. She would not
take to her bed – bed was the next stage to coffin and grave. She
ruled the little house of Strom, grim and feeble, from her chair
beside the fire.

'I can't go to the fishing and leave her,' said Andrew, 'What
am I to do?'

Dancey rolled up her sleeves and came down and milked the
cow of Strom and fed the few hens. Whenever she entered the
house the old one muttered darkly. She would shake her fist, but
feebly, for the strength was out of it.

'You'd feel better after a wash,' said Dancey.

'I'm cleaner than ever you were in your life,' said the old
woman.

'I'll make a little porridge,' said Dancey. 'Then you'll feel
stronger.'

'Don't touch anything in this house!' came the thin cracked
voice. 'I'm not hungry. Don't put a finger on pot or plate.'

She drowsed. And when she woke, she did consent to sip a
cup of warm milk. 'Thank you, Andrina,' she said. 'That's
kind.' (Andrina was the name of her younger sister who had
died of measles twenty years before.) Then she nodded off to
sleep.

'I'll help you into bed,' said Dancey.

'I'm not ready for bed yet,' said Mrs Crag. 'I feel more
comfortable in this chair.'

She drowsed, and woke in an hour. 'Where's Andrew?' she
muttered. 'Where's that boy? Is he home from the school yet?'

'Andrew's out in the boat,' said Dancey. 'He'll be home at sunset.'

'He's taken money out of the chest where I was keeping it. The chest under the bed. A shilling now and half-a-sovereign again. The money I was keeping for my wedding!' And she wept: soft, easy, soundless tears, to think that her son should take her dowry, last precious thing, from her.

'Who are you?' she said to Dancey another day. 'It's kind of you to come. Yes, that's more comfortable, the way you've put the cushions. There was a woman here today – did you see her? – a tinker wife. She stole the china teapot from the sideboard, the one I got for my wedding from the missionary's wife.'

'The teapot's still there, mother,' said Dancey. 'Look!'

'Well, there was a woman here and she was trying to take something. She thought I was asleep. But I was watching her all the time.'

Dancey took the wet warm flannel to her face while she slept and then dried her.

Mrs Crag woke when Andrew came in with a full basket of haddocks, lurching with it in a kind of slow heavy dance from door to corner. The thump of the basket on the stone floor wakened her.

'Oh Simon!' she cried. 'You never had a catch like that! Your tea's on the table. Come over to the fire and warm you first. Simon, I've built up a fine fire for you. Look!'

The golden hearth-shadows were all over the interior of Strom. (Simon had been her husband's name.)

'Simon,' she said, 'I never knew we had a lass – a daughter. She's been with me all day.'

'You should be in your bed, getting a good rest,' said Andrew. 'You've never left that chair for ten days past.'

The old woman considered this for a while.

'So that's it,' she said darkly. 'Once I'm in bed I'm finished. I'm out in the ebb. You can send for Tom Stanger anytime, once you get me in bed. First bed, then coffin. Then everything's yours, the house and land and boat and the money under the bed. You're cruel. While I'm in this chair, there's nothing you can do, you jail-bird!'

Exhausted by her spate of words, her head drooped again.

While she slept, Dancey heated broth for him and he ate it with buttered oatcakes, and afterwards beef and tatties.

He kept glancing miserably over at the chair where his mother was ripening for death, so slowly and mysteriously.

That night Dancey did carry her over to her wooden box-bed. But when she woke at dawn she flared up, like a lamp in a draught. 'I'm not dead!' she shrilled. 'I'll live longer than any of you . . .'

And when Dancey carried her over to her chair beside the rekindled hearth, she said, 'I have a lot of things to do in this place before I go.'

Andrew cried a little. Dancey had never seen the glister on his cheeks before. He turned away from her, put on his sea boots and oilskin. Then he kissed his mother and went out quickly.

'Who was that man?' said the old one.

She even, that morning, took two or three spoons of thin porridge from Dancey's hand. 'That was right good,' she said. 'Did you make it? Well, I pay you well enough for anything you do. Why are you neglecting the fire? It's very cold.'

Dancey piled peats on the hearth until it could hold no more. Still the old one complained of the cold.

Outside, the first daffodils were beginning to open in the schoolhouse garden. A few new lambs cried thinly from this field and that.

'I was never so cold,' said old Mrs Crag.

Dancey put the thickest shawl about her shoulders, and broke another peat into the blaze. 'Now then,' she said, 'be good till I come back. I won't be long.'

She went out and across the fields quickly to see if her own ewes had given birth. Her hens came against her in a fierce hungry red wave. Two lambs tottered round their dam in the spring sun. The cow Sybil blew her bugle again and again. 'Milking time!'

Dancey took some honey in a cup back to Strom: honey, if she could sip it, might put some strength into Mrs Crag.

No, she didn't want honey, or anything. 'My throat's frozen, I can't open it. I only remember one coldness like this, and that's the night they took the bodies out of the ship in the snow. I never saw coldness like that. There's a white shawl in the kist, put it on me. The dead woman in the barn of Eard! And then they brought the bairn in, out of the drifts. I was young then, not long married. I remember thinking, *Poor thing, you'd be better dead*. There was life in it still. Whether it lived or died I don't know. I can't remember . . .'

She took a spoonful of brandy, though half of it ran down her whiskered chin.

'Where's that boy?' she whispered. 'What I'd like Andrew to do is, I'd like him to buy a shop in Hamnavoe with the money I have put by. He'd be happy then, and his bairns after him. This crofting and fishing's a poor life. In Hamnavoe, Andrew'll get a good, respectable wife. Her hands would be clean always.'

When the sounds of the first ebb were all along the shore, the old woman said, 'I'm tired. I want to go to bed now.'

Before Dancey could get to her, she slumped sideways in her chair. She was dead when Dancey laid her out on the bed.

That evening Tom Stanger came with his tape-measure and boards.

Word was sent to the gravedigger, the doctor, the registrar, and the missionary. In every croft curtains were drawn. In the rich spring light, the valley would be blind till after the funeral. Before midsummer Andrew Crag and Mary Danzig Selquoy were married in the barn of Strom.

The wave of time went over the valley, and removed Shalder the beachcomber and the laird's shepherd and Tom Stanger the joiner-boatbuilder-undertaker. Somebody else had to make Tom's coffin.

And William Ness sat up at Eard, and worked his fields, unbeholden to anyone. Sometimes the harvests were good enough, and sometimes they were poor, but mostly they were adequate, no more. The people drew most of their food from the sea.

And time broke upon the valley, a slow wave, and carried away the old and the fated, but brought new children, scattering them in this croft and that. In the croft of Strom, the cradle in the corner was rarely empty. After twelve years, from the furthest side of the valley could be heard the medley all weekend from inside Strom, laughter and lamentation and chastisement and encouragement and chanted games.

Andrew Crag came home from the sea day after day and a wave of children broke about his knee.

'A poor catch that, on a fine fishing day! What ailed you, man?' And the small boy Stephen who was clinging too hard to his father's knee was sent reeling away by a mild sweep from Dancey's open palm. The child in the cradle then would join its thin wail to the yells of Stephen. And the other children would laugh all about the loud anguish.

'A fisherman needs patience,' said Andrew mildly. 'I'll tell you something else – that boat of mine won't last much longer. She's dangerous in a heavy sea. Tom would have patched her to serve for a year or two yet. What way can I buy a new boat?'

Dancey set a bowl of broth before him on the bare scrubbed table.

'It'll be a fair to middling harvest,' she said. 'Nothing to speak about. It's a good thing I'm here to see to it. Or we'd starve here at Strom!'

There came the summer of the golden harvest that was spoken about for a generation afterwards. That year the elements of sun and rain and wind were so exquisitely measured and scattered upon the furrows that the little black-ploughed fields sown with barley and oats had shallow pools of green soon and then the sloping rectangles were all green, all crammed with murmurings and whisperings in the wayward wind of early summer, and jewelled after a shower; and at morning and evening the lark stood high above the ripening stalks, and the blue hemisphere rang with the rapture of its singing.

The valley folk waited anxiously; many a year such promise had been ruined by a week-long deluge of August rain. And if an easterly wind came with the rain, a whole summer of work could be all but ruined.

The weather kept faith with the crofters. The corn changed overnight, from green to bronze, not uniformly, but croft by croft would receive the blessing. Then, after the pledge and seal of the sun, it was time to put the scythes in. It did not take the cockerel to wake them, those summer mornings. The crofters did not wait for their own ripening time. Whenever a field took the burnish, there they all went with their scythes, and before dark the last stook was set up. There were a few grumbles here and again. 'That's not fair! It should be our field for cutting in the morning, not theirs!' (Mostly it was the women who complained.)

The men would sit down under a stook, smoking their pipes, and discuss the rotation mildly. The women would pour ale out of the great stone jar – and usually before they dispersed it had been agreed whose field was next for cutting.

Always they cocked their heads, harkening for a smell or taste of rain on the wind. A few of the older men and women knew days before whether it would rain, and they always took into their calculation the airt of the wind and the phase of the moon. Even the sun held portents; too clear and intense a light portended prolonged rain, and that very soon. The best promise was a faint bloom of haar, or mist, along the horizon at morning and evening. Day after day of faintly diffused sunlight fell into the valley, and flashed from the swinging scythes of the harvesters. The swathes fell before them. The women followed after, gathering and binding. The children ran among the stooks, chasing rabbits and birds. There was no school till harvest was over.

There among the harvesters laboured the squat strong figure of Dancey. Only she did not stoop and gather like the other women; she swung a scythe with the men. With keen crisp susurrations the line of scythes went through the dense coroneted barley.

Old Billo Spence the ex-sailor licked his finger and held it up to the wind. His nostril flared. 'No rain for the next few days,' said he . . . The harvesters let Billo go home early, for he was crippled with rheumatics and couldn't keep up with the other men.

A child from the croft of Svert wailed suddenly! A bee had stung him. All the crofters worked together, in this field and that, except William Ness of Eard. William Ness had never been beholden to anybody. William Ness cut his own harvest. Let them keep to their own fields. Let the women especially keep away from his acres, with their gossip and inquisitiveness. Sometimes the harvesters would cast an eye up at Eard. The oatfield there was ripe for cutting all right – in fact one corner had been cut – but there was no sign of the solitary harvester. He must be all right, as far as anything could be right with the creature, for his door was standing open. But his cow in the field above was raising a great outcry.

The day dawned clear and fresh for cutting the two fields of Strom. The harvesters arrived, singly and in groups. Dancey had porridge and boiled eggs and bannocks on the table for them, 'to give them strength . . .' Andrew she sent to the fishing – 'he would be nothing but a hindrance'. She swung her scythe for an hour or two, but she had to break off every now and again to go inside and get more food ready for the harvesters, and replenish the ale-jar, and see to the infant in the cradle. The valley children had never had a day like it, leaping back from the flash and onset of the scythes, hurling themselves on the threefold stooks, chasing the rabbits that leaped and danced from their diminishing domain.

Once or twice Dancey, coming out with the cheese and oatcakes and ale-jar, cast her eye up at the croft of Eard and its bellowing cow.

'There's something wrong there,' she said.

The harvesters shrugged their shoulders. He had never needed them. Let him see still to his own affairs.

Andrew Crag came up from the shore with a full basket of crabs. The children were too steeped in bronze and ripeness that afternoon to pay much attention to him. 'I think it'll come to rain,' said Andrew. 'But not for a day or two.' He held out a mug to be filled with ale. 'Get inside,' cried Dancey.

By sunset the two fields were cut. The harvesters trooped home on half-a-dozen different paths.

Dancey put on her coat and took the steepest path up the hill.

'Get out,' yelled William Ness from the floor. 'Nobody asked you to come here.'

He was lying on a rag mat near the dead hearth, with his right leg splayed at a wrong angle.

'Get out,' he shouted. 'I fell, that's all. I tripped on a stone out there in the field and came down. I'll get up again when I'm ready.'

'Your leg's broken,' said Dancey. 'You need the doctor.'

'I want no doctor,' said William Ness. 'The leg'll mend. I can't afford doctors.'

'I don't care about you,' said Dancey. 'You can die for all I care. That poor cow of yours, Queenie, she needs milking. Listen to her. She's in agony.'

'Milk her,' said William. 'Then go.'

'And your hens are starving,' said Dancey. 'Where do you keep your oats?'

When Dancey had milked the cow and fed the hens, she came back and rekindled the dead fire.

'How long have you been lying here?' she asked.

'A day and a night,' said the man. 'I had just begun to cut the oats when I fell over that stone. Leave the fire alone.'

Dancey plied the bellows and the fire was all roaring yellow and red rags.

'I've just told Jacob Voe,' she said. 'Jacob's gone over the hill to get the doctor.'

'This house is private property,' said the man. 'You're trespassing. The laird will hear about this.'

'You must be hungry,' said Dancey. 'Let's see what you have in your cupboard.'

'You slut,' he muttered.

'O Lord, what misery!' cried Dancey from the open cup-board. 'A few bits of salt fish. A few tatties. Some mouldy oatmeal. I knew you were mean, but I little thought it was so miserable as this. I'll go home and get some hot broth for you.'

'You'll go home and you'll never darken this door again!' cried the man on the floor.

'I'll boil an egg or two in the meantime,' said Dancey. 'I'd better be here when the doctor comes.'

She boiled three eggs and shelled them and emptied them into a bowl, after blowing the peat dust out of it. Then she set the bowl of salted eggs down beside William Ness, with a horn spoon in it. 'Eat,' she said.

He wouldn't touch the spoon. He wouldn't even look at it.

'House-breaking,' he said. 'This is a serious business. A matter for the police.'

'I'm not going to force it down your throat,' said Dancey. 'If you want to die of starvation, you can. You've had plenty of practice.'

She found a broom behind the door and set about sweeping the floor all round the stricken man. 'We can't let the doctor see a hovel like this. I expect he's seen many a poor place in his time, but never a pigsty like this . . .' Sometimes she swept a spider's web with the broom from the rafters, or a hanging curtain of smoky filth from above the hearth.

'The doctor might be able to save your leg – it's hard to say,' said Dancey. 'The eggs are cold. But eat them. You'll need all your strength.'

The man closed his eyes, as if he was sleeping. But from time to time he moaned a little.

'Sore, is it?' said Dancey. 'Just wait till Dr McCrae begins to put you together again.'

It was time to light the lamp. Dancey 'tut-tutted' while she scoured the greasy lampglass with her apron, and trimmed the wick, and shook the bowl to see how much oil there was in it. 'I don't suppose it's been lit since last winter,' she said. 'And then only for a few minutes till you read your chapter and got into bed.'

They heard the clip-clop of hooves, the rattle of wheels, from the throat of the valley a mile away. When Dr McCrae arrived the inside of Eard was softly irradiated.

They heaved William Ness, moaning, on to his bed. 'A good thing you found him when you did,' said Dr McCrae. 'Another night and he'd have been a goner. Now, man, this is going to hurt you. Dancey, would you put on some water to boil? Your oatfield? It's your leg I'm worried about, man, not your oatfield. You'll be lucky if you can hobble as far as the door this side of Hallowe'en. Dancey, if you open my bag you'll find a big blue bottle with tablets in it. Yes, take it over . . .'

Next morning, Dancey left the neighbour woman Angela in charge of the children of Strom. She took a can of hot broth across the burn and up the side of the hill to Eard. She pushed open the door.

'Here's some soup, man,' said Dancey. 'If I can find a bowl that's passing clean. Broth like this'll have you on your feet in no time. Tell me if you want more salt in it. Here.'

William Ness let on not to be aware of her existence. He lay in the box-bed with his eyes lightly closed. He could have been dead but for the faint flutter at his lips and the pulse in his temple.

'I'll set it on the chair then,' said Dancey. 'When you're hungry, you'll eat. I'm not going to coax you.'

The man on the bed said nothing.

'Every cornfield's cut except yours,' said Dancey. 'It's a poor thin crop, like the man that sowed it. But it's a pity to let it lie waste. The rain's coming, Andrew says.'

She took the scythe out of the barn and whetted it on a stone and set about cutting the oatfield of Eard. By mid-afternoon it was all finished – the field cut and the stooks set up. She had done it alone. It was a very small field.

When Dancey went into the house to tell William Ness that his harvest was cut, he was still lying there with his eyes closed. The bowl of broth lay cold on the chair next to the bed, with the horn spoon lying in it.

'I suppose better men have died of starvation,' said Dancey. 'Anyway, your field's cut.'

Before she went home, she took in a bucket of water from the spring. 'Tomorrow, I'll tidy you up,' she said. 'The doctor and the missionary'll be coming to see you. I'll leave the broth. Even if it's cold it's nourishing enough.'

As Dancey went in at the door of Strom, she heard the clip-clop of the doctor's gig coming on the road between the hills.

Down at the shore, Andrew was setting his basket of fish on a flat rock. The sun took silver flashings from them.

William Ness lay as quiet as a corpse, but for the flutter of a nostril, while Dancey poured water from bucket into basin, and unwrapped a piece of green soap from a flannel. 'I ought to heat the water,' she said. 'But the cold water might put a spark of life in you.'

When she wet the flannel and soaped it to wash his face, he swung at her with his fist. The blow caught Dancey off balance and she reeled against the bed-post. 'Ah,' said Dancey, 'that's what I like to see. You're mending. You're getting your strength back.'

She wound one fist through his grey-black hair and held his head down on the pillow, and with the other hand she washed his face thoroughly. Once he tried to bite her – she took the cold flannel and whipped it across his mouth.

'You've got ten good years of life in you yet,' said Dancey, 'with all that strength.' Her flannelled finger went into his ear-whorls and nose-flanges. Then she took the towel to him and rubbed so hard that he let out a soft moan. 'I've brought a comb too,' said Dancey.

He made no resistance while she combed his beard and his hair. 'You'd be a bonny enough man,' she said, 'if only you kept yourself clean and tidy. What you need is a wife. I don't suppose any lass in this island would have you. But if you were to put an advertisement in the *Orkney Herald* . . .'

When she saw tears oozing out of his closed eyes, and glittering in his eye-pouches, Dancey said she'd go out and milk his cow. 'I think what you need is a mug of warm milk and a couple of eggs.'

He would not eat or drink, still. She left the milk and the new-boiled eggs and the oatcakes on the chair beside the bed, growing cold. 'The bairns'll be home for their dinner. I'll be back in the afternoon.'

He had bitten his lower lip so fiercely that a bead of blood stood there.

When Dancey returned in the later afternoon, William Ness was asleep. He hadn't touched the milk or the food. The pure breath of sleep came from his mouth, soft and rhythmic – he looked like a boy lost in the wonderment of falling snow. Dancey kissed him on the forehead. Then softly she left the house. She milked Queenie the cow in the upper field, then she went home.

When she returned in the morning, he was awake. The mug and the plate were empty.

'Well done!' cried Dancey. 'You'll get a fresh haddock for your tea. I should change your bed today. Are there blankets in that kist?'

'I don't want your charity,' said William. 'I'll pay you for the work you've done. There's a black box at the foot of the cupboard, far back. Be good enough to bring it here to me. The key is behind that loose stone in the wall – yes, that one. Bring it too.'

He unlocked the little black lacquered box and inside, in separate compartments, were gold coins and bank notes. The sovereigns spilled from his fingers back into the box, golden music. The notes looked like discarded mummy wrappings and had an ancient smell.

'How much do I owe you for your services, up to now?' said William Ness.

Dancey laughed. 'Lock it all away,' she said. 'You'll need it all to pay the undertaker and the gravedigger, and for the funeral whisky.'

Treasure box and key were restored to their separate secret places.

'You're a very strange woman,' said William Ness. The cow Queenie lowed from the field above.

When Dancey returned with the pail of milk, he said, 'My leg is not so painful today.'

He drank the warm milk so eagerly that his whiskers were festooned with white droplets.

As Dancey was leaving, he said in a low voice, 'I think I would like a piece of haddock with butter about it, and a bannock.'

Dancey met the missionary on the sheep-path. 'He's getting stronger every day,' she said. 'He'll be very pleased to see you for a change.'

Before the month was out, William Ness was on his feet again; though he hirpled on a stick for the rest of the winter.

One morning Dancey said, 'You can do for yourself now, can't you? You can milk Queenie and light your fire? And take in peats and water from the spring? Then I'll be off.'

'Thank you, woman,' he said.

Dancey never crossed the threshold of Eard again. It was plain to see by all in the course of the next winter that the croft of Eard reverted slowly to its former state of filth and neglect. The little windows lost the glitterings Dancey had put on them. But on a Sunday morning William Ness emerged from that withered door in his black suit with his Bible under his arm, and set out slowly on his staff to the kirk five miles away.

The accident had not put one drop of honey into his nature. He did his slow business – if he had to – with the other valley folk curtly and ungraciously. If a child wandered near his door he would swipe at it with his stick and utter some wild meaningless syllable. On winter nights the valley boys threw stones against his door. One night of snow a stone went through his window. Two days later the policeman from Hamnavoe arrived in the valley and sharply interrogated the pupils in the school. A policeman come for them! They were grey as cinders in the face at the thought of chains and dungeons.

The boy who had broken the window was never discovered.

And Dancey: for William Ness it was, between him and her, what it has always been, as if the affair of the broken leg had never happened. If they chanced to meet, on the peat road or along the shore, he would look through her as if she was made of glass.

Dancey always had a few words for him. 'It's time you were getting a new cow, man. Queenie is done . . .' 'Have you put that advertisement in the paper yet for a bride?' 'Watch yourself in this snow – it's very slippery up at the spring . . .'

Never an answer. He had ears of stone, going past her with the limp he always had now since he broke his leg.

As Dancey had predicted, William Ness lived for ten more years. Then, when no smoke was seen from his chimney for three mornings in April, the shepherd from the big house found him slumped in his chair, with a cold smile on his face, and a spider spinning a web between his dropped hand and the wall.

Only as many men as were required to carry the coffin attended the funeral. Andrew Crag was at the fishing that afternoon.

A month later the postman from the island post office five miles away walked down the valley with a letter for Andrew Crag, esquire, Strom. The address was typewritten, the flap of the envelope had a red embossed seal to it. Andrew opened the letter with trembling fingers (a letter like this boded no good). It was from the solicitor in Kirkwall. 'Dear Sir, I enclose a copy of the will of the late William Ness, of Eard. I should be glad if you could come to our office in Kirkwall as soon as possible, to sign the necessary forms and finalise the business. Yours faithfully . . .'

William Ness's will was short and simple. 'I leave all my worldly goods and assets to Andrew Crag of Strom in this island, to get him a new boat. Any man with a wife like he has got, with her clattering tongue and her interferences, needs to be out of the house as often as he can, among the silences of the sea. His old boat *Hopeful* is the worse for wear. Let Andrew Crag order a new boat from the yard in Hamnavoe. Whatever monies

are left over to be equally divided among his children, the poor
man . . .'

**John Agard** was born and educated in Guyana and moved to Britain in 1977. He was part of the All-ah-we dramatic group in the Caribbean and spent several years as a lecturer for the Commonwealth Institute. He has published several books for children and, with his wife, Grace Nichols, is co-author of a collection of Caribbean nursery-rhymes, *No Hickory, No Dickory, No Dock*. Most recent collections are *Mangoes and Bullets* (1987) and *Lovelines for a Goat-Born Lady* (1990), both published by Serpent's Tail. He was winner of the 1982 Cuban Casas de las Americas Poetry Prize. His most recent book is *The Emperor's Dan-Dan*, a calypso retelling of the fable of the Emperor's new clothes (Hodder and Stoughton, 1992).

**Brian W. Aldiss** has been interested in the pleasures and contradictions of Shakespeare's magic island from an early age. His latest novel, set in a contemporary and changing Europe, is *Remembrance Day* (1993), a companion piece to *Forgotten Life* (1988). His fifteenth collection of short stories, *A Tupolev Too Far*, is forthcoming. Aldiss performs in his own evening revue, *Science Fiction Blues*.

**Simon Armitage** was born in Huddersfield in 1963 and works as a Probation Officer in Manchester. He was the recipient of an Eric Gregory Award in 1988. He has published three collections of poetry: *Zoom!* (Bloodaxe 1989), *Xanadu* (Bloodaxe 1992) and *Kid* (Faber 1992).

**James Berry** grew up in Jamaica and came to Britain in 1948. He has written a number of volumes of verse and won the National Poetry Prize in 1981 for his poem, *Fantasy of an African Boy*. His collection of stories about childhood in the Caribbean, *A Thief in the Village*, was the winner of the Smarties Prize in 1987. He has a special interest in multicultural education and the development of Black British writing and has worked extensively for schools through writing workshops and radio and television. He was awarded the OBE in 1990 and won the Cholmondeley Award for poets in 1991.

**George Mackay Brown** lives in Orkney and has been publishing fiction, poetry, drama and essays since 1959. Among his novels are *Greenvoe* (1972), *Magnus* (1973), and *Vinland* (1992); his *Selected Poems 1954–83* were published in 1991. He was appointed OBE in 1977.

**Glyn Brown**, ex-signwriter and motorbike messenger, is a free-lance journalist whose work has appeared in the *Guardian*, the *Times Literary Supplement, City Limits* and *Blitz*, amongst others. She won the 1991 *Time Out* Short Story Competition; her story 'The Strong-woman' will be published in the forthcoming Women's Press anthology, *The Plot Against Mary*, and 'Flight' has previously been published in the anthology *The Word Party* (Centre for Creative and Performing Arts). She is now wrestling with her first novel provisionally called *The Fabulous Wild*.

**Amit Chaudhuri** was born in Calcutta and grew up in Bombay and was a research student at Balliol College. He is now Creative Arts Fellow at Wolfson College, Oxford. He has contributed fiction, poetry and criticism to the *London Review of Books, The Times Literary Supplement*, the *London Magazine*, and other literary periodicals. His first novel, *A Strange and Sublime Address* (Heinemann 1991) won the Betty Trask Award 1991 and was short-listed for the Guardian Fiction Prize. He is now working on his second novel.

**Robert Crawford** was born in Glasgow in 1959 and is Lecturer in Modern Scottish Literature at St Andrews University. His collections of poems include *A Scottish Assembly* (Chatto 1990), *Sharawaggi* (written with W. N. Herbert, Polygon 1990) and *Talkies* (Chatto 1992). He is co-editor of the international magazine *Verse*.

**Helen Dunmore** has published four collections of poetry, the most recent of which is *Short Days, Long Nights, New and Selected Poems* (Bloodaxe 1991), a Poetry Book Society Recommendation. Her first novel for young people, *Going to Egypt*, was published in 1992 by Julia MacRae Books and a second is forthcoming in early 1993. Her first adult novel, *Zennor in Darkness*, will be published by Viking in Spring 1993. She is currently Writer in Residence at the Polytechnic of Wales.

**Steve Ellis** was born in York in 1952, and lectures in English at the University of Birmingham. He is the author of two books of literary criticism, and of two collections of poems, *Home and Away* (1987) and *West Pathway* (forthcoming), both published by Bloodaxe. He lives uneventfully in suburbia with a wife, two children and two cats. He has just completed a verse translation of Dante's *Hell*.

**Patricia Ferguson** studied history at Leeds University and nursing and midwifery at London University. Her previous books are *Family Myths and Legends* (for which she won the Somerset Maugham Award and the David Higham Award), *Indefinite Nights* and *Write to Me*. She lives in Bristol with her husband and son.

**Roy Fisher**, born in Birmingham in 1930, is a poet and jazz musician. His long poem, *A Furnace*, and his *Poems 1955–1987* are published by Oxford University Press; *The Cut Pages* (1971) is available in a new edition from Oasis/Shearman. His poem 'Town World' is part of a text commissioned for the film, *Birmingham's What I Think With*, made for the Arts Council of Great Britain in 1991 by Pallion Productions.

**Esther Freud** was born in London in 1963. Her first novel, *Hideous Kinky*, was published by Hamish Hamilton in 1992. She trained as an actress at the Drama Centre, London, and has worked in theatre and television as both an actress and a writer. Her second novel, *Peerless Flats*, will be published in 1993.

**Carlo Gébler** was born in 1954 and studied at the University of York and at the National School of Film and Television. His first novel, *The Eleventh Hour*, was published in 1984. Other books include *Driving through Cuba* (1988), *Life of a Drum* (1991) and *The Glass Curtain* (1991).

**Sarah Gracie** was born in 1961 in Bahrain and grew up in England and Scotland. After taking a First in English at Oxford, she taught English in prisons and psychiatric hospitals. She has an MA in Creative Writing from the University of East Anglia and is working on a doctoral thesis on post-war British fiction at Oxford. She has won prizes for her poetry and short stories and is now writing her first novel.

**Alison Habens** was born in Portsmouth in 1967. She has a degree in drama and dance from the Roehampton Institute of Higher Education and an MA in literature from Sussex University. She is currently writing her first novel.

**Selima Hill**'s most recent book, *The Accumulation of Small Acts of Kindness* (Chatto 1989), has as its title the poem that won first prize in the Arvon Competition. Her fourth collection, *Cattle*, is forth-coming. She was Writing Fellow, University of East Anglia in 1991, judge of the Arvon Competition in 1992 and Writer in Residence at the South Bank Centre Dance Festival.

**Michael Hofmann** was born in Freiburg in 1957 and lives in London. His book of poems, *Acrimony*, won the Geoffrey Faber Memorial Prize in 1988. A new volume, *At Cuban Dusk*, is in preparation, as are translations of novels by his father, Gert Hofmann, and by Franz Kafka.

**Ted Hughes** was born in Yorkshire in 1930. His first book of poems, *The Hawk in the Rain* appeared in 1957 to wide acclaim; since then he has published many more collections, including *Crow* (1970) and *Wolfwatching* (1989). He was appointed Poet Laureate in 1984, and his Laureate poems are collected in *Rain-Charm for the Duchy* (1992). He has written poems and plays for children; his controversial and inspirational *Shakespeare and the Goddess of Complete Being* and his tribute to T. S. Eliot, *A Dancer to God*, were both published in 1992.

**P. D. James** has published eleven crime and detective novels, including *A Taste for Death* (Faber 1986) and *Devices and Desires* (Faber 1989). Her latest novel, *The Children of Men*, was published in 1992. In 1987 she was Chairman of the Booker Prize judges and is now a member of the Committee of Management; she was a member of the Arts Council of Great Britain and Chairman of its Literature Advisory panel from 1987 to 1992. She is also a member of the British Council's Board and a Governor of the BBC. In 1991 she was created a Life Peer under the title of Baroness James of Holland Park.

**Michael Longley** was born in Belfast in 1939 and took a degree in classics at Trinity College, Dublin. From 1970 to 1991 he was Combined Arts Director at the Arts Council of Northern Ireland. He has been awarded the Commonwealth Poetry Prize and an Eric Gregory Award. His collections of poetry include *No Continuing City: Poems 1963–1968; The Echo Gate; Poems 1975–1978*; and *Gorse Fires* which won the Whitbread Poetry Award for 1991.

**George MacBeth**, novelist and poet, worked with the BBC from 1955–76, mostly as a producer of talks and poetry programmes. He published numerous volumes of poetry, including his *Collected Poems 1958–82* (1989) and *Trespassing* (1990). His most recent collection, *The Patients*, appeared in 1992. His novels include *Anna's Book* (1983), *The Lion of Pescara* (1984) and *Dizzy's Woman* (1986). He edited many books of poetry, including *Penguin Modern Poets VI* (1964) and *Poetry for Today* (1984), and also published several children's books. His autobiography, *A Child of the War*, won the Angel Literary Award in 1987. George MacBeth died in 1992.

**Norman MacCaig** was born in 1910 and educated at Edinburgh University where he read Classics. He has been a schoolmaster, Reader in Poetry at the University of Stirling and Writer in Residence at the University of Edinburgh. He has been awarded numerous prizes and honorary degrees, including the Queen's Gold Medal for Poetry (1986) and was appointed OBE in 1979. His most recent book is *Collected Poems* (1990).

**John McGahern** was born in 1934 and brought up in Roscommon and different parts of Leitrim, where he now lives. He has written three collections of stories, *Nightlines, Getting Through* and *High Ground*; five novels, *The Barracks, The Dark, The Leavetaking, The Pornographer* (for which he is also writing the screenplay for a forthcoming production) and *Amongst Women*, which was short-listed for the Booker Prize in 1990 and won the *Irish Times* Aer Lingus Fiction Prize the same year; and a number of plays for radio and TV, which include *The Rockingham Shoot* (BBC). Among his many awards are the AE Memorial Award, the Society of Authors Travelling Fellowship and the American Irish Foundation Literature Award. His first stage play, *The Power of Darkness*, was produced at the Abbey Theatre in 1991.

**E. A. Markham** is Senior Lecturer in Creative Writing at Sheffield Hallam University. He has directed the Caribbean Theatre Workshop, been a media coordinator in Papua New Guinea and held writing posts in universities, colleges and schools. His books of verse include *Human Rites, Living in Disguise, Lambchops in PNG* and *Towards the End of a Century*. He edited *Hinterland*, the Bloodaxe book of Caribbean verse, and the magazine *Artrage* and *Writing Ulster*. His forthcoming books are *Letter from Ulster* (poetry) and *Neighbours from St Caesare* (stories). *Something Unusual*, a collection of short stories, appeared in 1986.

**Glyn Maxwell** studied at Oxford, then lived in Geneva and Boston, where he studied poetry and playwriting with Derek Walcott. His first poems appeared in 1986, and in 1990 Bloodaxe published his first collection, *Tale of the Mayor's Son* (Poetry Book

Society Choice and short-listed for the John Llewellyn Rhys Prize). In 1992 he published *Out of the Rain* and received a major Eric Gregory Award. In 1993 Chatto and Windus will publish three of his verse dramas, including *Last Crossing of Isolde*, as *Gnyss the Magnificent*.

**Deborah Moggach** was born in 1948 and has written nine novels, including *Porky, Driving in the Dark* and *The Stand-In*, which she is adapting as a Hollywood screenplay. Two of her novels, *Stolen* and *To Have and to Hold*, started life as TV drama serials. She has also written a stage-play, *Double Take*, and her short stories have been widely anthologised. A volume of her stories, *Smile*, is being reissued in 1992. She is just completing her tenth novel, *The Ex-Wives*.

**Edwin Morgan** was born in Glasgow in 1920 and is Emeritus Professor of English, Glasgow University. At present he is visiting Professor at the University College of Wales, Aberystwyth. His recent books include *Collected Poems* (Carcanet 1990), *Nothing Not Giving Messages* (interviews, Polygon 1990) and *Hold Hands Among the Atoms* (Mariscat 1991).

**Mary Morrissy** was born in Dublin in 1957. She won the Hennessy Award for short stories in 1984 and has published in several magazines and newspapers. She reviews fiction for the *Irish Times* and is currently working on a novel; her first collection of short stories will be published by Jonathan Cape in Spring 1993.

**Paul Muldoon** was born in 1951 in County Armagh, Northern Ireland. From 1973–86 he worked as a radio and television producer for the BBC. He now lives in the United States, where he has taught at Columbia, Berkeley, and the University of Massachusetts; he now teaches at Princeton University. Paul Muldoon's main collections of poetry are *New Weather* (1973), *Mules* (1977), *Why Brownlee Left* (1980), *Quoof* (1983) and *Meeting the British* (1987), all published by Faber and Wake Forest University Press, and *Selected Poems 1968–1986* (Ecco Press 1987). His most recent collection *Madoc: a Mystery* was published by Faber in 1990 and by Farrar, Straus and Giroux in 1991.

**Margaret Mulvihill** was born in 1954 and studied history at University College Dublin and at Birkbeck College, London, where she has lived since 1976. As well as two previous novels, *Natural Selection* (1985) and *Low Overheads* (1987), she has written a biography of Charlotte Despard (1989), a play for BBC2 and many children's history books. Her third novel, *St Patrick's Daughter*, will be published by Hodder and Stoughton in March 1993.

**Grace Nichols** was born in Guyana in 1950 and moved to England in 1977. She studied at the University of Guyana, Georgetown and worked as a teacher and freelance journalist. Her book of poems, *I is a Long-Memoried Woman*, won the Commonwealth Poetry Prize in 1983. *Come On into my Tropical Garden* was published in 1988 and *Lazy Thoughts of a Lazy Woman and Other Poems* in 1989. She has also written a novel, *Whole of a Morning Sky* (1986).

**Kathy Page**'s fourth novel, *Frankie Styne and the Silver Man*, was published by Methuen in 1992 and a collection of her short stories, *As in Music*, appeared in 1991. She graduated from the University of York in 1979 and for some years supported her writing and painting by working as bookkeeper, carpenter, signwriter and gardener. She has held writer's residencies in numerous schools, colleges and other institutions and has recently completed a year's work at Nottingham Prison. She is now working on a new novel, *The Divine Economy*.

**C. M. Rafferty** was born in 1958 in County Clare, Ireland. She is currently working on a collection of short stories and her first novel.

**Peter Reading** was born in 1946 and trained as a painter at Liverpool College of Art. He has lived in Shropshire and worked at an agricultural feed-mill for over twenty years. He received the Cholmondeley Award for Poetry in 1978 and has published seventeen books, including *Diplopic*, which won the first Dylan Thomas Award in 1983, and *Stet* which won the 1986 Whitbread Prize for Poetry. In 1990 he was the recipient of a major award from the Lannan Foundation.

**Christopher Reid**'s four published collections of poems are *Arcadia* (OUP 1979), *Pea Soup* (OUP 1982), *Katerina Brac* (Faber 1985) and *In the Echoey Tunnel* (Faber 1991). He is now Poetry Editor at Faber and Faber.

**Carol Rumens** was born in London in 1944 and studied at Bedford College, University of London. After working as a publicity assistant and advertising copywriter, she became Poetry Editor of the *Literary Review*. Volumes of her work include *Strange Girl in Bright*

*Colours* (1973); *Star Whisper* (1983); *Selected Poems* (1987); and *From Berlin to Heaven* (1989). She edited *New Women Poets* (Bloodaxe 1991) and is currently Writer in Residence at Queen's University, Belfast.

**Robert Saxton** was born in 1952 in Nottingham and started writing in 1985. He has had poems published in the *Times Literary Supplement, Poetry Review*, the *Spectator, PN Review*, the *Observer* and Faber's *Poetry Introduction 7* and other periodicals. In 1988 he was joint first prizewinner of the *TLS*/Cheltenham Festival Poetry Competition, was featured in the New British Poets issue of *Poetry Review* (Autumn 1990), and was one of the readers in the Poetry Society's 'Catchwords' Festival, also in Autumn 1990.

**Helen Simpson** was born in Bristol and worked on *Vogue* before becoming a freelance writer. Since then, her short stories have appeared in numerous publications and anthologies. Her first collection of stories, *Four Bare Legs in a Bed*, was published in 1990 and won *The Sunday Times* Young Writer of the Year Award and the Somerset Maugham Award. Her first novella, *Flesh and Grass*, was also published in 1990.

**Iain Sinclair** was born in 1943 and lives in East London. He has published fourteen books of poetry, among them *The Birth Rug* (1973), *Lud Heat* (1975), *Suicide Bridge* (1979) and the selection *Flesh Eggs & Scalp Metal* (1989). He has also written two novels, *White Chappell, Scarlet Tracings* (1987) and *Downriver* (1991) which won the James Tait Black Prize and the Encore Award for the Best Second Novel.

**Joan Smith** was born in London in 1953. She trained as a journalist in Blackpool, then moved to Manchester where she worked for a local radio station. Among the stories she covered were the Yorkshire Ripper murders which she later wrote about in *Misogynies*. She was a journalist on *The Sunday Times* from 1979 to 1984. Her first detective novel, *A Masculine Ending*, featuring a woman academic, Loretta Lawson (who appears in two subsequent novels, *Why Aren't They Screaming?* and *Don't Leave Me This Way*) has recently been filmed and shown on BBC television. She lives in Oxfordshire and is working on her fourth detective novel.

**Anne Stevenson**, born in England of American parents, was educated in the States and has lived mainly in Britain since 1965. She has published seven volumes of poems with OUP, including *Corre-*

*spondences* (1974), *The Fiction-Makers* (a Poetry Book Society choice in 1985) and *Selected Poems* (1987). She has written the first full-length study of Elizabeth Bishop and her biography of Sylvia Plath, *Bitter Fame*, was published in 1989. She lives in Durham and North Wales with her husband, Peter Lucas.

**George Szirtes** was born in Budapest in 1948 and came to England in 1956. He trained as a painter and published his first book of poems, *The Slant Door*, in 1979. Since then he has written another five books, most recently *Metro* (OUP 1988) and *Bridge Passages* (OUP 1991), which was short-listed for the Whitbread Poetry Prize in 1992. He received the Faber Prize in 1980 and the Cholmondeley Award in 1986. He is also a translator of Hungarian literature. He lives in Hertfordshire and is married with two grown children.

**Gillian Tindall** has a formidable list of novels and works of non-fiction to her name. As an urban historian, she has written *The Fields Beneath: the history of one London village* and *City of Gold: the Biography of Bombay* (1992); as a literary critic, studies of George Gissing and Rosamond Lehmann and *Countries of the Mind: the Meaning of Place to Writers* (1991). Her novels include *Fly Away Home* (winner of the Somerset Maugham Prize), *The Intruder*, *Give Them All My Love* (1990) and *Spirit Weddings* (1992). She has also published collections of short stories. She lives with her husband in London.

**Fay Weldon** wrote a verse television play in 1977, *The Tale of Timothy Bagshott*, which was produced on BBC1. When it resurfaced in 1992, she found it was remarkable and surprising how little had changed over fifteen years.

**Matthew Whyman** was born in 1969 and brought up in Berkhamsted, Hertfordshire. He was educated at Bournemouth Polytechnic and the University of East Anglia and now lives in France, where he teaches English. He is currently writing his first novel, *Honey Mouth*, based on the travels of the eighteenth-century explorer, Mungo Park.

**Hugo Young** was born in 1938 and read Law at Oxford. He has worked as a journalist since then, first for the *Yorkshire Post*, then *The Sunday Times*, and is now political columnist on the *Guardian*. He is the author of a biography of Margaret Thatcher, *One of Us*, the most recent edition of which was published in 1991. He has won several prizes for his newspaper columns. He has written and presented a number of television films and radio documentaries about public affairs and now also writes a column for *Newsweek*.

# Booker
# Prize

FROM ONE SUCCESS

TO ANOTHER......

BOOKER WELCOMES

NEW WRITING

AS A VALUABLE STIMULUS

TO LITERATURE

# BOOKER
**KEY LINKS IN THE FOOD CHAIN**

SPONSORS OF THE BOOKER PRIZE
FOR FICTION ESTABLISHED 1968

*Also available in Minerva*

Malcolm Bradbury & Judy Cooke

NEW WRITING

*New Writing* is a platform for the best, by writers of note and writers to look out for – a stunning collection gathered together in this, the first of a series of annual anthologies published by Minerva in association with the British Council. Comprising specially commissioned stories, essays, poems, drawings, articles, interviews and extracts from work in progress, it bursts with the literary talent of today.

Fiction – comic or tender, realistic or more experimental – displays its diverse pleasures alongside a variety of non-fiction, work which includes the polemical and the reflective, personal and broad-ranging by turns, in a volume to engage passions and stimulate debate.

*Gilbert Adair* • *Martin Amis* • *A S Byatt* • *Angela Carter* • *Geoff Dyer* • *Lucy Ellmann* • *Penelope Fitzgerald* • *Alasdair Gray* • *Michael Ignatieff* • *James Lasdun* • *Doris Lessing* • *David Lodge* • *Hilary Mantel* • *Ben Okri* • *Craig Raine* • *Graham Swift* • *Rose Tremain* • *Marina Warner* • *Dannie Abse* • *Paul Bailey* • *Christopher Bigsby* • *Mel Calman* • *Wendy Cope* • *Paul Cox* • *Valentine Cunningham* • *Fred D'Aguiar* • *Carol Ann Duffy* • *Suzannah Dunn* • *Lesley Glaister* • *Georgina Hammick* • *Peter Kemp* • *Philip MacCann* • *Glyn Maxwell* • *Clare Morgan* • *Peter Reading* • *Lorna Sage* • *Adam Thorpe* • *Anthony Thwaite* • *Hugo Williams* • *Adam Zameenzad*

Giles Gordon & David Hughes

THE MINERVA
BOOK OF SHORT STORIES 1

*The Minerva Book of Short Stories 1* is the first in a series of
paperback anthologies taken from William Heinemann's *Best
Short Stories* series. It combines the short fictions of leading
writers with those of an exciting wealth of new talent. Varied,
illuminating and enjoyable, this volume is a remarkable tribute
to the current richness of the form.

'A wide-ranging and impressive collection' *Independent*

*Christopher Burns* ● *Patrice Chaplin* ● *Jim Clarke* ● *Richard
Crawford* ● *Ronald Frame* ● *Sophie Frank* ● *Penelope Gilliatt*
● *Nadine Gordimer* ● *Georgina Hammick* ● *Hanif Kureishi*
● *Jim Mangnall* ● *Adam Mars-Jones* ● *Deborah Moggach* ●
*Salman Rushdie* ● *Graham Seal* ● *Lionel Seepaul* ● *Helen
Simpson* ● *William Trevor* ● *Guy Vanderhaeghe* ● *Marina
Warner*

Giles Gordon & David Hughes

# THE MINERVA
# BOOK OF SHORT STORIES 2

The second *Minerva Book of Short Stories* confirms that the genre is in robust health. This volume will appeal equally to acknowledged lovers of short fiction and those seeking a vigorous introduction. Taken from William Heinemann's *Best Short Stories 1989*, it includes new and established voices; realistic and more experimental writing; serious, comic and tender stories; and some which will shock. As the popularity of the short story increases, this volume – and the series to which it belongs – confirms the breadth, skill and sheer art of the form.

'A fine collection' Deborah Moggach, *Sunday Times*

'All 22 stories here are of excellent quality' *Observer*

*J G Ballard* ● *Peter Carey* ● *Angela Carter* ● *Adrian Dannatt* ● *Berlie Doherty* ● *Marilyn Duckworth* ● *Lucy Ellmann* ● *Robert Grossmith* ● *Howard Jacobson* ● *Penelope Lively* ● *Tracey Lloyd* ● *Bernard MacLaverty* ● *Adam Mars-Jones* ● *Edna O'Brien* ● *Ruth Rendell* ● *Patrick Rogers* ● *Carl Tighe* ● *Jonathan Treitel* ● *William Trevor* ● *Edward Upward* ● *Fay Weldon* ● *Kit Wright*

Giles Gordon & David Hughes

THE MINERVA
BOOK OF SHORT STORIES 3

The third *Minerva Book of Short Stories* continues the tradition of
its highly successful predecessors. Taken from William Heinemann's *Best Short Stories 1990*, it contains excitingly varied work
by twenty-five writers, some new, some established. Multi-
faceted and diverse, vigorous and unpredictable, these stories
range from the comic to the profoundly moving, the extravagantly inventive to the minutely etched. As the short story enjoys
a deserved renaissance, this anthology confirms that it is alive
and well and in good hands.

'An extremely bright gathering' *Independent*

'A highly-regarded and highly-rewarding series . . . excellent
and varied' *Oxford Times*

'The level of quality in this collection is reassuringly high'
Anthony Quinton, *The Times*

*Cecil Bonstein* ● *William Boyd* ● *Jenny Diski* ● *Janice
Galloway* ● *Jane Gardam* ● *Nadine Gordimer* ● *Robert
Grossmith* ● *Russell Hoban* ● *Desmond Hogan* ● *Janette
Turner Hospital* ● *Elizabeth Jolley* ● *Gabriel Josipovici* ●
*Francis King* ● *Hanif Kureishi* ● *Moy McCrory* ● *Steve
McGiffen* ● *Adam Mars-Jones* ●*Alice Munro* ● *Philip Oakes*
● *David Park* ● *Fiona Farrell Poole* ● *Frederic Raphael* ● *D J
Taylor* ● *Jonathan Treitel* ● *Charles Wilkinson*

Giles Gordon & David Hughes

THE MINERVA
BOOK OF SHORT STORIES 4

'If you never buy another book of short stories, buy this one –
no boring compilation of nearly-made-it writers here, but the
very best, culled from a myriad of impressive sources . . . truly
brilliant' Miranda France, *The List*

'Should be got straight away by anyone who wants the unexpected pleasure of finding [1990's] Booker winner going berserk in
a hairdressing salon' Robert Nye, *Guardian*

'As good as ever . . . The major authors have produced polished
stories, but the ones I found really moving – the masterpieces
for my money – were by the less familiar names' Carla McKay,
*Daily Mail*

'Those of us who love short stories have reason to be grateful
to Giles Gordon and David Hughes . . . The choice is marvellous
in its variety' Angela Huth, *Daily Telegraph*

*Margaret Atwood ● Julian Barnes ● Alan Beard ● William
Boyd ● Julie Burchill ● A.S. Byatt ● Michael Carson ●
Michael Dibdin ● Jenny Diski ● Nadine Gordimer ● Georgina
Hammick ● Tracey Lloyd ● Rachel McAlpine ● Shena
Mackay ● David S. Mackenzie ● Richard Madelin ● Deborah
Moggach ● Alice Munro ● Denise Neuhaus ● Colm O'Gaora
● June Oldham ● Frederic Raphael ● Rose Tremain ● William
Trevor ● James Waddington*

Judy Cooke

## THE MINERVA ANTHOLOGY OF 20TH-CENTURY WOMEN'S FICTION

Judy Cooke's anthology balances the seriousness of its aim – to encapsulate the best in 20th-century women's writing – with a lively eclecticism. In the more than thirty novel extracts and short stories included here, there's a nicely judged mixture of classic texts and new writing, of mainstream and avant-garde. Rosamund Lehmann – but also Angela Carter: Iris Murdoch – but also Marguerite Duras . . .

'Even the familiar stuff gets a fresh look through being seen in a different context – Fay Weldon providing, as it were, an ironic commentary on Virgina Woolf. And was it mere coincidence or something more deliberate which placed Jeanette Winterson's *Sexing the Cherry* after Edith Wharton's *Pomegranate Seed*? Definitely one to pack for the desert island' Christina Koning, *Guardian*

'An easy introduction that tantalises and encourages the reader to seek out the full-length originals for her- (or even him-) self' Anne Smith, *Scotland on Sunday*

Amit Chaudhuri

# A STRANGE AND SUBLIME ADDRESS

'Shot through with poetry. A small jewel of a work, perfectly cut and polished' Francis King

'Sandeep, who lives with his parents in a Bombay high-rise, plunges eagerly into the life of his uncle's extended family in Calcutta; everything he sees and hears . . . is touched with magic' *Independent on Sunday*

'Funny, delicate, sensuous, evocative . . . made me laugh aloud. The best portrait of India today I've read' Margaret Drabble

'A boy's world is conjured with total credibility, a way of life looked at with some sharpness, some tenderness, some irony . . . a perfect, small achievement' Isabel Quigly, *Financial Times*

'Numerous daily events – unremarkable in themselves – assume a bloated yet magnificent significance under Chaudhuri's tutelage' Simon Cunliffe, *Independent*

'This evocation of the routine, quotidian magic of normality strikes me as an extraordinary thing to have brought off . . . mesmerising' John Lanchester, *Vogue*

'Raptly luminous . . . there is no ordinary writer here' Christopher Wordsworth, *Guardian*

# A Selected List of Fiction Available from Minerva

While every effort is made to keep prices low, it is sometimes necessary to increase prices at short notice. Mandarin Paperbacks reserves the right to show new retail prices on covers which may differ from those previously advertised in the text or elsewhere.

The prices shown below were correct at the time of going to press.

| | | | |
|---|---|---|---|
| ☐ | 7493 9145 6 | **Love and Death on Long Island** | Gilbert Adair £4.99 |
| ☐ | 7493 9130 8 | **The War of Don Emmanuel's Nether Parts** | Louis de Bernieres £5.99 |
| ☐ | 7493 9903 1 | **Dirty Faxes** | Andrew Davies £4.99 |
| ☐ | 7493 9056 5 | **Nothing Natural** | Jenny Diski £4.99 |
| ☐ | 7493 9173 1 | **The Trick is to Keep Breathing** | Janice Galloway £4.99 |
| ☐ | 7493 9124 3 | **Honour Thy Father** | Lesley Glaister £4.99 |
| ☐ | 7493 9918 X | **Richard's Feet** | Carey Harrison £6.99 |
| ☐ | 7493 9028 X | **Not Not While the Giro** | James Kelman £4.99 |
| ☐ | 7493 9112 X | **Hopeful Monsters** | Nicholas Mosley £6.99 |
| ☐ | 7493 9029 8 | **Head to Toe** | Joe Orton £4.99 |
| ☐ | 7493 9117 0 | **The Good Republic** | William Palmer £5.99 |
| ☐ | 7493 9162 6 | **Four Bare Legs in a Bed** | Helen Simpson £4.99 |
| ☐ | 7493 9134 0 | **Rebuilding Coventry** | Sue Townsend £4.99 |
| ☐ | 7493 9151 0 | **Boating for Beginners** | Jeanette Winterson £4.99 |
| ☐ | 7493 9915 5 | **Cyrus Cyrus** | Adam Zameenzad £7.99 |

All these books are available at your bookshop or newsagent, or can be ordered direct from the publisher. Just tick the titles you want and fill in the form below.

**Mandarin Paperbacks**, Cash Sales Department, PO Box 11, Falmouth, Cornwall TR10 9EN.

Please send cheque or postal order, no currency, for purchase price quoted and allow the following for postage and packing:

| | |
|---|---|
| UK including BFPO | £1.00 for the first book, 50p for the second and 30p for each additional book ordered to a maximum charge of £3.00. |
| Overseas including Eire | £2 for the first book, £1.00 for the second and 50p for each additional book thereafter. |

NAME (Block letters) .........................................................................................................................................

ADDRESS ...........................................................................................................................................................

..............................................................................................................................................................................

☐ I enclose my remittance for .........................

☐ I wish to pay by Access/Visa Card Number ☐☐☐☐☐☐☐☐☐☐☐☐☐☐☐☐

Expiry Date ☐☐☐☐